day May 1st.

as these days at the end
declaration of war —
stancy, preparations being
of living — But the
silent anxiety, for the
huschill that is to herald
the beginning of another
we wait wondering if
or dying or dead or will
is x tried and their, and
i x feeling Hummler
gh to ulgoStrate through

haus
aintance strongly
ment of the Sodras of
I heard one man in

OUR HIDDEN LIVES

OUR HIDDEN LIVES

The Everyday Diaries of a Forgotten Britain
1945–1948

SIMON GARFIELD

EBURY
PRESS

First published in Great Britain in 2004

10 9 8 7 6 5 4 3 2 1

First published by
Ebury Press
Random House
20 Vauxhall Bridge Road
London SW1 2SA

Random House Australia (Pty) Limited
20 Alfred Street, Milsons Point
Sydney
New South Wales 2061, Australia

Random House New Zealand Limited
18 Poland Road, Glenfield, Auckland 10
New Zealand

Random House South Africa (Pty) Limited
Endulini, 5A Jubilee Road
Parktown 2193
South Africa

Random House UK Limited Reg. No. 954009

www.randomhouse.co.uk

A CIP catalogue record for this book is available from the British Library

Photographs on pages 10, 70, 112, 160, 484 are © Getty Images
Photographs on pages 44, 94, 128, 192, 248, 282, 318, 336, 392, 422, 448
are © Hulton Archive
Photographs on pages 226, 364 are The Advertising Archive

In Westminster Abbey by John Betjeman from Collected Poems reproduced by
permission of John Murray Publishers
Cover Design by Eleanor Crow
Text design and typesetting by Textype, Cambridge

ISBN 0 091 896959

Papers used by Ebury Press are natural, recyclable products made from
wood grown in sustainable forests

Printed and bound in Great Britain by Clays Ltd, St Ives plc

'For the growing good of the world is partly dependent on unhistoric acts; and that things are not so ill with you or me as they might have been, is half owing to the number who lived faithfully a hidden life and rest in unvisited tombs.'

George Eliot, Middlemarch, *1871*

'Think of what our Nation stands for,
Books from Boots' and country lanes,
Free speech, free passes, class distinction,
Democracy and proper drains.'

John Betjeman, from 'In Westminster Abbey', 1940

Contents

Introduction

In 1936 the anthropologist Tom Harrisson arrived back in England from the South Pacific, where he had been studying cannibals. Within weeks of his return he had arrived at a startling conclusion: remote tribes were all very interesting, but they were not more interesting than the inhabitants of Bolton, where Harrisson lived. What was needed, he believed, was an 'anthropology of ourselves', a study of everyday people living regular lives. He reasoned that the press was not providing this service, and the government did not understand the most basic attitudes, desires and fears of those they served.

At about the same time, two other men were reaching similar conclusions. Charles Madge, a poet and journalist, and Humphrey Jennings, a documentary filmmaker, wrote a letter to the *New Statesman* describing their plans for a new type of scientific survey, one which would enable ordinary people, for the first time, to explain the detail of their days. The letter appeared in the same issue as the only published poem by Tom Harrisson, and in this way the concept of Mass-Observation was born. Notices appeared in newspapers and magazines asking for volunteers who would be willing to share their thoughts. More than one thousand responded.

The methods of Harrisson and Madge/Jennings were very different. Harrisson employed a team of paid professional observers – journalists, social scientists, civil servants – to note down passing opinions and overheard conversations in pubs, factories and holiday resorts. Madge and Jennings sent out 'directives', questionnaires requiring ordered reactions to specific answers: what did they think of Chamberlain? Did they engage in any sporting activity? What were the advantages of having a royal family? New observers were presented with a simple task to get them in the swing: 'As a first test of your powers of observation, try the following: write down in order from left to right all the objects on your mantelpiece, mentioning what is in the middle . . .'

By September 1939 the tone had changed. A 'Crisis Directive', printed in red ink, asked for specific reports on gas masks, masking windows and bomb-proof shelters, and also this: 'Failing further directions being sent you, would you keep a diary for the next few weeks, keeping political discussion at a *minimum*, concentrating on the details of your everyday life, your own reactions and those of your family and others you meet.' This was the first request for free-form monthly diaries, and about five hundred people responded to the new challenge. They wrote from industrial centres, country towns and remote villages, completing their diaries after their work as secretaries, accountants, shop workers, scientists, schoolteachers, civil servants, housewives and electricity board inspectors.

In all, about one million pages found their way to the Mass-Observation headquarters at Grotes Buildings, Blackheath. Some arrived on scraps of tissue, some on scented notepaper, some neatly typewritten, many almost illegible. Some people wrote three pages a month, some wrote forty. Some commented merely on the weather and their journey to work; some wrote predominantly about the contents of the newspapers; but some kept highly compelling and detailed journals containing almost every joy, disappointment and quirk of their lives. In many cases, married couples kept their writing secret from their partners, often recording their days late into the evening or before daybreak.

Mass-Observation's small staff were swiftly overwhelmed by the flood of words they had released, and by the lucidity and diversity of its correspondents. After a few years the founders of the project squabbled over what use to put its assets and left for other work. New staff took over in an office in Bloomsbury and they claimed to read every submission that arrived. But the diarists received little feedback, and in time came to wonder whether their work often lay undisturbed in the sealed envelopes in which they were sent.

The diaries are now lovingly archived in cardboard boxes at the University of Sussex in Falmer, near Brighton, where they are frequently examined by students and researchers concerned with the build-up and progression of the Second World War. Most diarists had stopped by 1945 but a few kept writing as the country emerged to face momentous change and great challenges. The passage from war to peace is told in the simplest, most personal and moving terms, providing a singular window into the British temperament during one of the most under-examined periods of our recent history. Pure and direct, the impression that emerges from these writings is truly one of a vanished England, where a trip to the Charing Cross Road is a treasured event, and where a moment's slight by a neighbour is likely to be remembered for years.

The period from VE day in May 1945 to the birth of the Welfare State in July 1948 was a time of great austerity and dramatic change, of major economic and social reforms, of Cold War terrors and the threat of biological warfare, and of the worst winter in memory. Britain was increasingly unsure of its place in the world. The Empire was shrinking and India and Palestine posed intractable dilemmas. The economy became reliant on American loans and the balance of payments crisis, and the need to feed a starving Europe ensured that domestic rationing pinched as hard as it had during the war. The people who danced in Piccadilly in May 1945 did not entertain the possibility of bread shortages in July 1946.

This book cannot hope to provide a thorough history of the times (for that I recommend Peter Hennessy's erudite survey *Never Again: Britain 1945–1951*, Jonathan Cape, 1992, from which I drew some of my Chronology; for a brilliant series of essays on the period see *Age of Austerity*, edited by Michael Sissons and Philip French, Hodder & Stoughton, 1963), but it is an attempt to give a vivid portrait of how Britain coped with the decisions made in Whitehall and Washington, and to show how much and how little our lives and attitudes have changed. The diarists tackle national issues as they affect their daily routines, but they are equally concerned with their own engagements, their job prospects, the difficulty of getting a seat on the train, the big local murder case, the hem of their dress and the purchase of a new radio. A biro is a thing of wonder; a man may step from a tram in central London to borrow a book from Boots.

The five diarists selected here are not a representative group; because of their huge diversity there can be no such thing. The diarists themselves were self-selecting: they had time on their hands, they liked writing, they were usually nonconformists; and they just happened to have seen the original requests from Mass-Observation for volunteers. But they do, I believe, present an engrossing picture of Britain at an important turning point, and are true to the original ideals of Mass-Observation's founders; perhaps it is only with the passage of more than half a century that we can fully appreciate the value of their original concept.

These are invaluable records of quiet lives, sometimes despairing, often moving, occasionally bitter, frequently prescient, and, I hope, consistently rewarding. Occasionally they are just plain funny. There is Edie Rutherford, forty-three at the end of the war, a proud and sometimes sanctimonious housewife in Sheffield, married to a timber merchant and football fanatic, eager for news from her native South Africa, dismayed at the price of cod, delighted with the Labour government despite everything.

There is George Taylor, an accountant in his mid-forties, also living in Sheffield, a keen supporter of Esperanto and the Workers' Educational Association, unable to resist an offer of cheap linoleum, forever trying to finish a novel he had begun reading thirteen years earlier.

There is Maggie Joy Blunt, a lyrical and talented writer in her mid-thirties living in a cottage by Burnham Beeches, near Slough, eager to leave her job as a publicity assistant in a metals company, frustrated that she can't put her public school and university training to better use, forced by circumstance to take in lodgers, ever hunting down new supplies of cigarettes, once again failing in her ambition to have an early night.

There is Herbert Brush, seventy-two, a widowed retired electrical engineer living in south-east London with his housemates W and D and a cat, spending much time in the British Museum Reading Room and tending celeriac on his allotment, certain that one cannot eat a sausage roll in the Royal Academy, frequently ambushed by the local gossip, writing copious amounts of poetry about the fuel crisis, the fate of Hitler and his own mortality (possibly the only person in his neighbourhood to have considered rhyming 'barley water' with 'everyone ought'er').

And then there is B. Charles, a gay antiques dealer and tutor in his mid-fifties, once of Windsor but now of Edinburgh, previously a dresser in the theatre, a regular concert-goer, a man not delighted by Hollywood films or other trappings of the modern world, still bitter about the mysterious details of his father's will, a bold critic of high court judges, a regular prowler around the local bars in search of younger men who might benefit from his unusual course in 'personality development'. His writing reminded me a little of the post-war journals of James Lees-Milne of the National Trust, who

4

demanded impeccable social standards from all he knew ('Had tea with Margaret Jourdain and Ivy Compton-Burnett but really could hardly bear it and left early. These two women do not eat. They stuff. Ivy consumed eight cakes . . .').

The diarists never meet, but occasionally their lives overlap. With the exception of Mr Charles in Edinburgh, the diarists all visit the 'Britain Can Make It' exhibition at the V&A in the autumn of 1946. They all face the same hardships of rationing and power cuts. At one point they all think, 'But I thought we *won* the war . . .' They all value their basic freedoms. Most have clocks and cats that give them trouble. In February 1947 they all trudge wearily through the snow. Two of their neighbours are called Braun and Goebbels, and there is a neighbour's cat called Hitler. They all fear a nuclear war. And they are all vaguely or vehemently anti-Semitic.

If this were a novel, all the diarists would meet up by chance at some national event or street corner, or they would share a terrible secret. In reality, the closest they come to a communal happening is listening to the news on the radio and marking a national victory or festive season. Herbert Brush and Edie Rutherford may have crossed on Oxford Street on a few occasions, and there is the distinct possibility that Herbert and Maggie Joy Blunt made eye contact one day at the British Museum Reading Room. With this in mind, I sometimes questioned the technique of placing them side by side in this book, as if they were characters in a play, or Internet bloggers pursuing a complex thread (the web log, of course, is now frequently regarded as the digital Warholian equivalent of the traditional hand-written diary). I concluded that had they met at a party they would have many things in common, and their love of words, storytelling and dissent would have bound them in a way their disparate politics and interests could not. In time I think they would have valued each other, as I swiftly came to value them myself.

My relationship with the diarists has inevitably changed since the project began. My initial search was for a number of people – perhaps as many as ten – who wrote well and legibly from different perspectives and a variety of locations. I thought I might place a few months of one writer followed by a few months of another, but it soon became clear that a strict interwoven chronological approach would provide a clearer narrative, more scope for juxtaposition, and a fuller historical picture (there is a chronology of significant political and social events at the end of the book). Ultimately the diarists really chose themselves. I wanted each writer to contribute throughout the three-year period (there were only about twenty-five of these), and I wanted each to have a distinctive voice and engaging encounters. I was also looking for a certain frailty in their journals, and a sense that they were not writing what they thought was expected of them. As their lives unfolded I came to feel proprietorial towards them, and to empathise with many of their struggles. Some are easier to like than others – Mr Charles's anti-Semitism is particularly hard to endure – and they all display traits that a modern-day observer may find unattractive. But I hope the present reader will share my impatience when circumstances prevent a diarist from writing for several weeks. Throughout my work on this project I never once tired of their company, and I couldn't wait to see what illuminating or awful thought, or hilarious or despairing scrape, I was to encounter on the next page. I can't remember crying at the death of another person's pet before, but I was in tears when Maggie Joy Blunt's cat expired; with each new fuel or food cut I yearned for each of the diarists' lives to improve soon.

Unlike so many diaries written for a public readership, the Mass-Observation journals were written with a wider aim than self-promotion. This is not to say they are not occasionally self-serving or self-censoring; but it is evident that enough of the genuine character and true opinions of the writers shines through. And of course the entries included here are far from the full picture: the complete diaries of these five writers in this period run to more than two thousand pages and a million words. To accommodate this edit and clarify detail, I have very occasionally run two days' entries into one. Invariably I was drawn towards opinions and episodes that appear poignant today in a way they may not have done when they were written, and sometimes selections were chosen because they provide a counterpoint to another entry. On all these occasions I hope I have never created a false impression of what the writer intended. When the diarists were first contacted by Mass-Observation they were informed that their identities would be protected, and I have honoured this promise here by finding them new names. No other details have been changed.

Occasionally the diaries contemplate posterity. Herbert Brush, whose diaries were often submitted in the form of copies of letters to his sister in Hampshire, wonders whether 'anyone at the Mass-Observation office ever reads through one of these letter-diaries of mine'. But Maggie Joy Blunt, a biographer herself, foresees the worth of her history writ small. On 13 October 1946 she noted a letter she had received from Tom Harrisson, geeing up Mass-Observers to keep writing, assuring them that their work will 'be of great sociological and historical value in the future'. Ms Blunt ruminated: 'It makes me feel one is, perhaps, doing something worthwhile, though it seems trivial and unimportant at the time. Yet just reading through one's own [diaries] one is fascinated and amazed – they cover only a very small field of action. Multiplied and representing as much as possible of the social structure one can imagine and understand their collective value.'

I hope this is what she meant.

Chapter One

OUR TROUBLES ARE ONLY
JUST BEGINNING

The news is good this morning: the outbreak of peace in Piccadilly Circus.

'And now – Oh, what wonderful luck! At this moment . . . at this moment, how wonderful, Mr Churchill has come out onto the Ministry of Health balcony . . . he's wearing his boiler suit . . . and he has the audacity, shall I say, to put on his head his famous black hat. Nobody can say that it goes with the boiler suit, but you heard what a cheer it raised from the crowd!'

BBC radio broadcast, 8 May 1945

'God bless you all. This is your victory! It is the victory of the cause of freedom in every land. In all our long history we have never seen a greater day than this. Everyone, man or woman, has done their best. Everyone has tried. Neither the long years, nor the dangers, nor the fierce attacks of the enemy, have in any way weakened the independent resolve of the British nation. God bless you all.'

Winston Churchill from the balcony

TUESDAY, 1 MAY 1945

Maggie Joy Blunt
Freelance writer and publicity officer in metal factory, living in
Burnham Beeches, near Slough
Important hours, important as those days at the end of August in 1939 preceding the declaration of war. This is tension of a different kind, expectancy, preparations being made for a change in our way of living. But the tempo is slower. We wait, without anxiety, for the official announcement by Mr Churchill that is to herald two full days' holiday and the beginning of another period of peace in Europe. We wait wondering if Hitler is dying or dead or will commit suicide or be captured and tried and shot, and what his henchman are doing and feeling.

All the women of my acquaintance have strongly disapproved today of the treatment of the bodies of Mussolini and his mistress. I heard one man in the sales department when he was told that the bodies had been hung up by the feet say glibly 'Good thing too!' But RW and myself and Lys and Miss M are shocked and disgusted. Spitting on the bodies, shooting at them, seems childish and barbarous, and such actions cannot bring the dead to life or repair damage and is a poor sort of vengeance. What a state the world is in and what a poor outlook for the future.

I have worn myself out spring cleaning the sitting room. All Sunday and yesterday at it – it now looks so brilliant and beautiful I'll never dare live in it.

We had ice cream in canteen for lunch today – the first for two or is it three years?

George Taylor
Accountant in Sheffield
I noticed that the flags which were flying on the Town Hall yesterday, presumably in preparation for peace, have been taken down. Apparently the officials were premature in their preparations.

WEDNESDAY, 2 MAY

Maggie Joy Blunt
One can hardly keep pace with the news. 'Hitler Dead' the *News Chronicle* informed me this morning in 12-inch type across the front

page. Doenitz has either been appointed to succeed him or has seized power over Himmler's head . . . We discussed the situation all through lunch, wondering how much longer the war would now continue with Doenitz in control. At the office an atmosphere of suspense but little obvious excitement.

George Taylor
News of Hitler's death has caused little stir. I never heard it mentioned on my tram journeys to and from work, none of the clients I met breathed his name, and the only person who mentioned him to me was my thirty-two-year-old colleague. He doubted very much his death, but I said that in my opinion he was indeed dead, but that he had died from natural causes and not in the fighting.

I was completely surprised at 9.10 a.m. to hear of the surrender of the German forces in Italy. It has been a well-kept secret, and I should have been less surprised by a surrender in the West. Events are certainly moving now.

Herbert Brush
Retired electrical engineer, south-east London
Good news. Hitler is really dead. I wonder what sort of reception his astral form has received on the other side.

> I can imagine when he came
> And when his victims heard his name
> They gathered round him not to miss
> So good a chance to hoot and hiss
>
> But those on earth may all agree
> From torture he must not go free
> That God Almighty has some plan
> To punish such a naughty man

THURSDAY, 3 MAY

Maggie Joy Blunt
RW had a violent argument with a young woman (A) who works in our firm. RW says that her ears turn scarlet when she gets excited in conversation and when she came upstairs immediately after this

13

scene they were as brilliant as cherries. A is quite unbalanced as to what should be done with war criminals. She thinks they should all be shot without a trial and in some cases tortured. She would like to have seen very special torture done to Hitler and one of her suggestions was pulling out his eyes with knitting needles. When RW declared she would never do it if she actually had the opportunity, she did say she would want someone else to do it. She is a bright, intelligent, friendly person and an amusing conversationalist. One would not expect her capable of such savage inclinations. But she is Jewish and there is I suppose in all of us still a streak of the savage. I remember once dreaming of my father – seeing him, thin, pale, tottering as he was during his last fatal illness, being pushed about by someone most brutally. And in my dream I just went mad with rage and I attacked the attacker without mercy.

DJ gave me the afternoon off. About 8 p.m. the rain turned to snow. I ate my supper watching the enormous snowflakes fall, wondering if any other country in the world could present such a scene – snow on tulips and broken lilac blossom, snow falling through bursting beeches and the sky ash – snow on shivering pansies and wan forget-me-nots . . . A fantastic spring. Three weeks ago the temperature was seventy in the shade.

George Taylor

Now that there seems every prospect of VE day being celebrated in the near future, my audit assistant, a married woman of twenty-five, seems mostly interested in when we are to have the holiday. Her forecast is Saturday lunchtime, with the rest of the day holiday and VE plus one will be Sunday. I suppose that is ingrained pessimism.

Police duty on a wretchedly cold and rainy evening. During the patrol my sergeant was telling me of the arrangements to celebrate in the works. It seems that some are to pay time-and-a-half for the hours worked between the signal and closing down on VE day, and full time for the following two days. Another works has set aside £3 for all employees as pay for the three days. In his own office, a Friendly Society, the girls were asking about the holiday, and when he said that they would be working as usual unless they received specific instructions to the contrary, they were loud in protest. One, indeed, declared flatly that she would not turn in.

Herbert Brush

The news is good this morning. I am wondering now whether Hitler died from a clot on his brain, whether he was murdered, or whether he shot himself or took poison. I suppose that the details will come out in due course, unless they have had his body cremated.

They probably want his name to become a legend, something like our King Arthur, so that the young Germans in the twenty-first can be told what a wonderful person Hitler was, and how he died a warrior's death while fighting for his country against enormous odds.

I don't like the idea that we have to feed all the millions of prisoners taken. Most of them are young Nazis who never will be any good in the world now, after they were brought up. I am still of the opinion that all those under twenty-five should go into a lethal chamber, for the future peace of the world. It rained most of the night.

FRIDAY, 4 MAY

Herbert Brush

The trams are not running today owing to a strike. I guess there will be a lot of this kind of trouble when 'Peace' comes.

Maggie Joy Blunt

When the first newsflash came through the radio announcing the surrender of the German forces in north-west Germany, I was in bed mopping my ears. We had looked at the headlines in the *Evening News* in the office just before 5 p.m. and decided that the end *must* be near now, as the enemy was collapsing on all fronts.

I asked RW what she intended to do on VE day and she said that she didn't know. Her people keep a pub in Windsor and they have not decided whether they will keep open or not. If they do (and the brewers want them to) they will not have more than their normal rationed supply and will be sold out by 9.30 p.m. Her father thinks he will invite in all his pals and keep the pub closed to the public.

No one seems very certain what they will do. There are to be some Victory parades and special services and bonfires. It looks as though I shall spend the day and days following in close, solitary seclusion. My ears are a most revolting sight and even Dr B is baffled. He talks of sending me to a specialist but I am to treat them myself this weekend with rainwater and special ointment. I am worried and tired and do not want to go out or meet anyone. I have been going to the office every day this week after a visit to the doctor in the morning and coming home early. My friends are sympathetic and anxious but I feel rather a leper and imagine all strangers to be goggling at me.

I came home at 5 p.m., collected ointment from the chemist, and, while waiting for it to be made up, some new stock arrived including a small box of Wright's coal tar soap. I have not seen any of this for a long while and the girls said they would not have any 'for ages' so I bought two tablets. I bought lettuce, radishes, beetroot and mustard and cress, came home, prepared salad, Hovis and butter, glass of milk, honey and an orange, and got into bed and ate it there. Since when I have been dealing with the ears and listening to the news.

Girls in cloakroom were chattering excitedly this afternoon. 'Oh, I do hope it'll happen while we're at work! – It won't seem the same will it?' The official notice asks us all to assemble in the canteen where news of victory is announced over the works broadcasting system. We are then to have the rest of the day off and the two following days. The girls began twittering about their husbands – what group for demobilisation did each belong to? I left them, feeling rather old and forlorn.

Listening now to the repeat broadcast of General Montgomery from Germany this afternoon. My emotions at this moment are indescribable: enormous pride in the fact that I am British, wonder and excitement. 'Tomorrow morning at 8 a.m. the war in Europe will be over . . .' The war in Europe is over . . . This is a tremendous moment.

The war is over. I cry a little. I think of my dearest friends, my stepmother, my brother in Egypt, of those men in the fighting services I have known – and I wish I had taken a more active part; it is too late now. But it is not too late to take part in the new fight ahead. I am not moved to rush out tomorrow and wave a Union Jack in the village high street. I think it is a good sign that people are saying universally 'Our troubles are only just beginning', because it would be idiotic to assume they are over with the end of hostilities.

We want a better world and we must fight for it. That is where we must distinguish between pessimism and optimism. I believe with the utmost optimism, faith, hope and joy that we can have our better world (and note that one says 'a *better* world' – not the perfect or even best possible world) – yes, that we can have it if we know clearly what we want and fight for it.

Midnight news now being read. The announcer sounds tired. Pockets of German resistance still remain. I have been down and turned off the radio. For once I waited to hear the whole of the National Anthem, moved suddenly again to tears by this historic, this incredible moment. I stood with my hand on the radio switch listening to the National Anthem and to the voices of a thousand, thousand ghosts. They came over the air into that unlit, silent room, I swear it.

It's time I tried to sleep. One of the cats is outside my window waiting to be let in. Tomorrow and tomorrow and tomorrow stretch before me. Infinitely more full of promise and interest than the war years have been. I feel that new and exciting events await me. But that may be due to the influence of tonight's news. The atmosphere is charged with a release and potentiality.

And the bottom sheet, in an exceedingly frail condition from old age and much hard wear, is now torn beyond hope and redemption. I am sick to death of patching worn linen.

George Taylor
The monthly executive committee meeting of the Workers' Educational Association. As an experiment next year we are having a class on Appreciation of the Films, and a most attractive syllabus has been drawn up. The committee members are a little afraid, however, that the class may be used for entertainment purposes only, and they have fixed a class fee of 10/- to emphasise that serious study is intended.

SATURDAY, 5 MAY

Maggie Joy Blunt
Awakened this morning by neighbour Mrs C shouting something to the butcher. Don't know yet what he has left me – in saucepan in shed outside my backdoor. It has been pouring with rain from the time I woke and I am spending the morning in bed, reading the papers which repeat last night's broadcast news, attending to the ears which do seem a little better, and dozing. Have cancelled a hair appointment, intend to have an early (salad) lunch and then get up. Shall

light kitchen fire, tidy the kitchen, go into the village, return to kitchen tea, maybe have the kittens down, wash a very large collection of soiled 'smalls' and look out for material for making two new cushioned squares for the sitting room – that is my programme. Why do people 'wonder what I do with myself all alone?'

The radio has been on and will be while I am indoors lest I miss some important gobbet of information. One of the dangers I think of having the news brought to one so quickly when history is being as dramatic as it is at present is that it makes one want and expect life to move with the speed of a film towards some happy conclusion.

Herbert Brush

W and I went to the Capitol Cinema this afternoon. The German prison camp was shown: it was not very clear, but clear enough to make me want to put our Nazi prisoners in under the same conditions. Nothing less will make those sub-human beasts realise that it is wrong to torture other folk in such cruel ways. Even the women guards must have been sadists of the worst type, who enjoyed seeing and making their victims suffer. Judging by the short glimpse I had of these females' faces, I could easily imagine them singing and cursing as they beat their helpless prisoners.

One of the films was awful piffle, but the other with Wallace Beery in it was good.

SUNDAY, 6 MAY

Maggie Joy Blunt

The end of hostilities in Europe is to be announced within the next day or two, we are told, and before Thursday when Mr Churchill is making a special broadcast.

Lys came to tea and stayed the evening. Her friend C called in about 6.30. She left a spare pint of milk for us, two eggs for Lys and some ointment for my ears, which has, so she assures me, positively magic powers and has been used by people of her acquaintance who have had the same trouble and found it effective where other remedies have failed. We had a drink and wondered when the announcement would be. Lys thinks she will go home that day and read a good book. C, whose husband is in the forces and stationed nearby, expects to hear from him and have him home for two days.

I have, urged on by Lys, answered an ad in this week's *New Statesman* for a job in a publishing firm. Not that I expect any results but it is good for one's morale to make this kind of effort when one feels in a rut as I do.

George Taylor

A joint ramble with the Rotherham WEA. Did not think many would turn up, but twenty-two gathered at the starting point, including members from Parkgate and Worksop. We had a charming walk through the Porter Glen, superior in my mind to any of the commercial glens of the Isle of Man, to Ringinglow, and then along the ancient moorland road, known popularly as the sheeptrack, to Longshawe. The sheeptrack has been closed throughout the war, as the moors have been used for bombing practice. It was good to find it open once more, and the RAF dismantling their station. The RAF have left a Tarmac road behind, however, and I am afraid that this will be used by motors after the war and spoil another track for walkers.

Usually we go to the Ramblers Café at Longshawe – a clean and smartly run café managed by the Holiday Fellowship. It is usually very crowded, so our leader had booked at a neighbouring cottage. It was an unpleasant place, however.

MONDAY, 7 MAY

George Taylor

No news of VE day, so to the office as usual, and my wife went collecting rents. When I arrived back at the office after lunch, my thirty-two-year-old colleague said that his assistant, seventeen, had overheard a prominent solicitor say that peace would be announced at 4 p.m. Another person he had met, who was 'in the know', also gave the same time. A few minutes later I went out, and overheard a tram conductress say to her mate, 'Well, the war will be over at 4 p.m.' We did not settle down to any serious work at the office, and listened for the church bells at 4 p.m., but they did not come, so we lingered on till 5.30. Meanwhile, the office boy had brought in an evening paper which announced that VE day would be tomorrow.

Town was very busy, and there was a holiday atmosphere everywhere. It took me nearly a quarter of an hour longer than usual to get home, so I just missed the 6 p.m. news. However, my wife said there was nothing in it, so we did not know what to think. Hoping to see a news film we went to the local cinema, but they did not show even a newsflash, the whole time being taken up with *The Adventures of Mark Twain*. We were thoroughly disgusted.

Maggie Joy Blunt
Had a £1 note taken from my handbag at work this week. Like most women there I leave it about unguarded – we do not suspect each other of petty theft. Other people have been missing notes recently also and when I reported my loss to the works police I was told that they had their eye on a certain office boy. I hate everything of this kind happening and won't – I can't – accuse anyone, but I believe I know the boy they mean. He is a weaselly looking lad, impertinent and difficult to handle, but responds I find to a touch of humour – scolding only makes him sullen and disobedient. No doubt he thinks me a good-natured mug. My feelings about him are that he is a slippery, sharp, incurable type, always quite well dressed as though from a fairly good home, but there is something about him, some destiny in his face and manner. No remand home or schooling will make any difference. He won't listen. He will just follow the force that is urging him along a certain path.
From Italy, S wrote on 1 May:-

'Last night German resistance on the northern Italian front ended. I was at my desk with two very young officers and my OC who was a captain with me in Greece in 1941. He said, "It's been a long road." We opened a bottle of Scotch and had a lot. Yet the old real Desert Rats – my old 7th Armoured Division – are still battling around Hamburg. The youngsters felt more exhilaration than we. My thoughts, strangely, were on the safari track from Bug Bug to Maddelena – two graves long since covered with sand. The end is near now and a great sense of emptiness. A new desert of emotion to be explored and fought over . . .'

Herbert Brush
I went to the Royal Academy exhibition in Piccadilly. My word, it was hot walking in the sun, and by the time I arrived there perspiration was standing on my forehead. The show cost a shilling.

I put a pencil mark in the catalogue against the exhibits that were able to keep me in front of them for more than five seconds.

No. 31: *Girl Resting* by A. R. Middleton. She is naked, but it was the position of her left foot that caught my eye and I wondered how she could pose in that position without getting cramp.

No. 88: *Snow in Nottinghamshire* by Henry Moore. The reason I looked at this is because there are hills and valleys in the background, and I could not remember there are hills in Notts.

No. 184: *Still Life* by Frederick Elwell. There is a cold ham with a nice wide cut in the middle showing the inside lean part, and a pork pie with a couple of bottles of spirit alongside. It made me feel hungry, and I remembered that I had a sausage roll in my pocket, but I could not eat a sausage roll in the Royal Academy.

I left the exhibition at 2.45 p.m. I walked as far as the Haymarket and caught a No.12 bus. A crowd was waiting at the end of Downing Street, presumably waiting to see the Prime Minister, who is expected to declare Peace today.

TUESDAY, 8 MAY

George Taylor

There was the stillness of a Sunday when we woke, and this continued all morning. I spent the morning doing some useful work in the garden, and then, as it started to rain, stayed in during the afternoon. Although we knew what Churchill was going to say at 3 p.m. – or at least what we hoped he would say – we switched on the radio and continued listening until nearly 5 p.m.

After tea we went for a short walk and found quite a few flags displayed by the houses, although there was nothing elaborate. From the look of the trams we thought there could have been very few in town this afternoon, but a friend we met told us that there had been thousands. We still cannot realise that the war in Europe is indeed at an end. It is true that I have removed some more of the blackout today, as I promised myself on Peace Day, but somehow I still have a sneaking feeling that it may be wanted again any time.

In January 1941 we purchased some tinned chicken, and as we have never been called upon to use it, we promised ourselves a treat on Peace Day, and we did open it today. As with many things, it proved somewhat of a disappointment, for although it is genuine chicken – bones, skin and meat – it is spoilt by aspic jelly. Another long cherished tin, of sausages purchased in November 1940, proved much more acceptable for lunch.

Herbert Brush

I wonder whether any two of the millions of people in London will think the same thoughts today about the date when the change in their lives from War to Peace commenced.

I heard Mr Churchill at 3 p.m. declare that war will end at 12.01 tonight. I wonder why the extra minute was added? Then an account of the various crowds collected in London and elsewhere, which made me glad that I was not in one of them.

I nearly swore this afternoon when I found that nearly all my runner beans had been eaten before they put their tips above the ground. I shall have to sow them all afresh: luckily I have plenty of my own seed.

10.30 p.m. Listened to the King's broadcast at nine o'clock. W keen to see a bonfire so we went down the road to the place where a bomb had made plenty of firewood available and saw quite a good fire. W wanted to see another, but one was enough for me, so I returned and wrote this note.

WEDNESDAY, 9 MAY

George Taylor

Finished taking down blackouts at all windows and fanlights, and parcelled them for storage in the loft, ready for the next war. If we do leave this house before then, they will go along with the fixtures. I hope, however, that we shall be able to forget their existence. Bank holiday crowds everywhere.

Herbert Brush

7 p.m. I have been on the plot most of the day. I believe the judges in the competition come round for their first visit before the middle of May, so I have been busy trying to make the plot tidy. I have fixed up another seat at the end of plot close to the hedge so that I can sit in the shelter during showers. This was the spot where I pressed myself into the hedge with the bucket over my head when a rocket burst overhead and bits of it came down all round me.

Edie Rutherford
Housewife and clerk in Sheffield
Where to begin? Well, we came home from work on Monday evening, 'bewitched, buggered and bewildered' as a friend of ours used to say. We had our office wireless on hourly without getting any satisfaction.

Then at 9 p.m. we got the news that the next two days were holidays. That was enough for me. The following day I had promised to go to help my friend who is still clearing up her house, so husband came with me. I had stood in a queue for two small brown loaves for them. There were bread and fish queues everywhere all along the bus route and our tram route to town.

A neighbour brought in her portable radio at 3 p.m. so that we could listen to Churchill. He spoke well and seemed in good form. Everyone agreed that we have been well blessed in having such a leader. I felt once again great gratitude for being born British.

Left at 5 p.m. and walked to nearest tram so that we could come home via town centre. Thousands round City Hall for a service. More thousands just wandering about. All the little mean streets had their decorations just as for Coronation and Jubilee. I find them pathetic though courageous.

We got home and had a meal and sat quietly till 10 p.m. when we decided to go and have a look round. These flats had a neon 'V' right on the top flat roof which looked effective. Also our corridor balcony lights were on for the first time since blackout began. At the street corner, our shopping district, a radio shop had fitted up loudspeakers and music blared out. We saw many people the worse for drink, in fact most that we saw were in that state. Either looking very sorry for themselves or just merry, and we also saw vomit about, ugh.

Met up with a spinster who lives alone on this floor who asked could she stroll with us so of course we said she could. Came home about 11 p.m., decided we were hungry and what about looking at reserve food put by years ago. To our surprise and pleasure found a tin of asparagus tips and tin of tomatoes. Had these with cheese and water biscuits and margarine. Miss S found a stout for husband at her flat and one gin and ginger for herself and myself. Then we sat and talked till 1.20.

Went to door to see friend off and found terrace floodlit and loudspeakers giving music for tenants and their friends to dance, and they all seemed merry. Kept it up till 2 a.m. when, I heard since, someone on a higher floor threw water over them.

We woke next morning about 9 a.m. to find all quieter than any Sunday. I did some washing and ironing and sewing and housework, and in the afternoon we went on a tram ride through town and to Bingham Park which we had not seen before. Called at a pub in that neighbourhood to find it shut. So back to town and while I waited in a queue to spend a 1d., husband had an ale at a nearby pub. Said it was packed tight.

I thought, as always, that the King's speech was marred by his speech, but on the whole his stammer wasn't so bad. Maybe if he were to speak to us more often he would learn to relax so well that he would not stammer at all. I have decided these last few days that 'Rule, Britannia!' is a far better tune than 'God Save The King'.

Goering need not imagine he can get away with it by calling his ex-colleagues nasty names. He is an arch villain and should hang for it. As to all the reasons for defeat given by various German generals – it is clear they lost because material might is NOT right, never was, never will be. It is good that the Channel Islands are free and I hope we will get food to them quickly, plenty of it.

There are several Nazis not yet accounted for. And I shan't be happy about Hitler till the body is found. What guilty consciences they have who commit suicide. Is it possible they really thought once they'd get away with their villainy?

I laughed when it was announced that the Japs had told the world that Germany's surrender would make no difference to them. Won't it indeed? They'll soon see just what a difference it is going to make.

I keep thinking our few windows are all unblacked and keep finding a pane that isn't. Amazing how long it takes. Thought I had done yesterday when husband smilingly pointed to two small top windows in bathroom. Drat. I'll scratch the paper off sometime this weekend if I get time.

Weather forecasts are a welcome return and we don't care how many deep depressions threaten from Iceland or anywhere. We can bear that kind of depression now. Anyone want tin hats and two gas masks?

George Taylor

I was alone for lunch at home, and noticed there was a symphony on the radio, so switched on for company. It was Beethoven's Fifth. Some fortnight ago I had booked for the Hallé concert in the evening tonight, and to refresh my memory as to the programme I turned up the advertisement in the daily paper. Lo and behold, the programme had been altered, and Beethoven's Fifth Symphony included there. Twice hearing in one day is pretty good going.

At the Hallé concert there was a very thin attendance, the poorest I have seen for some time. To start, we had three national anthems, I presume the American and Russian played in full, then the British. When we sat down my neighbour remarked, 'It's a good job they didn't play the Chinese.'

TUESDAY, 15 MAY

Edie Rutherford

Yesterday I had a cable from my goddaughter in Natal – rejoicing about our victory and assuring me I am in their thoughts at this time. Kind gesture.

Friend tells me that he gave a talk to Jewish Youth at a club in town one night last week and was amazed at the intelligent questions afterwards. I listened and told him that in my opinion the Jews need to sort out their own minds, i.e. they want Socialism because they believe it makes no distinction of class, colour or creed; yet they want capitalism because so many of them are capitalist.

Shops now display notices that they have plenty of torch batteries . . . GOD BLESS OUR LADS FOR THIS VICTORY is painted on sides of houses near where I work. Others thank Monty, Churchill, Roosevelt, Stalin. Clear that decorations were planned some time ago as all show Roosevelt; or is it that folk feel he should get the credit?

Churchill sounded tired when he spoke on Sunday. I think he should be put to grass, as he calls it. Can't understand why he doesn't admit it and be done with it.

I notice the Ford factory at Cologne is working again. Seems there is truth in the oft-heard statement that we didn't bomb places which concerned our rich owners.

Burning Belsen is the only thing to do.

Wanted to buy a sponge in town today – but they started at £4 each. Used to be 18/6d. before the war. I did NOT buy, will stuff shoes with newspaper rather than give in to such wicked profiteering.

1/- for a small lettuce . . . oh well. No cress about just now. There are suggestions that we are going to be worse off than ever for food. I believe I would not mind that if the variety could be improved. My husband is quite definitely suffering from poor nutrition today. He needs more milk, butter, cream . . . I'm terribly worried about him.

WEDNESDAY, 16 MAY

George Taylor
The news of the restoration of the basic petrol ration has brought no joy to me. One of the great blessings of the war has been the reduction of motor traffic on the roads, and I dread seeing all the private cars back again. I think that peacetime public transport services should have been restored before private motoring was let loose on us again.

Gardening and typing in the evening. I also listened to the BBC broadcast 'Tribute to the RAF'. It was good to hear one of these feature programmes not messed up with incidental music.

THURSDAY, 17 MAY

Edie Rutherford
In all the news of the past week in papers and BBC, I have yet to hear a word about what happened in the Dominions at V time. One person to whom I commented said, 'But it doesn't mean anything to them', which is just typical of the general ignorance from high up to low down. Now that we don't need so much help from our Empire, it can go to the devil again.

Just done a wonderful make do and mend with pyjama coat of Husband's. They were bought in Durban thirteen years ago so must have been good when new. They had gone where husband's shoulder blades always cut open his clothes, and at top of sleeves. Have made a new top half of back.

Yesterday in a rash mood I bought myself two bunches pyrethrums, 3/- the two. One bunch would not have made a decent vase full. It is an outrageous price but when I've been without flowers for months, as I often am these days, I break out . . .

SATURDAY, 19 MAY

Herbert Brush
Roger the dog did not give any trouble during the night but he is now wandering about the house like a lost dog. Went to the Duchess Theatre to see a play by Noël Coward, *Blithe Spirit*, a weird fantasy in which the spirit of a dead wife made things uncomfortable for a man who had married again. Irene Browne was good in her part as a medium. It is some years since I went to the theatre, and I am not sure what I prefer – theatre or cinema.

SUNDAY, 20 MAY

Edie Rutherford
I just haven't had a chance to see to this diary. On Friday husband woke with temperature so I bullied him into staying in bed, rang his brother and took the opportunity to tell him how worried I am about Sid these days, and that I won't be satisfied till he has been screened; also said Sid should have two weeks' holiday this year as he needs it. Harold says he would mention the screening to Sid, and see that he gets the latter. So I hope I have achieved something. One has to go about things so carefully.

WHIT MONDAY, 21 MAY

Maggie Joy Blunt
At rest now, in the domestic respectability and peace of a suburban garden. Warm sun, large clouds, cool wind, neighbours' voices, one or two aeroplanes, birds full-throated, joyous.

Saturday morning I went to have hair done in Windsor, did some shopping, had lunch, came home, cycled into village to order rations, take shoes to be mended, collect some paraffin oil in bottles. Collecting milk from next door, Lady A bears down on me with a triumphant, exultant gleam in her eye: 'I have always said that our troubles would begin when the war was over – now everyone is out for himself and there is a clash of interests everywhere. Power goes to heads of these people who have not been brought up to rule . . .' I agree that the future promises to be chaotic and that there will be trouble with Russia but can't believe it will be as black as she seems to think. I go in, have tea, do some chores and cooking and start preparing myself for CL's party.

I leave – suitably clad over afternoon party frock and taking one of my few remaining pairs of real silk stocking and shoes to change into – on cycle for Windsor about 8 p.m. and arrive just before 9 p.m. Fully intended to cycle home after the party but a friend CL was expecting couldn't come so she has a spare bed and insists that I stay. A pleasant gathering. Rep theatre people, one or two Service men, a couple of Canadian RAF, a woman I recognise as having lectured a Red Cross unit on gas two years ago. We sit and talk, drinking orange gin, champagne cider or cider cup and eating delectable snacks prepared by CL. They roll back the carpet and we dance but not for long, as there isn't much room and people evidently prefer to talk.

Spent the weekend with stepmother Ella (Aunt Aggie also there). Listening to the report of Ellen Wilkinson's speech on the one o'clock news I was suddenly struck by the thought of how extraordinary it was that the BBC should allow Labour propaganda such prominence. At her statement that the Conservative Party had carried out very few reforms during their long term of office I heard Aunt Aggie snort and wondered how I could defend that view. When I am with Conservatives I find myself agreeing with Conservative opinion, when with Liberals with Liberal, Labour with Labour, Communist with Communist. It is all very confusing. Conscience and the fact that my politically minded friends will expect me to, will probably make me vote Labour. (The election may be held, we are told now, in July, which seems too soon, too much of a rush. But why should we have to put up with the present Government until the war with Japan is over?)

N thinks we have not heard the last of the Nazis – their apparent collapse has been too quick and easy. She is not alone in this opinion. Note a new film released and reviewed this week: *The Master Race*.

There are people even now who have never used a ration book for themselves. For example, an elderly female cousin of Ella's and Aunt Aggie's, of fantastic wealth, who has been living with an elderly companion in a remote part of Scotland during the war. They have not, either, heard a gun. They are now in London staying in a hotel near

Welbeck Street. Two useless, parasitical old women. How my Communist friends would love to denounce them. And what a lot of apparently useless people there are in the world living on money someone else has earned. Is it entirely their fault? I am not at all sure that unearned income is not more demoralising than dire poverty. When no effort has to be put into living the character grows fat, flabby, feeble. I'd rather see it twisted and hard.

10 p.m. A pleasant, lazy day. Have done nothing but sit and knit, listen to gossip and be fed excellently at regular intervals. My dear relatives. They were up I think about 7.30–8 a.m., brought me my breakfast about 9 a.m. Spent the morning washing (an electric washing machine simplifies this for them) – Aunt Aggie dealing with the clothes, Ella hanging them in the garden. Then I borrowed the iron and mended two tears in my mackintosh with Mend-a-Tear, dried up the lunch crockery which Ella was washing, sat in the garden while Ella hoed the garden path and clouds gathered like mountains. A gin and lime, supper (herrings in tomato sauce, salad, stewed gooseberries from the garden and blancmange). Rain began to fall.

TUESDAY, 22 MAY

Herbert Brush
I took a bus to Regent Street and walked towards Oxford Circus, and seeing a big queue going into the *Daily Express* exhibition of German camps, I joined the queue and went in, as entrance was free.

Awful pictures, enough to make one feel ill, but everyone wanted to see them. Heaps of human skeletons, some of them alive though they seemed to have only skin on their bones. It is difficult to understand the mentality of the German guards who could treat people in such a way, even though they were ordered to do so by the beasts in command. The ghouls even had dental forceps with which they extracted teeth from their victims if there was any gold in the stoppings.

I was in there for about five minutes but that was enough for me to see all I wanted to see of those photographs. Every German prisoner of war ought to be made to go to an exhibition like the one in Regent Street.

At Westminster Bridge I noticed a large crowd had gathered to look at the U-boat which had just come to the landing stage.

WEDNESDAY, 23 MAY

Herbert Brush

I wonder what made Churchill resign so suddenly. Probably he knows that he will have a better chance to return if the election is soon.

Edie Rutherford

The world seems in a mess. All reports that come are of unrest and at home we have all this acid between P.M. and Labour Party, with an election looming. A man I spoke to yesterday, a Liberal, reckons Labour will win and God help us, riot and revolution are the only things to follow that. I said they haven't won yet and I refuse to fret till they do, and even then I don't know that they would for sure make a mess of things, though I can believe they might.

Husband reckons Labour isn't fit to rule. Well, whoever gets in, the voters put them there, and you can't get away from that. All I want is good men and true and damn what party they belong to, but I know that is asking a lot. (Good women and true also!) Was interested to see that Bevin admitted women had turned out the equal of men in industry in this war.

What an awful war our men are fighting out East. The Japs are such beasts that our lads have to do things which must disgust them to their souls' depth. Ugh. May it end soon.

THURSDAY, 24 MAY

Edie Rutherford

Discovered at work yesterday that I was the only one who has ever voted. I felt like Methuselah as I explained things. One girl asked, 'Was Asquith P.M. in Queen Vic's time?' They'd never even heard of Bonar Law. One girl had the idea that we are behaving disgracefully and what will the rest of the world think? I told her a general election always means a rumpus, and Churchill's resignation is only going through the motions connected with same. She thought it would look like ingratitude to Churchill, and had the idea an election would be a peaceful affair, done in quiet and orderly fashion.

Everyone seems resigned to food cuts, but all think Germans should be put on the rations they thought sufficient for occupied countries, and that anything we go without should be for those occupieds now. I do too. What makes me mad is, our Government has spent thousands advertising dried milk and dried egg and now that folk are at last getting the idea that they are not synthetic and can be eaten, enjoyed, and help to keep them well, we are told both will be in short supply.

Yesterday our recently married typist didn't come to work at all. Boss was fuming – sent someone in his car to her home. Her mother said she was in the dark: the RAF husband had turned up on Monday and they'd gone off, she didn't know where, and hadn't seen them since. The husband phoned in the afternoon to say they went to visit friends and missed the last train back on Monday. He was coldly listened to.

FRIDAY, 25 MAY

Herbert Brush
I wonder whether death by prussic acid is very painful: I hope so, as Himmler chose that way out.

My feet were like ice when I went to bed this evening, after listening to *Pride and Prejudice* on the wireless. I have a nasty boil on my back just where I can't reach it.

Maggie Joy Blunt
I should be writing to N, to S, or to poor, shamefully neglected Julia. I listen to Chopin's Waltz in A Minor, wait for my supper to cook, consider the washing and mending I should do and how nice it would be to sit and knit while I listened to the broadcasting of *Pride and Prejudice* later this evening. And all the while a story is bubbling up inside me (it has been bubbling for weeks) begging to be given coherence and shape. Should I disregard my duties and pleasures – ignore, cloak, suffocate them and give the story its chance? Is it really important enough? Would the result be worth the sacrifice of the other things? I don't know. Probably not. This is what always happens when I want to write a story. I have to wake up my mind to abandon all other activities for the time being – and pay for it dearly later, and then find that the story isn't at all what I intended or wanted it to be.

I am having help in the house again, after three years without. A woman recommended through friends is coming every Thursday morning, and came last Thursday for the first time. When I returned

31

from the office the place had a spuriously tidy look. Certain things had been put back on their shelves and ledges with the symmetry so beloved of Mrs Mops. The electric fire had been placed on the sideboard in the sitting room. The bedroom floor had been polished and looked very nice, the kitchen stove blackened, the parts of the stone floor I could see washed, the stairs swept. But the carpet hadn't been touched and a mat carefully arranged and disguised the fact. A table by the bed, in a rather dark and difficult to get at corner, had not been dusted. And so on. This sort of slackness and cheating enrages me. We have to pay 2/- an hour for it and be thankful. I gave her something for one of her children, told her to make herself tea, showed her where the biscuit tin was and intend to let her have flowers as she likes. My manner to these women is always kind and sympathetic and I always hope not patronising. I feel sympathetic to them and like to hear about their families and troubles. I am probably too kind, too trusting. Yet if I were here to supervise I am sure I could get her to do everything I want done and to do it well.

SATURDAY, 26 MAY

George Taylor
I left the office early to get home early, but a tram just ahead of ours caught fire, and we were held up for nearly half an hour while the fire brigade came to put out the flames.

In spite of the continuous rain during the morning, seventeen WEA members turned out for the historical ramble to Bradfield. The leader, Professor Potter, came complete with raincoat and attaché case, but he struggled manfully on, and gave us an interesting talk about the history of the church, and the size and importance of the county of Hallamshire.

MONDAY, 28 MAY

George Taylor
My wife tells me there is a lot of dissatisfaction about the reduction in rations. Most people had been expecting a lifting of rations, not a reduction – five years of struggling with food difficulties have been sufficient strain. One woman remarked that the fat ration would not

be sufficient to grease the frying pan, and another, somewhat sarcastically, said that it would not be enough to cook the weekend joint!

TUESDAY, 29 MAY

George Taylor
At the annual meeting of a brewery. The chairman has now lost an eye, twelve months after an accident in the blackout. This is an unrecorded war casualty.

FRIDAY, 1 JUNE 1945

George Taylor
Coulton's *Fourscore Years*, Readers Union choice for May, reveals an intellectual world that is quite foreign to the ordinary man. Compared with Coulton I realise how ill-read I am, and how mentally sluggish. And yet it seems almost as unbalanced to devote so much time to monasticism like Coulton as I am compelled to spend so much of my life working out tax computations. Still, Coulton becomes somebody, which I shall never be.

SATURDAY, 2 JUNE

Edie Rutherford
Well, this diary has been sadly neglected. The day I last attended to it, our friend Alex MacLeod turned up and from then on I had two men to look after, and one to entertain. Alex stayed just a week and I think he enjoyed himself. I took him out the three afternoons this week when I was free after work.

He went down two caves (Blue John and Speedwell) and, as he is a mining engineer, he liked that. (He told the Germans he was a barman, as he did not intend going down their mines.) We went to Bakewell and to cinema to see Will Fyffe in *Give Me the Stars*.

Russians liberated Alex's camp, near Chemnitz. He had pneumonia at the time, but when fit he walked with others thirty miles to where American lorries took them to an airbase. They flew to Belgium, went by train into France, and air to England. Alex said he could have got out via Russia but he was scared of them. They give little value to human life. Shoot too readily and, well, women as well as men, and use hand grenades to play handball. Alex says he had to bury the dead after we strafed Chemnitz and Dresden. Says the destruction we did is quite unbelievable. It was just impossible to get rid of the dead. They buried for a month, and tried to burn but it wasn't possible so they had to abandon it. Red Cross parcels kept them going. The German sentries would swap anything for a bar of chocolate. The Nazi boss of the camp lived like a king – several cases of Scotch intact in cellar when the end came, not to mention all the looted stuff from France and elsewhere.

Alex hasn't seen his six-year-old daughter since she was twenty months.

SUNDAY, 3 JUNE

Edie Rutherford
The Pope is late in denouncing the Nazis . . . He makes me sick. I think Mrs Churchill is speaking with great wisdom on her Russian visit. Without envying them, in the stupid way our Communists here do, she feels for them and pities them. That seems okay to me.

I hope we aren't expected to feel sorry for the Swedes if they go a bit short of food in order to help Finland and Norway. It is their job to help their neighbours. I shall never regard Sweden with anything but contempt for the rest of my life, along with all the other so-called neutrals.

MONDAY, 4 JUNE

Herbert Brush
I listened to Churchill this evening and after hearing his speech concluded that I was quite right on being a Conservative Nationalist, even though I know scarcely anything about politics, beyond what comes to me through common sense; which sense seems to be sadly lacking in some people who say that Socialism is the best thing for individuals.

I was a little doubtful about whether I have a vote after all these years; but W found out that my name is down on the voters list at Lewisham, so I shall once again make my X.

TUESDAY, 5 JUNE

Herbert Brush

When walking along Thorpewood Avenue this morning a woman showed me a large hedgehog which was lying near the steps which lead up to her house. She was afraid to touch it so I put it in her front garden, saying that it would be a useful pet. Its spikes were so sharp that I felt them on my fingers for half an hour afterwards. The animal had evidently tired itself out trying to escape from the pavement under its feet, but the only way was up the steps and I don't think that hedgehogs can climb steps.

I went to the National Gallery to have a look at an exhibition there, but when I walked in a girl at a desk near the door said that the entrance fee was 1/-, so as it was only a modern home exhibition I retreated.

I looked across to Nelson's Column and as usual there is a big advertisement on the lower part. I was struck by the foreign look about the first word. GIUE – certainly looked like a strange word and I had to read the line before I grasped what it meant. GIVE THANKS BY SAVING. But the V is distinctly a U.

Edie Rutherford

The slanging has begun, and Churchill at his worst doing it. I did not tremble at his bogeyman, Socialism, because I know the other side to the picture. Only the ignorant will fall for that Mr Churchill, but unfortunately there are plenty of ignorant folk who have a vote. Ah well. The way I feel now, I shall not vote at all. A friend says that is wrong. I say no – if one can't vote for any candidate because one doesn't like their ideas, it is better not to vote, then when someone else thinks of putting up for Parliament, and looks over a constituency, surely the one where most don't vote will be considered a possible place where they want someone good to vote for?

One of the grand things about life these days is hearing all the time of ex-POW men returning home. The joy of it. I hear this morning that my cousin Nellie is to be wed on Saturday. Her boy has been POW since Dunkirk. Poor kids.

My young brother in Birmingham reports that, contrary to expectations, and to his son's delight, their car still runs, though he says it will be too expensive to do so.

35

Maggie Joy Blunt

Prisoners of war returning now thick and fast. Their stories differ tremendously. An acquaintance of Jacky's, for instance, has come home looking well, tanned and happy. Speaks well of the ordinary German soldier – the non-Nazi – who shared parcels of food with the prisoners.

On the other hand, RW met a friend in the RAF who has been a prisoner for two years. He was so thin she would not have recognised him but for the uniform. He was in an army prison with Russians and conditions were always bad, apparently, where there were Russians as prisoners too. All were fed in this camp on cabbage water soup and bread – one loaf between ten men a day. They were so hungry they would steal rotten turnip peelings as they were carted through the camp. The Russians would keep the bodies of dead comrades as long as they could and take them into roll call in order to get the extra rations.

Punishment for the slightest offences were severe – R's friend had frostbite cracks between the toes from having been stood out in the winter cold for two hours at a time. Russian Cossacks liberated them. They had not sufficient food for the prisoners but allowed them to roam the town and loot what they could. Men were shooting cattle and pigs and gorging themselves on these. Some died from it. A month later he was flown to England, medically examined and given six weeks' leave.

An extraordinary cigarette shortage since VE day. For at least the last two weeks, when I have been in London, ordinary Virginian brands have been unobtainable. They have been increasingly scarce here, locally, but so far I have managed to get at least twenty a day from the canteen kiosk (but not my favourite brand) and sometimes from one or other of the local shops, but all shops appear very short of supplies.

Returning prisoners of war, returning evacuees, relief from night fears of enemy attack, no more blackout, factory sirens again, people talking of getting their cars on the road once more, a young girl I meet on the bus now wanting to give up her shorthand and typing and take up singing as a career – and the old familiar faces at the office disappearing one by one . . . So do the changes from war to peace happen, slowly, little by little.

George Taylor

For the first time since its return to Sheffield we visited the Playhouse. My wife was severely critical about the immediate desertion of Sheffield by the company upon the outbreak of war, and did not feel like patronising them again. However, having received two complimentary tickets, we went to see *Kind Lady*, described as a thrilling adaptation of a story by Hugh Walpole. The story may have been thrilling, but the play seemed too far removed from reality to grip.

WEDNESDAY, 6 JUNE

Edie Rutherford

A year since that momentous news of the landing on the Normandy beaches.

We reckon Attlee walked rings round Churchill. He was constructive and lucid. Man at work said to me yesterday that he would always vote Tory because he believes in freedom. He wants to be free to walk out of his job to another when he likes. So I just said, 'And free to walk into the dole queue when there isn't any job?' and left it.

Teachers next door tell me their benevolent fund has bought two houses in which elderly teachers will live, and be regularly visited by a nurse. It appears it is not unusual for old teachers to die alone and neglected; one old woman actually lay dead four months before she was discovered.

Husband sent a further five guineas for bio-chemic homeopathic remedies. Practitioner sends further treatment and is pleased to inform Husband he is better! I shall be more impressed when Husband FEELS it, and when he eats some food, and puts on some weight.

Fetched new ration books yesterday. Not much queue, was about ten minutes getting fixed up. Girl at library said the fiancé of a friend of hers is mad keen to go to India and is trying to join the army there. Said she could not understand it. Thought it terrible. I asked why? She had some vague idea about foreign parts. I said that if we are to hold the Empire together we'll have to look after it and that it is a good job certain folk are willing to do the looking after, and that I personally would go anywhere in the world without a qualm.

Herbert Brush

Raining since the morning so I am making myself useful in the house by topping and tailing gooseberries.

I have been playing with No. 37 today, a very remarkable number. A prime number multiplied by 3: the product is 111, by 6 it is 222, by 9 it is 333 and so on by multiples of 3 up to 27.

After that it gives other remarkable numbers which I never expected. For instance, you may put down any digit twice, such as 66, 44. To turn these into figures which will divide by 37, without remainder, you only need to take two digits the sum of which is 6 or 4 and place one in front and the other after the chosen digits, making 4662, 2664, 5661, etc. and find that all these numbers divide by 37 without remainder. For the 44, place the figures like this 1443, 3441, 2442. There are many other arrangements, but I have given as many as I think you will care to investigate and check.

THURSDAY, 7 JUNE

Herbert Brush

I notice in the paper this morning that Hitler's body has been identified by his teeth.

George Taylor

I took a pair of flannels to be mended by a Jewish tailor in business in one of the poorer parts of Sheffield. Talking about clothes, I suggested that his business would soon decline with everyone buying new outfits instead of patching old ones. He did not agree. 'People had hard times after the last war,' he said, 'and it will be just the same again.'

Edie Rutherford

The Honours List today makes me want to be sick as usual. Are there no men who serve because they love their fellow men and realise that if they have the God-given ability to serve them, it is reward in itself?

I should not be surprised if that is Hitler's body they've found.

FRIDAY, 8 JUNE

Edie Rutherford

One short at work yesterday. What a mess we're in when one is away, now we are already short-staffed. In my next incarnation, if I have a say, I'm going to be male. They leave dead on time always; draw the big salaries; sit down to meals prepared for them and put up their feet while some female clears it away . . . talk about equality of the sexes. Women are for the most part far superior to men.

SATURDAY, 9 JUNE

Herbert Brush

Went to the Capitol Cinema in the afternoon. The film *Between Two Women* was good with Lionel Barrymore in his usual part of a doctor in a chair.

Gave the tomatoes a little 'dried blood' to try and urge them on to grow faster.

SUNDAY, 10 JUNE

Herbert Brush

Raining and dull. Topping and tailing gooseberries. I see in the *Dover Express* this week that H. E. Osborne (Mournful Moses) has resigned from the Electricity Department after forty years and retired on pension. Mournful Moses used to get on my nerves so that sometimes I would have liked to kick him, but I think he was honest and conscientious in his work.

I also noted that 'Dr' Clarke is dead. I used to play against him at cricket many years ago at Wingham, and knew him very well. He kept the Red Lion at that time and many a good meal I had there.

J. Robinson – we always called him Captain – lived close to the Red Lion. He was the man who broke my left thumb with a cricket ball more than thirty years ago. My thumb has been quite stiff ever since.

Edie Rutherford

So Hitler may be alive, and with a wife. And with Bormann and Ribbentrop too presumably? Well, the earth is just not large enough to hold those folk and we must get busy and rout them out and finish them off, if alive.

I have a hunch we shall have the Tories back in power. Folk are torn between fear and ignorance, and will vote for no change. I hope I'm wrong, but . . . I fully expect the Tories to throw a sop to the masses before polling day.

Husband bought from his firm two camp beds, two mattresses, two pillows, five blankets for £2 – fire watcher's stuff. My sister is having her half, but I must get all cleaned before I can rail them to her. Oh for a drop of petrol to get the things to the cleaners, and fetch them when done. Life is irksome in irritating little ways these days.

Yesterday my cousin Nellie married her boy who has been POW since Dunkirk. The ceremony was in Bodenham church where my mother, grandmother, and all my aunts and uncles and cousins, have married. I would have given much to have been there yesterday. Bodenham is that rarity, an unspoiled English village, and I'm proud my folk had their roots in that neighbourhood. The tombstones round the church have our family names over and over again.

In the street the other day, while I waited in an outside queue for new ration books, I watched a woman with a baby in a pram, child white as death, about a year old it looked, obviously ill, listless and with that pitiful look a sick child always has. Another woman comes along, the mother tells how poorly the child is, and the woman takes a bar of chocolate from her basket and gives it to the child, 'It's nice, chocolate, luv, eat it, luv.' The little one sat there with the chocolate drooping from its hand, too weak to hold it up, wanly trying, but failing to respond. Were she mine, I'd have been in a panic about her, or him.

Awful case in this town last week, inquest held, young woman had a baby in a local nursing home and when it was a few days old it was gnawed by rats in the night nursery, and died next day from poisoning and pneumonia. Coroner exonerated the home from all blame. It is not a cheap home, one of the costly ones of this town. Bad enough to die in a war without dying at home when born healthy.

George Taylor
I was on police duty in the evening. I went into the station to collect my subsistence allowance, and found the telephone operator very upset, as she had been told that the women police would not be

released until two years after the end of the Japanese war. The war police look like being the last civil defence service to be disbanded.

MONDAY, 11 JUNE

Herbert Brush
The ever-increasing amount deducted from my monthly pension cheque is worrying me considerably. My income tax is now making a considerable contribution towards the war effort, but all the same, it is becoming more and more difficult to make both ends meet.

TUESDAY, 12 JUNE

Herbert Brush
I suddenly decided this morning that I would go and see Eisenhower's reception in Fleet Street on his way to the Guildhall, so I took a No. 62 tram and went to Savoy Street and walked to Temple Bar. The crowd kept on gathering and soon they were three deep behind me, as I kept my position on the kerb. I fancied that my size annoyed some of the small folk behind me but that did not make me move.

In about a minute the mounted police came along, followed closely by an open carriage drawn by two horses, and I got a very good view of the smiling face of the General as he sat on the back seat with another man. Cinema cameras were following up and I had to dodge an American jeep which carried one. The jeep had the name 'Dream Boat' on it.

Chapter Two

AT LAST THE PEOPLE WILL HAVE
A CHANCE TO GOVERN

Each time there were more Labour gains: a woman votes for her husband still stationed overseas

'I must tell you that a Socialist policy is abhorrent to British ideas on freedom. There is to be one State, to which all are to be obedient in every act of their lives. This State, once in power, will prescribe for everyone: where they are to work, what they are to work at, where they may go and what they may say, what views they are to hold, where their wives are to queue up for the State ration, and what education their children are to receive. A Socialist State could not afford to suffer opposition – no Socialist system can be established without a political police. They would have to fall back on some form of Gestapo.'

Winston Churchill, election speech, May 1945

'We have great tasks before us. Let us look at those tasks and not underestimate them. We intend to conquer and overcome all difficulties. We have first of all to finish the war with Japan . . .

Here at home . . . we have to bind up the wounds of war. We have to reconstruct our ruined homes – a great task in itself. We have to bring back in due course the workers who have been working on war to be workers for peace. We have to build up in this country the highest standard of life that we can achieve for all.'

Clement Attlee speaking at Central Hall, Westminster, on the night of his election victory, Thursday, 26 July 1945

WEDNESDAY, 13 JUNE

George Taylor

I heard the first reference to the pending general election on the tram today. During the day, too, one of our partners spoke of the election. He thought that the Labour Party were trying to draw red herrings across the trail, but then the Labour Party is always wrong in his eyes. He was also disturbed at the working of the popular vote. 'It is absurd to give the vote to boys and girls of twenty-one,' he said. 'My daughter has been asking for whom she is to vote as she has had no time to think things out for herself.'

Herbert Brush

I have had a couple of hours on the plot; there is always plenty to do there, although I have every square foot planted with something or other.

That reminds me, I dreamt last night that I had lost the hoe, but it was a mixed-up dream and at one time I was an assistant detective and had just been sent to Northampton to await instructions in connection with a murder. I forgot what else happened, except that my hoe disappeared in a strange manner, after I had seen a land girl with one very fat and one very thin leg walking across the wet ploughed field in a pair of huge boots.

THURSDAY, 14 JUNE

George Taylor

At 9.31 p.m., when I was on police duty, a man came rushing up to me and, in an agitated voice, told me that a gas oven was on fire at his house. I called out the fire brigade and in four minutes a salvage tender, another tender, the section leader's car and a police patrol car were on the scene. At 9.45 p.m. it was all over, all vehicles had returned, and I was left to make out my report from what few details I had collected. It was surprising what little I had gathered, but with the help of a friendly officer I made out my report and hope it will be accepted.

FRIDAY, 15 JUNE

Herbert Brush

Are you interested in bats? I read this morning that the way they manage to dodge things in the dark is by the use of very high-pitched sound which they make when flying in the dark. The echo of the sound comes back to them from any object nearby and they can tell exactly where that object lies. This is the same principle as 'Radar' which uses wireless beams which are reflected from a plane and gives away its position. So we are a million years behind bats.

SATURDAY, 16 JUNE

George Taylor

Nine from Sheffield, nineteen from Rotherham and twelve from Worksop took part in the joint WEA ramble to Roche Abbey. At Maltby we had the most shocking tea we have had for a long time. The caterer had been informed of our visit, and of the numbers to be expected. We arrived on the minute, but found nothing ready. Scarcely had one cup of tea each been served, when we were informed that the milk had run out. For this we were charged 6d. each.

Herbert Brush

I looked up a list which Caldwell once gave me showing the birthdays of the Brush family. Here it is:

Caldwell	25 February 1866
Horace	27 December 1869
Basil	6 January 1871
Herbert	17 October 1872
Con	29 May 1874
Nora	14 June 1876
Christine	16 February 1880

It's a long time since we all sat at the same dinner table.

W and I went to the Capitol Cinema this afternoon, but the films were not up to much. *Under the Clock* and *The Great Mike*. I certainly should not have remembered the titles had I not had a programme. Not interesting enough to keep W awake, but I just managed to do so by sucking sweets.

Went with Bill and Maggie at Dulwich to supper and stayed until 10 p.m. Took the car for the first time for years.

SUNDAY, 17 JUNE

Maggie Joy Blunt

Catering difficulties increase rather than decrease. There is a shortage of potatoes, soap, fresh fruit and greens. The cigarette scarcity continues. Our fat, cheese and sugar rations are being cut. Fish is fairly plentiful but one has to wait in long queues for it, and it is expensive. I have not seen any strawberries, gooseberries or tomatoes in any greengrocers, though that may be because I am never able to get to his shop when he has them.

I have had one lot of cherries. Peas are now in but there is little else as a vegetable except cabbage. We have had nothing but cabbage on the menu in the canteen for weeks and weeks (I mean as a second vegetable to potato). A woman who shops in Slough was told by the managers of two big food stores recently that they expected this winter and next to be the worst we have yet known. There are now no food reserves in the country and supplies are going to Europe. She was told: 'We are having to do it because the Americans won't. Why should we? We've gone without willingly all through the war because we've known it's been going to Our Boys. But why should we feed Europe? I resent the idea of helping the Germans or the French . . . But I have a family of young children to feed and I think the essential foods should at least go to them first.'

There are some people who in all seriousness thought that as soon as the war ended the shops would be filled with pre-war goods and we should be free to buy what we liked.

Have Huxley's *Eyeless in Gaza* out of the public library. Yesterday Ella and I went to see the Aluminium exhibition at Selfridges, lunched at the Bolivar and then went to see *Arsenic and Old Lace*, in its third year, I think. Really delightful entertainment, though it has not pleased everyone.

TUESDAY, 19 JUNE

Maggie Joy Blunt
Some evacuated children do not want to return to their own homes, and their foster parents don't want to let them go. Jacky talking this morning of a young cousin: 'My uncle's little girl was taken at five years old, by a wealthy family in Scotland at beginning of war. They have adopted her as companion to their own daughter and given her the same education, clothing and attention. Now she's a proper little lady. She won't want to go home – her people being rough and ready farmers . . .'

THURSDAY, 21 JUNE

Edie Rutherford
On Monday morning at 9.20 a.m. I had just started washing when there was a knock at the door. I went and there stood my young sister's brother-in-law, ex-POW. 'Are you Mrs Rutherford? Oh, I see you are – Edith all over again.' I said, 'Come in, Ross, I'm not so much like Edith as all that, why I'm ginger and she's got brown eyes and are you staying a bit or what?'

Well, there was plenty to talk about. He is an extremely nice young man and I am very glad we had the chance to meet him. He left late yesterday afternoon for Birmingham to visit my brother there. Day before yesterday I met him from work and we got the 1.30 bus to Bakewell where my South African friend got half an hour off from her job to have a cup of tea and chat. Ross amused me in the store where Alice works – he went up to the girl at the cigarette counter and said nicely, 'Miss, would you let me have one of those boxes of matches you have under the counter somewhere?' She did! There is no doubt my countrymen have a way with them. No wonder so many have already married here since liberation.

For myself, I must say I have enjoyed having my countrymen around. Their manners are perfect, and after eleven years of uncouth Yorkshiremen it is lovely again to be with men who have been properly brought up. Ross says that, when in a bus with his three companions he has gone around with, they were one day told off by an Englishman for giving up their seats to girls. 'It is no longer done in England.' When they protested that they were still going to do it, and felt they could not do otherwise, they were told, 'Well, you will be taken for sissies.'

Herbert Brush
The man who lives next door to here has a large garden, also a family of at least three young sons. He has bought each of them a horse, and this evening they are riding round and round the garden. He also has a billy goat, a dog and a cat and a sick wife, so he must be very fond of animals and have plenty of money to spend.

W and I went to the Capitol Cinema this afternoon. I always like a film when Wallace Beery is in it, and *Rationing* was very good; the ugly man always being amusing.

George Taylor
My policeman friend called in for a cup of tea. We started talking about the election. My friend thinks there should be a strict limitation on the size of private incomes. I pointed out that this was already effectively done by income tax and surtax, as a result of which all the people with incomes of £6,000 or more, net, could be put into a single double-decker bus. He was not convinced, however, and said that although the income was taken, the power of holding vast properties remained. He was not going to vote for the Conservatives because the first thing they would do would be to reduce Income Tax. My counter to this that the working man, too, would feel relief, did not carry much weight.

MONDAY, 25 JUNE

Maggie Joy Blunt
Some extracts from S's letters from Italy:-

26 April. The Rome I knew of in 1937 stands as ever – historically – but its life has changed as has that of London. Les Americans of course. As in London they dominate the cabarets and bars. They have certainly succeeded in forcing up the value of tarts. It's a question of relative values. In 1937, a reasonably good-looking tart would be valued at say 180 lire for the night. And dear at that. About 37/- at sterling rates then. The Yanks pay – the fools – up to 3,000 lire, or over £7.

Tonight I prowled around, as I enjoy doing, on my own. I dined well at a club, reserved for British officers on a pre-war gastronomic level – ravioli, lamb, apple fritters, cheese and coffee, superbly cooked at 100 lire (5/-). I went to a nightclub, danced with appalling women, half obviously syphilitic. For every British officer there were ten Yanks, mostly very, very young and behaving as adolescents. They are mocked, swindled and despised by the Romans. The British are swindled and, I think, pitied. They cannot understand why Britain – to them a great power – does not pay its soldiers on the same level as the Yanks. The only Englishwomen here are ATS. All little suburban tennis-clad girls whose heads have been turned by mass-men desire, and are gawky (to me anyway) and undesirable in contrast to the worst of the locals.

30 April. I'm scribbling this on my bed in the tent. I shall probably head north very soon. My batman, now snoring, said tonight, 'The War's nearly over – then the real one begins, xxxx it!' Comment of one officer: 'The next war centre is Tehran – oil interests.'

Can you read this? My wrist pains me a little tonight. Means rain . . . Will finish this tomorrow.

2 May. 2nd General Hospital. Now in hospital. In an hour's time they take out my blasted appendix. Was taken ill at 3 a.m.

4 May. I am weeping weakly because I can't stop pain in my belly and three days without food, and on top of it the emotional storm of the great victory.

Let me weep. Six long years, my dear. And I end them here, in a shabby Italian barracks . . . but my complaints are for the wounded who cannot celebrate. Funny. I have never wanted to weep so much before and I know others are weeping silently. Physical weakness, I expect. The radio blares victory after victory after victory . . . A soldier I knew in the desert brings me water as he has done before. I haven't seen him since 1942. He says 'You are much better, sir.' And he, poor devil, has lost a foot and awaits the ship home.

Later. Rockets climb the skies outside. Once to be watched with spectacular fear, now weariness. The fitter group of five in this ward are talking. One will soldier on – 'I know no other life now.' He is twenty-eight. Two others see war with Russia in fifteen years, one less. I raise my voice to protest. They seem hurt and surprised. 'Everyone knows,' they say, 'that Russia wants the whole of Europe.' I cannot answer them logically. So I turn to my one-footed orderly, 'All I want is what I'm going to get,' he says. 'A nice little council house in Ruislip and a job on the council.'

7 May. Weakly scribbling still. Radio says expect announcement hourly of end of war in Europe. Thank God. Little celebrations here. Much political talk.

Nothing to read except Yank magazines, dog-eared and worn. Lots of patients make slippers or toys – this is called 'taking the mind off'. My visitors tell me that there are little signs of celebration outside, just a strange emptiness – 'Thank God I'm alive, but now what?' Queer to think what I shall do. I have lost all ability to plan but retain a great Micawberish certainty of 'Something going to turn up'. Meanwhile my only immediate plans are to get fit again . . . I can hear a military band somewhere playing in Eastbourne Pier-style. Very hot here. Part fever, I know. Can see from window – my bed below it – only blue sky, white roof edge and the thin green top of a fir tree. Tired now.

8 May. So it's over . . . Listened to Churchill's speech. Surprising end to it – 'Oh Britannia! God save the King!' Then came, to us, the most pleasing thing – the thin clear notes of the 'Cease Fire'. And so I snuggled down to sleep. Wonder where Hitler, Goering, Goebbels & Co. swine are. Possibly we shall hear of a Terence O'Goebbels editing the *Cork Courier*.

10 May. I shall probably be demobbed about December if I can; in the meantime I shall fix myself up with a job in the consular service in the Balkans (or it may be The Hague) or if this fails try for a journalistic or British Council job in the Balkans or France. My main personal worry now (after demobbing anyway) is getting enough money to feed my family without returning to the old journalistic racket in which I could not keep pace with the younger Smart Alec. Nor want to. That is most important. Nor want to . . . I want to sit in the sun for six months, God knows how. Most in this ward just want to get home and out of uniform – even to the dole if need be, but get out. Home means so much to them.

16 May. In the shade of the poplars beside the swimming pool. Your charming VE day's description letter came today. I read it to an appreciative ward.

19 May. This is a beautiful place (BRC Convalescent Home, Sorrento) perched prettily on the towering green cliffs above the incredible blue Bay of Naples. I just sit in the sun – not allowed to swim yet. My room looks over the sea. This morning I heard the fishermen singing at their nets – not rowdily as British workman but in lonely harmony 'La Donna é Mobile'. There are women as well as men here – nurses and ATS officers more efficient than beautiful. I prefer to read Robert Graves' admirable *Wife to Mr Milton*. So we are to have more medals and be as decorative as the Yanks. Pity the Government couldn't increase the pay by 1d. a day instead of dishing out medal ribbons. I shall now have to wear five! 1939–1940 Star, African Star, France Germany Star, Italian and Greek medals. Fantastic . . .

25 May. So there's to be an election. Mother will vote as my proxy. Left, of course (and cancel her Tory vote!). This snap election may lose Labour much of the military vote, but it has a 2:1 chance of winning. I fear its foreign policy but welcome its internal plan for nationalisation. The pledge to the Jews in regard to Palestine is especially dangerous. May set the Arab world ablaze – and more poor British tommies will die in a cause they profit not by.

27 May. Lady Louis Mountbatten (with motorcycle outriders) came yesterday on inspection. I refused to be inspected, so with the gunner sailed in our dinghy to Amalfi. She was still there on our return, flinging a party for the more respectable convalescents. But the gunner and I waffled one of the reserved lobsters and bowed stiffly. Overheard from one of the female staff: 'She's EVER so nice, really she is EVER so!'

The gunner is twenty-seven, tall, broad, ginger and inarticulate. Will vote socialist purely because Barclays refused him an overdraft. Can play 'Bluebells Of Scotland' on bar glasses . . .

TUESDAY, 26 JUNE

Edie Rutherford

A. V. Alexander [local Labour MP] speaks here this evening at 8 p.m. I had thought he'd be missing something if he didn't make a target of these flats, as here he has close on six hundred folk all congregated who need go only a few steps to hear him. I shall go downstairs to hear what he has to say, and see what he looks like.

The town is full of Australians. Last week I noticed them and, not being a cricket fan, wondered. Then when I remembered the cricket . . .

It looks as if, reading the programme in the park, we won't have a beastly fair this year to rend the air with its hideous alleged music. Thank God if that is so. It was one of the horrors of war.

Herbert Brush

I listened to *The Brains Trust*, though I do not consider it as interesting as it used to be. One of the questions was on the Theory of Chance. I read the other day that someone had tossed a coin ten thousand times and that heads turned up 50.7 per cent of the total, so that there is a better chance to win if you say 'heads'. It is suggested that one side of the coin may be a little heavier than the other and would fall downwards, but, after looking at a penny for some time, I can't decide which side is likely to be heavier than the other. I tossed a penny just now and had six tails and four heads out of ten throws.

WEDNESDAY, 27 JUNE

Edie Rutherford

Last night Albert Victor Alexander came to speak to us. The meeting was in the open air, on the terrace. 8 p.m. He looks older than his photos and knows his stuff.

He got a fair hearing (opened up with the remark that it was the best setting yet, after so many stuffy schoolrooms etc); only one woman at the back kept interrupting with comments about letting Churchill down. I got a look at her once and imagine she was a bit mental. Dorothy Holmes (whose cat on fifth floor we care for when she goes away – spinster and clerk) sitting next to me, asked would it not cost a lot of money to finance all the nationalisations, etc.

Alexander said it would but that the money was there and would be better invested by Government than left to private folk who bungle and contrive and scheme with the profit motive.

Then she asked would it not take thousands of workers to carry things out – in short, a greatly increased civil service. Alexander said he didn't think so, but that if it did, if folk were doing a USEFUL job, surely it was a good thing.

I suppose it was a good meeting though attendance was poor, as is usual in these flats. They seem uninterested in things. I noticed some of the Tory tenants stayed at home, leaned over the balconies laughing.

The *Daily Express* this morning has Churchill in Manchester yesterday with thousands around him. I don't see how the opposition parties can stand up to the tremendous power Beaverbrook wields. If only all the Left parties would unite. Disunity is their weakness and will lose them this fight. It was said at the meeting that Churchill had been advised to sidestep Sheffield in his tour as his reception here would not have made pictures for the press. I wish there were such a thing as a newspaper that prints the news just as it comes, no views, no leading article, no editorials. Just the news of home and world, and let folk read and form their own ideas. Surely that is not too much to ask?

After the meeting I was speaking to a woman tenant who has a brother-in-law who was a Fascist, I should say *is*, and was interned some years. Now free, he boasts they are as lively as ever they were; I must say I was disgusted to hear of the Fascist salutes that went on outside the court the other day. We are a dopey lot. The things we stand for, after all we've been through.

SUNDAY, 1 JULY, 1945

Edie Rutherford

Last evening Lieutenant Hobart, the Tory candidate, came to address tenants, so I went. It was a very lively meeting – our Communist friends were there prepared, our Conservative friends were there to defend. What a racket. I noticed our Fascist who, before the war, swanked in a black shirt, vehemently stick up for Hobart. I don't like his pals when they are that kind.

Hobart is a nice youngster, public school obviously. Speaks well, but, poor man, only one eye and his one good one doesn't seem to be much good. I pitied him. Whether he thinks he is now so handi-capped that Parliament offers him a career he can cope with, I don't know, but it seems likely.

Supporting Hobart was Alderman Bearcroft, an old man, Irish with a rich brogue, but intensely Tory and both he and Hobart appear to worship Churchill, and Eden too. I enjoyed it all; much better than the pictures and no price.

When I got in, Husband told me about Churchill's final speech, which I have this morning read for myself. Same old thing, and he'll get in, and all his pals, because most folk are still dead in ignorance in this country.

A pouring wet day again – paper says wettest June for twelve years. Husband saw in *Punch* this week about the American who was asked what memory of England he'd take home, and he said 'The magical way in which spring merges into autumn . . .'

TUESDAY, 3 JULY

Edie Rutherford
School of one of the teachers next door was burgled Saturday night. Staff tea for two months went, also some money – the burglars made themselves tea in the staff room. Police suspect louts, old pupils who know their way about. Teacher says petty theft among school-children these days is appalling.

WEDNESDAY, 4 JULY

Herbert Brush
W and I went to the orchard plot near Strood and gathered what was left of the cherries, about 5lb. or so. Not worth going all that way for, but W does not like the idea of leaving a cherry behind if it can be got.

Churchill was making a tour in this part of London this evening so W, D and I went to London Road near Horniman's Museum to see him go by. We got there about 6 p.m. but it was 7.10 p.m. before he went past in an open car. He was sitting high up, making his usual V sign and I only caught a glimpse of him as his car went quickly down the hill towards Forest Hill. The last time I saw him was thirty-odd years ago, when I met him in the door of a second-hand bookshop in Smargate Street, Dover.

THURSDAY, 5 JULY

George Taylor [on holiday in York]
We set off to the nearest shopping town, Hinderwell, in the morning, but midway I flicked some flies off the side of my face and in so doing sent my glasses flying into the road. Fortunately neither lens broke, but a section of the frame broke into many pieces. My wife performed wonders with a bit of sticking plaster.

It was election day and there was a polling station at the school opposite our farm to which the villages had to come from a radius of three or four miles. For the better part of the day there seemed to be absolutely nothing doing, but in the evening there was a diminutive trickle of farm labourers, and even a rush of three or four just before 9 p.m. We watched a car come for the ballot box about half an hour later.

FRIDAY, 6 JULY

Edie Rutherford
Well, we both voted on our way to work yesterday, both for A. V. Alexander.

In butcher's this afternoon, woman ahead of me in queue gave a South African half-crown, which butcher noticed and handed back, 'This is no use, it is African.' Poor woman, she said, 'Oh, is it? Someone passed it to me.' So I said, 'Never will I stand by and see my country's money spurned, especially in the mother country,' and I swapped it for her. Why can't there be an arrangement within our Empire whereby banks honour the coins of each other?

TUESDAY, 10 JULY

George Taylor
To the bay morning and afternoon, then as a drizzle set in we went to the cinema at Hinderwell. The main show was Wallace Beery in the *Barbary Coast Gent*, not too bad in spite of its title, and the shorts included a very interesting one dealing with the manufacture of glass.

Soon after dark we were awakened by a man raving just outside the farm, then passing into the distance still shouting. We found he lived at Port Mulgrave and had these outbursts at intervals after witnessing the death of his mother in a motor accident.

Edie Rutherford

Delighted to hear in this morning's news about our extra heavy bombing of the Japs. I wish every Jap could be killed. Horrid little yellow beasts.

I sometimes wonder who did win this war. When one thinks of the way the Germans looted with each conquest and gloated publicly to the world about it, and then contrast it with a cut in rations which followed our victory.

Just been for rations – English eggs this time, so I hope they'll be fresher than the Canadians we've had for months past.

WEDNESDAY, 11 JULY

Edie Rutherford

A cinema in town, by no means the best, is being turned into a News Cinema. We have none here, and I'm sure it will pay well. I have never been inside this cinema; it is centrally situated, but looks drab and buggy. I asked Husband had he ever been in. 'Not for twenty-five years.' Then, it was THE cinema here. Its only rival was the Palace (now also third-rate) where one could not pay more than 9d. and for that got a tray of tea with fancy biscuits all in. Gosh, already we can speak of the 'good old days'.

It looks as if several national dailies are saying queues should be abolished. Well, I have said all along, and still say, some of us just have not the time to queue, so we don't. It has been unfair all through the war years that the women who have loyally gone to work have had to go without extras. While the women who went on calmly living domestic lives have stood around to get the plums.

Herbert Brush

I met Miss Hudson, the ninety-three-year-old nurse, in the road yesterday as she was coming up the hill and she said that she did not feel very well and had been to the doctor for medicine; so I offered to take her some spinach from the plot. She is a remarkable old lady, with a voice like a foghorn. Old Ing told me once that she can drink beer by the pint.

FRIDAY, 13 JULY

Herbert Brush

W dropped me at Camberwell Green this morning and I went to Peckham to change my library book and get my hair cut in Rye Lane.

A barber earns a shilling in less than five minutes nowadays. He does nine-tenths of the work with electric clippers and then takes half a dozen snips with his scissors and the job is done. He calls out 'Next Please' and one is expected to vacate the chair as quickly as possible; but he is never in too much hurry to hold out his hand for a tip.

The book I took out is *Brideshead Revisited* by Evelyn Waugh. (I wonder how he pronounces his name.)

Edie Rutherford

I hear there is a prefabricated house on view on a site in town, and one of the girls at work saw several of the houses now erected at Totley. She says they look awful, but are well fitted up inside. She swears they'll never stand up to a bad winter. 'I would not mind living in one' is the general verdict. Given the right spot, we would not mind one, in fact we'd LOVE one. Was told they cost £900 each, which seems terrible when one thinks of what one could get for that sum pre-war. Well, I still say that anything is better than mother-in-law.

Twice lately I have found a bug in our second bedroom, on the ceiling. I say they come from wood, Husband says from filth. Well, I am not a prize housewife, but I'm not as bad as that. When we bought our furniture we were very hard up and bought cheap stuff from a Jew firm with a gentile name. I suspect the furniture, or, maybe that rotten wood was used in these flats. Anyway, though I don't like bugs, I was raised in such an insect-ridden land that I don't get hysterical about them as folk here do.

SUNDAY, 15 JULY

George Taylor

On arriving home we found the son of one of my Special pals with a basket of eatables and a pint of milk ready for us. This is more assistance than we have ever had from our neighbours.

Both my wife and I disliked putting the clock back by an hour so early in the summer. Double summer time has been one of the two blessings of the war in our opinion, the other being the disappearance of public motoring.

WEDNESDAY, 18 JULY

Edie Rutherford
I must say I think it is rotten bad taste to advertise so much all the food, drink, etc, we've poured into Berlin for the Big Three affair. Apart from the vulgar swanking of it, the Germans don't get enough (oh yes I know we are the victors; and I know they'd have done the same and more so had they won) but it isn't right that we should do it while all of us are on rations.

Herbert Brush
Up at 5 a.m. and left home at 5.45 on our way to Truro. Travelled via Kingston, Staines, Egham, Camberley, Basingstoke (bypass), Salisbury, Shaftesbury, Sherbourne (stopped at the 'Rest Awhile' café). Kept nearly 30 mph all the way up. We crossed the Tamar into Cornwall and on through Launceston and Bodmin and arrived in Truro a few minutes before 6 p.m. Horace and Dolly Bacon were quite well and expecting us about the time we arrived.

THURSDAY, 19 JULY

Edie Rutherford
Husband dreamt last night he had taken over a boarding house. Was looking it over, found one room with two double and one single bed in it and in another room he found Yates, one of his firm's lorry drivers. Just as he was pondering the various problems the place presented, someone said, 'Time you thought about tonight's dinner, you know. There will be only six in tonight, but if I were you, I'd make a start as it is late . . .'

That for my Husband comes under the heading Nightmares.

Herbert Brush
Before leaving Truro, W got three gallons of petrol in the car, then we started off along the St Austell road. A man was lying unconscious by the roadside, with a policeman and a nurse near him; his car was up against a telegraph pole. We could do nothing, although W offered her first aid kit.

The cottage stands on the cliff side and a narrow footway leads past the door to the other cottages about twenty feet above the harbour which lies just below. It is unfortunate that another house stands even nearer to the cliff edge, right in front of this window. It is named 'Sea View' and entirely blocks my sea view.

During the afternoon W decided that she wanted to drive the car somewhere, so we went to St Austell to post a letter.

FRIDAY, 20 JULY

Herbert Brush
There is no WC in this cottage and one has to go down to the Public Lavatory on the quay side, about 50 yards away and 20 feet down. No paper supplied.

Edie Rutherford
Yesterday afternoon I went straight from work to visit Lowfields School. The Head Teacher is a charming woman, about fifty, silver-haired, soft brown eyes, gentle expression. As for the kids, it is a poor neighbourhood and they are a non-washed (for the most part) smelly lot, with poor clothes but not ill-nourished. That, thank God, is seldom the case today. Well, I talked to them about South Africa and Australia and had quite a riotous time. It is clear they have learned a lot about the Empire and showed it. The school has 250, fifty-three in the class to which I spoke. It is one of the most hideous, badly built and non-planned Victorian schools. I'd like to sweep it out of existence.

They are going on to study USA and USSR so I promised to see what I could get for them to help. I was asked for my autograph by a bright lad aged about eleven. First time in my life!

My sweetshop today actually offered me surreptitiously a quarter pound Cadbury's Tray Chocs. I nearly dropped. I bought them.

SUNDAY, 22 JULY

Herbert Brush
Horace got up early and went to church. I got up early and went to the WC on the quay.

This afternoon we went for a picnic on Penewan Beach. Talking to a man and woman at the harbour later, the woman mentioned the fact that no villagers go on the sands where we had been: there were too many mines left by the Americans, even after they were supposed to have cleared them all. Probably if we had been told before we went there we should not have rested on those sands with such comfort.

MONDAY, 23 JULY

Edie Rutherford
Oh ho, a to-do-ment about the woman who got a divorce because her husband would not agree to her having a child. I could get a divorce on that if I wanted, then, but it so happens, I don't – I should say, WE don't want one.

Went to dentist yesterday. He has a queer mind. Said he was sure of a Tory majority, adding that we weren't so decadent as to let Socialists rule the roost. I said I also thought Tories would get in but with a smaller majority than before, for which I would be very glad as they have had it all their own way far too long.

Herbert Brush
A fine, warm morning and I had to pay two visits to the convenience on the quay side.

Today we went to a beach and stayed there all afternoon. The sands here are really composed of small grains of granite and are painful to walk on with bare feet for a man of my weight. A mother left her small son in my charge while she went to get her tea, and for the first time in my life I looked after a small boy to see that he did not drown himself in the sea, of which he seemed to be very fond. I was not sorry when his mother returned.

TUESDAY, 24 JULY

Herbert Brush
We took the picnic gear and went to Porthluney Cove where we remained until 6 p.m. Basking in the sun, paddling and bathing and picking mussels off the rocks at low tide. Six Italian prisoners of war were engaged in the task of taking down the anti-invasion fence. They did not overwork themselves.

A man and his family had a large rubber ball to play with in the water, and they allowed it to escape and it drifted quickly out to sea.

The man chased it for a long way, but he could not swim fast enough to catch it and it was soon a dot on the water. It seemed to go on the rocks to the east of the cove and the man, who did not want to lose the ball, as they are now nearly impossible to buy anywhere, signalled to a boat in which a party was fishing and asked them to get his ball, but the fisherman in charge would not take his boat near the rocks, and I don't blame him. That man did not give up, however, and he walked about half a mile along the top of the cliff, climbed down and managed to recover his ball.

THURSDAY, 26 JULY

Edie Rutherford
Yesterday at work a twenty-four-year-old girl told me, seriously, that ever since the election was mentioned she had not put a penny in the bank because, if the Tories don't win, her money will be grabbed from her. I told her I found it hard to believe that anyone of average brains could think that way, but she was vehement about it. She thinks Torywise, her young husband Communistically, and they have endless and violent arguments.

Speaking to a German friend last evening, she said she cannot yet attempt to communicate with her parents in Berlin, but feels it can't be very long now, and is very heart sore. Her Czech husband sent a cable to his home two weeks ago and every day looks for a reply.

Last Friday, grocer sold me six 'cooking' eggs for 6d. Every one was bad. Trust the Ministry of Food to be generous with bad eggs.

George Taylor
It was with dismay that I heard the first announcements of election results from a loudspeaker in the city. Each time I passed there were more Labour gains, until I dreaded coming within earshot. During the afternoon, our senior partner came in to tell me that Labour had secured a majority. He did not seem unduly disturbed, although he is a staunch Conservative.

I took my Scotch friend to my brother's at Totley. My brother, of course, is appalled by the election results. He thinks it is a disaster from a foreign policy point of view, and then my friend suggested that the reverse might apply. Discussing the causes of the swing to the Left, my brother thinks that Churchill has caused a lot of this by his bellicose election talks on the radio.

On reflection I think it is a redeeming feature that the attempt to exploit the personality of Churchill has failed. We want no little Hitlers here.

FRIDAY, 27 JULY

Edie Rutherford

Well, well, well, who'd a thought it? Not I. Damn bad prophet me, but how GLAD I am. At last the people will have a chance to govern. Pray God they get His help so that they don't make colossal blunders. There's is the heaviest task any Government has ever faced in all our history. I would not be anywhere but in England this day.

At work the two girls in my office were quite unmoved. Say it makes no difference, things will always be the same. I replied, 'Well! It is said pessimism goes with age, optimism with youth, but I, at twice your age, have more optimism than you.' That made them go very quiet.

Another girl in another office, stout Conservative, was terribly upset. This is the one who told me she had not banked any money lately. She said all she could think of against the Labourites. Only one worth recording is this fantastic rigmarole, told her, she says, by her husband, recently returned from North Africa:-

Ellen Wilkinson [parliamentary secretary at the Home Office, soon to be Minister of Education] wanted all men back from abroad to wear a special armlet to distinguish them, so that English girls could avoid them. Why? Because they are so riddled with VD. Further why? Because Ellen has an illegitimate daughter who got VD from a returned soldier. I said I refused to accept a word of it and treated it with the contempt such a yarn yells aloud for.

Husband very pleased and, like me, amazed and interested. We wonder now – mines nationalised? Railways?

I'm surprised the Communists haven't done better. Makes you think. Also surprised Liberals haven't done better. Too indecisive perhaps.

Man who has little shop nearby where we get our papers says, 'If they take my son from the university and put him to a job he'll leave the country.' I said, 'Don't be daft. Your son and thousands of other sons are more likely to stay at universities longer and under less strenuous conditions.'

Secretary at work was delighted, says he had lived all his life for this day.

Nice to have a Prime Minister whose wife does some housework and her own shopping.

Herbert Brush

We arrived home about 5.45 p.m., both very tired, but tea soon revived us. Two hundred and seventy-one miles.

I can't help feeling sorry for Churchill; he can't have expected all this. What a lot can happen to a man in a couple of days.

A man came along my plot path this evening and stopped to talk. 'What do you think of it now?' said he. Of course I easily guessed what he meant and answered, 'It depends on your politics; for my part I don't like it at all.' That started him off and he said that he felt sure that something dreadful would happen before long. He added that he was eighty-eight years old and that he did not like the idea of young men governing him or the country. What could they know of life or the wiles of foreigners?

WEDNESDAY, 1 AUGUST 1945

Edie Rutherford

Yesterday a Czech friend of the boss, a coal merchant from Prague, came to the office on a visit. He spent thirty-nine months in a concentration camp, and saw his mother and brother gassed. He bears lashes on his back still. He's a 12-stone man, but weighed 90lb. when liberated. He says nine million died in his camp alone. He knows that isn't believed here, but says after first census is taken in Europe we will know he speaks the truth. He maintains that the death toll in camps will far exceed German losses in the field. Poor man. How he can still smile and be courteous is amazing. He is in this country to see about trade.

My hairdresser yesterday said Attlee is a nonentity, without character and so on. But we just don't know what kind of man he is. I think, and hope, the world will find Attlee is stronger and worthy of the great work he has just undertaken. Anyway, let us give him a chance.

THURSDAY, 2 AUGUST

Herbert Brush

W took the necessary steps to get new ration books this morning and we had to go to the police station to have our signatures witnessed by a police sergeant. I worked on the plot and was soon soaked with perspiration and the day getting hotter and hotter.

3 p.m. I have been sitting in the summerhouse where the temperature is 74°F; the thermometer placed outside in the sun for a few minutes registered 107°F.

> It is now too hot
> To go on the plot
> So I'll sit indoors a while
> And drink barley water
> As everyone ought'er
> Who suffers a little from bile
> In the heat of the sun
> I feel nearly done
> It's a little too warm for me
> So I'll follow the rule
> To sit in the cool
> Now I'm nearly seventy-three.

4.15 p.m. The ration books came back. What a lot of trouble can arise from the loss of ration books.

Edie Rutherford

I suppose it is a good sign that the King has gone out of his way to meet President Truman. Shows willing. Makes him more human.

Had lunch in town with a friend yesterday. Cost her 6/- for the two of us. I thought it poor value. Soup, a miserly piece of cod with three tiny new boiled potatoes, about two dessertspoons of peas. Then a scrap of pastry and three small plums. We noticed that the male regulars in the place (they call all the waitresses by their Christian names) all got a very different lunch from ours, ample and varied.

All that nonsense in the House of Commons yesterday . . . how childish. Why not get down to things properly the way other folk have to do after a holiday, or when they start a new job? I regret that 'The Red Flag' was all the new Government could think of to sing. They ought to have known that the sore Tories would whistle to keep their courage up. That's what their public school training teaches them to do.

FRIDAY, 3 AUGUST

George Taylor

On the way home I called at the Town Planning exhibition and also visited the Demonstration Prefabricated House. This latter seems well off for gadgets but to live in that tiny space, neither bedroom being large enough to take a full-size bed, would become very boring. To those without a home, a prefab will certainly be better than nothing, but I hope that permanent houses may soon become possible.

Edie Rutherford

Girl at work cornered me yesterday: 'There you are, I told you it would happen.' Me: 'What would happen? Girl: 'First thing they're going to do is nationalise the Bank of England.' 'What of it?' 'Well, that means our savings go.' Me: 'Don't be daft, it simply means control, and won't affect your little bit.' 'Oh, but it will. Supposing I want to build a block of luxury flats, I won't be able to.' Me: 'You might. It all depends. For instance, if you want to build luxury flats while poor people live in slums, then you will not be allowed, nor should you be, should you?' 'Yes, I should. I should be free to do as I wish with my own money.' 'Well,' I replied, 'that is not God's idea of freedom and I prefer God's idea to yours', and marched off, furious inwardly but outwardly calm. Folk who can't see will have to be MADE to see.

Chapter Three

IT WAS MIDNIGHT WHEN THE NEWS CAME THROUGH

The triple victory of the common man: Chinese waiters delight in the Japanese surrender

'All over England, in a thousand English towns and villages, the Yanks are going home. And as each American says good-bye, kissing his English "Mum", and tweaking the ear as he hands out the last bit of gum to his adopted kid brother or sister, he mutters, being rather inarticulate, "Well, thanks a lot, folks." And the family replies: "You're welcome!"'

Picture Post *marks the departure of the GIs, September 1945*

'Titles. Authors. Reviews. Subscriptions. Never a spare minute. Like most other people these days, the Librarian leads a busy, worrying life; and her overworked nerves are grateful for a soothing cup of Rowntree's Cocoa.

Many a hard-pressed housewife, too, after a long, tiring day of cleaning, cooking, washing-up, bedmaking and shopping, finds that Rowntree's Cocoa calms her jangled nerves and aids digestion. Unlike so many other drinks, it contains body-building protein, energy-giving carbohydrate and fat.'

Advertisement in Illustrated, *August 1945*

SATURDAY, 4 AUGUST 1945

Edie Rutherford

Last week when I asked one of the men in our works what he was doing with his week off, he replied, 'I think I'll have a week at loggerheads with the wife.'

I like all the shake-up in the Government. What matter if we've never heard of many of the new ministers? All the better, say I. Everyone has to become known some time or another if they have aspiration.

TUESDAY, 7 AUGUST

Edie Rutherford

Met char on stairs this morning and she says yesterday the kids had to play in the communal room because of the weather, and they pulled the electric light brackets right out of the ceiling with a lot of plaster, and cut chunks out of walls with knives . . . Dear little children.

Only time my Husband wants children is to book them two seats in front of ours at cinema. Says he'd feed 'em on gin to keep them small enough for that.

Oh my God, this atomic bomb. Mankind will exterminate itself and this earth if we don't soon exercise some restraint. Surely the Jap war is over today. They can't possibly go on now.

George Taylor

When I glanced at the paper this morning and saw the heading about the atom bomb my first thought was of the fragmentation bomb and I said to myself, 'It's a lot of fuss about nothing.' However, when I looked closer I found that it was indeed a vastly more important affair, an affair with awful possibilities.

Herbert Brush

News of the first atomic bomb dropped on Japan; what an awful weapon judging by the papers. Where should we be now if the Germans had made them first? It is probably a painless death to die by atomic bomb, and all your friends would be with you when you went into the unknown.

W has official permission to purchase a new car.

There was a great crowd in London today, judging by the crush on Oxford Street and I think that a great many were country folk judging by their attempts to cross the streets; going halfway and then running back. I should not be surprised to read that some of them met with accidents.

I wanted to go into a waxwork exhibition in Oxford Street but when inside an extra charge of six pence was required to see the German Concentration Camp. I did *not* go into that, and the effigies of Hitler, Musso, Monty, etc were so bad in the main part of the exhibition.

8 p.m. Repaired Ida's vacuum cleaner.

WEDNESDAY, 8 AUGUST

Edie Rutherford
Last evening we saw the film *Wilson* at local cinema. A good film. [Woodrow] Wilson had vision far beyond that of his fellows. The only other item on the programme was the newsreel, in which we saw the mess Berlin is in and was tempted to feel sorry for the people till one recalled to mind Belsen etc. We also saw Monty getting the freedom of Chiswick (always seems to us a silly business) and in his speech he emphasised the need for stressing spiritual values in reforming Europe. I wish folk who speak in public would not refer to spiritual values just as thât – don't they know that millions of folk don't know what they mean?

If the new Food Minister does restore the fat ration, he will make a good start from the housewife's point of view. Good for Bevin to say yesterday that some nations could and should contribute more to nations in need. We won't mention any names but the flag with stars and stripes on it belongs to the country who could do most.

THURSDAY, 9 AUGUST

Edie Rutherford
Russia has come into this war as the Yanks came into the last one – in time for the end. Well, she had to do it to have a say in the peace. Japan gets her second atomic bomb. How many before she wakens? I brought up the subject of the new bomb at work yesterday. Horror of its power is definitely the chief reaction.

Papers and BBC say that grapefruits have arrived for Scotland. I see that my country has offered this country some thousands of tons of meat, cheese, fruit, jam and sugar. Let us hope the new Food Minister will get the ships for transporting it, as it is no use howling for food if ships are not available. One trip by the *Queen Mary* would no doubt get the whole lot now offered by the Union over to Europe and in shorter time than any cargo ship.

All at work commented on the cost of this atomic bomb research and remembered the howl that always goes up if 2/6d. weekly is suggested for adding to old-age pensions. We live in a mad world.

George Taylor

I travelled home with an ex-tram inspector. He pointed out a poster urging us to 'Use Less Electricity' and said, 'You should have seen the trams at Meadow Head last night. It was like fairyland. They do not need more that half the lights. It is some use talking to us about economy when they waste like that.'

I did not agree with him, saying that I was glad to see the lights again.

Herbert Brush

The British War Relief Society of the USA sent packets of seeds to allotmenteers again this year, and we are asked to send letters of thanks, so I am writing a few lines of verse to the Mayor of Cleveland, Ohio.

> The kindly folk in USA
> Encourage all old men like me,
> By sending seeds from far away
> To help us dig for Victory.
>
> That mighty nation in the West:
> May friendship with it thrive and grow
> Like seeds, which are the very best,
> Supplied from Cleveland, Ohio.

I'll keep it a day or two in case I think of some better lines.

4.30 p.m. I have planted out a row of 'celeriac' this afternoon. This is the first time I have attempted 'celeriac', and I don't even know what it looks like.

FRIDAY, 10 AUGUST

Edie Rutherford

One wonders what the announcement is that the Japs intend to make to the world. Seems to me quite possible that they too have an atomic bomb. Why not? I see in the *Daily Express* that a Spanish newspaper pictures a Jap scientist in his lab busy on splitting the atom. If two can play at that game, the outlook is appalling. In fact – is there any future?

A boot and leather shop on the way to work, noted for its catchy phrases, has this week: NO SANDALS. NO PLIMSOLLS. NO KIDDING.

George Taylor

On my way to a client's this afternoon I noticed a couple of workmen leaning out of the windows and heard one remark to the other, 'I should laugh if he had to put it in again.' I did not understand to what he was referring but about an hour later, when I was in the Commercial Manager's Office, I saw a flag floating up past the window. The manager remarked, 'Hello, what's that? It must be the end of the Japanese war. Let's look and see if any more flags are going up.'

We did so and saw a neighbouring firm putting up a flag so we concluded that the war must have ended, although I had not the slightest inkling that this might be possible.

When I went for a tram I saw the evening paper declare that the 'Japs quit the war' but, strange to say, there was not the least excitement and I did not hear one person, either in the waiting queue or in the tram itself, during the journey home, make any remark on the news.

Naturally I switched on the 6 p.m. news with keen anticipation but found it very disappointing as the Jap offer was not unqualified. I hope, however, that the offer will be accepted.

SATURDAY, 11 AUGUST

Edie Rutherford

So the Japs make a condition re surrender. Atomic bombs make no distinction between Emperors or commoners. And anyway, from all I've read and heard, that Emperor of theirs is a menace, largely responsible for the Japs being the way they are. Cast him out, I say. What matter if he is head of the constitution? We must revise the Jap methods from the ground up. And all our poor POWs – those who have survived – are they hearing that liberation can't be much longer delayed?

Herbert Brush

I wonder how the Allies will fix up a peace with Japan and still leave the Emperor on the throne. The best thing we could do would be to lock him up and make the Japs understand that he is not a divine creature after all. I guess that most of them know that well enough now.

Now, what shall we do with our stock of atomic bombs? There is no place in the world to drop them on except Japan. It may not be too dangerous to unload them in an office, though I should not like to take on the job.

5 p.m. W has got her new car this afternoon. HGC 869 in place of FYV 180 which she had in 1940. Another 'Standard 8'. Everyone seems to want to look at it as it is the first new one in the neighbourhood for civilian work since the war began.

SUNDAY, 12 AUGUST

Edie Rutherford

Husband says the pace of life is too swift for him, V day, election, tommy bomb, Jap surrender . . . he is left behind gawping. I agree.

George Taylor

Sunday morning buses have been reinstated on some routes today for the first time since pre-war days, although the service is very sketchy. However, we decided to try our luck with the 9.40 a.m. Holmesfield bus, which in peace time was usually full when it reached our stop. Today very few people appeared to know that it was running again and we easily secured seats. There is still no news of the ending of the Jap war.

MONDAY, 13 AUGUST

Herbert Brush

I wonder what little game the Japs are playing now. I expect that we shall have to drop another atom bomb before they make up their

76

minds to allow the Emperor to take orders from a soldier, a foreign devil.

3 p.m. I went to the British Museum this morning and had my ticket renewed for another six months. Afterwards I walked along Charing X Road to have a look at the bookshops. I was tempted to buy once or thrice but a glance inside at the price destroyed the temptation.

I went into the National Portrait Gallery to have a look round, and found that all the space in one room open was filled with portraits from the Kit-Cat Club. Forty-two of them, every one clean-shaven and dressed in the garments of the wealthy in the eighteenth century. Every picture includes a hand of the man, as though this was an important feature of the club. A booklet about the pictures was on sale but I did not feel like spending sixpence to learn all about the Kit-Kat Club.

I sat down to rest in front of Turner's large picture *Crossing the Brook*. A soldier was evidently explaining to his girlfriend how the picture *should* have been painted.

Electric lamps in reflectors are placed in front of the National Gallery in readiness for the 'Peace with Japan', but as I was looking at them I noticed the headlines on a paper being read by a man, that if Japan does not hurry up and surrender we shall drop some more atom bombs on her cities at six o'clock this evening. Serve her right if we do it to the second, as she is so damned artful that she may have some scheme to minimise the result if she is given time enough to prepare.

TUESDAY, 14 AUGUST

Edie Rutherford
The 8 a.m. news just now tells us that acceptance is due at any moment. So I suppose the holidays will fall tomorrow and Thursday and then Husband and I go to work Friday morning and start holidays that afternoon. However, one's personal affairs don't count of course. Only it could have worked out so that we could have had the two days extra.

Hairdresser tells me they will work right through regardless of holidays as mostly just now folk are either going away or having weddings, and they don't see how they can let them down by cancelling all appointments. I said, with relief, that I thought it noble of them, and so I do. I had resigned myself to the possibility of going away with my hair the mess it is at the moment, but now all is well. Praise be. I always maintain that it is up to each one to keep his or her individual flag flying bravely, without getting an undue idea of one's importance in the entire scheme of things.

One girl at work maintains that because of the atomic bomb we are as bad as the Japs. I hotly repudiated the idea. Bombing like that gives a quick, clean death, whereas the tortures inflicted on our men by the Japs makes a drawn-out and appalling end for a man.

Seems to me that if the seventy thousand civilians this island lost in air raids etc had gone in one night, we'd have had over five years in which to pull ourselves together, whereas having lost them in six years we are going to take years yet.

Came through town yesterday. Packed. Queues for meals, queues for ice creams . . . but if folk will do it, well, I spare them no pity.

WEDNESDAY, 15 AUGUST

Edie Rutherford

8 a.m. It was midnight when the news came through – were fast asleep when suddenly a man's voice shouted 'Jap war's over. Hurrah!' Both woke with a start which gave Husband a headache which he still has. Recognised the shout as the voice of man in a flat on floor below ours.

Then the fireworks started and for about an hour youths and girls went about the street singing most unharmoniously. Eventually we got off to sleep again. Got up as usual this morning and had 7 a.m. news on to confirm things, and there we are with two days hols.

Later. I hate to think of the amount of bread wasted through the Emperor of Japan in the last few days. The bakers have baked nothing but the 2lb. National loaf which one has been obliged to buy far in excess or need. The only folk I know who eat bread to a finish are the two teachers next door. Others take it for granted that bread a day old is uneatable, let alone a week old . . . Whole loaves lie in our pig bins, great hunks lie all over the grounds. A Belgian woman spoke of it to me this morning, and an Italian woman yesterday. Such people have more perception than our own folk. I have said for years now that bread and flour should be rationed, and I consider it even more urgent now.

Each day folk have thought the holidays might come the next day, and so they've bought up far too much. This has gone on since last Friday. Crazy.

Have just been out to shops. Awful mess. I wanted to get rations for this week to post on, but my grocer hasn't got any bacon yet, so I'll have to see to it on Friday. PO won't accept parcels till Friday anyway.

I did a pile of mending last night. Never have I mended and made do as now. Actually had to do more handkerchief darning last night. And as for darning over darns on Husband's socks . . . Ugh.

George Taylor

The sound of fireworks woke me from a deep sleep early in the morning but I was merely annoyed at them, thinking they were a continuance of those I had heard last night. I got up as usual, prepared for the office and over breakfast switched on the 8 a.m. news. I was quite surprised to hear that the Jap offer had been accepted and still more astonished to learn that today and tomorrow were to be general holidays. Both my wife and I suffered from an illogical sense of annoyance about the shortness of the notice.

Having prepared to go to work we decided to go into town after all. Quite a few people were streaming in but there was little to see and only a few flags were out: even the Town Hall being so surprised that there were only three flags available and no other decorations. The chief occupation of the morning seemed to be queuing and at all confectioners and firework vendors there stretched long lines of people anxious to buy. Fortunately we had ample stock of bread and, having no children, had no need to buy any fireworks.

From the city we walked over to Hunters Bar to see my mother-in-law who lives on her own. My wife does not like her to be alone when there are any celebrations. We stayed for lunch there and then called on my brother at Totley. His youngster of ten was particularly excited about the bonfire which a neighbour had prepared, so we had to stay and see that lit, and watch the guy of Hirohito burn away.

Herbert Brush

The Prime Minister tells us all to take a holiday today, but when I suggested that to D just now she said that she was too busy, and I can hear her now scrubbing away in the kitchen.

I met old Ing in the road. He had been down to the bottom of the road to buy bread, but there was a long queue and by the time it was his turn all the bread had been sold, so he came back with an empty bag.

As usual he told me a few tales about London life when he was a member of the Force, most of which were about the 'tarts' he came across in his younger life. He gave me a tip which may be useful to you if you have any stale bread in the house. 'Hold the loaf under the tap for a short time, then put it into the oven, and it will be like new bread.'

However, I think there must be a trick in doing it properly or everyone would do it and there would not be so much bread in the dustbins.

THURSDAY, 16 AUGUST

Edie Rutherford

Tele-Radio had fixed up loudspeaker music on first-floor balcony over our foyer, facing street, and dance music began at 7 a.m. Crowds and crowds. We met the two next-door teachers and they asked us in for two helpings of gin and French vermouth.

We slept till 9.15 a.m., got papers from hall, had tea in bed and lazed there till after ten. Now it is midday. I don't mind how many Japs kill themselves from shame. All the less for us to curb and control.

King & Queen seem to have had a day of it yesterday. I think Clem Attlee has acquitted himself well in his first appearance. King sounded much better last night. He seems unafraid now. When he gets stuck in he goes to it and blurts it out. One imagines that before he used to sit in terror and the more fearful he got the more incapable.

I expect the next momentous event this nation will have will be the betrothal of Princess Elizabeth, though who on earth can be a worthy consort is outside of my knowledge. Husband says it should be an American, to further bind the two nations together. On that argument, why not a Russian?

FRIDAY, 17 AUGUST

Edie Rutherford

Dancing again last night till 2 a.m. Husband didn't budge but I watched for two to three hours and saw a display of jitterbugging by two girls, very good. Clearly a dance for the young and a sort of 'wrestling to rhythm' as one woman put it. I like to see it but would not like to do it myself.

Speaking to German woman while watching dancers last night, she tells me she has heard from her mother in Berlin, Charlottenberg, the British Zone. Her father was taken to Belsen two years ago, aged sixty-seven, and has not been heard of since. Just because he was always unwilling to be a Nazi, not give to Party funds or give the Hitler salute. But was not a big mouth – kept a still tongue and spoke when spoken to only. The mother, sister and nephew are well, and say the five days fighting over their heads before Berlin was taken were sheer hell, the worst horror of all the war.

MONDAY, 20 AUGUST

Edie Rutherford

We left on the ten something train for Euston. Platform 2. We waited. The voice bawled 'Platform 3'. We rushed, got into empty train and settled. Voice bawled 'all change, Platform 4'. Imagine the rush . . . It was all right at last, we got seats and away. Had our lunch with us and enjoyed it.

When we got to Euston, Husband wanted a pub . . . we found most shut, got inside one, only to be told 'sold out'. Awful place anyway. As we had to get to Liverpool Street we decided to go there and try. Got inside the only one there and same news greeted us. Another lousy place it was also. I'm particular what pubs I grace my presence with.

Arrived at Hadham station, no one there. Halfway to the house the two nephews met us, on bikes, so they did not carry stuff. A bit further on my sister and her husband met us and they did help. Spent the rest of that day talking and inspecting the place after five years of not seeing it. My sister is much better off than she was, better off than we are in fact. Their inheritance from his people has made a wonderful difference to them, praise be.

Herbert Brush

We went to the Hutts last evening and Bill showed me a short method for squaring numbers with his algebraical explanation. Later we played Lexicon until after the nine o'clock news.

Why do some people get so excited on Peace Days and think that they have a right to break things up, especially if the things are public property? I say that because when I boarded a tram today I found that I had to sit on one of the double seats as the long ones near the entrance were full up. The man next to me said, 'They ought to have been smashed to bits on Peace Night, then we should have better ones to sit on.' It struck me that he looked like a man who would get excited and think he was at liberty to smash things as soon as he got sufficient beer.

Oxford Street was packed with people again today and there was a hawker every few yards selling elastic, combs and odds and ends which many people bought at high prices.

TUESDAY, 21 AUGUST

Herbert Brush

I decided to go to Oxford Street and see that Jap exhibition. After a long queue I started by going through the dark and steaming jungle. It was so hot inside there that my collar soon became a damp rag round my neck.

The sounds of birds and beasts around were realistic, but I could hear the scraping of the gramophone needle which spoiled the illusion a bit.

Then I came out of the jungle and entered a room with big photographs of Jap scenes and a picture of the Emperor. An insignificant little man.

Further on were pictures of Jap manufactures, such as well-known English razors and blades and many other little things which the Japs used to turn out cheaply and by the million for our use. A Jap girl was shown working a typewriter which had an alphabet of 2,400 letters; a bit of a handicap I should say.

I looked down on it from a platform above while a running commentary was made through a loudspeaker on the events of the war, and each point was marked as it was mentioned, by coloured lights.

I was not sorry to get out into the cool air and wipe my forehead with an already wet handkerchief. When I went round to the front again there was a queue along a good stretch of Oxford Street and some way up Newman Street, four deep. There is nothing like a 'free show' to draw the people from all parts.

W went to the hospital today to have her throat examined by a specialist. He says that it is not cause for worry and advised her to eat as much as she could and suck barley sugar all the time. But he did not tell her where to get all the food or the barley sugar. She had to wait her turn for three hours, but the specialist's advice cost only one shilling. That is one of the advantages of paying 3d. per week into the Hospital Saturday Fund.

WEDNESDAY, 22 AUGUST

Edie Rutherford

We took the two boys to Bishop's Stortford for the day. Shopped, had lunch at the George, said to be the best place there. Awful lunch. 18/4d. which seemed to me sheer robbery.

Then went on to cinema, where I was glad to see manager let a soldier in free. Somewhat restored my balance which had been upset by the dud lunch. We had tomato soup so weak and thin that it was a disgrace. Then a piece of plaice, boiled so that all the flavour was gone. Five half potatoes and some marrow. The boys would not have marrow so they had two half spuds each. Pudding was plum tart. It looked awful at the next table but as I was still ravenous, we decided to have some. The other two said not. Ate one spoonful each. If that was pastry, then what I make is super pastry and I'm no pastry maker. As for the plums I don't believe any sugar at all was used. Husband asked for coffee. Not served.

We got the five-something bus back, and at bedtime the two small boys came and said in chorus, 'Thank you for taking us out today', so obviously told them by Pa . . . We laughed. They are nice kids. Chimpanzee stage. Climb on every darn thing they can.

Herbert Brush

I have been creosoting the garden fence this morning. It is rather a slow job, so many people stop to talk about the weather and the iniquity of small boys who like to damage garden fences.

W came back from Norwich and on the road came across a large bag of potatoes dropped from some lorry, evidently. The bag had burst and potatoes were all over the road, so W collected about 25lb. in a small bag she had in the car.

THURSDAY, 23 AUGUST

Edie Rutherford

I went to London, met a friend I hadn't seen for twelve years, after spending a couple of hours shopping in Oxford Street, especially Selfridges. Bought six yards of knicker elastic from a hawker at 8d. a yard and glad to get it. We then wandered down Oxford Street and in and out of shops, and did bits of shopping. My friend Nanette expects that she and Neville will be back in SA by Christmas so I'm glad I saw her. She kept repeating that in twelve years I am unchanged. Preposterous statement and quite untrue. She has changed and for the better. Is much softer and generally nicer to know. Nanette left me at about 3.30 to return to the BBC where she works.

I snooped about some more, went to Fortnum & Mason. Heavens, things not on points are pricey. I used all our sweets coupons. Got Fullers, Mars, etc, etc, which we never see owing to zoning, so I took the chance. We are enjoying them now.

FRIDAY, 24 AUGUST

Edie Rutherford

I went to town again, to get train out to friend at Hitchin. I left my sister's at 8.30 a.m. but found when I got to King's Cross that there was no Hitchin train till 12.25, so decided to ring my friend as she had expected to lunch me. Now this is what happened:-

I stood in a queue for the phone at King's Cross, wanting to shoo every Yank ahead of me off this island. Eventually got a phone. Asked for my number. Silence. Then about five minutes later a voice said, 'Sorry to keep you.' I answered amiably. Long interval. Then a voice said, 'Put two shillings in the box.' I knew it was too much but obeyed. Then a voice answered, 'Brixton or Bexhill' or some such. Oh dear. We both rang off, and I tried to start at the beginning again. At long last I got someone and told my tale of woe. I was told to hold on. I did. Then 'Can I help you?' Feeling by this time in despair, not to mention asphyxiation in that smoke-filled box, I said 'Oh, I wish you would!' and told my tale again. Hold on. I did. Nothing happened. So I decided to say 'Hello hello hello hello' like that till someone gave me something for my two bob. After a bit a voice said VERY rudely, 'Oh do stop saying hello like that.' 'I will not stop,' I said firmly, 'till I get my call.' 'What do you want?' So I told my story again. Oh dear. Reply was, 'Well, what do you think we are?' I said promptly, 'Dead and buried, obviously.' 'Don't be rude', I was told. 'You started it,' I said. Immediately I was put through, spoke to my friend and that was that . . . Wonderful things telephones, so handy, so convenient, so up to date . . .

Sunday was the twentieth anniversary of our wedding day. I walked with Husband to village for pre-lunch half pint (pint for him), having had a pre-breakfast walk earlier. It was a super perfect day. In the afternoon I picked blackberries for my sister from her briars in the garden, and packed parcels to be posted home – mostly dirty linen we had accumulated.

Monday was Husband's fortieth birthday, another perfect day. I got him *Animal Farm* by Orwell, pending getting him a blue shirt, his small size always hard to get, and I had no coupons then. We both enjoyed *Animal Farm* very much.

On the train back we took charge of three small girls travelling alone at the request of an elder sister. One of these results of evacuation to the North, all returning visits and forming lasting friendships.

THURSDAY, 30 AUGUST

Herbert Brush
On the plot this morning I cut my thumb on an old razor blade which was in the ground. The allotment judges have awarded me a certificate of merit for my plots this year, but no money prize. Personally, I am of the opinion that my plots are better than last year, but evidently the judges don't think so, as I am No. 67 on their list against No. 50 last year, and there are fewer competitors.

Edie Rutherford
Letter from Husband's elder brother to the effect that 'to celebrate the triple victory of the common man' he was cancelling all debts owing to him. He advanced the cash for my passage when I came to

England eleven years ago, and we've paid annual interest every year except once, when Sid had one of his breakdowns, lost his job and generally life had been bloody for us. We are much relieved to be rid of this annual drain on our still slender resources. We know the brother can afford this gesture.

FRIDAY, 31 AUGUST

Edie Rutherford
I bottled 7lb. cooking apples so that we may have muesli through the winter months. Though I suspect there may be some apples on sale from abroad this winter, I'm taking no chances.

We had a nice country walk in the evening. Kids blackberrying everywhere. We realised that hereabouts, compared to Hertfordshire, where we were, there are too many kids and too few berries.

Herbert Brush
W dropped me at Camberwell Green this morning and I changed my book at Boots in Peckham. The book I took out is by H. Blood-Ryan: *Goering, The Iron Man of Germany.*

SATURDAY, 1 SEPTEMBER 1945

Herbert Brush
Had my hair cut in Sydenham. I notice that my bald patch has increased in size lately. The hairdresser gave me a kind of soldier's crop, very short round the back and sides but hardly any off the top. The sides are now nearly white.

I soon read enough about the wonderful skill and bravery of Goering so I changed the book in Sydenham and took out *Chungking Diary* by Robert Payne.

Maggie Joy Blunt
I received this letter from my friend S with our army in Austria:-

'We wear, on orders, our best uniforms to compete with the Russians and Yanks, so I am brass-buttoned and beribboned. Last night, as I stood alone, at an allied dance, a smart young Russian officer (white double-breasted high-collared jacket, bottle-green trousers and gold epaulets) saluted me and asked, "If you are alone, please to join me and make merry." The turn of phrase delighted me so I bowed assent and joined him with two chic Frauleins. We talked a motley of Russian, German, French and English – my Russian is limited to twenty words and German to fifty – but we get around and dance and drink the carafes of beer at 3d. a pint. Then a rather tight Russian Colonel joins us and there is much saluting and bowing. Surprisingly, for a man with the face and figure of a pork butcher, he says to us in halting French, "I agree with Chekhov – *le monde c'est triste, la vie terrible.*"

Then we are whisked off to a luxurious flat which is a Russian officers' mess, where sober, stiff, disciplined soldiers serve us with caviar and vodka. There are about twenty officers and a number of Austrian girls all well dressed and crowding round an elderly officer who is playing Chopin on a grand piano. A senior officer with a ravishing blonde enters, and she says to me in lilting French "I am a displaced person", and gives me her hand to kiss. Suddenly they all begin to sing magnificently in harmony, a wild rousing song that on inquiry I find has the delightful, incredible title of "Yo Ho For The Day, The 10,000th Tractor Cut The First Furrow at Ekaterinoslav".

The Colonel announces that he will sing an English song and with a voice to challenge Paul Robeson sings with fervour "Daddy Wouldn't Buy Me A Bow-Wow". He then turns to me and asks what the words mean, for he learned them by heart without knowing the meaning. I hadn't the heart to tell him the truth so I said it was called "The World Shall Be One People".'

MONDAY, 3 SEPTEMBER

Edie Rutherford
I took a copy of the magazine *American Home* [to steelworks] for girls to see in lunch hour. They wanted to lynch me. Such lovely foods. 'Take 1 tin Del Monte peaches . . .' 'Take it where from?' they ask. They are all fed up to the teeth re food, and reckon it is time the USA went without more.

TUESDAY, 4 SEPTEMBER

Edie Rutherford
Paper this morning says pregnant women are going to be allowed to stand at the head of any queue. What nonsense. The thing to do is to

abolish queues. And anyway, pregnant women these days are robust and as fit as the unpregnant, well able to stand up to the last four to six weeks. It is the decrepit sixty-year-old women with dropped wombs and fallen arches who should not stand around in queues.

When we got back we found our radio wouldn't work. How long it will be in hospital we don't know, but we sure do miss it. I have to force myself to make do and mend, as usually I only do it to the radio.

Herbert Brush

I had a pile for a few days and yesterday it seemed to burst with a certain amount of blood. It seems better today, but I must be careful.

In the afternoon we went by car to Leicester Square. Parked the car within fifty yards of the place and went to see *Johnny Frenchman* at the Leicester Square Theatre Cinema. It was very good and very interesting to us all because the picture was taken in Mevagissey and the two principal actors were Tom Walls and Mme Rosay. We recognised all the places we knew; even the little cottage where we stayed and the steep and narrow passage leading up to it. It was almost like visiting the place a second time.

THURSDAY, 6 SEPTEMBER

Edie Rutherford

Amused at work yesterday – when I got in the girls were still having their lunchtimes, one was playing piano for another to sing. I went downstairs to do some filing and foreman chap said to me, 'I used to sing a lot when I was young.' I replied, 'So did I. Good for one. Good fun and splendid exercise.' And he said, 'And learns you to talk proper.' Deadly serious too. How I kept my face straight I don't know, and rather suspect I didn't entirely succeed in doing so.

When we got back from holidays we heard from many quarters about the marvellous children's Victory party here, the Saturday after we went away. The balance sheet has now been displayed ... my, my, nearly £40 spent. I should think it WAS a good party. Item: five gallons ice cream, £5. Oh well, it is a good example of what can be done even in our circumstances.

The street dancing also kept up for two Saturdays after VJ day but apparently got so riff-raffy, plus many tenants complaining about noise, that it has now stopped.

FRIDAY, 7 SEPTEMBER

Edie Rutherford
Looks as if I shall go to London alone on Saturday of next week, for Leslie Keith's wedding. All the office was to go but what with prior engagements and holidays, no one can go but me. Husband says I'm mad to go for such a slight thing, but I'm content to be mad me if the events of the last six years have been sane. I intend now to let up on personal restrictions after years of denying myself. If I can get a bed, I'll stay overnight too.

George Taylor
Our annual outing to Monyash gathering mushrooms. We made a poor show of it this year, getting only about half a pound, instead of returning laden. In the evening we went to the cinema at Bakewell. There was a long film showing the liberation of Paris, a short of a trial explosion of the first atomic bomb in Mexico, and an amusing production of Flanagan and Allen 'Dreaming'. We were lucky for a change.

It was Navy Comforts Week in Bakewell, and the square was to be illuminated and dancing was to take place. So we strolled about until 8.45 p.m. until the lights went up (a solitary spotlight) and dancing began. However, no attempt whatever was made to stop traffic and, as the square is the busiest spot in Bakewell, the dancing was somewhat a dangerous game.

SATURDAY, 8 SEPTEMBER

Edie Rutherford
Daily Express yesterday said that by Christmas all rationing in the USA would be over. I could spit. How can they be so callous? Quite apart from us, they know the hunger in Europe. In another place the same paper reports that next year American tourists expect to come here in thousands. While we are still on rations? If they really love us so much that they want to come and stare at our victorious discomfiture, they can stay put and use the ship space to send some of their good things to us.

Herbert Brush

This afternoon, W and Horace and Dolly came to Catford to see me get my allotment certificate for Digging for Victory from the Mayor of Lewisham. The function took place in a big marquee in the Private Banks Sports Ground near Catford Bridge. My number was sixty-five so it was a long wait for my turn to come. I was a long way down the list with 132 points out of 200 against 155 points out of 200 last year; and all the time I thought I was doing better.

Herbert Morrison [Deputy Prime Minister] was speaking in the tent when we arrived and afterwards we had to listen to Arthur Skiffington, MP for West Lewisham and the man I voted against. I now have three Certificates of Merit from the Ministry of Agriculture and am sticking them in a book as a record of my work on the plot.

SUNDAY, 9 SEPTEMBER

Edie Rutherford

All these disclosures about the tortures to our Far East POWs makes one wonder what on earth we are going to do with these beastly Japs. They are not human as we understand the word. Seems that in the past we have treated them with Christianity only to get this. Should we go on being kind or should we give them some of what they gave our lads?

George Taylor

In the evening I finished off a book I commenced thirteen years ago. It is Balzac's *Le Cousin Pons*.

MONDAY, 10 SEPTEMBER

Maggie Joy Blunt

Last entry made in June. Have been ill on and off through July and August and having holidays. Illnesses not severe – further ear trouble and bad flu cold. Generally run down like so many people. We are all feeling effects of war strain and now the tension is relaxed our resistance has gone. Numbers of people with summer colds.

I spent last week in Hove and feel much better, though could do with another three weeks at least. A fortnight's holiday in the year is absurd and no good to anyone. I would most earnestly urge for longer holidays for everyone.

At the office great changes have been taking place. Managing director W resigned in July and took various key people with him. Many others have gone too and the firm is constricting in every direction and no one seems to know what is to happen next. The General Manager (HG) is I think the only director remaining and is now in control. We are now a 'full member' of a big group of aircraft and motor manufacturers who financed us from the beginning. We are told to 'carry on', which we all do in a very half-hearted way, but in every department are complaints of lack of work. One hears every day of people looking for other jobs. I could, I am sure, go too if I wanted to, but it suits me to stay on at present until pushed or guided.

In Hove last week the holiday crowds had abated but there were still many visitors on the beach and seafront and in the cafés and cinemas and dance halls and shops. Weather was grey, cold, disappointing, but children paddled and hardy adults bathed, although there were no huts for dressing (I was told that on VJ night a pile of huts and chairs and other such oddments was burned by the populace gone mad). Children had their spades and buckets and shoddy products were on sale in the shops for them. Deck chairs one had to carry from a pile for oneself and notices asked visitors to replace them as labour was lacking. A couple of elderly men went round collecting 2ds and tickets were often old band concert tickets.

The front and gardens are wonderfully restored. All barbed wire removed and the long grass cut and flowers planted. The Hove Town Hall was reopened while I was there for dancing. It had been the Food Office during the war. Many troops still stationed there, but going gradually. A group of South Africans next door to a friend of mine nearly all gone. The Aussies still occupy some of the big Brighton hotels.

Not much in the shops and local inhabitants grumbled. Food where I was staying was plain, plentiful, well cooked and satisfying. We had fish every evening and roast meat midday three or four times a week. Sometimes we had powdered milk for breakfast. I had breakfast in bed several mornings. Meals served by small girl of thirteen – one of a family of nine and pleased to earn something during her holidays. For all this I had to pay one guinea a day.

Cigarettes as difficult to get there as in London. I walked round The Lanes one evening but saw little of interest in the famous antique shops. Bought a utility all-wool twinset which I don't think I could have done in London, not of the quality and for the price. Went to two dances, saw Norma Dawn in a variety show (sheer curiosity – she is young and very pretty but has a hard face). Was taken to two fortune tellers, crawled round many pubs and did not bathe once.

WEDNESDAY, 12 SEPTEMBER

Herbert Brush
The wireless set has gone wrong: I think that the insulation of a small condenser has broken down. We took it to Philips in the Purley Way and then went to Rochester to pick apples.

7.30 p.m. I was going to the plot this evening when the postman was clearing the pillar box near the garden gate. A man in a large car drove up and wanted to hand a large envelope to him to put in his collecting bag, but the postman would not touch it and said that the man must put it through the slot. To do this the man had to get out of his car and walk round it to reach the slot, and then had some difficulty in getting the wide envelope through; he had to double it up before it would go through the slot. However, he did it and the postman then picked the letter, or whatever it was, out of the pillar box and put it in his bag.

Then the man began to curse him and gave him a few unpleasant names.

I looked round several times as I walked down the road with my bucket and hoe, and they were still at it when I turned into Charlecote Grove.

THURSDAY, 13 SEPTEMBER

Edie Rutherford
Hairdresser did almost all my hair, to my disgust, not just the ends. She won't do as I ask, always comes back with an explanation why she can't. I think that as I don't know about hair, she must be right, but am never pleased with the result and always wish she'd do as I first asked.

George Taylor
Cancellations of bookings for the WEA Weekend School caused me some trouble today. It is not good enough cancelling within two days of the School. I feel like refusing to refund the fees.

I paid off the Building Society mortgage on our house today.

Chapter Four

SHAFTESBURY AVENUE
A DISGRACE

Small compared with Nelson's Column: the V2 rocket in Trafalgar Square

'Good evening. I am talking to you about Germany. That is a concept that many of you may have failed to understand. Let me tell you that in Germany there still remains the spirit of unity and the spirit of strength. Let me tell you that here we have a united people . . .

. . . You may not hear from me again for a few months. I say, "Ich Liebe Deutschland!" Heil Hitler, and farewell.'

From the last, drunken, broadcast of William Joyce, aka Lord Haw-Haw, the Nazi radio propagandist, speaking from Hamburg as British troops entered the city, 30 April 1945. Tried in a British court for treason, he was found guilty and hanged on 3 January 1946.

'What is your first thought when a tang comes into the air and lengthening autumn evenings urge you to seek the comforts of your fireside? A Lamp and a Book . . . a temporary escape from the workaday world into the realm of reading. WH Smith and Son's Library, with its five hundred exchange branches throughout England and Wales provides the ideal home recreation – unlimited reading. The 'A' Service at £1 a year is the most popular as it gives access to all the books in the library. The 'B' Service, while not necessarily providing the newest books, costs only 10s. a year.'

Advertisement in Homes and Gardens, *October 1945*

SATURDAY, 15 SEPTEMBER

Herbert Brush
I heard the roar of planes about 12.45 and caught sight of a few of them going over Peckham Way. There were three hundred according to the newspapers, giving London an exhibition to encourage everyone to buy saving certificates. I wonder whether the planes will cause the sale of one certificate, or make one person decide that he ought to buy one. I might if I had any money to spare, but needless to say, I have not. The Income Tax people take care of that, and deduct more than a third of my pension before I get it.

MONDAY, 17 SEPTEMBER

Edie Rutherford
Well, I got the 9 a.m. train on Saturday for London, and stood for four hours all the way. We stopped five times and every time more and more servicemen got in. The air was foul with cigarette smoke. Twice I sank to the floor, legs and feet under luggage places (RAF lad crouched in each place), to get some air I could breathe. Near St Pancras I struggled to powder my nose, and one of the RAF lads said nicely, 'One side has too much powder.' So I made him put things right, as there just wasn't enough space to hold up a mirror. Train was half an hour late so that meant a taxi to get to the wedding in time.

What a beautiful church is St Paul's, Knightsbridge. The bride looked marvellous, her husband looked grand. The reception was very posh and the bridegroom's parents were so snooty that I was disgusted. They are of the aristocracy but were quite boorish in their manners. The mother was frigidly polite – just – the father not even polite. Not even a murmured greeting, not even a slight bow of the head. One usher was a lord, and the best man was also titled. I'm damned if they LOOK any nicer or better than hicks such as they no doubt thought us.

Eventually Nanette and I went to bed and talked for ages in the dark – I heard Big Ben strike three (and was thrilled about it too) and later six.

Just found a seat on train home when one of the girls from office found me and said they had a compartment so I joined them. Two Americans there also and the hour they were with us we had a spirited conversation. One bloke from Georgia told me I ought to be a critic. I said, 'Of what?' he replied, 'Of anything.' They gave us gum, orange juice, chocolate, candy. Americans are very insular. They know nothing outside the USA and seem to be not interested in anything outside the USA.

Herbert Brush

I went to Hyde Park to see the captured German aeroplanes which are parked there, surrounded by a fence. I noticed a few bullet holes in one of them and wondered whether the German who flew the machine had died there. I hope so.

There were hundreds of people walking about, with little crowds near each plane. One young man had bought his chair close to the fence, and with his face pressed close to the railings was staring in a sort of fascinated way at one of the planes, as though he wanted to memorise every detail. I watched him for some time, but he never moved a muscle.

I got a seat under a tree and ate my lunch, and I forgot to look for the young man when I came back. Probably my thoughts were on the chances of a ticket collector coming along and charging me 2d. for the chair.

George Taylor

My Special police friend called for a chat in the evening. He is a married man of over forty, has three children, all boys, and yet takes up a new study most years. Last year it was music, now he tells me he intends learning bookkeeping. In spite of this he took little interest in the WEA classes when I told him about them.

Naturally I did not press him, as I do not believe in thrusting my ideas on other people.

TUESDAY, 18 SEPTEMBER

Edie Rutherford

Good leader in *Daily Mirror* today about how the Government should take the public into its confidence. I am sure that all the grumbles about the new Government doing nothing could be blown away if we were told that something IS going on, as I am quite sure it is myself.

George Taylor

On the way to Chesterfield today I heard two colliers discussing the Belsen trial, and its cost of £1,000 per day for fourteen days. One of them said, 'Somebody must get money out of it. They would have done differently in Russia.' I presume that he would like the accused to have been shot out of hand, rather than have a trial.

Herbert Brush

On the bus at Peckham a lady was about to get off but, as the conductor was on top and had not collected her fare, she handed the money to the lady opposite, to give to the conductor when he came down. The conductor was a long time on top and the lady changed her position on the bus and moved up several seats. I watched when the conductor came for the fares. He collected only one 2d. fare from the lady and she said nothing about the fare handed to her by the woman who got out. I think she sold her conscience for 3d., though it may have been 2d. She lives in Lordship Lane.

WEDNESDAY, 19 SEPTEMBER

Edie Rutherford

Looks as if that creature Joyce will get off . . . I'm not surprised. The Americans can have him. Surely someone will bump him off some dark night?

I remember talking to a soldier as I stood all the way to London. He said that he and his pals are nervous of demobbing being speeded up, and fear it will increase unemployment, and therefore would rather be slow getting out than on the dole.

Herbert Brush

Have you noticed how much darker in colour the postage stamps are?

THURSDAY, 20 SEPTEMBER

Edie Rutherford

So that b*****d Joyce has not got off. I hope his appeal fails. Talking to a friend last night I remarked that the amount of alarm and despondency Joyce had caused was enough to convict him, but she said that no one needed to listen to the man, and that she never had. Well, we heard him three times in all, and then not for more than a few sentences. But I still think he had no right to foul the atmosphere.

I have heard of two instances of our soldiers in Germany writing home to say how splendid the German people are, that they'd like to live there, and that they can explain Belsen when they get back here. As if anyone can explain Belsen!

Maggie Joy Blunt

Office situation grows worse and worse. The aim and object of this firm is to manufacture good light alloys and to make bits and pieces for the engineering industries. Metallurgy and engineering – I couldn't be less interested in either of those subjects. I know of no one who is content with their job and people are leaving for better jobs on all sides. Almost at any time during the day you can go into the cloakroom and find girls there knitting or reading because there is nothing for them to do. Today I have felt I would like to walk out and never go back. I can see my advertising department just folding up and no one being very much the wiser. If I could scrape together some capital I would retire into rusticity and try to get back in to freelance writing again.

The comic thing is that one of the fortune-tellers in Hove told me most emphatically 'to stick it'. She saw the firm as a big concern! 'There's promotion for you. You'll be asked to do work you'll resent but do it. Through it you will get a much better job and better pay. You have been very browned off with it all, haven't you? Well, don't worry. Stick it.'

I have never felt less like sticking it the whole time I've been there. Why on earth should I try and stay when I have enough money to live on without another job for at least several months? And a brother, who although with a family of his own, would never see me starve? I've been in this job too long. Why does one fall to the fascination of these old witches? I wish I'd never been near them.

FRIDAY, 21 SEPTEMBER

Herbert Brush

W dropped me at Peckham where I changed my book, taking out *Born to Adventure* by K. D. Young.

SATURDAY, 22 SEPTEMBER

George Taylor
The police gave me an urgent ring today; asking for my attendance at a parade on Saturday. By this short notice I gather that they are having difficulty in getting a decent muster.

We went to the matinee at the Playhouse to see James Bridie's *It Depends What You Mean*. There was a much larger attendance than usual. Evidently Bridie is popular, although enigmatic.

MONDAY, 24 SEPTEMBER

Edie Rutherford
Girl at work was saying this morning that yesterday she had tea at her friend's home where her brother was home on leave from Germany. He says the Germans greedily accept chocolate ration our men say is uneatable – sounds as if it is that black, sandy chocolate one used to get from the Continent. This man is full of pity for the Germans, says they have convinced him they could not help Hitler being where he was and doing what he did, and that they could not stop the concentration camps. Maybe not. But he should have been stopped long before things got that far. Looks as if our men are going to be sucked in again by the Germans as of yore.

Herbert Brush
I still occasionally dig up bits of the bomb which fell near my allotment. Or they may be some of the bits that fell all round me when a V2 burst overhead and scattered itself all over Sydenham.

However, the V2 in Trafalgar Square seems small compared with Nelson's Column, and Nelson has his back to it. I wonder what his reactions would have been to a weapon like that. Scared stiff, I expect.

George Taylor
I cannot wax enthusiastic about Readers Union choice for September. Probably because my mind has been so occupied with more topical matters, I could work up no deep interest in the life of William the Silent.

TUESDAY, 25 SEPTEMBER

Edie Rutherford

Their Majesties visit Sheffield today. Hope our Mayor won't leave all his aitches behind him. I'm told he has improved a lot since he took office. Good. There was plenty of room for it.

Tuesday later: I saw the King and Queen. I was under the drier when hairdresser came and said if I came to the window I could see them go past. He was in his navy fancy dress, Admiral I suppose. She wore a beige hat, upturned as usual. But her face is too fat for beauty. They were in a closed car but glassed so that we could see them. He sat rather still, looked bored, poor lad. She smiled and bowed and moved her hand the way she does.

My hairdresser sisters were closed last week while they went to London for a holiday. But London's scars distressed them, especially the amount of bombed churches. Admitted food was hard to get and complained bitterly about the swarming Americans. Noticed one thing, I did – the way they go to some depot or other and walk about the street with good things, candies, tinned fruit without any wrappings. We are a law-abiding folk, and so we let them get away with it. They said that in the theatre the Americans get all the ices, stand on their seats and grab. The hairdressers have decided they don't like Americans.

For the past two years I have managed to buy tissue paper at one shop in town. Today they had none and say no knowledge of further supplies. The horrors of peace.

George Taylor

Spent the evening shepherding students to the WEA classes commencing at the university. Psychology attracted between thirty and forty, a large number for us, and both Biology and Drama had good groups. Social Aspect of Towns was a complete failure, however, only two students arriving, and one of these transferred to Psychology. The new one dealing with Films attracted nearly twenty students – a relief to me as there had been very few inquiries at the office. British History was a very doubtful starter, however, only half a dozen, including one soldier.

WEDNESDAY, 26 SEPTEMBER

Herbert Brush

I have been creosoting the garden fence this afternoon. First the postman came along and said that I was making a good job of it; then old Cousins, who is seventy-six, stopped to tell me oak-creosoted posts put into the ground did not last as long as oak posts without creosote.

He had just won £8 10s. for 6d. in a football pool and added that he did not know anything about football but put down his 1s and 2s and Xs at random. Then Nicholson, an allotmenteer and gardener, who was wheeling a load of manure into a garden opposite, offered to get me a load of manure for £1.

Edie Rutherford

Everyone talking today about how the King's face was obviously made up with tan make-up. Oh well, they are on a stage in a sense.

Maggie Joy Blunt

I replied to the Save Europe Now appeal launched by the *News Chronicle*, that I would be willing to have my rations cut 'if thereby alone men, women and children of whatever nationality may be saved from starvation'. I received an answer this week asking me to collect signatures which I set about doing at the office yesterday. Lys was very sympathetic but the two men I next approached (both well educated and progressive in outlook) were definitely 'hard'. The first said No before I had had time to explain the matter; the second had seen the *News Chronicle* appeal and noted that only the conditions in Germany were mentioned. What about Holland, for instance? It is true. There is a feeling here among people of 'Why should we help the Germans?' I have heard one of the typists at lunch expressing very strong anti-German views, saying they should suffer as they have made other people suffer.

I have since seen S who is just back from Vienna and will be finished with the army this week. He says, yes, conditions are appalling. Food is the currency – not cigarettes. Eight tins of corn beef will pay for the rent of a flat in Vienna. If I took my normal rations for one month I could live like a queen and get all I want. But, he says, the food is there – in the soil – and all that is necessary is to get it into production again and properly. The problems are ones of labour, organisation and transport. And the Russians. He tells shocking stories of Russian treatment of the Germans. They are doing just what the typist above wants to see done. S says he would quite willingly sacrifice some of his food if he could be sure it would go where it was really needed. But there is no guarantee that the Russians won't confiscate it en route. We, the British, have had to put armed guards round the stores for the defeated peoples.

THURSDAY, 27 SEPTEMBER

Edie Rutherford
I find folk are grumbling more now than they ever did in the war years. It is easy to see why. Whilst the war was on we realised the need for economy and going short, and we grimly did it with the belief that the end of the war would see some let-up, though we knew the world would be in a mess and we could not have everything at once. As peace has so far brought us less than we had in war, and as we realise how well off USA and others are, folk are getting restive, and I foresee riots some not too distant day if we don't get some of the blessings of peace, instead of all disasters.

Herbert Brush
I have done a little more creosoting to the garden fence. A young woman bemoaned her misfortunes as she had had to go to the hospital twice a week since a bomb dropped and damaged her foot, and that she only got 9/- per week and had to depend on her mother and father to keep her. An old woman stopped and began to lecture me on the future life, and said that everyone had some duty to perform before they passed on to everlasting life. I replied that I hoped to finish the garden fence sometime before the end of the year.

Another woman remarked that it was a long job. I guess that most of them know me in this road by now, and even though they are Londoners they speak to a stranger. I did not know a single one of them.

George Taylor
We caught the 7.15 a.m. train to London. After lunch at the hotel I took my wife round St Paul's district to have a look at the damage, and we called for a bit of tea at the Kardomah Café in Fleet Street.

We had booked for Wyndham's Theatre, where we saw *The Years Between*, dealing with the problem of a man who returned from the war having previously been reported dead. The returning warrior, Clive Brook, played a very domineering part, and I was sorry for the wife, who had seemed to have gained her freedom after his reported death.

It is the first post-war play I have been to in London, and I was surprised to find the wartime hours still in force. For a performance to finish shortly after 9.00 p.m. seems very early. We were very disappointed with the street lighting in London. Oxford Street seemed very patchy, and Shaftesbury Avenue a disgrace. Our own road at home, although only in a Sheffield suburb, is much better lit than either of those two famous streets.

Maggie Joy Blunt

Have started Dutton's Double Speed Longhand – a contracted form of longhand and useful substitute for shorthand for anyone like myself who has no intention of becoming a shorthand typist but would like a means of taking notes quickly. Lys is very interested – what intrigues her is the fact that one can learn to speak 'Speedword' too. She takes the book during lunch and makes the oddest noises at me, which I try to interpret.

This evening I washed my hair. Hate having to do this but have lost step with my appointments with Windsor hairdresser and will have to wait a week or two to get another one on a Saturday afternoon. Have been going through my stockings – had to start wearing them again this week as the temperature fell abruptly. Stockings are all in a shocking condition, so have been experimenting with a tube of Mendahol which I bought sometime during the war. Wish I had bought more of it. It is a rubbery mixture which you smear round the edges of a patch cut from an old stocking and stick over the hole, over an upturned tumbler. It seems highly successful. Have thereby salvaged six pairs of stockings I might otherwise have abandoned.

Cat Dinah has had four more kittens and I still have one left from the spring batch. She moved them all the other day from the house into the woodshed.

FRIDAY, 28 SEPTEMBER

Edie Rutherford

Daily Express yesterday showed the midday meal of a German POW here, and a friend I went to see on Wednesday said her husband works alongside Germans who are digging foundations for prefabs, and he too complained that they are much better off for food.

One of the teachers next door said it went against the grain to praise Germans but you can't beat the truth, and the British workman is jealous of the industry and tries to get his own back by mentioning the food. This workman said the POWs should be sent home as it will lead to endless trouble if we keep them, as bosses are already preferring the industrious German to the loafing British workman.

George Taylor

A morning looking round the Oxford Street shops with my wife, and the afternoon discussing company flotation with a client. In the evening we went to Studio One to see *Fantasia*, a film I regretted missing in Sheffield. My wife did not like it too much: it seemed noisy and somewhat frightening to her. I like it immensely, however, and would have loved to sit it through again.

SATURDAY, 29 SEPTEMBER

Herbert Brush

W and I went to the State Cinema to see *Henry V*. The early part of the film was very slow, I thought, and I yawned at least a dozen times and nearly fell asleep once. The battle scene was exciting for a short time, but even that did not seem very real to me. In the queue to get in, two small boys, brothers, had two or three fights and grown-ups had to part them at least twice as they lay struggling on the pavement. I guess that they would enjoy the battle of Agincourt.

SUNDAY, 30 SEPTEMBER

Edie Rutherford

To think there was once a time when we used to throw sugar on the fire to get a cheerful blaze . . .

Talking on Friday to a friend due for demob any day. He says he reckons there will be riots in this country in the next year or so. He bases his belief on the conversation of men serving, says they won't put up with what their fathers endured. He said that this war has come too soon after the last for that to happen. But I welcome unrest as it shows folk are waking up and realising what they ought to have, and doing something about it.

MONDAY, 1 OCTOBER 1945

George Taylor
I had to go over to Mexbro to deal with the affairs of one of our clients who had died suddenly while I was away. In spite of his sixty-seven years he had been active right up to the day of his death. Even on his last afternoon, he had driven himself back to the office, helped to load a lorry with goods for the branches, and only then, feeling what he thought were indigestion pains, returned home, to die of heart failure soon after midnight. He was one of the straightest businessmen I have met, and a credit to the pawnbroking fraternity to which he belonged.

WEDNESDAY, 3 OCTOBER

Edie Rutherford
There is at least one man on the radio in this country who won't feel sorry for the Germans who are eating grass. He has twice told us on the air how he thrives on lawn clippings.

What to do about the Jews who are landing in Palestine without leave? And with the protection of their own armed guard. That must have been well planned as you can't get ships and an armed guard all in a few days. Now who is behind it all?

All this talk of the demob. Husband says that what his firm can't get is labourers. They have a perpetual request at the Labour Exchange and now and again a man round seventy from the old men's home turns up.

Have just put a cake in oven, to send to nephew in RAF. He says the food where he is now, North Luffenham, is awful. At Wing, Beds., it was all right. Queer how it varies. Have put a lot of dripping in this cake. Had to. Fat is such a problem.

George Taylor
A lecture at the WEA Political Forum on Proportional Represen-
tation. As I feared, there was only a very small attendance, probably
about thirty. The absence of controversy, which had been a feature of
the first meetings, and the complete lack of interest in electoral
reform, were no doubt the reasons for the small audience.

THURSDAY, 4 OCTOBER

Edie Rutherford
Two men tenants called last night to tell us the Government is going to
put a hut on the site of one of our three tennis courts, with stage,
kitchen, dressing room, toilets and so on, for various activities. Before
this is done, the tenants have to show they have funds to furnish the
place. Hence the visit. The proposal at their last meeting was 5/- down
and 6d. weekly. We gave our blessing but no more than that.

Herbert Brush
I went to the Institute of Electrical Engineers to hear the new
President's speech this afternoon. Prof. Dunsheath gave a mass of
detail about what electrical engineers had done in the war; in fact,
they almost won it on their own.

If I was asked 'What is a Klystron?' or 'What is a Magnetron?' I
should be stumped for an answer. There was a short length of
PLUTO on show; this is the three-inch pipeline laid across the
Channel to convey petrol for the forces at a pressure of 1,500lb. to
the square inch; a really wonderful bit of work. Also short lengths of
buoyant cables used for blowing up magnetic mines, and many other
little gadgets which I did not understand, as such things had not been
thought of in 1937.

Sir John Anderson was there and gave a little speech after the
President had finished. Sir John's face reminds me very much of a
comedian I sometimes see in the films.

FRIDAY, 5 OCTOBER

Edie Rutherford
In library porch yesterday I was interested to read that those
industries who can employ cripples will be obliged to employ a

percentage. Husband objects, says it's against nature. As I pointed out, we go agin nature at every point of civilisation – that it is obvious that crippled folk are better off themselves and for the community as a whole if they learn a trade and follow it.

SATURDAY, 6 OCTOBER

George Taylor
The opening rally of the WEA, with the new Director of Education as speaker. He outlined the likely developments under the new Education Act. After the talk we had a social, a very poor affair. In one corner our President took half an hour to arrange a spelling bee, while our treasurer, who had been pressed to act as MC in the absence of the MC billed, struggled to keep things moving.

MONDAY, 8 OCTOBER

Edie Rutherford
In the first year of the war I bought a 1lb. tin each of Parkinson's mints and boiled sweets. Yesterday I opened the mints – perfect condition, and oh so much nicer than any sweets we buy now. I was amused to note that the printed slip in the tin advises one to buy sweets in tins, so MUCH better, and then asks if you have remembered to buy this week's supply of old-fashioned humbugs?

Herbert Brush
Went to the British Museum today and when I left there was a big procession which seemed to contain thousands in Oxford Street. They were bomb-damage workers who want less work and more pay for knocking people's houses about under the pretence of carrying out repairs.

TUESDAY, 9 OCTOBER

Edie Rutherford
One of the girls at work has a boyfriend in Burma, a private. She had a parcel from him on Saturday sent by an Indian firm. None of the things is quality stuff. The sultanas had fermented and were a wet and stinking mass – we didn't see them as they had to be put on the

108

fire. But they had soaked through the sheets and pillowcases and left a stain which a first boiling has not removed. The handkerchiefs are child's size. All I can say is, one Indian firm has its own way of getting its own back on Britain.

I have just finished reading *They Build a Bridge* by Marie Worsley, a novel which is laid mostly in USA in the 1800s. Writing in her diary in 1887 the heroine, while on a visit to this country, comments thus: 'I love England, not just because of the gay time we are having here but because of its mightiness. America's great ideas originated here, they thrived as a plant does in new soil, they advanced and improved; in fact, these two nations are like the same tune, played in a different key. I hope the day is not far distant when our two destinies may be as one.' Which suits me and suits this era.

Herbert Brush

I spent a few hours playing with figures, more especially the figure seven, which always interests me. I have finished creosoting the fence. A good many people stopped to talk for a few moments. One old lady who was very deaf told me that the lips of young women ought to be creosoted.

Chapter Five

DELICATESSEN SAVOURY

The Moscow Dynamos had better go home: the first Russian invasion at Stamford Bridge

'I haven't long, Judith,' he said swiftly, kissing her. 'I shouldn't be here at all – But I had to see you! Here – let me look at you. Oh, how pretty you are – prettier even than I remembered!'

She clung to him desperately, thinking that she could never let him go again. 'Oh, John! John, darling – how I've missed you!'

'It's *wonderful* to hear you say that! I've been afraid – But it doesn't matter, does it – that our parents are quarrelling? We love each other just the same—'

'Just the same?' she cried, her throat choking with tears of happiness and dread. 'Oh, John! We love each other more! I never knew how much I loved you till you were gone and I was afraid that – Oh this terrible, terrible war! I hate it! When will it end, John? Will it end soon?'

From the Prologue of Forever Amber *by Kathleen Winsor, set in 1644, published in 1944 by Macdonald & Co., London*

'Now that the brief visit of the Dynamo football team has come to an end, it is possible to say publicly what many thinking people were saying privately before the Dynamos ever arrived. That is, that sport is an unfailing cause of ill-will, and that if such a visit as this had any effect at all on Anglo-Soviet relations, it could only be to make them slightly worse than before.'

George Orwell writes on 'The Sporting Spirit' following Moscow Dynamos' tour of Britain in the autumn of 1945. The violence on the pitch and the aggression on the terraces led him to his famous conclusion that sport was nothing less than 'war minus the shooting'

WEDNESDAY, 10 OCTOBER

Edie Rutherford
Two days ago I overheard a man where I work talking to a man from a firm across the road – a slanging match against the French. Both could not think up enough derogatory things to say of France and French folk, and each heartily concurred with the other as fast as the slanging fell from each pair of lips. Inwardly I was choking with laughter. What ignorance. As if you can dispose of a whole nation like that.

Last night as we listened to *The Brains Trust* I sewed patches on Husband's underwear.

FRIDAY, 12 OCTOBER

Edie Rutherford
Instead of our Minister of Food person coming to the microphone on Thursday morning as promised last week, one of their woman gave us a recipe for suet crust without suet, which I call letting the side down.

SATURDAY, 13 OCTOBER

George Taylor
Eight members from Sheffield joined the Stocksbridge Branch WEA Weekend School at Great Hucklow. After tea we had a Round Table Conference on the WEA pamphlet 'Making a Fresh Start'. One of the teachers present objected to the word 'Workers' in the title of the Association.

TUESDAY, 16 OCTOBER

Edie Rutherford
Friend called last night whose husband was just home from Italy on leave. She said he had travelled nine days and arrived with a beard. Was unable to eat his first meal till he had fingered the tablecloth and taken in the fact that the crockery was decent, cup had handle, etc, etc. Made his wife and mother weep to watch him.

WEDNESDAY, 17 OCTOBER

George Taylor
I went to Mexbro for a Pawnbrokers Annual Meeting. It seems that already they are getting quite a few of the new demobilisation suits in pawn.

Herbert Brush
My seventy-third birthday. Seventy-three years ago, father went to a sale at Marnham and when he came back recorded the fact, and also that a baby had been born. I suppose the nurse turned him out of the house when I was expected to appear.

A lot has happened since then, but I can't help wishing that father had put a little more detail into his diaries. A description of me when first he caught a glimpse of his new baby might help me to visualise the small lump of flesh which I inhabited. It probably had a small, snub nose on a big head, large hands and feet and a good pair of lungs. A woman in the village, who was considerably older than I was, used to tell me about the first sight she had of me in my 'pram' and the nurse who was pushing the 'pram' told her that the baby's name was originally Charles.

THURSDAY, 18 OCTOBER

Herbert Brush
I paid my usual visit to my bank manager for him to certify that I am still alive. I gave him a couple of large tomatoes.

Edie Rutherford
Hurrah, the Director of Public Relations at the Food Ministry came on the air this morning, as he had said he would, and gave a worthwhile talk too. Hurrah for restored fat and cheese ration. Only bacon remains cut now.

I see that my idea, that folk with room to spare in their homes should be asked by the Government to share with those less fortunate, has come off. Seems so obvious.

Husband a bit pleased about the boy shooting the schoolteacher.

FRIDAY, 19 OCTOBER

Edie Rutherford

The woman who cleans corridors, foyer, lifts, etc to these flats was going off the deep end terribly yesterday. She had just swept two French letters out of the phone booth in the foyer, and one out of the biggest lift a little earlier. She says she's sick of such work.

My boss is still trying to locate his mother. She was arrested in Prague a year ago and taken, it is thought, to Leipzig. He has put all into the search that he can think of, and would go himself to search if he could. He is positive her record is clean so he can't understand why she was arrested in the first place, unless it was simply that she didn't like the Nazis. What a lot of trouble we have brought on ourselves through our own folly in the years when Europe looked like a playground.

Herbert Brush

A lump has come up in the flesh in the middle of my back. It is not painful and I did not know it was there until W told me. It is just in the position where I can't reach it with my hand, either from above or below. W is going to rub it with Iodex.

SUNDAY, 21 OCTOBER

Edie Rutherford

On this beastly dock strike. Goods piling up for export, soldiers sweating to unload imports. How will it all end? I do think they might give our new Government a chance.

Really, old Churchill is silly. I listened to his speech in 9 p.m. news last night – the man doesn't know when he's had enough. Lovely letter in *Sunday Despatch* today suggesting that our new Government has caused strikes and international tension, and that Churchill and Eden should be restored, the present regime being in power not by virtue of superior qualifications but through the hazard of the hustings.

TUESDAY, 23 OCTOBER

George Taylor
K. B. Hathaway's autobiography, *The Little Locksmith*, Readers Union choice for October, is a thoroughly wholesome story of a sensitive-minded cripple girl and her development into maturity. She never really grows up, although she thinks she does, and she has ideas, which are naïve in the extreme. For instance, in her new house she proposed to invite young lovers to associate freely, and she intended to provide them with darkened rooms suitable for the occasion. Fortunately, for her reputation, she never put her project into operation. The book is certainly a change from the sordid filth now being turned out by many modern writers.

So the budget is out, and what a deception. In spite of all the fine proposals of reduction, I calculate that I shall be just 17/6d. better off in a year, after taking the cancellation of post-war credits into account. My socialist, Special Constable friend would scarcely believe my calculations when he called in for a chat.

WEDNESDAY, 24 OCTOBER

Edie Rutherford
What a splendid budget. Husband and I both think so. We like the sound of Mr Dalton too – firm, clear and kind and understanding. Let the Tories say what they will, it is a good budget. *Daily Express* praises with one hand this morning and damns with the other.

George Taylor
I visited our Film Appreciation class and found a dozen there. The tutor showed one reel of a film, *The Last Laugh*. Unfortunately, the laugh came in the last reel which he did not show, so I had the misfortune of suffering what is probably the most horrible film I have ever seen. And I had to endure its showing twice.

Herbert Brush
Went with W to Ramsgate this morning. The reason for the visit was to collect six ducks and a goose. A further reason was that her firm are giving her a lunch to commemorate the fact that she has been with them for twenty-five years, and as no one seemed able to get the

necessary food she was asked to get it from her friends. We went via the Thanet Way.

FRIDAY, 26 OCTOBER

Herbert Brush
W dropped me at Camberwell Green this morning and I changed my book at Boots, taking out *Forever Amber* by Kathleen Winsor. It begins with a very clever description of a childbirth and the agony of the mother, who dies while listening to her crying baby. I don't know how many lovers Amber managed to get during the two or three years covered by the eight hundred pages of fairly close type, but there must have been more than a dozen, including King Charles II.

TUESDAY, 30 OCTOBER

George Taylor
We made a special effort to see Disney's *The Three Caballeros* and were bitterly disappointed with it. The opening section, giving the story of a penguin that sets sail on an ice floe to see the world, is amusing and enjoyable in the true Disney style. After that, however, glamour girls are introduced, and the sound becomes just formless and very noisy jazz. Apart from the clever designs, such as when Donald Duck takes on the form of a vibrating violin string, the final two-thirds of the film require a real effort to endure. Disney has certainly degraded his art, in my opinion. The only compensation to the evening was the documentary dealing with the Channel Islands during and after the occupation.

THURSDAY, 1 NOVEMBER 1945

Herbert Brush
W and I recorded our votes for the Conservatives in the Borough election about 8.30 a.m. Very few people about. That lump on my back does not vanish, as I had hoped, and she still rubs in Iodex.

W has gone to her firm to be inoculated against catching a cold. This has to be done three times to be effective, or maybe to give the doctor a paying job.

FRIDAY, 2 NOVEMBER

Edie Rutherford
As we don't take the local paper I don't know yet how elections went, but according to BBC 8 a.m. news Labour has had nationwide gains. Good.

Husband says that yesterday a businessman friend called on them and said his solution to the Palestine problem was to send the English there, and let the Jews have England – they already have most of it anyway. Ha ha. In the timber trade (my husband's line) they do resent Jews keenly, and with good reason.

SATURDAY, 3 NOVEMBER

Herbert Brush
I voted for the losing side again. I wonder how long this state of things will last and whether we shall be any better off at the finish. It seems to me that the world in 1955 will be a funny, disagreeable place to live in, and it will be difficult to do anything without running foul of some law or bye-law.

Bertha Hardy came in during the evening and we played a few games of darts. I won each time, but I think she was hungry and hoping that W would produce something to eat. A little later Seaden came in. He has grown a beard during the time he was away on an aircraft carrier in the Pacific. He has been away for a year, though it does not seem so long to me. Everyone was interested in his beard.

George Taylor
The WEA Annual Meeting. The attendance was very thin, only some 7 per cent of the members troubling to attend. The President, in a very outspoken speech, criticised the operation of the new Education Act. He thought that too much lip service was being paid to the slogans of equality, parity and uniformity: to say that all are equal is to ignore the facts. It was his opinion that the effect of the act would be a levelling down of education, rather than a raising of the standard. This brought a member of the local Education Committee to his feet to deny any intention, on the part of the Sheffield authorities, to give anything but the best.

TUESDAY, 6 NOVEMBER

Maggie Joy Blunt

Last entry 27 September – am shocked by the speed with which time passes. If asked what I have done since then I should reply, 'Nothing much', yet I have been too occupied to keep up this diary. It should be so simple to make one or two entries during the week or after I am in bed before turning out the light but I don't do it. I wait for an evening such as this one when nothing more urgent claims my attention.

Office situation much the same. My boss cannot find other work and RW has given up looking for something else, deciding that she might find herself in a worse job. The position with regard to typists' is curiously inconsistent. Some apply for their release and get it without difficulty, others are refused, and others are made suddenly redundant for no apparent good reason. Work in our department as boring as ever. Have not yet received layout from the agents of my building pamphlet, which DJ says I am to approve.

June and I have birthdays in October so we decided to celebrate together and throw a joint party in her Hampstead flat. Asked everyone to bring a bottle of whatever they could get to drink, and we provided sandwiches and other snacks. I was busy for a week making oddments such as cheese straws, peanut butter sweets and biscuits, etc. Packed them, and various sauces, cheese, margarine and so on into two large parcels which I sent from the village by registered post on the Thursday, expecting they would arrive by the Saturday for the party. No parcels came. They were not delivered until the following Wednesday when June posted them straight back to me *un*registered. One arrived here the next day and the other the day after, only because a bottle of Worcester sauce had broken and soaked through and the parcel had to be replaced. So in future if I want to be sure of parcels reaching their destinations quickly, I must send them unregistered.

We had, however, more than enough to eat and drink. Plenty of sandwiches, fillings as follows: liver sausage, watercress, delicatessen savoury, scrambled egg and tomato, cheese and onion. Someone sent a jar of prawns and June had bought a jar of pickled sardines and these I arranged on plain cream cracker biscuits and small scones split open, decorated with watercress. There was more than enough to drink too – someone brought some rum and made a small quantity of rum punch. I got some cheap British port from my grocer and someone else contributed half a bottle of sherry. Everyone seemed to enjoy themselves hugely. About sixteen to eighteen turned up, several of the men still in uniform. But so many people had to go early to catch the last trains and buses. Our last guests left soon after midnight, but June and I decided to clear up at once and were not in bed until 2 a.m.

The young woman who worked in the village hairdresser's, who did my hair so well and left to join the volunteer nurses in the navy two or more years ago, has returned (married), much to my joy. She has persuaded me to have a 'Liberty' cut which I had done in time for the party, and it was generally approved. But naturally curly hair, as I grow tired of trying to explain to people who profess envy of it, is highly temperamental and never obedient for more than a few days at a time. It will take several trims and sets to get this new style into working order, but it promises well.

WEDNESDAY, 7 NOVEMBER

Edie Rutherford
A remark of the woman in next cubbyhole at hairdresser's yesterday: 'My husband says he doesn't know what I do with my money. I tell him I'd like him to have the spending of it.' I wonder if there is any marriage where such a situation isn't all the time arising. I have often offered my Husband the wifely job, but he shies away instantly. He may be mystified about what I do with his allowances to me, but he apparently would rather go on being mystified than take over the job. Dear knows, there are times, often, when I'd be glad to have no money to handle. Like royalty.

George Taylor
Tonight a class on 'Environment and the Ego'. A keen little group . . . Tonight the subject was mainly climate, and the tutor quoted at great length an Italian writer of whom I have never heard. According to him, genius is encouraged by warm but not hot climates, by mountains and access to the sea. He has collected statistics to show that at least in the case of mental defectives, sudden changes in temperature or barometric pressure have a disturbing influence on the mind.

FRIDAY, 9 NOVEMBER

Edie Rutherford
Yesterday I wrote to Howie & Co., florists in SA, and asked them would they give me an agency for chincherinchees, the flower which travels and lasts three months in water, and which blooms just right for midwinter here when flowers are scarce and costly. Maybe shipping space will not be available for Christmas 1946. I would like to do this business as it would not only give me monetary reward but also it would please me to know I was bringing pleasure to people. I think hospitals, hotels, churches and so on should all buy the flowers, and a big business could be worked up. Not much advertisement would be needed as the flowers sell themselves. I used to pick them in the veldt as a child but in those days their keeping powers had not been discovered, or at any rate not commercialised. If Howie's won't play, I'll write to their chief opposition.

Maggie Joy Blunt
Day off today. Hairdo first thing this morning, then sweep came to clean kitchen and sitting room flues.

I have a chance now to be transferred to the library. My friend Dr RL has taken the librarian's place, one of the chief assistants has just left and the young woman who has been doing all the work since is married and wants to leave at Christmas. Dr RL seems to think I should be suitable to take her place. Can't say that I have any ambition to become a librarian, but it would be better than my present, very unsatisfactory, position and it would be one of those nice steady jobs with opportunities for advancement if I care to take them. I shall probably accept.

SATURDAY, 10 NOVEMBER

Edie Rutherford
Teachers next door tell me of a colleague who, in 1939, was offered an old railway coach seaside shack for £5. Thinking it was ramshackle they refused it. Last week it sold for £250. Opposite where my sister lives in Hertfordshire there is a weatherboard cottage with a small piece of land, sold by auction the week after we visited them this summer. It fetched £1,400. Could never have cost half that originally. We live in a mad world.

SUNDAY, 11 NOVEMBER, ARMISTICE DAY

Edie Rutherford

We have had a church parade along the road, although our local Church of England has no vicar at the moment. Last one has taken a living in London and the last few Sundays a callow curate has been tearing along the road in his cassocks on Sundays, presumably deputising. I have no time for all this Legion annual nonsense – if ever a body was corrupt the British Legion is the one. More than time it was investigated and exposed and finished.

There have been several burglaries in this district last week. I am not convinced that it IS a good idea to turn off street lighting at midnight. It may save fuel but it just suits burglars and in the end lots of people may lose more than the corporation saves. In one robbery £8 was taken from the drawer in the public library – they have no safe – but I say it serves them right for not having a better arrangement for dealing with cash.

MONDAY, 12 NOVEMBER

Herbert Brush

I went to the British Museum today and read more about Derbyshire. I have never been to Derby, but I am interested in the county because the Brush family in years gone by were very important people, and I should be pleased to find out for certain that our family are an offshoot.

In Derby in 1732, a man gave an exhibition of what was called 'flying' in those days. He fixed a rope to the top of a church tower and slid down to a spot about 150 yards away, while everyone in Derby watched the performance. He did so well and earned so much that another man copied him soon afterwards, and slid down the rope with a board attached to his chest on which he lay with his arms and legs stretched out. The friction on the rope set the board on fire and he left a trail of smoke behind him as he came down.

But he was not satisfied with sliding down the rope himself. He made an ass do the same thing, with half cwts attached to each leg to keep the animal upright as it came down. They kept the animal on the roof of the tower for several days, with nothing to eat, so that it might advertise the show by braying for food. However, when the ass was sliding down, and had nearly reached the bottom, the rope broke and the ass fell on the crowd and knocked down scores, but did not receive any injury itself. No one was killed which I think is remarkable, if the donkey really had half a cwt of lead attached to each leg. I wonder whether there was a Brush in the crowd; probably there were several.

About the same date, a man did the same kind of show at Dover, but he used the top of a high cliff as a starting place and slid across the old harbour to the wonderment of the natives. How would you like to be back in the days when this kind of show was considered wonderful? I would not, because I don't believe that there ever were any 'Good Old Days'. If you had lived then, it is fairly certain that you would have caught smallpox or died before you were five years old.

I remember when I was a boy seeing men with their faces pitted all over with smallpox, which they may, of course, have had when they were young, but I was always scared when I went near one of them. No, the 'good old days' are a myth for discontented people to talk about.

TUESDAY, 13 NOVEMBER

Maggie Joy Blunt
How different I feel tonight. My weekend orgy of cleaning left me completely exhausted and last night was in bed by 8.30. Meant to read but fell asleep, woke at 11 p.m. and turned out light and slept until 8.30 this morning. Last week a doctor was reported in the press to have said that most of us were suffering from food shortage. One of the symptoms was an unusual feeling of fatigue and particularly after doing extra work. The only advice he could give his patients was to cut down their activities as much as possible and get more sleep. Many people I meet seem to suffer from this fatigue. Lys is one and has been to her doctor about it (she says 'One's heart feels almost too tired to beat').

Today at lunch WS spoke of some tablet she had been taking and of how much better she felt since she had done so. They turned out to be Fersolate, which I have been taking since my holiday in Hove and they do seem to help.

S writes that after the party at Hampstead he missed all his last trains and buses for Victoria and stopped a car near the Heath tube station. He was still in uniform and demanded of the astonished occupant in the back, who was a Jew, that he be driven at once on urgent military business to his rooms. The Jew, in evening dress, spoke up and the driver said he was taking him only as far as the Spaniards and would then drive S where he wanted to go. The driver turned out to be an old Desert Rat and a good time was had by all.

Patching and darning all this evening. Poked a toe through a sheet last night. So sick of Making Do.

WEDNESDAY, 14 NOVEMBER

Edie Rutherford
I hope the Russian footballers are pleased with their reception. I should think every Communist in the country was there, though they could not ALL have had a grandmother to bury. I had to laugh at the description in *Daily Express* today of the bus clippies after the match yesterday trying to enforce this new 'no standing' law on 85,000 football fans . . .

I was sorry to become aware the other night on the air that Aneurin Bevan has a stammer. Apart from that, his Welsh voice is quite pleasant. Extra rations for Christmas. Hurrah.

THURSDAY, 15 NOVEMBER

Edie Rutherford
Glad the Lord's Day Observance lost their case yesterday. Not because I think kids should go to cinemas on Sunday afternoon, but because the LDO are such nosey parkers.

Got a piece of beef at the butcher's today. Neighbour thinks she may be able to get us a rabbit – under the counter – this weekend. Nice when such things become easily available again. Poor little rabbits though.

SATURDAY, 17 NOVEMBER

Herbert Brush
I am disappointed with my celeriac; it has grown bulbs as large as a tennis ball, and most of the tops had maggots in them and turned brown before the right time.

Wife and I went to the Capitol Cinema in the afternoon. Two very good pictures were on the screen. One was about the canals and other waterways of England, which was interesting. The other picture was *The Son of Lassie*, a coloured film of the adventures of a collie dog during the war. Certainly this dog is worth watching. It seems to understand exactly what it is doing, and why it is doing it.

Chapter Six

MADE SOME DROP SCONES
IN THE AFTERNOON, WHICH
WERE NOT A SUCCESS

They ought to have shot him immediately: a notice at Wandsworth Prison states that Lord Haw-Haw was hanged for treason

'Hess was strained and taut; his dark, roving eyes were continually roving about the court when they were not absorbed in a Bavarian novel he had brought into the dock with him, and he smiled cynically when at the outset the batteries of floodlights were switched on overhead for the cameramen . . . Sometimes he engaged Ribbentrop on his left in animated conversation; once he made a remark to Goering, but Goering, chin in hand, and gazing thoughtfully at nothing, ignored him. As for the others, they might almost have been attending a business convention.'

The opening of the Nuremberg Tribunal, The Times, *Wednesday, 21 November 1945*

'As the number of turkeys available this Christmas will not be sufficient to meet the demand, the Ministry of Food asks turkey retailers to spread the limited supplies among the largest possible number of families by cutting birds into two parts before sale. Half a turkey, he believes, will supply a good meal for most families.'

The Times, *Saturday, 15 December 1945*

MONDAY, 19 NOVEMBER

B. Charles
Antiques dealer and tutor in Edinburgh
Filled in the November [Mass-Observation] Directive in the evening, and made up my mind to keep a daily diary.

Went to a sale of furniture and left a commission with the auctioneer for a pair of pretty Adam vases to be used as tea caddies. I had never seen any before like them, and was told they were very unusual. I said I would give £6 but they made £8 10s., I hear. The prices of all furniture are rising tremendously. I think this is largely owing to the coupon business, and to rationing of foodstuffs. People are so tired of saving that they are determined to spend on something.

Am very disheartened at the renewed Compulsory Billeting, which is all this 'Sharing your Home' is. I have decided that it will be better to sell my house in England and buy one in Scotland, where the billeting is not likely to be anything like so acute.

TUESDAY, 20 NOVEMBER

B. Charles
Made some drop scones in the afternoon, which were not a success. It was the first time I had ever cooked on a girdle. Went out in the afternoon to pick up the things I had got at the morning sale and had to walk all the way back, as the trams were so awfully crowded. It is the same every afternoon. Hordes of women cluttering up every-where, with apparently nothing whatever to do except joy-ride on trams.

WEDNESDAY, 21 NOVEMBER

B. Charles
This afternoon I went to a shop near here and asked for a pencil. The man said he hadn't one in the shop, and that, nowadays, it was hardly worthwhile having a shop, as so many things were utterly unprocurable.

A letter from a friend this afternoon, in which he writes that in London the Poles are very dangerous and many of them are running many of the brothels in the neighbourhood of Victoria and Maida

Vale. I should think it is quite likely. There certainly is a very great deal of anti-Polish feeling about.

Herbert Brush

I have been reading about Harry Price's book on poltergeists in England and it makes me wonder whether it was a poltergeist which worried me when I lived in Rose Cottage, River, near Dover. The noises got so bad that I was glad to leave the house.

I never managed to explain the things that happened to me there. I might be reading a book by the fireside in the evening, when suddenly my back hair would seem to stand up, a cold shiver would run down my spine and I felt sure that someone or something was behind me in the room. I asked a local spiritualistic medium to come and investigate, so he came with others, and presently he went into a trance, or seemed to, and said that a man who used to live in the house, and who committed suicide years before, objected to me very much.

THURSDAY, 20 NOVEMBER

B. Charles

Went to Kirkcaldy this morning to see Robert. When I got there he told me he had been in Edinburgh last night, and asked if I had noticed the number of women about, cluttering up everywhere. I told him it was usual to see hordes of women trailing about the town doing nothing except trail about. Can't imagine what these women did in pre-war days. We had lunch at the usual restaurant, and again there were hordes of women, the working class, lunching out, and spending a good deal of money on the food. This 'eating out' for all classes is one of the most remarkable results of the war. It is a habit that has come to stay, I feel sure. It is remarkable how much money there seems to be about nowadays.

I had a very interesting conversation with a naval petty officer on the train home. He said he feared the nationalisation of industry and he thought, as a result, Compulsory Direction of labour would remain. The only thing he wants to do is get out of the service he has been in seventeen years and get a good civvy job and a home of his own. He is married. I told him I thought the navy had changed very much during the last twenty years, so far as the Lower Deck was concerned. I thought the films had been largely responsible. I told him I thought another war would happen within the next ten years, and in all probability much sooner.

I intend, if I can get the time, to reread all the novels of Jane Austen again. This will be a sort of 'escapism' from all the dullness of these post-war days. Mr Woodhouse and Co. will make delightful company.

Maggie Joy Blunt

At lunch today someone mentioned problem of Palestine. 'I don't think the Jews should be *forced* to leave a country – let them go to Palestine if they want to.' 'Jews get such a financial hold on a country.' 'That's true – all the same, a country is nearly always better off where Jews are powerful – they may make big money, but they circulate it.' 'They produce much talent too.' 'Pity they have such unpleasant characteristics.' 'Only due to long years of persecution – aggressive trait has developed.' 'Well, we all get aggressive don't we, when we feel looked down on?'

Have not yet moved to the library – some typical hitch of which I am kept in ignorance.

FRIDAY, 23 NOVEMBER

Herbert Brush

W dropped me at Camberwell Green this morning and I changed my book at Boots, taking out a Wild West book for a change. Sometimes I feel that a book of this kind will do me good, especially when the weather is foggy and cold. Even to imagine oneself in the wide open spaces of the west is refreshing, when you can't see the house next door for fog, thick smoky fog which clogs your breathing apparatus and makes you feel that the world is not a happy place to live in.

Edie Rutherford

A parcel from Brisbane, Australia, today. Peanuts, sugar, dried fruit and actually some cherries among the fruit!

Oh dear, all this trouble in Calcutta now. Let us GET OUT and if the Indians are bent on killing, let them kill each other.

Now we have this farcical trial of major war criminals which Husband reckons will last a year. All the world knows every one of them is guilty over and over, so why the trials? We are all mad.

We didn't get that rabbit last weekend.

SATURDAY, 24 NOVEMBER

Edie Rutherford

Today I hear of the death of one of my oldest women friends, Maud Bennett, spinster, with whom I lived in digs in Birmingham when I left home at the age of twenty-one because of my stepmother's barbarity. Poor Maud, she had been ill for years and the loss of her mother last month was more than she could take. She was in the fifties. Far too young to die but life has held little for Maud for years.

I think the Moscow Dynamos had better go home. Far from fostering friendship I can foresee worse relations as a result of their visit. Already there are recriminations about assault during the game . . . Our men are bound to get madder with each lost game and I don't kid myself that our lads are above a dirty blow if they see a chance.

B. Charles

I went to Lyon & Turnbull's this morning, to see about this miniature of Lady Blessington. Very lovely, but rather sad-looking. I left a commission for it, up to £9 10s. and hope I get it. That is as much as I can afford, but I have an idea that, as it is 'reputed' to be by Cosway – this is written on the back, that it will fetch a great deal more.

I see by this evening's paper that the Nazis on trail at Nuremberg intend calling some of the Cliveden Set to give evidence! I expect any sensational material will be 'censored' and not allowed to appear in the British papers. I always was astonished that, on one occasion at least, Queen Mary dined or had tea, I forget which, with Lady Astor at Cliveden. I always thought all that lot extremely weird. I see Hess proposes to call the Duke of Hamilton.

Just going out for a stroll, so won't enter up the budget expenses until I see if I spend anything on having a couple of 'wets'.

SUNDAY, 25 NOVEMBER

Herbert Brush

I went to see a doctor this morning about the lump on my back. He said that there was nothing to worry about, as it is only an accumulation of fat which will do no harm. Maybe if I live to be a hundred it might grow large enough to be worth cutting out. He charged me only 5/- for telling me this.

MONDAY, 26 NOVEMBER

Edie Rutherford

Poor old London does cop it. The dock strike which must have affected thousands there, then no standing rule, then gas strike. Is anyone satisfied?

Listening to the talk after 9 p.m. news last night of UNRRA [United Nations Relief and Rehabilitation Administration] and its gigantic task, one wondered why we presumably give three meals a day, shelter, medical care and a fair trial involving months of time and work to the beasts who are responsible for it all. The person who wrote in the *Sunday Express* yesterday that Hitler had launched a secret weapon to make us all mad, had something in my view. And a new society started in this country last week . . . Hitler the Messiah. Imagine anyone paying £500 for a bust of Hitler.

B. Charles

A thoroughly vexing day; this morning I went to see if I had got the Lady Blessington miniature, to find the fellow I left the commission with had forgotten all about my order. The miniature was sold for £5. I had left a commission for £9 10s.!

I see by the *Telegraph* that the Russians have raided the British HQ in Berlin. The reason given being that they were looking for deserters from the Red Army. The Russians seem to have struck terror into everyone's heart, including the British, so that no one seems to feel inclined to tell them where to get off. I still think that, ultimately, we shall be sorry we were in the position of having to join forces with Russia during the war. I am quite sure our relations with Russia will worsen, and before long.

I asked who had got the miniature of Lady Blessington, and find it is Mackintosh, in the Grassmarket.

WEDNESDAY, 28 NOVEMBER

B. Charles
An interesting morning; I met a very pleasant lad in the post office and got talking to him. He is at the university on an agricultural course. He is English and comes from near Princes Risborough. He is seventeen, and has a very good amount of the modern 'poise' and assurance, without, however, being in any way cheeky and pert. A nice lad. I gave him my address, and asked him to come and have a chat sometime. The modern young people have far more 'poise' and assurance than we had, but they are, generally, unpleasantly assured and off-hand and rude. When, however, one meets a well-behaved, assured, young lad or young girl, they make a very good impression, I think. I wonder how it is they have this greater assurance? And they are better looking than their fathers and mothers were. No doubt the films have had something to do with this.

THURSDAY, 29 NOVEMBER

Edie Rutherford
How mad Churchill & Co. are that they were defeated at the election. They are now done with being polite and resigned. The fury they really felt is gradually seeping through. Churchill's speech to the Conservatives yesterday was malicious, spiteful, petulant, jealous and entirely unworthy of him. If he knows no better than that, thank God he is no longer Prime Minister. I hope Attlee will make a point of publicly answering Churchill's outburst, as, to many who are ignorant, it will cause fear for which there is – as yet – no cause.

B. Charles
I went to Mackintosh to see the miniature of Lady Blessington he got last Saturday, and found he was only charging £7 10s. for it. As he gave £5 for the miniature, I didn't think this price at all excessive. It is really a lovely piece of work and I thought it would be foolish not to buy it.

FRIDAY, 30 NOVEMBER

B. Charles
I went and bought Lady B. I am charmed with it, and it looks very lovely in my room. I inquired about the name of that biography about her I read a few years ago, and find it is called *Blessington D'Orsay* by M. Sadleir, published by Constable. I have written to Sadleir this afternoon, to know if he can throw any light on this miniature, and am eagerly awaiting his reply. If it is by Cosway it will be worth £50–60.

I am going to the concert tonight. No soloist, but it is called 'Music for Ballet and Film'. It doesn't sound specially interesting to me.

SATURDAY, 1 DECEMBER 1945

Edie Rutherford
Goering's lawyer complains that he is liable to burst if he is not allowed to speak. Let him burst then. Good end to one beast.

I am counting the days to the end of my job now. One of the men came to see me yesterday and said he had heard I was leaving. I said that was so, so he said, 'I'm deeply sorry.' Then he said he had never known anyone work as industriously as I do, and that in part-time I have done a full-time job. I said I was of course aware of it.

Yesterday I saw a pikelet shop has opened – haven't seen one for years. Can't think why as fat for spreading is surely the reason for pikelets disappearing, and that position is still the same. The oat cake shop which has lasted through the years has often had a queue. But not me in it.

George Taylor
My wife and I went to a client for shopping. It is not often I trade with clients, particularly in scarce goods, but when I was offered some linoleum, which we are wanting so badly at home, I could not resist.

B. Charles
The concert last night was interesting, but not as much as some others I have seen. I like the William Walton, *Introduction to a Spitfire Fugue* for some film or other, quite well. Couldn't make head

or tail of Vaughan William's *Job, a Masque for Dancing*. Modern music, so called, leaves me quite cold.

During the morning I went to the free library here and read all about Richard Cosway in the *Dictionary of National Biography* to see if there was any mention of his having painted a miniature of Lady Blessington. There was not, but it seems all the society leaders used to delight in frequenting his London house, so I expect she went with everyone else. I have just written the *Sunday Times* to know if any of their readers can tell me anything about a miniature of Lady B by Cosway.

The shoemaker told me this morning that the question of shoes and boots is far more acute now than it was some months ago. There is such a feeling of 'unsatisfactoriness' everywhere. I may go out tonight to have 'one or two'.

I have just returned, after visiting various public houses, to observe the behaviour and to hear the conversations of as many service people as possible. There is no doubt at all that there seems to be money galore in the services for drink and smokes. The pubs were packed and almost all with service personnel who were drinking as hard as they could. The behaviour of sailors, in particular, has altered a very great deal even since the outbreak of this war. The old-time sailor has given place to a much more sophisticated, and, on the surface more 'genteel' young gentleman, but I suspect, underneath the present-day sailor is inferior in common sense to the old-timer, and he is certainly far less cheery to talk to.

Herbert Brush

I met Mr Ing in the road and asked him whether he liked artichokes, 'Not 'alf,' he said. 'Help yourself,' said I, thinking that he would fill his pockets as the artichokes were quite clean and white; but he produced a bag from a pocket and helped himself to about half my bucketful. He was going shopping, but he returned home with the artichokes before going down the hill again.

I learn that Smut has been busy again and the result is another family of three kittens in Mrs Sparks' house, two doors away, and the mother is Hitler, her cat.

Went to the Capitol Cinema with W this afternoon. A documentary picture, *Queen of Hearts,* was interesting as well as instructive; it showing many pictures of interesting places in Herts.

SUNDAY, 2 DECEMBER

Edie Rutherford

A bitterly cold day with watery sun. I got washing done, scrubbed the pesky kitchen floor, and, feeling as virtuous as a South African brought-up woman must do after such exertions, hied me the library to. Met a German woman in the park who says that her father, whom the Nazis took from his Berlin home a few years ago because he would not toe their line, is alive after all. In a concentration camp in Austria. Too ill to be sent home, and her mother cannot go to him from the British Zone in Berlin. Her mother lost 60lb. in weight due to the war. Mrs Braun longs to go to see her and wonders if she dare hope it will be possible next summer.

Girl at work had twenty-six bananas from a boyfriend in the Azores. She brought us in a third of a banana each. I have brought mine home to share.

B. Charles

I read a review of a book on this new insecticide, DDT, in this week's *Cavalcade* and have written the authors to know if it is any good to kill woodworm.

There were two queues in the post office. This queue business is simply amazing. I can't think how it was that there were none of them prior to the war. When I was coming home on the tram I spoke to a naval officer and his opinion is that, now people have become so 'queue-minded', they just fall into a queue instead of hanging about the counters of the shops, as they used to do before the war. He thinks the vast majority of people are so determined to get all they can, that they queue so as not to miss anything. I feel sure, too, that a great many women LIKE queuing: the queue is, really, the 1945 edition of the Mother's Meeting.

Herbert Brush

I walked along Charing Cross Road to see whether I could find a book giving prime numbers up to five million or so.

I don't know how many bookshops I went into with the question, 'Have you a book giving prime numbers up to, say, 5,000,000?' but every bookseller said 'No', without any hesitation. Even Foyles could not help me.

MONDAY, 3 DECEMBER

Edie Rutherford

Hairdresser today astonished because I think there is some good in our Government. Most of her clients are of the moneyed classes who damn them.

She went off deep end today regarding clothes. I do think folk are getting ready to revolt about coupons and poor quality, and coupons for curtains and towels. We have been asked now to stand as much as we will stand, when we can see plenty all round. Hairdresser said nothing would make her open her home to anyone. I asked if that idea wasn't as Christian as Socialistic? She didn't like that, as she is a Christian Scientist.

I'm sure terrible trouble is coming soon to India and do wish we'd scram out while we safely can. Methinks this Government is mistaken in carrying on as Tories would do about India, Dutch East Indies, and other places where we have no real business to be. One day the people will show they aren't standing for it any more. We've had enough war and our lads should be getting home now. And without plane accidents as they come too. What is wrong that there have been so many lately?

TUESDAY, 4 DECEMBER

Herbert Brush

I have not been away from the fire at all today and as it is raining fast I am not likely to do so, with my nose running like a tap. I'm remembering the day that father took me to Elsemere College and presented me to The Revd Bullock, the Head Master. Bullock asked me some question in the rudiments of Latin and I did not know, and father got angry.

On the first night of a new boy's arrival at this school, he was 'crowned' as soon as he got into bed. Several boys held him down while another boy fished out the chamber from under the bed, and while the other boys held him fast, put the chamber on his head and held it there for a few moments. I remember that I was lucky because there was nothing in the pot.

For some reason, my nickname was 'Curly Ginger'. I don't know why and I don't think that anyone else knew. My particular pal was a very pretty boy with red cheeks and fair hair. He was in my dormitory, which was a dormitory of plain-looking boys and he told me that a master wanted him to be put into a dormitory where all the boys were pretty to look at. But he would not go; he had heard things which scared him and he did not want to be a plaything for a black-browed brute. I did not understand what he meant, but I was glad that he was to stay in my dormitory.

How I did hate the black-browed brute, and he was not at all fond of me. Near the end of term there were examinations and he stood on a kind of stage with a big stick, watching us to see that no boy cribbed from the next boy.

For some reason he thought he had caught me cribbing, so he called me up to the side of the stage and told me to bend over, which I had to do, though I really did not know why. He gave me three strokes on my tight trousers and told me to go back to my seat, while he put my name in the black book he had on the stage. I wanted to question why he did this, but I was scared to say anything, for fear I should get some more. I'm sure he liked doing it, and I was fortunate that he did not make me lower my trousers, as he did sometimes.

I never forgave him and even now after more than sixty years I should like to take a kick at that black-browed brute.

At first I could not eat the food they gave us, but it did not take me long to get over that, as there was nothing else, and all my money soon went in the tuck shop. While I had chocolate cream in my pocket every boy was friendly.

There was one master in the school who was good and kind, who taught me prayers to say when I was miserable, and asked me to always come to him for advice. I can still think of him now with pleasure, and I kept a book he gave me and believe I still have it somewhere, stored away.

B. Charles

A letter this morning from Doris, in which she asked me to let her have the address of Mass-Observation as she would like to work for them. She said she had never heard of them, but if it was at all similar to the Gallup Poll, she thought it an excellent idea. Surely if I have managed to hear of Mass-Observation, she, with so many more advantages in a great many ways, so many more friends and opportunities, could have done so.

I know perfectly well that had Father done what was right to me, taken an interest in my pursuits, encouraged me to do what I always wanted to do, and spent a little money on furthering my aims, that there is NOTHING that I could not have done, and done well. Yet, in spite of all, I certainly have had a very interesting life, though it has been hard and difficult, at times. And it is so funny that so many people really envy me! I never can get over that, in a way, and yet, is it so queer, really? Perhaps not, when one realises that nothing in the usual, common or garden way has stood in my way of getting and doing what I have always wanted. I have never cared a row of pins what people have thought about me. Almost everyone I have ever heard of is terrified of 'what the lady next door thinks'. And of course this terror of the lady next door cramps their style. I would never, never advise anyone to flout the aforementioned 'lady' unless they have the courage to spend most of their life quite alone.

Well, it is a strange world and I have led a strange, eventful life, and I suppose I shall continue to do so until the end of the chapter. I was, of course, born original, and if one is born like that, one's life is, I think almost always, hard in many ways. It would not have seemed so hard, had I had some great friend to confide in, but this had been denied me. It is a bit odd, really, as I have always been so keen, so anxious for this friend. Probably I have tried too hard to gain this person.

There was also a letter from Sadleir regarding the miniature of Lady Blessington. He seems to think that it is most probable that it is by Cosway. I wrote him this afternoon that I will bring it to London when I come shortly and, if he is interested enough in it, I can meet him in the West End.

I may go out this evening for a couple of 'wets'.

WEDNESDAY, 5 DECEMBER

B. Charles

In last Sunday's *News of the World*, two men have got six and seven years' penal servitude for some sex offence (both first offenders). It would be very interesting to know how often a non-sexual offender gets the maximum sentence – especially if he is a first offender.

I have noted a great many very savage sentences for sex offences during the past year. I often wonder if the reason for these savage sentences is that the judge who tries the case is (shall I express it?) a bit jealous HE hasn't done the same! These sentences want careful watching, I think.

Maggie Joy Blunt
Have just been listening to BBC's *From the London Theatre* series – an excerpt from *Private Lives*. Saw Gertrude Lawrence and Noël Coward in the first production of this evergreen, then the film version. An incredibly fascinating play about really very stupid, tiresome people. Such delicious, delectable love scenes – that's what makes the play so appealing. All the women in the audience see themselves as Amandas, and see their men as Elyots. What, one wonders, are Elyot and Amanda like when they are not being brilliantly witty?

My move to the library has been cancelled. JT suddenly changed his mind. Said he had decided not to replace Miss F after all. I know what is at the bottom of this, though it hasn't been said to me directly. I expect Miss F's salary was about the same as mine and JT considers I would be too expensive, now that the firm is on the down and down. Dr L is disappointed and disgusted. I am left in an unfortunately redundant position as DJ and I both agreed there was no work for me in his department. DJ suggests that in the circumstances I look round for something else, and take my time about it, as it is the firm's fault entirely. 'Stay three, four, five months if you want to, Miss B,' he said.

THURSDAY, 6 DECEMBER

B. Charles
When I went out to do the shopping, I saw a woman in trousers. I couldn't help thinking how funny it is that everyone appears to approve of women dressing in trousers, and aping men. Yet if a man goes out in the street dressed as a woman he is liable to be arrested, and, if charged, can get imprisonment. Can this aping of men by women be in any way responsible for the drop in the birth rate? Perhaps. And then the law with regard to homosexuality is utterly different for men and women. It is no offence for women to have homosexual affairs, yet men are regarded as criminals! A mad world, indeed! I remember so well, when there was all the fuss about *The*

Well of Loneliness, there were ever so many people who stoutly affirmed that there was no such thing as female homosexuality.

FRIDAY, 7 DECEMBER

Edie Rutherford
Churchill is rapidly becoming what George Orwell aptly called some other politician: 'a hole in the air'. Rent collector of these flats said yesterday that in his view a Tory ought to be captured for the British Museum while there is still one about.

Herbert Brush
I expect that all these robberies that are taking place in London now are carried out by young men who are so used to excitement that they can't do without it now that the war is over. After a few years with a gun in one's hand it is not likely that a hungry man would hesitate for long if he knew where to find plenty of money.

SATURDAY, 8 DECEMBER

B. Charles
The concert last night was really excellent, and Beecham conducted with his usual brilliance and genius. The climax, in the *Trojan's March*, Berlioz, was thrilling. Beecham possesses great virtuosity; and he is another instance of my having been right in my judgement when I was quite young. I remember, when I saw him conduct first, about 1910, I thought him wonderful. I think he is as fine a conductor as I have ever seen, though I have not yet seen Toscanini.

I saw Robert at the concert, and we JUST exchanged greetings. Of course I blame Gordon for the 'coolness' though I may of course be wrong in thinking he had anything to do with it. At all events, I do not wish to see Robert again. It is better NOT in every way. I thought he looked very seedy and 'played out'.

SUNDAY, 9 DECEMBER

Edie Rutherford
Opinion seems very varied on the matter of our financial arrangement with USA. I have bought five Sunday papers of different

outlook to see if I can get at an average view. Meantime, the crime wave spreads. I do feel that we are at fault in that our education system is wrong and we therefore send young folk into the world with such wrong ideas that we get all these social problems. Take all these deserters from the services who are existing somehow on this island without identity cards or ration books, hunted things. They are those who never learned self-control, or were mother's spoilt darlin's. Whatever the cause they are just about forced to be criminals now to survive at all. Pardon the lot, I say, and let's start afresh. I am interested and relieved to know that Russia is having a crime wave also. It shows that human nature is much the same no matter what government rules.

Elizabeth Craig recipe for Christmas cake in *Sunday Express* today includes almonds which is just the sort of thing that annoys me – almonds from where? If anyone had any, I don't know how they got them.

B. Charles

I had better begin to get some Christmas letters typed, and the few presents I am going to give off. I am always glad when Christmas is over and done with. I haven't enjoyed it for years. It seems to me a most unsatisfactory time of year. Being merry 'to order' sort of thing does not appeal to me. On such occasions I usually feel like bursting into tears! I am not a good mixer and never was. I like to be in the company of one person at a time, and enjoy talking to them. It always seems to me that when one is in the company of a lot of people altogether, that it is impossible to enjoy any sort of intelligent conversation at all. Just a lot of silly chatter and empty laughter.

MONDAY, 10 DECEMBER

B. Charles

The first Christmas card of the season arrived this morning from Dicky Challen, such a nice one too. A regimental one from the Royal Horse Guards. He has decided 'possibilities' and I think he ought to do quite well.

This morning I went to see if the book *Curious Relations* I want to give Doris for Christmas has arrived. It had not, but I looked at H. G. Wells' book *Mind at the End of Its Tether*, and thought it very prophetic indeed. I think too that civilisation, in fact life in general on this planet, will be quite wiped out in the near future. The atomic bomb has just put paid to all life on the earth.

I saw an American soldier this afternoon who confirmed me in my theories as to the reason of their great popularity with English women. Their manners and gestures are exactly what the average Englishwoman likes and understands. Personally, I find them somewhat aloof, though I fancy they mean to be very pleasant. I must try to get into conversation with some more of them.

Maggie Joy Blunt
New time schedule began at office today. Hours 9 a.m. to 5.30 p.m. (instead of 6 p.m.) and lunch hour for all staff and works 12.30–1.30.

In view of shorter working hours we are asked to arrive punctually in the mornings – rumour had it last week that the names of all staff arriving a minute late would be taken, and that if they arrived a minute late a second morning they would be sacked. This place gets worse and worse.

Coming home tonight I and others spoke of the Christmases when everyone received full, untaxed bonuses and large amounts of holiday compensation money. A £5-a-week salary would bring in nearly £15 at Christmas! Now we are not getting even a tax-deducted bonus. Have decided definitely to plunge back into freelance work and agreed today to leave at end of February.

TUESDAY, 11 DECEMBER

George Taylor
I went on a Public Works contractor's audit. They have been responsible for the first estate of American prefabricated houses in the country. Our clients were told to wait for the arrival of an expert from London before starting erection, but when, after waiting, this official arrived, it was found he had not had his course and knew less than our clients about the matter. Again, they were advised to search for a book of instructions, which was to be found in one of the crates. After a diligent search they failed to find any book. Eventually they were informed that the book had still not been printed.

WEDNESDAY, 12 DECEMBER

Maggie Joy Blunt

Our slack days at the office are definitely over. I cannot bear this sort of niggardly discipline – I never did like it at school, although I am sure it was good for me and I have never had to submit to it since. I may be suffering like other people from war fatigue and under-nourishment, but I have *always* been unable to get up early and eagerly – I hate getting up, and I hate going to bed. There is something rather degrading in being kept to 'clock time' and spied upon.

Herbert Brush

I am constipated despite a dose of salts this morning. Constipation is always dangerous to old people. Did a little digging on the plot.

As I was talking to Ing in the road along came a little man in a huge overcoat, walking with his wife who carried a small baby. Ing, who knows everybody, said, 'Hello, Ron, where have you come from?' Ron had been demobbed and was in his old clothes, and I could hardly help laughing at his choice of overcoats. He stands about five feet three inches, and his coat would have been loose on me, a double-breasted garment which reached to his boot tops. His wife was very thinly clad and looked frozen, but Ron did not seem to worry much about her. After a time I recognised him as the man who keeps prize canaries.

B. Charles

A letter from Peter this morning, in which the following passage occurs:-

(He has been demobbed from the Guards about two months, and was with them on active service for about four years. He is a reliable person.) 'I'm sorry I can be of so little use on the subject of VD but then it is not easy to get details, as I understand it is now cured within a matter of hours. To the best of my knowledge and belief there was very little in the regiment. I only knew of one case during my wartime service, although naturally it would be ridiculous to suppose there wasn't more. With regard to the natives of the various countries on the Continent, I didn't have first-hand knowledge of a single case, although vague rumours used to be bandied around of girls being

146

specially left behind by the Germans, their task being to contaminate the allied armies.

'I consumed fifteen new-laid eggs during my final week in Belgium, all bought in cafés. STARVING EUROPE! I entered this war having come to the conclusion that 99 per cent plus nine-tenths of what one hears in Merry England and outside, is just sheer, unadulterated LIES.'

Went out this afternoon and, as I was going to pay the dentist's bill, I saw Roy Allen, with another lad, leaving school. He is extremely pert for his age, but he looks younger out of doors than inside. NOT a nice lad.

THURSDAY, 13 DECEMBER

Herbert Brush
I wonder whether a Tory Government would have been able to get a better loan from America than the one we are talking about now. Maybe the USA doesn't trust our Government now that it's socialist, and I can hardly blame them. I reckon that in a few years' time no one will trust them, not even the young inexperienced electors who put them there.

Edie Rutherford
I got the 9.30 a.m. bus to Totley to visit friends there and take their Christmas gifts also. They are Tories and I had to listen to a lot of the usual Tory claptrap about present events. I too said my piece as I could not sit and hear Attlee, the Christian that he is, called what he was called. The defence was made that 'I was brought up to be a Tory', and so I was. I replied, 'My old Dad would turn in his grave to know I'm not one now. But I have thought things out for myself since I grew up. All right-thinking people are Socialists.' That last was probably not a little rude, but some folk have GOT to be roused.

SATURDAY, 15 DECEMBER

Herbert Brush
It must have been lively in Piccadilly last night, with thousands of policemen stopping everyone and making them produce their identity cards. I never go out without mine.

B. Charles
Last night's performance of the Choral Symphony was, of course, far from perfect. Isn't it always? The choral portion just does not 'come off'. And Beethoven certainly does not write well for the human voice. Much of the choral portion ends in just a lot of screaming.

This morning I went to the museum with a wooden vase thing I got the other day, and asked Mr Wallace if he could identify it. He had no idea what it had been used for but he does not think it is more than a hundred years old. I do, and I think it has been used for snuff. I shall give it to Doris for Xmas.

Mr Wallace seemed very nice and told me some amusing things about Queen Mary, which did not, however, surprise me. It seems, when she went to the museum some time ago, she asked the price of the lining they have in the cases. Wallace says she is dreaded by many private collectors, because when she knows they have certain valuable things, she invites herself to see them. First of all, the Lady-in-Waiting says to the owner that Her Majesty admires such and such a thing very much indeed and is MOST interested in it. If that is not enough to make the owner offer it to her, she speaks to him herself, and hints broadly that she wants it. I have heard before how frightfully mean she is; in fact most of the members of the royal family appear to be similarly afflicted. She generally walks off with one or two things. Wallace said whenever she comes to Edinburgh the only shops she patronises are the second- and third-rate antiques dealers, so that she may manage to get what she wants for practically nothing at all. I don't think the royal family do any active harm; they are quite innocuous. In fact I think 'the Smiths' a very good name for them. But I DO think they are redundant.

This afternoon I went to hear Marjorie Lawrence, and her rendering of the closing scene from *Götterdämmerung* was one of the most painful things I have ever heard in a concert hall.

Edie Rutherford
Only thirty-two deserters found out of fifteen thousand the police detained last night. How ridiculous. Scarcely worth while I should think.

That kid I am training at work helped me wash up coffee things at work this morning. I notice about her what I notice so often about young folk today – i.e. they don't even know how to wash up. All the things are put on draining board right way up so they don't drain, and half of them still dirty. I told her the right way to place cups etc to drain but she went on the old way.

SUNDAY, 16 DECEMBER

B. Charles

I feel vexed this afternoon, owing to Mrs Irving having had the telephone moved into her own room. This afternoon she told me there had been a phone call for me, but the caller hadn't left any name or message. I expect it was nothing of any importance, but one never knows. I do hope so very much that I shall be in my own house by next Christmas. I am tired of this unsettling sort of existence.

Just as I finished typing this, a ring at the bell. On opening the door I found that very nice lad I met in the post office a few weeks ago! I was delighted to see him, such a charming kid, with such nice manners. He came in for a very few minutes; he couldn't stay as he was going on for tea with friends. He wished me a very happy Christmas, and I gave him 10/- for which he was much obliged. I told him about Mass-Observation and he said he had heard quite a lot about it.

MONDAY, 17 DECEMBER

Edie Rutherford

One of the girls at work has a friend who is a schoolteacher. A small boy who had been at school in the morning wasn't there in the afternoon last Monday. Teacher asked why, and he said, 'We've got a new baby at our house.' She wanted to suggest that it would have been better had he been out of the way at school for the occasion but decided to let it go, and asked, 'Is it a boy or girl?' to which he replied, 'Don't know, Miss', and a small girl's voice from the back of the class piped up, 'They'll have to wait till its hair grows to tell, won't they, Miss?'

Himself has got out of being a godfather. I told the parents that I was dead set against it as he is not a suitable subject for that privilege, and so they have let him off, with a good grace I'm told. He is very relieved as of course he should never have got himself involved in it.

TUESDAY, 18 DECEMBER

Edie Rutherford
I went to the Little Theatre last night to have tea and see *The Frogs*. Well put over, all players anonymous. I found to my surprise that the theatre is in a club of intellectuals, the sort of place I did not know existed in this town, but have often felt was needed. I met the man who runs it, Arnold Freeman, and asked why in eleven years here I had never heard of the place. He said he was sorry, they have little money for advertising. I remember reading about a year ago Freeman's book on Rudolf Steiner.

B. Charles
There is a letter in today's *Daily Telegraph* from some man in the Midlands, to the effect that the Germans are far better workers than the English. I think this is pretty self-evident if anyone watches the German prisoners of war working in the streets. I remember when they were working near the British Restaurant here, one of their guards told me that one of these men did more work in a quarter of an hour than a Britisher did in a whole day! I wrote a letter to this effect to the *Scotsman* but it was not published.

WEDNESDAY, 19 DECEMBER

B. Charles
A letter from Bobby this morning, in which the following passage occurs: 'Honestly, London gets worse as the days go on. And it's so dangerous. You never know when you are going to get a knock on the head and robbed.' Who would have thought that London would ever be dangerous before the war? I shall never forget, as long as I live, the squalor and dirt in the Imperial Hotel, when I stayed there in July. Really I can't make out why London is so utterly impossible today. Of course the air raid damage was colossal, thousands and thousands of houses, and buildings wrecked, and there appears to be no material, or labour to get them in order. Yet I saw that in preparation for Queen Mary's visit to the film *Caesar and Cleopatra* hordes of workmen were working feverishly at all sorts of decorations. There were many angry protests.

I see the Picasso exhibition at the Victoria and Albert Museum is causing a lot of fuss. I don't think I have ever seen any of Picasso's pictures but I expect they are a lot of tripe; just painted to get a lot of cheap, and rapid, notoriety. I don't blame him in the least. It is the public's own fault for going to see them!

Herbert Brush

I daubed scarlet paint on laurel leaves this afternoon to make Christmas decorations. Rather effective. The same kind of thing is being sold in the shops for 5s. a branch. The wireless set has gone wrong again, something amiss with a valve.

THURSDAY, 20 DECEMBER

George Taylor

Had lunch with a group of file manufacturers. The 'under counter' dish was fish, and as I am not fond of fish, I had to take meat pie as my special.

During the talk the usual point of labour supply cropped up. It seems that all the manufacturers have full order books, and could increase their turnover considerably if they could only secure the right type of labour.

B. Charles

When I went for the milk today I asked if it would be possible to have an extra half pint, as I wanted to make a blancmange. The man said he couldn't let me have it, as nowadays it is impossible to let anyone have more than they are entitled to. He went on to say that the Government hope 'next winter' to let everyone have two pints a week. If anyone is still labouring under the delusion that rationing is going to finish soon, they will be rudely awakened from their fantasy. What a curse this last war is proving.

I am a little surprised that there is nothing for Christmas from either Doris or Erica so far. Well, it can't be said that we are a united family!! What an evil day it was for us all when Tootie arrived! Who could have thought that when Auntie inserted that advertisement in the *Yorkshire Post*, all those years ago, that I would have been the quite unconscious cause of all the evil that Tootie has wrought in our family! With such a Father and Tootie: what else could have been expected, except what has happened?

Herbert Brush

9 a.m. W has taken the radio set to the makers at Croydon, but has doubts about them doing anything this side of Christmas. One misses the radio when it is not available, but sometimes I am glad to turn it off, particularly when some female decides to sing through her nose.

11 a.m. W brought back the radio set from the makers, repaired, so it is all right now.

I wonder how long it will be before we have a reformed calendar which begins each month on the same day of the week. There have been plenty of schemes put forward, but I think that the best is for thirteen months in the year, with twenty-eight days in each month, and the odd days made into special days at the end of the year. If every month began on Sunday, Sundays would always be on the 1st, 8th, 15th and 22nd and the months would end on Saturday night.

One would never have to consult a calendar to find out which day of the year one's birthday fell on, though I own that those born on the 29th, 30th or 31st of any month would have to shift their birthdays into the next month. I think that the benefits would be worthwhile.

FRIDAY, 21 DECEMBER

B. Charles

Last night Joe Gyness came and spent the evening with me. He has decided possibilities (I think he is a bit of a Jew). He has artistic leanings, and seems to like old furniture and is interested in intelligent conversation. He told me he is a lorry driver for a big firm of ironmongers in Oxford. He has had no advantages, so-called, yet is well above the average person in mentality. He hung the fine Dresden bracket mirrors for me very well and thinks them very lovely indeed. He is getting demobbed tomorrow and says, in a great many ways, we will be far worse off financially than he is in the army. He told me his pay is £3 a week, and that his wife gets another £3 for herself and the children. It is just 'money for jam' in the services now. Joe told me he has hardly heard of any VD in the army. He says they get issued with early treatment outfits and he thinks it is owing to the use of these things that it has decreased so tremendously. I forget to ask him if he has known of any cases of VD being treated with

152

penicillin. It seems that gonorrhoea is cured in a matter of hours with this drug. I want to get some first-hand information about this.

SUNDAY, 23 DECEMBER

B. Charles

I read an interesting article in which it said that only three hundred thousand less turkeys were available this year than in an ordinary pre-war year. But where, in 1938, only one family in seven had turkey, either from choice or inability to pay for one, today almost everyone wanted bird, and were quite able to pay the price.

People are so afraid of letting anything 'get by them'. Take fruit, for instance. I feel sure the average working-class person hardly ever bothered to buy oranges except at Christmas, but now, as soon as it is rumoured there are oranges or apples on the way, everyone spends hours looking for them. And I know, perfectly well, that before the war thousands and thousands of people never had one salad in the whole course of the year. Whereas now they all seem to want salads.

Herbert Brush

11 a.m. Norah came in to arrange about the feeding of Smut while we are away at Christmas, and I gave her one of my three-year calendars.

11.30 a.m. Ida came in and brought me a box of chocolates. I gave her a calendar.

MONDAY, 24 DECEMBER

Herbert Brush

7.30 a.m. Up early as we have a long way to go in the car. We arrived at Felixstowe about 12.30 p.m. and by two had had lunch in the Ordnance Hotel. My bedroom is No. 6 on the third floor, and the view from the window is towards the sea across the tops of several rows of houses. Quite far distant enough to be safe should one of the many mines adrift in the Channel choose Felixstowe as a landing place.

Edie Rutherford

All these gales and drifting mines. Blast war. It was a year this early morning since we had our first and only fly-bomb attack.

I've had mail from my country for Christmas but none from USA or Canada. Maybe that will follow. As usual I have given heaps of gifts and as usual got far less in return, but that doesn't worry me an iota, honestly.

We got our Christmas fowl: 12/- plus 1/- for pulling insides out and well worth it as the thought of it puts me off the bird entirely. Husband scrubbed kitchen floor for me while I was out shopping this morning. I was staggered when I got in and discovered what he'd done. He had gone out for his pre-lunch walk and ale when I returned so I haven't seen him to thank him yet. I call that a really grand Christmas present. Never before has he done such a thing though he has done the bathroom floor (smaller) for some months now, not often mind, but at intervals. On Sunday mornings.

CHRISTMAS DAY

George Taylor

We had the usual fun over presents and succeeded in getting quite a variety, in spite of the shortages and rationing. We still miss the little things, such as 'spice pigs' and well-boxed chocolates.

We had the usual quiet Xmas day, and did not switch on the radio even for one minute at Totley. As there was no public transport service after 6 p.m. we stayed the night.

B. Charles

Such a quiet Christmas Day, but in a way not too disagreeable. I have got a bit of cold, so only went out for my dinner to the British Restaurant. It would be impossible to cater for oneself on the amount they charge you for a meal. Today I had a good plate of soup, then two slices of roast mutton, sprouts and mashed potato and Xmas pudding and custard to follow. And all for a shilling. I came straight back, and have been indoors all the afternoon, and quite alone in the flat. No one has been to the door at all. I often think I should like to have more company, but at all events, when one is alone one can do exactly what one likes, and one need not listen to all sorts of silly chatter. To be with a lot of foolish people is too tedious for words. How I hope I shall be back in my own house next Christmas! It seems too stupid to have a nice house and to be an exile from it. I guess no one during the war has suffered more from the billeting curse than I!

154

Herbert Brush

A fine morning but a red sky. Went to the parish church and had to queue up at the door to get in. Mostly women or white-haired or bald-headed men. The vicar gave a good and short sermon, and I enjoyed singing the Christmas hymns at the top of my voice.

W insisted that I should don my dress clothes for dinner, so I did so rather unwillingly, and for a time felt uncomfortable as I and one other man were the only ones to do so. A kind of amusements committee arranged a programme for the evening when the dining room was cleared of tables and chairs to make room for dancing and other games. I helped by showing some of my tricks with string, sticks and corks.

It caused a fair amount of amusement when I tied up two young fellows and they tried to get apart using all kinds of antics, but without succeeding.

THURSDAY, 27 DECEMBER

Edie Rutherford

Well, I have had the nicest Christmas for years, and all because I was in the company of people I love and who love me.

I did a bit of dashing round to kiddies in various flats with odd-ments, found excitement each time of course. Then to help friends with whom we were having midday dinner. Goose was perfect and we had a lovely lunch, wash up, rest, tea, and played solo whist till 1 a.m. with a short break for a snack. Yesterday, Boxing Day, we reversed it – they came here to share our fowl, which I'm glad to say I had steamed an hour before roasting as it turned out to be a chicken's grandmother.

Herbert Brush

After breakfast we packed our baggage and said goodbye to the numerous friends of two days' standing. The old couple, the Edwards from Ipswich, the Hynes from Ipswich and Mrs Green and party from Newmarket.

Drove until we reached the Blackwall Tunnel, in the middle of which the car met with an accident. There was a traffic hold-up and another car ran into the rear and damaged the number plate badly and pushed us onto the car in front. The sudden jerk knocked my hat off.

W had words with the man who drove the car behind, and finally made him go to a police station to report the accident, as it was his fault. A police sergeant came out and took down particulars.

Curiously enough, no damage was done to the other car, but the man had to prove that his brakes were in a satisfactory working order. It was about 3 p.m. when we arrived home, and Smut gave us a great reception.

FRIDAY, 28 DECEMBER

George Taylor
To a Philharmonic concert with the Hallé Orchestra, conducted by Malcolm Sargent and Max Rostal violin soloist. The highlight of the evening was Cesar Franck's Symphony in D Minor. The audience was very thin.

Maggie Joy Blunt
Another Christmas come and gone. We had from Friday evening until yesterday morning. Last-minute Christmas shopping in Windsor, but I was not able to look for good and interesting presents this year and my friends and relatives had to be satisfied with Readers Union books, soap (from my store) and cards. For Ella and Aunt Aggie I packed up a box of oddments such as Rinso, lard, tea, hand cream etc – it was just like a hamper for poor relations in pre-war days, but met with tremendous welcome. I did manage to get an attractive emerald scarf for Lys and oddments for the various young children I know. Myself, I received book and gift tokens, books, one pair of fully fashioned stockings, flower seeds for the garden and a homemade mince pie, shoulder covers for hanging clothes (made from blackout material and bound with bright tape), a much needed sponge bag, a lovely small glass bowl filled with homemade toffees, calendars, many cards.

N came for the holiday on Saturday at tea time. Julia came for the day on Sunday – to get some holly with berries on it as prices for it in London were exorbitant. On Sunday the young Canadian scientist RS also came, whom N had known in Canada in the thirties as a schoolboy. He is now working at Cambridge and having a thin time of it, and was glad of the invitation to spend Christmas with us at the cottage. An acknowledged authority on penicillin in North America, he has done much work on its production during the war, but doesn't receive the same recognition in England. One of these quite brilliant but detached modern intellectuals – full of Ivory Tower aristocratic scorn for the ordinary human being – like Aldous Huxley's Tony in *Eyeless in Gaza*. I think though he enjoyed his visit here – he was pleasant and interesting and helpful – chopped much wood for me and filled the coal scuttles.

Yesterday the office seemed quite unendurable. Most people returned tired and bad-tempered. Mrs Mop didn't come yesterday. Maybe she is ill or worn out with Christmas too, but I wanted to shoot her when I got home last night.

SATURDAY, 29 DECEMBER

Herbert Brush
Went with W to the Capitol Cinema to see *The Wizard of Oz*, a picture for children rather than grown-ups. A child near me was frightened at some of the scenes and howled at the top of its voice. I was somewhat disappointed.

B. Charles
I received a letter from Boots head office, Nottingham, re the suitability of using DDT for the destruction of woodworm. They are looking into the matter, and will write me in due course. I fancy I am the first person to have thought it might be good to destroy these pests. If it is, I think the Antiques Dealer's Association ought to make me an honorary member. I shall feel like that obscure Gloucestershire milkmaid, whose chance remark set Jenner on to the tract of vaccination.

I see that Lord Haw-Haw is to be hanged on 3 January. I don't think he ought to be really, as he was treated just as a huge joke, and he provided many millions with a great deal of fun at a very depressing time. If anybody took him seriously they only have themselves to blame. It was quite evident that he would be hanged once he was arrested. If they wanted to kill him, they ought to have shot him immediately he was arrested, without all this hypocrisy of a 'trial'. I have no patience with this lamentable English trait. I shan't be sorry when this year is gone and done with. I wonder what 1946 will bring forth?

SUNDAY, 30 DECEMBER

Herbert Brush

Had a little trouble getting home from the Hutts. When we got to Forest Hill we ran into a blanket of fog so thick that I could not see the curb at my feet. I had to walk in front of the car and guide W with my torch.

MONDAY, 31 DECEMBER

B. Charles

I am interested in some parts of this so-called 'will' of Hitler's that is reported in the papers today. It is amazing what devotion he inspired in many of his followers. I see this Eva Braun merely came to Berlin to die with Hitler, and Goebbels, apparently, refused to quit Berlin and leave Hitler in his darkest hour. There is something very fine in not valuing his life except in so far as it is serviceable to his Führer. His wife too, seems to have expressed the wish to die in Berlin with her husband. Such people are fine. I often think that the Germans deserved to win the war.

It is a constant source of amazement to me how France has got away with it for so long. A treacherous, false nation, if ever there was one. They have been utterly effete since the death of Louis the Fourteenth, with a short rebirth of glory at the time of Napoleon Bonaparte. It would be a good thing, in a great many ways, if the whole of France could be swallowed up in an earthquake, along with the entire population! They are no good.

The Scots continue to make a great deal of fuss about the New Year celebrations.

Maggie Joy Blunt

We have had no oranges yet. Greengrocer's stock this morning was depleted. No sweets either. Went into village this morning urgently requiring paraffin oil but there was none to be had until supplies come tomorrow. Reminder of wireless licence renewal arrived.

And so Good Night. We wish all our readers a Happy New Year.

Chapter Seven

'THEY HAVEN'T THE BRAINS TO RUN THE COUNTRY,' SHE SAID

Every convenience on a small scale: pre-fabs go up in Watford

'The Bill for the National Health Service, which is a necessary part of the structure of Social Security, has got its place in the queue of major measures and will probably be before the House by Easter.

The real test of the Bill . . . is: does it take care of the patient? Parliament will apply that test to the Bill when its details are disclosed, but it can be assured that in design and scope it will provide a completely comprehensive service – from before birth, in the form of ante-natal care, until death. The people of this country will get clinics, a family doctor service, consultants, hospital treatment, rehabilitation, dentists, drugs, oculists and opticians and a lot more. All free . . .'

Editorial in the New Statesman & Nation, *2 February 1946*

'Great art or not, the work undoubtedly has enormous powers of horrification, and of suggesting the frightfulness of a civilisation that is in imminent danger of disruption.

At the moment we are convalescing from a surfeit of horrors, which probably accounts for the outcry. But when the world has put its head back in the sand of complacency and the aggressively-minded are refurbishing their armour, would not an exhibition of this sort of work do a little towards stimulating the untiring vigilance which is our only hope of existence? If it should prove to have this effect we should welcome it with enthusiasm, whether it be great art or mere hocus-pocus.'

The Picasso debate rages in the Listener, *here from correspondent E. A. Terry, 3 January 1946*

NEW YEAR'S DAY 1946

Herbert Brush

A lot has happened since last New Year's Day. Then we were busy dodging doodlebugs and rockets and sleeping in the dugout, and it is nice to compare the quietness of the present time with the noisiness of last year.

When turning out a box today I came across . . . [a] Rudyard Kipling signature on one of his cheques in the New Oriental Bank which went Smash. Caldwell gave several of these to mother and two or three to me. I don't suppose that any value is attached to them.

Edie Rutherford

A cold, dark, foggy morning. We expected a noise at midnight last night, as before war, but no. Church bells faintly heard at various times 'tween eleven and twelve, but not one factory hooter, a few feeble street revellers . . .

And now all these New Year's honours. Shucks. Makes us tired. The really meritorious folk are unknown and get no rewards. So let us laugh at honours.

B. Charles

I see by today's paper that they are beginning a rumour that the twelve-year-old boy's photo, found along with Hitler's will, may be his son! When I saw, yesterday, that a boy's photo had been discovered, I immediately thought some silly person would start up a tale of a sort of 'Lost Dauphin'! It is just absurd. I don't believe Hitler was married and I don't believe he had a son. In a way, I feel quite sure Hitler is popular in England. He has got a sort of glamour since the end of the war, and in time this glamour will become more pronounced. I think there are a great many people in England who are utterly sick and tired of all the mediocrity there is about today, and are only too willing to become a bit hypnotised by Hitler's personality. It may well be that, in time, Hitler will be canonised by the Catholic Church! There is a letter in today's *Telegraph* stating that the copy of Hitler's marriage contract, published in some paper, shows several errors in German, and was not typed on a German machine. The writer suggests the whole thing is a fake.

Maggie Joy Blunt

I went to bed early last night but couldn't sleep, and was reading when the bells and hooters let the New Year in. It is, I thought, a coward's trick to make no resolutions because you know they will be broken. So I made the following three:

1) To make more effort over this diary.
2) To go ahead with my plans for freelance writing with determination, whatever people say. (When they hear that I am not looking for another full-time job they tend to say 'Oh!' and look very glum.)
3) To read again, several times until their meaning has soaked through me and been digested, Katherine Butler Hathaway's *The Little Locksmith*, and chapter three of Esther Harding's *The Way of All Women*.

Bought sweets tonight on my way home. One lb's worth – I felt wildly extravagant.

WEDNESDAY, 2 JANUARY

Herbert Brush

I often get little purple patches under the skin on the backs of my hands. The patches come suddenly and then die away in a few days. I thought at first that I must have knocked the place to break small blood vessels but I can't remember doing so, and am beginning to think it is something which comes with age.

B. Charles

Tonight I got into conversation with a young soldier on the bus who interested me by saying I spoke 'such VERY King's English' and used words he hadn't heard for quite a number of years! It is extremely queer how so many people tell me I talk so very posh, and I appear to give people the idea that I am very grand. I fancy what it really is, is that I never try to put on this absurd, so-called, Oxford accent. And of course I speak, I think, with a slight Yorkshire twang, in addition to speaking very distinctly. Nowadays the vast majority of people, thanks largely to the BBC, try to talk all exactly alike. It is a very mistaken way they have of trying to make people 'genteel'.

The weather is bitterly cold tonight and I think there will be skating tomorrow.

THURSDAY, 3 JANUARY

Herbert Brush
I have literally hundreds of [eldest brother] Caldwell's letters stored away in a tin trunk. If only he could have used his hands as efficiently as he used his brain, he would have gone a long way in this world.

He never even learned to shave, though when he was at Oxford friends sent him several razors, but without result, and he never learned which way to turn a screw or how to tie his tie. He thought he knew how to dig with a spade, but I did not agree with him on that point.

FRIDAY, 4 JANUARY

Edie Rutherford
A girl at work told me that two days ago she and her mother sat down and cried with cold. I know that feeling. It is horrible and needs instant treatment as is most lowering, but as they were both taken with it there was no one at hand to stir things up. Well, thank God, the forecast promises us something warmer today.

Herbert Brush
I wonder how the office boys who return to their pre-war jobs with the rank of colonel or major will like to be ordered about by the men above them in the office. I can foresee trouble when someone says, 'Here you are, Major, take this letter to the post, and be quick about it.'

SUNDAY, 6 JANUARY

Maggie Joy Blunt
Went to local pantomime with CL and party on Thursday evening. Costumes for finale were made of shiny plastic – colourful and effective but just a little too reminiscent of bathroom curtains.

We were accompanied by two Grenadier Guards. The guards were helping the GPO at Mount Pleasant over Christmas and they had some amusing stories to tell. Apparently at Christmas time all parcels are brought to this one centre and sorted and sent out again from there. They are piled to a height of 15 feet. The parcels posted very early naturally are at the bottom of the pile and don't get sent out until last.

Our escorts were not regulars and hoped to be out of the army soon. I asked one of them what he wanted or would like to do as a civilian. 'Nothing,' he answered. 'I would like to be a director of something where I didn't have to appear, or on the Stock Exchange, or something in the City without having to work in the City. But you need a lot of money for a job like that.'

B. Charles

I have cut out a small piece from *Newsweek* and stuck it in my book. It records the death of the late Archbishop of Canterbury, and says he was the principal single force who compelled Edward VIII to resign (I mean abdicate). And I fancy this is true. It is a great mistake for people to think the established Church hasn't much power. It certainly has, worst luck!

I enjoyed the concert last night, better than I expected. Saw Robert there, and the fair lad I once met on the hill. I shall go out this evening and have a chase round for a bit.

TUESDAY, 8 JANUARY

Herbert Brush

I think that I have caught a chill in my bladder, as I have done little else beyond unbuttoning and buttoning my trousers, until I am half inclined to leave them unbuttoned.

Maggie Joy Blunt

Time off in London. Caught the 10.24. Went to see Paul Klee exhibition at National Gallery; then Picasso at South Kensington. Preferred the Klee to Picasso, if one can compare them. Picasso so boosted. Klee such an excellent draughtsman – his line dances. Such careful, delicate work, though moons and arrows in his pictures get boring. Liked watercolours and pen drawings best. Picasso has, of course, magnificence. As someone else says, if his pictures appear revolting to the average viewer, one must remember that certain aspects of this age are revolting. This is how he has seen and suffered

165

it. We may not like to be reminded of it, but there it is. On the other hand, I can't help feeling that some of those pictures were done with his tongue in his cheek. Later, DJ tried to be knowledgeable – said Picasso had been encouraged to paint those pictures by the 'Jew Boys' who were making packets out of the exhibition. 'Picasso was at one time a very good artist.' Well, I think he still is and wonder if DJ ever recognised him as being good without being told.

WEDNESDAY, 9 JANUARY

B. Charles
Saw something for sale at Lyon & Turnbull's this morning that I have never seen for sale before: a mummy complete with case. I imagine some person must have brought it back from Egypt. The case was open and you could see the skull. I spoke to Mason there and he told me about Boyd, Scott and Co. being prosecuted for overcharging for some second-hand stuff. The fellow in question was at the sale and Mason told me he is a JP; I need hardly add he is a Jew. As I have before remarked, how do they get away with their sharp practices?

Got a letter from Boots of Nottingham about DDT and its suitability for destroying woodworm. They seem to think it may be good for killing the insect, but they are uncertain if it might damage the patina.

Maggie Joy Blunt
Visited bank manager and arranged to sell some shares. These particular ones now worth only 9/-. Bought in 1937 at £1.

THURSDAY, 10 JANUARY

B. Charles
The Mummy fetched 7/- yesterday, and was bought by some private person. Perhaps a doctor. I see in today's *Daily Telegraph* that Mr Tom Williams says milk rationing will probably go on for a long time, and, in an adjoining column, we are told that at the banquet last night given by the King to inaugurate the start of the UNO meeting, the Gold Plate was used, and we are given the whole of the menu. It is an outrage that such guzzling should go on at this time. I feel so indignant about the matter that I have written a letter to *Cavalcade*.

Edie Rutherford

Got some rather unpromising-looking liver from butcher, stewed it in a casserole in oven and it was good. Austerity banquet off a gold plate.

Much discussion in office about a local family whose home was burnt last week, two of four children being smothered with smoke. Father got out first, mother handed out two kiddies and left the other two. Coroner said he had to assume the father did right but hoped he in such circumstances would have been last. A fund was started and over £1,000 has already been subscribed for the family. Also gifts in kind have been showered on them, which those who reckon to know reckon will be in the pawnbrokers, and the money with the publican, in short time. They are just that kind of family. The council found an empty house the next day, magically.

Maggie Joy Blunt

Felt too tired to live. At lunch as I sat with elbows on table and head leaning on hands, WS remarked, 'You look as though you'd collapse if your arms were removed.' We all felt like that. Lys had had neuralgia again.

Mrs Mop arrived.

Herbert Brush

I did not sleep at all last night, and heard every hour struck from 1 a.m. to 6 a.m., except 2 a.m. which I somehow missed. I don't know whether it was due to the presence of Smut in the room, asleep on a chair, but I can think of no other cause.

FRIDAY, 11 JANUARY

Herbert Brush

Last night I turned the cat out of my room and afterwards slept like a top; so maybe my sleeplessness the night before was due to the presence of pussy. I felt like a piece of limp rag all day.

Edie Rutherford

I am trying to find a home for a stray dog a friend on first floor has had some weeks. I expect the poor brute was set adrift rather than pay licence. The old story.

George Taylor

Went over to one of our clients who has made a mushroom growth during the war, and now has factories in several towns, and a swelling organisation all over the country. His books are in a dreadful state. There is no proper day book, the cash book does not fit in any way with the bank and no additions are done. Posting of expenses to the nominal ledger have not been made, and no lists of ledger balances exist. The neglect is almost criminal, but all the blame is put on the head girl, who has been sacked.

B. Charles

A letter from Len Bull this morning. I am interested to note that he says he now has two children and he would very much like me to see them. I always noticed how very fond he was of the little girl: he used to come round to see me pushing the pram with her inside, and he was so pleased when I asked him to bring her inside. Perhaps, when I see parents so fond of their children, it makes me a little jealous when I think of my own childhood. Certainly, I am sure that the average parent IS very fond of their children.

I am writing to the Admiralty tonight to see if I can trace Fred Bassett. It was a pity Fred Bassett married in the way he did: Marion was such a dreadfully ordinary sort of person.

TUESDAY, 15 JANUARY

George Taylor

The marvellous electricians who are rewiring our house have left us so that we could have neither the electric clock nor the radio at the same time as the radiator. As I particularly wanted to hear *The Brains Trust* I had to make a temporary set-up myself, and linked up my set with the drawing-room light by means of the vacuum flex, added to the kettle flex and that of the iron. It was a bit of a Heath Robinson outfit, but it worked.

B. Charles

A letter from Doris this a.m. I wonder if any other family has ever had so much quarrelling as ours?! And all, really, on account of Tootie! What an evil day it was when SHE arrived! Then two more servants who have exercised quite extraordinary influence on our fortunes:

Ellen and Hilda. They, with Tootie, are responsible, in a way, for Father's will. It seems a pity that there has been all the quarrelling in our family there has been. Of course money has been at the bottom of a good deal of the trouble, AND Tootie.

WEDNESDAY, 16 JANUARY

Edie Rutherford
Frost, frost, frost. Skaters must be getting excited. Hairdresser commented yesterday on the pregnancy of Duchess of Gloucester. I said that meant a few more thousand pounds from the masses. She said, 'Oh well, this Government is squandering shamefully and so can't complain about someone else doing it.' I said nothing whatever to that as I just won't waste time on such hopeless folk.

THURSDAY, 17 JANUARY

Edie Rutherford
Had a letter from Howie's of Jo'burg, in reply to mine asking for an agency to sell chincherinchees in this country. They say they have had an agent here for years, that shipping is the problem, and will I write again in August.

When we get clear of this patch of woe I never want to hear the words austerity or utility again.

SATURDAY, 19 JANUARY

Maggie Joy Blunt
Hairdresser this morning said it was more difficult than ever to get supplies. Says that the Jews got everything – or rather people who got to the wholesalers first got first choice of whatever was going and these people always seemed to be Jews. When she came out of services she made inquiries with a view to setting up a shop of her own, but apart from not being able to get premises there is no equipment available (e.g. rubber tubing for sprays). Only alternative to buy an established business, but prices asked prohibitive. So, fortunately for me, she came back to local shop.

TUESDAY, 22 JANUARY

George Taylor

Our local WEA had arranged a lecture by Mr Bosson, the Director of a Swedish Folk High School, but although some 750 notices had been sent out, only one hundred came. Unfortunately, Mr Bosson's command of English was so poor that I lost interest in the lecture and set about drafting the programme for our spring series. I brightened up at the film, but this did not last for long as so many shots were of singing classes; what is more boring than to see an exhibition of mouths opening and closing on a silent film?

B. Charles

I have thought about Mother so often today, on this, her eighty-eighth birthday.

For years we have concentrated on quite unimportant things in life and have completely neglected the important matters. A typical instance of this attitude is the attitude of the authorities with regard to 'vice dens', 'cleaning up dens of iniquity', and so on and so forth. Jailing a few old prostitutes instead of getting on with important matters, they dissipate all their energies on utterly piffling things, things that don't matter a tuppeny damn. In the atomic age I think that grandmotherly legislation is just a lot of drivel.

I sometimes wonder if this grandmotherly way of life has anything to do with the part women now take in public life? Before women interested themselves in public affairs to the great extent they now do, England seemed a good deal more virile. I may be wrong, but I have a shrewd suspicion that women, in public life, are a very great mistake. I'm sure the way the police spend their energies on piffle is one of the reasons for the present state of crime. Possibly, too, all this 'closing down' this, that and the other, has some bearing on the case, as if people can't get amusement in one way they will get it in another. I should think that, if public houses were open, as in the old days, and if there was sufficient drink to be had, crime would, in all probability, decrease.

I wonder if I decide to sell the house in Windsor, whether I shall be able to get one in Scotland and, if I can, whether I should be able to make myself happy? It seems a bit difficult to get any interesting friends here. In a way the people are very friendly, but when one is over fifty and in a strange place, it isn't easy to make new friends.

WEDNESDAY, 23 JANUARY

Edie Rutherford

Husband reckons, and I agree, that the present wave of flu etc is due to wrong eating. On Monday while I was doing the washing I realised that it is all of eighteen years since I spent so much time as half a day in bed. The most I have felt obliged to do is go to bed early. I have been feeling grateful for this ever since. Not one of my colleagues at work could equal this.

Fuel economy indeed? In this weather. The Government is optimistic. Asks the almost impossible. Only way will be to withdraw it at source, and by the erratic behaviour of our electric clock, they are doing that.

£1 for radio licence still cheap at the price and I hope it won't be too hard on some folk. For most I am sure it is not. Yesterday on the BBC I heard the most clever bit of acting I have ever heard. In the Galsworthy serial, where Soames Forsyte rapes his own wife, Irene, it was perfectly put over. I bet they get some protests from stuffy minded folk though.

B. Charles

Have had an extremely pleasant evening with the Reids. Ken told me it is not at all impossible to buy a house in Edinburgh. He has some most delightful china, as I was sure he had. He has a lovely, tiny Chelsea piece of a squirrel. Most attractive. His Medusa, a tiny Portobello model, which acts as a whistle, is immensely pleasing. They are both well travelled and interesting. I shall try to 'cultivate' them, as it is very nice to have a place to go to where there is something of interest.

Ken said he had met the late Duke of Kent quite often, and that he was always made up: coloured cheeks, lips, etc. I am not surprised at this. I always had the idea that he went in for that sort of thing.

THURSDAY, 24 JANUARY

Edie Rutherford

I'm glad the man Nettleton won't hang for killing his nagging wife. Having once lived in a house where the wife nagged her husband, we have concluded that murder is the only remedy for such. I am amazed that the judge should suggest that a man who is nagged may leave his wife. I'm all for it myself though. Once knew a man who just disappeared from his nagging wife. He said it would have ended in murder otherwise and she wasn't worth it.

A twenty-five-year-old typist at work yesterday told me she was listening to the Galsworthy episode the day before, and what was Soames doing to Irene when she sobbed so? I said, 'What do you think?', so she said, 'Well, we didn't think it could be that.' This girl is engaged but I have always thought her a virgin so now I think it is so for sure.

FRIDAY, 25 JANUARY

George Taylor
For the third time I was sworn in as a Special Constable, and have decided to carry on, and about two dozen Police War Reserves have joined us. The duties are only light: there is not another parade until April.

Herbert Brush
It is a week today since I went to bed with the flu and it has seemed like a month or more. There is still the sound of a rattle deep down in my lungs. I have just managed to get rid of six days' growth of beard. It took nearly half an hour.

It is curious that whenever I get a bout like the one I have just had, my thoughts always go right back to my early youth when I had a touch of pneumonia. I can still feel the awful terror that came over me when a huge shadow on the wall formed itself into a monstrous dragon coming always nearer to my bed, and I must have set up a loud yelling until I heard mother tell father that I was scared of his shadow on the wall near the door.

Edie Rutherford
I am all for this new [National] insurance scheme . . . Makes growing old not so frightening.

Later: with one exception, everyone at work was against the new insurance. The exception was the foreman, who sided with me in upholding it. All the others are furious, and say, first, income tax is so high that few can also afford the weekly contribution. Second, the amount sick will be paid is not much more than they get now and certainly doesn't make up for the big difference in contribution. Third, that folk who keep well get no benefits and no rebates so it is unfair.

SATURDAY, 26 JANUARY

Edie Rutherford
I think the round-up of women in London last night was not too soon, as if even only a part of the rumours about prostitutes during the war is true, a clean-up was needed. Mind, the trouble is economic and educational. These swoops were tinkering with symptoms, our usual stupid way of coping with our problems, national and personal.

SUNDAY, 27 JANUARY

Maggie Joy Blunt
New complications at the office. I am doing myself no good at all by remaining. The big chemical lab, one of the most expensively equipped in the country's industrial laboratories, has been stripped and is to be used as a drawing office. Everywhere one hears the same story of discontent and gloom. People who can find better jobs are leaving every week and nothing is done to stop them or to improve the firm's team spirit – there is no team spirit. But all firms are not like ours. One of the draughtsmen in the design drawing office has landed a job at £1,000 per annum with a film studio, sketching sets. Lys has left. She is now, under doctor's orders, taking a rest cure. Like so many people she is tired out and badly in need of a real holiday and relaxation. I think the war has drawn so much on our nervous and physical energy that we have few reserves left and are suffering in consequence. I know that this awful feeling of fatigue pursues me and I would give almost anything not to have to go into the office this coming week at all. Did not get up today until nearly 3 p.m., although it has been a gorgeous day . . . have spent most of the time on the living-room sofa.

WEDNESDAY, 30 JANUARY

Edie Rutherford
My hairdressers consist of two sisters. The one who attends to me doesn't like our Government but isn't venomous about it. Her sister,

however, is so full of hate for them that she is incoherent. I once attempted to say something conciliatory a few weeks ago, and I have an idea since that she therefore goes out of her way to be over venomous when I am behind another curtain. So I am clam-like, as I long ago learned it is folly to attempt to talk to anyone eaten up with anger and/or hatred.

Yesterday I was amused to hear her customer say she had converted her thirteen-room house into two flats and taken in a couple with two children, and that she had felt sure she'd be forced to have someone in time, so she had guarded against it herself. I was jubilant, but hairdresser expressed sympathy with client for the nerve this Government has.

She told an earlier customer that the country would be ruined by this Government and then someone decent would have to build us up again. 'They haven't the brains to run the country,' she said.

THURSDAY, 31 JANUARY

Maggie Joy Blunt
Was told the other day that for the thirty-eight prefabs recently put up by council there were 1,600 applicants, and these had to be forces people or people with family of two. For another small lot of prefabs, there are two thousand on waiting list – the rent is 12/6d. All this is causing much discontent.

Met young EJ on bus the other morning. A soldier friend of hers just off to Italy had given her his entire book of coupons and she had just indulged in orgy of clothes buying including six pairs of fully fashioned silk stockings which her mother collected for her from small shops where she is known.

Saw *Pink String and Sealing Wax* last night with Hy. Not very good . . . too much altogether of Googie Withers. Also a news flash of parade of American troops in New York. Hy exclaimed, 'Good Lord! I've never seen a GI marching, have you? They were always leaning up against something.'

Edie Rutherford
A girl at work this morning brought to show us a hat for which she paid ten guineas three years ago. A cute thing, a delicious shade of mauve, a few small ostrich feathers, a scrap of velvet . . . but ten

174

guineas! We haven't been able to get it out of our minds all morning. Strange thing is, we all had it on and it suited every one of us! I said she ought to hire it out and get her money back.

I saw a bedroom suite, without bedstead, for sale in local shop in town on Tuesday. £730. Also a small scarf 22/11d. Are we going mad, the lot of us?

FRIDAY, 1 FEBRUARY 1946

George Taylor

I attended a police dinner for the Specials but was thoroughly disgusted. I knew there was to be a bar, but did not imagine it was to be the all-important feature. The speeches were mere trimmings, and I could hardly hear them for the chink of glasses. Again the whole place was disturbed by the wandering about of guests between the speeches, all too obviously caused by the drinks. When finally the meeting was officially adjourned to the bar, I gave it up and came home. It will be the last dinner with bar to which I shall go.

Herbert Brush

I have burnt my backbone on a hot-water bottle and now have an intensely painful blister. The pain seemed to go right through me, worse than a tooth extraction without gas. This makes me think that the Nazis probably make use of a victim's backbone to make him squirm.

I had to get my bank manager to certify that I am alive at the end of the month so that I receive my cheque.

MONDAY, 4 FEBRUARY

B. Charles

A most disturbing letter in last week's *New Statesman & Nation* from a man called Maurice Cranston. It seems that Havelock Ellis's *Studies in the Psychology of Sex* and Marie Stopes' *Married Love* are now on the pornographic shelf at the British Museum and, before one can get them, one has to get the permission of the supervisor. All this goes to prove what I have been certain of for quite a while: that there is now a veritable outbreak of savagery with regard to all things sexual. No doubt the Powers That Be, knowing full well that World

War III will happen within five years, are anxious to have as much cannon fodder ready as possible, so are terrified of people getting any sort of knowledge of contraception.

Herbert Brush

Went to the BM. Legs a bit weak still, but it was nice and warm in there. I meant to go to the Victoria and Albert Museum to see Picasso's pictures, but I put it off until too late. Now I wish I had gone as I have just been looking at illustrations of some of them in *Everybody's*.

I never saw such hideous pictures of females, but some people must see something in them which I cannot see, and I should like to find out what it is. After looking at several of these things for a long time I can't help thinking that the artist must be mad in some way. I can't even make a start on his *Lady in Green*, although she is supposed to represent the spirit of the age. A hideous lump under her claw-like fingers resting near her middle may represent a coming baby, but this idea is enough to make one feel sick. Get an *Everybody's* and have a look. I advise you to look at something pleasant afterwards to take away the visual horror.

TUESDAY, 5 FEBRUARY

Herbert Brush

I read that the Americans say they have had echoes back from the moon on their radar sets, the actual beam taking a couple of seconds to do the journey. Maybe radar will enable us to find invisible objects, little satellites of ours which we have had for millions of years without knowing it. These things are interesting to speculate on, though they are not likely to be of any practical use to mankind as far as I can see.

I met the RSPCA man in the road and he told me that every Saturday now there was quite a procession of people to his house bringing their cats to be put to sleep. I suppose it is not possible for people to get food for the cats now. Judging by the cost of feeding Smut I am not surprised that people prefer the money to the cat.

I wonder how much longer the Nuremberg Trial will last. It seems to me like a cat playing with a mouse, as no one can possibly expect the prisoners to escape the death penalty, and they might just as well finish the job quickly. The longer the trial lasts the more likely are some to get off with long terms of imprisonment, which I don't think the general public of any country would agree to without a lot of fuss.

WEDNESDAY, 6 FEBRUARY

Herbert Brush
After listening to Ben Smith on the BBC last evening I don't like the outlook at all. England, as usual, helps to feed foreigners at the expense of her own people, and I don't mind doing that up to a point, or living on brown bread, but I don't like the idea of eating only one slice of bread when I want two slices.

B. Charles
Everyone seems excessively angered by the new food cuts, and I am not surprised. All this 'austerity' is largely bunkum; I strongly suspect the cloven hoof of Big Business at the bottom of it all. I think if the Government continues to force this austerity nonsense on us that people won't stand for such twaddle. Were I in my thirties, instead of my fifties, I would, by hook or by crook, clear right out of Europe. Europe is completely finished. I can't help wondering if all these cuts are an attempt to try to force people to eat out more than they are doing. With all the rations it is almost imperative to get at least one meal a day out.

Met Freddie for dinner, and he showed me a photo of Rowland. He has got into a most attractive-looking lad. He has improved in looks out of all recognition. He used to be most ordinary looking. As I told Freddie: Rowland is now the best looking of them all.

SATURDAY, 9 FEBRUARY

B. Charles
I went to London on the *Flying Scotsman* and had quite a good journey. I found London extremely dull and tiresome and all the bomb damage appalling. Although I had seen a lot of it before, I thought it worse than I had ever realised. I took a bus from Charing X to East Ham, and Bobby, who was with me, agreed that it will be quite impossible ever to rebuild all the devastated areas. Probably, ultimately, satellite towns will be built all around London, and London itself, largely nothing but offices. But this will take about a hundred years, I think.

I took the miniature of the Lady Blessington to Guerault and find it is not by Cosway, but is a fairly recent copy of his work. Guerault said it is worth 'about £25'.

On Monday went over to New Malden to see Jack. Jack says things are 'very difficult', and is of the opinion that the emancipation of women has, in a large measure, contributed to this state of affairs. Also the Scout Movement.

The train I returned on last night was extremely crowded and uncomfortable, largely on account of a great number of soldiers who were on their way to get demobbed. When I got to Waverly I went into the British Restaurant and had some dinner. I was surprised to learn Frank McKew had left. Apparently some row over an omelette.

SUNDAY, 10 FEBRUARY

Edie Rutherford

I have been unable to do this diary for over a week as my husband came home from work last Friday last with flu, and I hope he will be fit for work tomorrow.

On Wednesday I went for a free X-ray. Women were invited and thousands took the opportunity. There was a queue but the job was soon done. If one did not hear in ten days, all is well with one. So now I wait. Looking at the queue of semi-nude women awaiting photography, I realised we could all live off our fat a long time. In fact, I was a shrimp of a woman compared to most there.

MONDAY, 11 FEBRUARY

Maggie Joy Blunt

Spent three days in London last week. Saw Ralph Richardson in *Henry IV Part I*. Excellent. Should now read the play again, but know I won't. Stayed two nights with June – making her my HQ.

Some time spent shopping in West End. Bought oddments including a grater gadget with a handle. Cheese, breadcrumbs and so on may be grated by revolving perforated wheel instead of against the usual straight contrivance which often grates my fingers as well.

Also exchanged Christmas book tokens for Shaw's *Political Guide* and bought one of the escape maps now being sold to the public. These maps are printed perfectly on squares and oblongs of silk or cotton. I found a good square of white silk of a large part of Europe (5/11d.) and wore it to the office the other day as a scarf with navy jumper and skirt and navy and white belt. Spent most of the time taking scarf off to show people. Roger now wants me to get two oblong ones if I can for Meg to make into a lampshade.

My position at the office now clarified. A replacement has been found and I leave on the 22nd.

Edie Rutherford

Today Sheffield Wednesday play here. None of the big factories have opened. Thousands of work hours lost, thousands of pay packets less, apparently that is OK. At this crisis in our lives. Because I live a few minutes from Wednesday's ground, I had a job to get home at 12.30 today, and if I look out of the window now the men are still streaming along the one way, thousands and thousands of them. It is more than time that weekday matches ended. Husband says a man he knows ventured to say in front of several workmen that men who go to weekday matches are equal to Haw-Haw: traitors.

George Taylor

The managing director of the engineering company at which we had a board meeting this morning rushed through the business so that he could attend a football match in the afternoon. He has put up a list in his works for the men to indicate whether they wish to go. One added to his name PB, and when asked as to the significance, said it meant Pall Bearer, presumably referring to the poor prospects of the local team. Later a wag added to the managing director's signature Chief Mourner. The whole works was closed in the afternoon, although the firm has an order book full to overflowing.

THURSDAY, 14 FEBRUARY

Edie Rutherford

My elder sister writes that when her nine-year-old son had his first banana last week, he was disappointed. Not in the taste, but in the size. Asked why, he said he thought they'd be about a foot long. My sister grows cucumbers so I think they must have something to do with David's mental pictures.

Maggie Joy Blunt

Yesterday I tasted banana again. One of the girls brought sandwiches and gave us all a portion. I have seen them about. A young girl in cinema queue near me the other day was holding one in her hand. The children are getting them. But I have heard of one or two of the very young ones who have never seen a banana before – who are *frightened* of them. I suppose that adults have been talking about them so much that the children have the idea there is something mysterious or magical about them. Their shape, colour and characteristics are all strange, too – there is no other fruit comparable to them. One little boy had his banana brought to him as a special treat when he was in bed. It was ready peeled but he would not eat it until the light was turned out.

Mrs Mop didn't come this morning. Last week she left the place looking extra specially tidy and bright, and I only hope now it was not a 'farewell do'.

On doctor's recommendation have been taking Vimaltol. But what are we all going to do, tired out, run-down as we are and food situation growing worse, and few of us with opportunities of really long, recreative holidays?

FRIDAY, 15 FEBRUARY

Edie Rutherford

The people groan for coal and the Government announces that some thousands of refrigerators will be available soon. Lunatic asylum.

I have been surprised at the way the young women with whom I work send and receive Valentines. I never had such a thing in all my life. This revival must be more recent than my era. Damn silly, anyway.

SATURDAY, 16 FEBRUARY

Maggie Joy Blunt

Throughout the recent cigarette shortage our canteen has always had what seemed to be an inexhaustible stock of a few brands, and anyone could buy as many hundreds as they wanted at a time. We grew to rely on the canteen supply and thought it would never fail us, and it was a shock the other day when we found only Kensitas or Weights on sale. I know no one who likes Kensitas.

Why do we smoke? That question was put to the Brains Trust this week; a learned Trust, too, including Bertrand Russell and Julian Huxley. Not one of them could give an answer. Russell said that he started at eighteen years of age because his friends smoked, and now he smoked because it was less painful than not smoking, but he found no pleasure in it. So why *do* we smoke?

SUNDAY, 17 FEBRUARY

Maggie Joy Blunt
Listened to and enjoyed an instalment of *The Diary of a Nobody*.

Priestley's three broadcasts (the last tonight on Russia and Fraternity) – I like his rich feeling for humanity, but surely it's going to be difficult to persuade the USSR to let down her barriers and declare herself an open city when there is so much hard prejudice and hostility towards her. They have to foster the 'capitalist' bogey in order to keep the people united in repairing and restoring the country after the ravages of war.

Herbert Brush
I was very sorry to see in the *Dover Express* this week that William Pullman is dead. Pullman was a fitter in the electrical works when I went to Dover in 1895 and I always liked him and I think that he liked me. Many years ago Pullman fell from a scaffold and damaged his testicles, which ever after accumulated water, which he had to have removed periodically at a doctor's, and he always asked for time off to go to have this done. He was, I believe, a teetotaller.

TUESDAY, 19 FEBRUARY

Herbert Brush
The touch of lumbago I had yesterday is somewhat better, probably due to the rubbing of 'Sloans'.

Edie Rutherford
Communist friend was telling me how someone had told her he knew a man whose wife had actually had to give him raisin sandwiches to take to work as she could not get meat.

City libraries have banned *Forever Amber*. Oh yeah? 'Because children have access to the books.' I then offered to go round the shelves selecting the not discussed yet filthy books being circulated.

FRIDAY, 22 FEBRUARY

George Taylor
I went to a lecture on the Pennine Way, but was very disappointed. The lecturer was poor, he was probably somewhat bored, having given the same lecture 180 times. He scarcely ever mentioned the Pennine Way itself, and certainly gave no help to would-be walkers on it, and the slides were unimpressive. The best feature was the speed with which he caught a bus home.

Maggie Joy Blunt
Last day at the office.
7.15 a.m. Alarm. Put on newly cleaned Harris tweed and left house at 8.45 exactly. Very cold. Frost had made the Christmas roses droop. Outside two little boys had been flying a kite – it was caught on the branch of a tree. 'Look what happened!' said young J as I passed and very patiently and determinedly went on pulling on the string. I felt grand. My last day of bondage! I walked on air.

On the bus met Sy. 'Feeling excited?' she asked. 'You'll miss us, surely?' 'Yes, I shall miss the daily contact with people', and I expect I shall, that feeling of being part of an organisation, having a place in a community, but not much. I feel I am starting on a new life and have no regrets for the old. Don't cling to things that are dead. I amused her by repeating O's comment yesterday when he asked if my boss was sorry I was leaving. I said I had seen no signs of it and O said, 'Well, what can you expect? The man has the mentality of a blancmange . . .'

A junior came to collect 2d. for my mid-morning cheese roll. Went through drawers in my desk – had taken most of my belongings home, but found some useful scraps of paper which I pinched. Went through an old notebook.

Phoned photographer for DJ and then had no more to do. It was 11.40. Was persuaded to buy 1/- ticket in raffle for hand-made leather handbag. Then decided I must clean out top drawer, full of powder and tobacco dust and old cigarette boxes. Then read February's *Building* until lunchtime.

Last lunch in canteen with Sy and Mrs G. Spam salad. Cold cooked vegetables, mashed potatoes, roll, butter, dates and custard, coffee. Bought sixty Craven A and some biscuits at the kiosk, watching the familiar faces pass by. How many shall I recognise in, say, a year from now if we meet unexpectedly elsewhere?

After lunch went through final explainings with RJ. Signed my letters and left her to pack them for the post. Went round saying a few farewells and came back to browse through an old copy of *Life*, wondering how soon after I'd collected my money and cards I could get away. Little man from Personnel came with more forms relating to my release.

Tea arrived. I distributed chocolate biscuits to sales girls as a farewell tea contribution. Then went to Wages for my money. Stitched hem of skirt and talked to RJ who sat beside me. About 4.45 went in to DJ. He was pleasant as always, said he was sorry I was leaving but it was the firm's fault. I couldn't go into all that again and said goodbye as quickly as I could. 'Come and see us,' he repeated. There was no life in his handshake. It was like grasping the end of a dead branch.

Collected my things. Went to the cloakroom. Said more goodbyes and then to the Commissionaire's at 5 p.m. 'You can take my name for the last time!' and out of the main door.

All over. Four years. Going home felt extraordinarily flat, threatened with depression. Curious. 'You'll feel it, you know,' said Sy to me this morning and I didn't believe her.

SATURDAY, 23 FEBRUARY

B. Charles

On the tram returning home this morning I got into conversation with a young air force chap from Cornwall. I happened to see, in a paper a man was reading in front of me, that there is a possibility of the Home Guard being retained. I remarked to this air force fellow that I wondered why there was this idea of retaining the Home Guard, now that the war was over. (I said this to try and draw him as to his ideas.) Immediately, without the least hesitation, he replied, 'For the war with Russia.' I think so too.

MONDAY, 25 FEBRUARY

Herbert Brush
In the afternoon yesterday W and I went to see Bill and Maggie Hutt at Dulwich. Bill and I invented a new game with the Lexicon cards, but it did not go down very well with the ladies. It seemed to make both of them very sleepy, judging by their yawns.

Maggie Joy Blunt
Feel better already. It's the relief of knowing you have *time* to yourself again. It doesn't matter if that pair of stockings isn't mended or those shoes not cleaned, or that the washing isn't done and you may not have a fire again in the kitchen for two weeks. These are the sort of things that wear a woman down. No time to manicure your nails because you had important private letters to write when you got in from the office. You simply had to iron a blouse to wear the next morning and if you weren't in bed by midnight you knew you'd never get up when the alarm went.

TUESDAY, 26 FEBRUARY

Edie Rutherford
Last evening I bought a sewing machine. Have wanted one all the twenty years of my marriage. I was passing the notice board in foyer at 5 p.m. when I saw the notice 'Sewing Machine for Sale, Jones, in perfect condition, £9'. Luckily walked into a friend who has a Jones and who gladly agreed to come with me to see the machine about which I know nothing. She told me it was a bargain – last week she saw its twin fetch £15 from a dealer. So I paid for it. Much against Husband's judgement. To him it is a waste of money.

Herbert Brush
Judging by the papers this morning we shall not escape bread rationing after all, if we allow thousands of tons of wheat to go to Germany instead of coming here, in our own usual English way of thinking first of the foreigner and secondly of ourselves.

We have received papers for both the Labour and Conservative candidates for the London County Council asking for our votes, and of course we shall all vote Conservative on 7 March, even if we don't go to any of the meetings.

WEDNESDAY, 27 FEBRUARY

B. Charles
I see in the *Daily Telegraph* that the Odeon Cinema in London has been fined for illegal decorating. This was the cinema being done up for the visit of Queen Mary to *Caesar and Cleopatra* some few weeks ago.

I have learned a lesson today. I went to the sale at Dowell's this morning to bid for the two lacquer mirrors Mason and I saw yesterday. I wasted the whole day there, got the things for far more than I originally intended to pay, and, when I took them to Mason to inspect and got the paper off the back, we found they are quite modern! He seemed as surprised as I. I gave £3 15s. for them. But it has been a good thing for me to get 'done' like this, as it will make me more careful in future.

Herbert Brush
I met Ing in the road and he told me a few yarns, and held forth for a while on the prevalence of syphilis. His description of the disease was enough to make me feel sick. When a policeman gets it he is told to hand in his uniform and go at once. According to Ing, there are plenty of young girls about with the disease, a great danger to all young men.

THURSDAY, 28 FEBRUARY

Edie Rutherford
My forty-fourth birthday. Woke to snow. I took a large cake to work this morning for all to have a piece. On tram a girl of about ten was sitting next to me. Woman of about fifty got on, and child didn't move, so I gave her a gentle shove. She got up and the woman sat down, turning to me to say thank you. I said if a child doesn't know, it must be told, and anyway, I felt privileged today as it's my birthday. So the woman said 'It is also MY birthday!'

Two girls at work gave me a beautiful painted glass bowl. Next door gave me a ream of pre-war typing paper (wonder where they got it?), niece a painted jar with a screw top, husband £1 and a wash-up bowl to follow, brother sent bottle of South African sherry, brother-in-law some blue writing paper with printed address, sister sent five large leeks, some shallots and greens. A friend sent me a quite hideous pinafore. Girl who works in Boots promises to get me a fireproof glass casserole as they have some in. The supply seldom gets further than the staff.

Boss came and asked me this morning if I am leaving on Saturday. I said yes, so he bade me goodbye and went off to London. Thanked me for much. I am relieved as I had an uncomfy idea he'd ask me to stay on a bit. I know they want me to.

George Taylor

On audit at a multiple grocer's. Through quite casual conversation in the office about the scarcity of goods, I was offered a tin of that rare commodity Nescafé and some unpitted bottled plums. When I received the parcel, the warehouse manager had put me in two tins and two bottles. I suppose that the branch shops never see these rare goods, but the management takes them all.

FRIDAY, 1 MARCH 1946

Edie Rutherford

So steel is to be nationalised. What did they expect then, all these folk who are expressing surprise?

This is my last day at work, henceforth I am housewife only, hurrah. I said to my husband last night, 'I have a good mind to go sick tomorrow morning for the first time!' He said, 'Oh no, go out with trumpets sounding.'

Herbert Brush

Frost during the night, and snow still lying thickly on the ground.

The book I had last week, *At the Tiller*, was interesting but did not encourage me to go yachting in a small boat off the north-west coast of Scotland.

It is very disturbing the way that England has come down in the world and has to borrow money where she can. At the time of Napoleon every country came to us for loans and we always had enough to finance them. Now even Canada is going to lend us millions. Maybe it is like a mother getting help from some of her children.

SUNDAY, 3 MARCH

Herbert Brush

I was sweeping snow off the pavement outside the garden when Ing came across to talk and to tell me that I was committing a statutory offence by sweeping the snow off an LCC pavement after eight o'clock. But if I lived in Penge district, only a little way from here, I should commit an offence if I did not do it. As he is a retired policeman he knows all these little things, and often tells me of his experiences. He told me this morning of a coalman who was delivering coals in Westminster, but he was entirely ignorant of the law; Ing had to take his name and that of his employer, and eventually both of them were fined a pound for delivering coal to a householder after eight o'clock.

Maggie Joy Blunt

Feel much, much better. Thursday a brilliant and lovely day – Mrs Mop came. I put on my red suit and went shopping in Slough and Windsor. Fell for some very pretty shoes and spent coupons I couldn't afford.

Meg said to me the other day, 'Don't you think people (meaning the middle-classes) are going *down* – they speak so badly.' She meant that society was deteriorating, cultural standards were being lowered. But I think what she sees is due to people always coming *up*, like several people I could mention at the office. For instance, the young typist TB whose father is a workman in one of the shops – she is now in the 'clerk' strata. The branch manager, now very important and highly salaried, was a moulder in the sand foundry, and so on.

These sort of economic advances are going on everywhere. A person can make money relatively quickly and improve his family's position materially within a few years, but cultural advance takes very much longer. It is extraordinary what a lot of wealth there is among the middle classes. An old local lawyer who died recently left £100,000 – someone else left £48,000 and there are others I know of who are probably worth as much. Quite apparently unimportant, insignificant people, with no place at all in what is known as 'society'.

Called on the S family. Their father, now deceased, was the vicar of this parish for I can't remember how many years. Anyway, I have

187

known them all my life and like them immensely. Four girls, two boys, one of them a well-known ballroom dancer and broadcaster (he once received a letter from a distant relative, saying 'After listening to your broadcast my sister went upstairs and died').

MONDAY, 4 MARCH

Maggie Joy Blunt
We listened last night to Attlee. I am afraid the speech depressed me. I think the Government might give some sanction and encouragement to civilians taking a few weeks holiday before calling on them to renew their labours and work for the peace. Men and women from the services are receiving several weeks' leave with pay but there must be millions of civilians, particularly women, who have had no break at all. I think now of the women I know still working hard at the office, and who have worked throughout the war. They are tired out. 'Permanently tired.'

To see *Brief Encounter* this afternoon. An excellent, excellent film. I can find no fault with it.

TUESDAY, 5 MARCH

Edie Rutherford
Did I feel a heel when Attlee asked married women to keep on working in his radio talk last Sunday evening. However, I just can't do everything and it's no use pretending I can.

Having pancakes, made with dried egg, for tea today, as it is Pancake Day, and also, Husband likes pancakes, and thirdly, we have oranges/lemons to squeeze.

WEDNESDAY, 6 MARCH

George Taylor
Clearing queries at a motor distributor's. While I was there a girl brought in a wad of £200 in part payment for a car, and the managing director remarked that he had never seen so many notes in his life as during the past few weeks. Many people were now paying for cars in cash, and they were even pressing him to accept the money now, although delivery might not be made for another twelve

months. 'Of course, I know what it is for,' commented the director. 'It is all black market or untaxed and undisclosed income.'

THURSDAY, 7 MARCH

Edie Rutherford
We have decided to buy a pressure cooker. Husband's teeth are all false and meat is a sore trial to him usually, unless I'm lucky enough to get a lucky bit, or veal which is always tender. We've often thought about this and at last are spending £9 on the smaller size. I have friends who use them and who look on all who don't as belonging to the Stone Age.

George Taylor
Engaged at a dye manufacturer's. I note that a circular has gone to the travellers pointing out that khaki is not a popular colour now, and therefore the company had ceased making it. In its place lavender had been put.

FRIDAY, 8 MARCH

George Taylor
For many years now my wife has kept a small builder's books, devoting about a day and a half each week to the task. At 9.30 tonight a knock came on the door, and the builder concerned was there. He came to tell my wife that he had now the promise of a sixty-five-year-old man who was willing to give his whole time to the books, and would charge for this the noble sum of £3 10s. per week. Unless my wife was prepared to do the same, she had finished. It was very much of a surprise, but my wife was not prepared to put in full time. The effect was that she has finished at an instant's notice, and has not even received a word of thanks for the effort she has put in during the past years. And this treatment was from a man who is supposed to have been my friend since boyhood.

SUNDAY, 10 MARCH

B. Charles
I am amused to see, in today's *Sunday Times*, a letter complaining of the modern use of the word 'pretty' in quite an incorrect sense:

'pretty bad', 'pretty awful', etc. I have written a letter to the Editor. I much doubt if it is printed.

Edie Rutherford

What is one to comment on the deaths at that football match in Bolton yesterday? Of all the unnecessary ways to die, and it's no use saying it has happened before – all the more reason why it should not have happened. Well, so long as sport is more spectator-like than participatory, England will have that kind of senseless tragedy I suppose.

I have come to the conclusion after a week off work that the trouble with many women is that they persist in thinking in terms of 1939. They want all they had then at the prices they paid then. Younger women are not so grouchy because they cannot make the comparison. Older women don't want the fag of thinking up food and making do. I had another SOS from the office this morning. But I am not going back.

Chapter Eight

CALLED IN AT DREAMLAND, BUT THE PLACE IS CLOSED AT PRESENT

Some of those Nazi thugs think they'll be let off: left to right, Hermann Goering, Rudolf Hess, Joachim von Ribbentrop and Wilhelm Keitel

'The question is asked – can we afford it? Supposing the answer is "No", what does that mean? It really means that the sum total of the goods produced and the services rendered by the people of this country is not sufficient to provide for all our people at all times, in sickness, in health, in youth and in age, the very modest standard of life that is represented by the sums of money set out in the Second Schedule to this Bill.

I cannot believe that our national productivity is so slow, that our willingness to work is so feeble or that we can submit to the world that the masses of our people must be condemned to penury.'

Clement Attlee puts the case for the National Insurance scheme to the House of Commons, 1946

'Arranging the programme is not nearly so easy as it sounds. As well as seeing that too many dances of the same kind do not follow one another, I have to select numbers that will enable my four vocalists to sing more or less in turn, and I have also to make sure that all the different publishers get an even break. I never want it to be said that I play more of one firm's numbers than another's. Finally, I must include tunes for which there have been several requests in my mail lately, and also make allowances for special requests from dancers during the evening.'

'Medley King' Charlie Kunz explains his programming decisions. His British performances in the spring of 1946 were accompanied by rousing communal renditions of 'Clap Hands, Here Comes Charlie!'

MONDAY, 11 MARCH

B. Charles
On the way to Kirkcaldy, I read an account in the *News of the World* about the menus Sir Ben Smith has been having in America. Surely it is extremely unwise to publish all this senseless extravagance?

I saw a pair of black glaze china dogs and they sold them to me for 15/- the pair. One of the eyes is missing but I can get Gardiner to take an eye out of some dog at the Lane, I think. When I had got them I went to have a talk to the man in the china shop and I was interested to learn from him that EVERYTHING is being exported. He says he has dealers from all over, England included, trying to buy up anything for export. Shiploads of stuff is leaving Great Britain for Canada and America. Soon there will be absolutely nothing at all left.

TUESDAY, 12 MARCH

Herbert Brush
Planted three rows of shallots on the plot. Another man in the next-but-one plot also put in some shallots, so I asked him if he had taken the plot over, and he replied that he was doing work for the owner, a lady. She has had the plot for several years and pays a different man every year to dig it up and plant something which she never gathers. By the middle of summer the plot is a bed of docks and long grass which scatter all over the place.

I can see the same thing happening again, judging by the way the present man is working. After he had put in his shallots he did about five minutes' digging, then he left and presumably went to collect his payment. When he had gone I went across to inspect his work, and his digging showed about as much knowledge of gardening as his planting of shallots, so I guess that the poor lady will be cheated again this year.

Edie Rutherford
Last evening I went to City Hall to hear Stanley Leif talk on how to keep 100 per cent fit, in connection with the efforts of the British Health Freedom Society to combat the new Health Act, which bars all but the orthodox doctors. As if they always cure! As if they know it all! It was worth a doctor's fee just to go and hear Leif. Keeler, the

Secretary of BHFS, said there are more vegetarians registered in this town than any other, yet membership of the BHFS was only fourteen.

So Vera Lynn has a baby. My, my, I'm all het up, I don't think.

THURSDAY, 14 MARCH

Edie Rutherford

I didn't get down to this yesterday as I started distempering. Ugh, what a beastly job. How anyone can say they like doing it beats me. I was tired by the time I had moved furniture ready to begin. However, I gave ceiling one coat and walls two, and that is all I intend to do. It doesn't look marvellous but it is clean. Husband started to criticise but I cut him short. At the moment only thing on Husband's mind is how to get a ticket to see Derby County play on the Wednesday ground.

What have Goering's early life and childhood to do with his infamous behaviour after he joined Hitler? Nothing. It is irrelevant and such evidence should not be permitted at that court, which is taking far too long as it is. One gets the idea that some of those Nazi thugs think they'll be let off. Surely not.

Herbert Brush

I went with W on her journey to Rochester today. We went on to Hoo, and then on to Stoke. We meant to go to Allhallows, the place which a vicar is reported to have said is the loneliest place in the country. But we did not go as far as that; the country around Stoke is certainly dreary enough.

We had a look at some prefabricated homes they are putting together in Hoo. These are certainly the best I have seen, and seem to have every convenience on a small scale. The homes were arriving on lorries, almost a third of a house on each lorry, and put together on concrete foundations. The homes are supplied by the Government to the Borough, which pays for them in twenty years. I have an idea that in twenty years they will be in a very dilapidated state unless constant repairs and plenty of paint are available.

George Taylor

Our provision shop manager friend and his wife brought along their little evacuee for tea. This little girl had gone back to her mother in

London, but had been so troubled on her return that she had pined, and her mother had written asking our friends to bring the child back to Sheffield. The mother has decided that it would be better for her to leave the child here, and our friends are adopting the youngster. They have certainly made a very well-mannered little lady out of a real slum child.

FRIDAY, 15 MARCH

Edie Rutherford
Found stray cat on stairs. It had been kicked around all day and I had seen it and told myself it wasn't my affair, but there it was to reproach me. Well, we kept it all night. It is a female, undersized, full of babies, back legs weak, sits like a kangaroo. Will have to be destroyed and hope to arrange for someone to take it today.

George Taylor
No fuel at the dye manufacturers where I am on audit, so we donned our overcoats. It seems to be Gilbertian to be surrounded by collieries, and yet be without a fire.

B. Charles
I was interested to see, in a back number of the *Sunday Dispatch*, an account about Vera Lynn. It seems this woman admits she has never had a singing lesson in her life, never practises, can't play the piano, yet manages to earn, so we are told, £1,000 a broadcast in Australia if she goes there. She seems undecided whether to devote all her time to her forthcoming baby or proceed to Australia. I think it fairly certain she will go to Australia and leave the baby to the care of a nurse, or someone. I have never heard Vera Lynn, and I certainly do not want to. But the idea of her getting £1,000 a broadcast for making a noise over the air seems fantastic. Money, really, has ceased to have any value.

WEDNESDAY, 20 MARCH

Maggie Joy Blunt
Just returned from short visit to London. Lunched with S today. He has been invited by the War Office to join the army again. They are

very short of trained officers, have been demobbing too quickly. We must, he says, be able to take a strong line with Russia, must feel sure that we can. Trouble is that though Russia 'has no will to war, she does not fear it. We have no will to war and fear it.' He full of gloomy Fleet Street prophesies. Sees no end to current chaos and confusion everywhere. Thinks we shall eventually leave India and then there will be frightful civil war there.

A difficult, transitional period. S hopes for nationalisation in a big way because then the Government will *have* to discipline its own people. Now there is none: 'Workers can be as rude and slack as they like because they cannot be easily replaced.'

THURSDAY, 21 MARCH

Edie Rutherford
The new Health Bill has been launched, and it will be interesting to see the repercussions. Am amazed that it won't start till 1948. By that time it will be so near an election that agitation against it should be effective, if serious.

FRIDAY, 22 MARCH

George Taylor
Visited a WEA psychology class. I found the men there quite enthusiastic about the Health Bill in which the Government propose taking over the voluntary hospitals. The charity of such hospitals was not wanted. I think I would prefer charity, however, to bureaucracy.

SUNDAY, 24 MARCH

Edie Rutherford
I fear the laughing, jolly pictures of [Food Minister] Ben Smith in papers today, on return from USA, won't go down well in his own land, nor his reply to journalist question that his own paunch is the only fat he brought back. I have heard several women say this week just what they'd like to do to Ben Smith . . .

Yesterday I used our pressure cooker for the first time and found the vegetables I tried in it so delicious that I was content to have them only for my lunch. Today I'm doing the pork in it, vegetables on top.

A boy living in one of the flats, aged six, went into the shop on the ground floor one day last week, tendered 3d. for a large loaf, saying his mother had no change and would pay rest when she came in. A few moments later the caretaker's daughter aged ten came in to report the boy had broken the loaf into pieces and he and others were kicking them about and throwing them at each other. Mother, told, said: 'Well, he lost his ball yesterday so I expect he wanted something to take its place.'

Husband had a stand-up ticket for match at Wednesday ground yesterday but I begged him not to use it, so he gave it to one of the clerks, who was very pleased. I know he badly wanted to see the match, and could he have got a sit-down seat I would not have minded. My husband is not robust and would be just the type to get jostled underfoot and I have no wish to be a widow so needlessly.

MONDAY, 25 MARCH

B. Charles
I am very glad indeed to see in today's *Daily Telegraph* that J. B. Priestley slated soundly, in a speech at Birmingham last Saturday, the smutty American film now showing at the Empire in London called *Getting Gertie's Garter*. It is an outrage on good taste that this tripe should be shown at all, much less at the Empire of all places. All this sniggering smut wants putting down with a vengeance. Crudity, yes, if you want it, but this sniggering, suggestive filth is so utterly debasing. There can be no doubt whatever that in general the taste, or lack of it, of the USA is simply shocking. I feel certain I am right when I feel that the USA is just like a HUGE Woolworth store.

THURSDAY, 28 MARCH

Edie Rutherford
Husband jubilant because Derby won yesterday at Manchester. But it looks as if too many went to that match again.

Got a dozen lemons at greengrocer's today. Can't beat them for internal cleansing. Other day when I said to another woman that I found Octim cleaner splendid stuff, she said, 'I have no time for such things, give me a brush, some soap and elbow grease and I'm happy.' Of all the out-of-date minds. Such a mind isn't worth while. Anything that will lighten labour, I receive with wide-open arms.

Yesterday came parcel from Texas, posted 16 December. Talk about the horrors of peace.

FRIDAY, 29 MARCH

Edie Rutherford

This morning I saw a banana skin in the street – first I've seen for years. Very nice to hear and read about smokeless Britain, but methinks the average person in this country prefers an open fireplace and the smoke is so usual that they don't mind it. I seldom find anyone to agree with my abhorrence of the filthy air here.

Last evening my husband said I ought not to spend money on reading matter. I spend 1/- on weeklies and 1/6d. on monthlies, which I consider very moderate for a person of my tastes. I retorted that my spending that way is my only personal luxury (and he reads them, then they go overseas), that they cost little, certainly far less than his tobacco and ale. No more was said. Even the most oblique threat to his little luxuries silences him.

SATURDAY, 30 MARCH

George Taylor

A half-yearly General Meeting of the WEA. Over five hundred notices had been sent out, but only thirteen members attended. The president was absent through illness, both vice-presidents were away, the treasurer was absent, and seven out of the nine non-official committee members did not attend. A representative of a Working Men's Club attended, and somewhat beerily suggested that we should have to simplify things for the ordinary working man who was easily frightened. He apparently was not aware that membership of WEA classes usually results in one being convinced that most simple problems are highly complex, and that most simple solutions are bad ones.

MONDAY, 1 APRIL 1946

Herbert Brush

W and I went to the Capitol Cinema in the afternoon. The pictures were very good, especially one showing the flight of a 'Helicopter', although I think there must have been a lot of fake about it.

D made an April Fool of me by telling me to look at the dirt on my tie.

TUESDAY, 2 APRIL

Edie Rutherford
Letter this morning from old flame, his mother died last week, buried today. Poor Norman. Both he and his mother openly used to moan that he did not marry me when he could have done. Yet, if truth is to be told, he threw me over and at the time I was broken-hearted. They thought I wasn't good enough for him – all except Grandma, she always insisted I was too good for him! Ah well, it is all old stuff now and when I look at Norman I am so thankful I didn't marry him, but of course had I done, he might have been quite different now.

WEDNESDAY, 3 APRIL

B. Charles
When I went to the baker's this morning, I saw a pamphlet on the counter, imploring people to try to stop the nationalisation of voluntary hospitals. It seems so odd that, after voting for a Labour Government, which promised to nationalise everything, now that it is doing so, hordes of people seem to be up in arms about the matter. A strange world, my masters. All this nationalisation will be a huge mistake, I am sure.

A letter from Brenda this morning. She says a whole lot of her underclothes have been stolen during her move from Borough. She has gone to the CID about this matter.

THURSDAY, 4 APRIL

Maggie Joy Blunt
Went to see Meg yesterday afternoon. Government has refused licence to builder who was going to build them a house. New regulation means that there must be four council houses to every private one built. Meg full of rage and despair. Does not know what they will do or when they will now get their house. Everything being done now for '*those* sort of revolting people' – indicating a nearby house where some poor families now living. They are dirty, noisy people, she says.

All this talk about the decreasing birth rate – but no encouragement being given to the ordinary middle classes. If the Government wants better *quality* children the poorer ones will have to go without.'

FRIDAY, 5 APRIL

George Taylor
A Youth Committee meeting of the WEA. The secretary wished to resign on account of the ill health of her mother, but I think she was not quite prepared for the attitude taken up by the majority of the committee. Almost without exception, the members thought that the lectures provided for youth organisations had been a complete waste of time. Youth clubs existed only to provide cheap dances, and no attention at all was paid to any serious subjects.

My wife cut her rent collecting round short so that she could go with her mother to visit her sick father in hospital. She is spending as much time there now as possible.

Herbert Brush
I must look very old when I go with my bucket and tools to the plot: several times I have been spoken to as 'Dad'. Today a lorry man pulled up and said, 'Which way to Round 'ill, Dad?' So I replied, 'I don't know where Round Hill is.'

As the weather keeps me in I shall listen to the Grand National, although I do not know one horse from another as regards its ability to jump. I guess that the favourite Prince Regent will not win, as the rain must have made a great difference to the course.

3.30 p.m. Prince Regent did not win. The name of the winner was Lovely Cottage. It was an exciting race, and probably the most excited man there was the BBC commentator near the finish.

SUNDAY, 7 APRIL

B. Charles
My fifty-fourth birthday. So far I have not seen anyone at all. The lad arranged to call this afternoon, but I doubt if he will be able to come along, though it will make a nice change if he turns up. I thought there might have been a letter of good wishes from Brenda yesterday, but no doubt it will come in the morning.

[Later] Well, the lad I was expecting came along and stayed for three hours! He is called James Paterson and has decided possibilities. He seems very intelligent, especially for his age, and is extremely keen to learn everything possible. It is odd, and at the same time interesting, to meet a lad who is keen to learn and who is, further, above the average in intelligence. We discussed all sorts of things, and I was fortunate in being able to 'draw him out', and get at his ideas. I fancy the Scotch Education is above the English in a good many ways. He has arranged to come again next Sunday. He suggested coming on Tuesday, but I thought it better not to see him again this week, so pleaded an excuse that I hoped to go to Inverness on Wednesday and should, therefore, be occupied on Tuesday with preparations for departure. I also told him I might have to go and pick up an old corner cupboard. Next time he comes we will enter into the question of period furniture!

MONDAY, 8 APRIL

Herbert Brush
On the tram today I sat next to a young woman who wore one of the absurd little hats which so many wear nowadays. She jumped up to leave the tram and her hat fell off onto my knee, and I handed it back and received a smile of thanks. The hat was about suitable for a fair-sized doll, and I could not see any means to fix it on her head. It did not weigh more than an ounce and she might easily lose it.

B. Charles
A letter from Brenda to wish me a happy birthday. Her underclothes have NOT been recovered.

Davy's train was an hour late. Davy looked very well; he was in uniform, which rather surprised me, as I imagined he would arrive in civvies. We had a very nice dinner at the NB [North British Hotel] and then went to the hotel where he is staying and he left his luggage. He has got a good room and the place seems clean. He then came back with me here and stayed about an hour. I was amused to see how very much he admired my room. He seemed to have thought I was living in some sort of garret. I proposed we go to *Pygmalion* tomorrow evening. He wants to go dancing one night, and, as I have a ticket for the Eileen Joyce concert on Wednesday, he will go dancing that night. I hope, and think, his visit here will be very pleasant for me.

Before I went to dinner I took an advertisement for exchange of Windsor house for one in Scotland to the office of the *Scotsman* for insertion. It will be about two months before it can appear.

TUESDAY, 9 APRIL

Edie Rutherford

It is quite cold again but the sun shines. The racket of the little factory next door is one of the worst features of life here. Clang, clang, clang, all day long.

So the poor old League of Nations is finished. And what of that huge edifice at Geneva? How stupid mankind is. Why can't the same place house UNO? Economy is needful these days, or so we're told. But I think the war is really over: I got some potato crisps yesterday, and with salt in the packet!

Herbert Brush

Where a rocket had fallen in the school grounds about sixty yards from my plot a bulldozer has been at work pushing out all the house rubble which was thrown into the hole. Six men are carefully handpicking the rubbish as though they are searching for hidden treasure. I don't think any of them will be tired out with hard work when they go home tonight.

WEDNESDAY, 10 APRIL

Edie Rutherford

We are delighted with budget and Dalton's speech on the air about it. There is no doubt we have the right man in that job. We loved his consideration for ordinary folk in subsidising essential foods and keeping prices of them fixed. We also loved his dig at those who leave two million of which he'll take one million, leaving the inheritors to struggle along on half a million. Ha ha.

Husband would have liked purchase tax off radio sets as we want a new one. Feel like waiting still longer just in case. And, anyway, looks as it if will be worth our while to consider a television set soon.

B. Charles

Such a sad anniversary. The fourtieth one of dear Mother's death! I remember the day she died so well. Father came in to tell me she had died in the night. He made what to me then seemed a peculiar remark: 'Your Mother told me I had been a very good husband to her.' I was only just fourteen at the time, and I am sure, had he not said this, that I should have thought this, without him having said so. In the light of latter discoveries, I think this remark extremely suggestive.

THURSDAY, 11 APRIL

B. Charles

Went to fetch Davy as usual and we went to town. As there was no sale on we had a coffee at Mackie's and then went to book two seats for the second house at the Empire. He is a very good sort of lad and I am enjoying his visit. He seemed to have enjoyed his dancing at the Palais last night very much, and is now off again for the afternoon session. He is meeting me at 6.15 in the Raglan. He wanted a bath, so I sent him to the Spottiswood Street baths, and gave him my towels and soap.

The show at the Empire was quite good. I particularly enjoyed some extremely clever performing collie dogs and a pair of extremely good acrobats. Charlie Kunz was on the bill, but I thought his act extremely dull, and can't understand why he has such a big reputation.

FRIDAY, 12 APRIL

George Taylor

My wife was very troubled on her return from hospital at her help-lessness in the face of her father's illness. She cannot aid him to recover, nor assist his passage out of the world. It is a very pathetic situation.

Later my brother-in-law rang to say my wife's father passed away at six o'clock. His death is a real release, although it is bound to be a shock for his widow.

SUNDAY, 14 APRIL

Edie Rutherford

Yesterday I brought what purported to be filleted haddock. Put it to soak out some of its salt and all the colour left it, leaving our old friend cod. So the same old deception is still going on.

It is a lovely day, Palm Sunday. The bong bong bong of damned RC church bell woke me from a delicious sleep at 8 a.m. Wish the bell ringer would die. However, no doubt some poor priest would be roped in then, and we'd have no option, or they'd electrify it or something. The man who built that church, an RC priest, was buried last week and that bell tolled for him three times in twenty-four hours . . . I wish he had taken it with him.

MONDAY, 15 APRIL

Herbert Brush

I was weighed the other day on one of Woolworth's machines – 15 stone 6lb. That is 216lb., which is 6lb. cubed. Of course that includes my clothes, which probably weigh a stone.

London streets are getting worse and worse with the increased traffic along them. What will they be like in a few years' time when everyone has a car . . .?

Have you ever heard of or seen an 'everlasting' match? A match which can be struck several thousand times? I learn from the *Irish Times* that Bryant & May have entered into a conspiracy with American and Swedish firms to keep the everlasting match off the market. I have not seen this mentioned in English papers.

B. Charles

On the way back from the sales I saw a lot of Yankee sailors and was amused, when I was having a drink in a pub, when an English sailor told me that he expects there will be a lot of black eyes floating around as the Yanks are so fearfully overbearing and boastful when they go with a lot of 'spare' women. And they were busy trying to get hold of any 'spare' women who were about. I have heard repeatedly that the Yanks are excellent to work with, both as soldiers and sailors, so long as they keep away from women.

When I got back there was a letter from Davy. One of the nicest letters I have ever had in my life. He seems to have had a very happy time here.

I have been inquiring from various people if they think that bread rationing will come into operation. No one seems to think it will. Neither do I. I never believed in the 'Invasion' scare, and I do not believe in bread rationing.

Maggie Joy Blunt

Saw CL, who does not like Medical Bill proposals. The idea of doctors being 'directed' and 'controlled' – men coming back from forces have had six years of it and want freedom. The proposed insurance payment under Social Security scheme – between 3/- and 4/- per head every week – she thinks excessive and will amount to more than she ever pays her doctor in a year as it is. If one is really hard up one can get free treatment now, so why alter it? And who wants Health Centres?

TUESDAY, 16 APRIL

George Taylor

My father-in-law's funeral this morning. His widow wished for cremation, a little to our surprise. She is seventy-two, and cremation is a modern idea. However, one of her points is that not only is it more hygienic, but that it will put a definite end to the long period of nearly six years during which she has been visiting the hospital. She does not want to follow with a grave which wants attention. Yesterday my wife went with her sister to the hospital, hoping to have a last look at their father before the funeral. However, they arrived too late. I was not very keen on her going, as it seems a bit of a ghoulish business to me.

THURSDAY, 18 APRIL

George Taylor

Our senior partner gave me a leaflet which his doctor is distributing, urging opposition to the new Government Health Service. The main point made is the change-over from individual attention to that of a state official, depending for promotion on the goodwill of his superiors and not that of his patients. I heartily agree with the circular, and have no use for an official health scheme. I hope that I shall never have to resort to it, although I shall be compelled to pay my contribution for something I do not intend to utilise.

We walked over to my wife's mother in the afternoon and explored a part of suburban Sheffield on the way which we scarcely knew at all. While at my mother-in-law's I had a lengthy read of *Hansard*, quite one of the most interesting periodicals I have found. Until last week I had never seen a copy, but we are getting selected numbers at our office under the finance service of the Stationery Office, and I bring these home for a pleasant hour's reading.

GOOD FRIDAY, 19 APRIL

Edie Rutherford
All a-flutter here re nationalisation of iron and steel industry. Posters on all hoardings warning against nationalisation octopus with gruesome picture of octopus behind the words. Reminds me of King Kong beating his breast in rage and to no purpose finally.

It is a lovely day, marred only by the incessant hammering from the factory adjacent, and the awful racket the children on holiday make. They are badly brought-up kids here – just because one or two ground-floor tenants ask them not to walk on their gardens outside their flats, and not to uproot plants, the mothers get into a fury, and, judging by events, instruct the kids to go and jump on the plants hard. What can one do with such folk?

Herbert Brush
At 6 a.m. we started off in the car for Torquay, and I am writing this while W is having a rest. I am boiling the kettle on a methylated stove, and it is quite pleasant sitting here on the grass by the roadside a few miles from Chard, though a trifle awkward writing. W's new car is certainly an improvement on the old one, and we averaged between 40 and 50 mph over long stretches.

SUNDAY, 21 APRIL

Herbert Brush
We went to the Pavilion last evening to see *A Desirable Property*, a farce, but the seats we had were so far from the stage that I could not hear more than half of the dialogue. However, I enjoyed it.

3.15 p.m. Have been sitting in the lounge, reading and dozing in a comfortable chair. I feel fairly certain that the people in this lounge are curious to know what I am scribbling down, and the faster I scribble, the more curious they become. An old chap sitting close to me is very deaf and uses an electric machine to aid his hearing, holding an earphone to his head. He is bald-headed and small, and he seems to be captivated by a woman half his age and twice his size. He is always trying to interest her in his doings. He has not known her for more than a few days, but he is already beginning to call her his dear when no one is near. I heard him this afternoon when he thought I was asleep in my chair.

MONDAY, 22 APRIL

B. Charles

There is a report in yesterday's *News of the World* stating that thousands of babies have been born to US women during the past fifteen years through artificial insemination. And it seems that one physician found all the babies so born – that he examined – 'above the average'. This artificial insemination seems to me to be quite unnecessary, and, therefore, like aviation, probably productive of a great deal of downright harm to the human race. In theory there should be no limit to experiment and the acquisition of knowledge, but in practice there are certain things that should NOT be experimented with. And this artificial insemination, for human beings, is one of them. No matter what benefits may possibly accrue to humanity from aviation, the downright harm it has caused to the world at large will, forever, far outweigh any benefits. It has been the greatest curse the world has ever known; and this artificial insemination ought to be left alone.

There is another report from America in which a doctor, Clifford Adams, in the magazine *Pageant*, states that 60 per cent of the women marrying in 1946 will have had pre-marital sexual intercourse. He says that pre-marital chastity is declining so rapidly that it will have reached almost vanishing point in females born after 1940. Among several causes, as he sees it, he stresses the cinema's influence as being one of the most potent: I agree. Everywhere one sees a positive glorification of prostitution. I should think it must be somewhat difficult, now, for an out-and-out prostitute to make any sort of livelihood, when so many pseudo-prostitute women are about.

TUESDAY, 23 APRIL

B. Charles

Shakespeare's birthday! How well I remember this day twenty-seven years ago today. I was with the Fagan Company at the Royal Court Theatre, and we all went to play at the Birthday Performance at the Memorial Theatre, Stratford-upon-Avon, and returned to give the usual evening show at the Court. I thought the Memorial Theatre beautifully situated, and remember, during the intervals, I went on to the banks of the Avon, which flowed right alongside the theatre.

Herbert Brush

8.30 a.m. We are not leaving before lunch and it will be necessary to spend one night on the road home.

7.50 p.m. Salisbury. The Chough is a rambling old hotel and I have difficulty finding my way along its passages. Horace and I are to share a double bed tonight so I hope that he will not be restless and that I shall not turn and twist about in my sleep.

A lot of smoke is rising above the houses and nearly blocked out my view of the cathedral spire. It may be a fire, as the fire engine has just gone in that direction, but I feel too lazy to go out and investigate. It seems that I am losing my bodily energy when even the excitement of a fire cannot make me run towards it.

> A man like me may think that he
> Has walked quite far enough,
> And after tea prefers to be
> At rest within the Chough (chuff)

WEDNESDAY, 24 APRIL

Herbert Brush

Not such a good night's rest as Horace kept on moving about.

George Taylor

One of the tenants on whom my wife calls for rent is a waitress at Thorpe's, a well-known café in Sheffield. My wife wanted to introduce me to this waitress so that I could get good service for lunches, so she reserved a table for tea tonight. The table was reserved all right, but when we arrived, nearly everything was sold out, and we had to have Welsh rarebit, made out of cheese powder.

For years we have deplored the non-existence of a News Theatre in Sheffield, and we said that if there were one we should be frequent visitors. One was opened last September, and tonight we went for the first time. We saw the film *Hitler Lives*. It was one of the most subtly produced hate films that I have seen. Caution is certainly needed in dealing with the German people, but repression is certainly impracticable, even should it be desirable, which I doubt. I cannot think that films such as this help to solve the problem.

FRIDAY, 26 APRIL

George Taylor
An Organisation Committee meeting of the WEA. We drafted the first list of classes for next session, including new ones in Philosophy, Nutrition and Towns and Buildings. I sent circulars to all our four hundred members asking for details of classes desired. Only twelve replies.

SUNDAY, 28 APRIL

B. Charles
Bobby sent me a report of the review of a book, *Antoine* by Antoine. This is, apparently, an autobiography by the celebrated French hairdresser. The review of this piffling book makes the most lamentable reading. Why on earth it was ever allowed to be published now, when we are assured there is a paper scarcity, I can't think! It is all very well for people to argue that the inane goings-on of the so-called Smart Set are of no importance whatever. Here I disagree entirely. I feel convinced, since the Americanisation of Europe, plus the great influence of the cinema, plus the radio, that the vast majority of the female population is immensely influenced by the behaviour of the so-called Smart Set. When Mrs Smith of Golders Green reads that, according to Antoine, the Duchess of Windsor has her hair dressed three times a day by a coiffeur, or a maid, the poor lady in Golders Green is bitterly jealous and tries, in her feeble way, to imitate this stupid woman. Lady Mendl, who was the wife of the British Ambassador in Paris at the beginning of the late war, wants a different hair 'do' every day, and got

Antoine to retire from view for several weeks, to try to evolve a good hair dye for her. This nonsense will, I feel certain, make thousands of women in Great Britain fearfully jealous and unhappy, because they can't requisition the services of some hairdresser to evolve some dye for their hair. When one reads such drivel it makes one think that Hitler was quite justified in thinking the English were utterly effete and wouldn't fight.

TUESDAY, 30 APRIL

Edie Rutherford

I note that the hoaxer who called for fire engines yesterday is being blamed 100 per cent for the killing of children by the fire engine. Seems to me some responsibility belongs to the driver of the engine. One can blame a brewer for an accident by a drunken man, but the courts don't.

Husband came home last evening with the news that his diabetic nephew Tony was involved in a car smash on Saturday night outside Sheffield. Car belonged to father of one of the young folk in the party. Damage £300. Tony is whole but in bed suffering from acute shock. Police brought him home about 2 a.m., moaning. Children are such a blessing, I don't think.

Got cheddar cheese at grocer's today, first time for three years.

THURSDAY, 2 MAY 1946

Edie Rutherford

Two nights ago when the Cup arrived in Derby, VE and VJ nights were nothing in it by comparison for joy and crowds. I give up. A world war ends but nothing like the excitement that silly football cup causes.

Herbert Brush

I went with W on her journey to Margate and Ramsgate. While I was parked in Sandwich a man I used to know as a bowler came across the road, having spotted me in the car, and told me all about his feats on the bowling green. I don't know his name, but that does not matter among bowlers. I inquired after Atkinson, the Borough Accountant of Sandwich, and was sorry to hear he has been in bed for the last eighteen months due to his bad leg, which always seemed to handicap him in the games.

In Margate we had cups of tea in a British Stores on the front. Called in at Dreamland, but the place is closed at present. Butlin, the holiday club magnate, is trying to take the place over.

FRIDAY, 3 MAY

B. Charles

I had a talk to Manson about the house, 56 Bruntsfield Place, that is going to be sold soon. He thinks it is a very good sort of house, and I agree. He fancies it will fetch more than £3,000. In many ways it is exactly the sort of house I should like and to look over it can't do any harm. I think I ought to get well on to £4,000 for the Windsor place, but it is impossible to tell.

Had a talk with a policeman this morning, re the difficulty of the food situation and he thinks it will be years before things improve at all. The idea of having any 'Victory' celebrations is simply farcical.

SATURDAY, 4 MAY

B. Charles

I couldn't help remarking this morning what a lot of very good-looking young people, of both sexes, one sees about now. They seem to be better looking than their fathers and mothers were, but, as soon as they speak, in many cases, the good looks are completely nullified by their manner: so off-hand, so superficial, and they seem to lack all charm. Their manners, certainly, are extremely unattractive. And I think they will age very rapidly. The girls, especially, look years older than they are in reality, and when they get to be about twenty-four or twenty-five, they begin to look so hard and raddled.

SUNDAY, 5 MAY

Edie Rutherford

Last evening we went on a walk through Beeley Woods, cuckoo noisy and lots of other birds singing. Fields masses of dandelions. Disappointed to come upon a notice by Corporation that a road is to be made as far as Underhill Farm. A rash of urban houses, then a bus service. So we lose another country walk, and the city of Sheffield accommodates its citizens.

MONDAY, 6 MAY

B. Charles
I had forgotten, until I read it in the paper, that it is a year today since the Germans collapsed. And it is a year, too, since Davy came to spend the night with me, at Marchmont Road, on his way south. What a dismal year it has been, to be sure!

Herbert Brush
I went to the Tate Gallery to have a look at the Braque and Rouault pictures. Before I could tell what these pictures represented I had to buy a catalogue, price 6d., and even when I found out what the picture was about I could not always find any part of it which looked like its name.

I wanted to laugh out loud when I looked at the picture of a billiard table. People were walking around and looking at these pictures, but I never saw even one smile on a face. I wish I could find out how to appreciate these pictures, if there really is something in them to admire. Maybe sometime I will enthuse about the beauty in *Judge's Head* or *Kitchen Table*.

TUESDAY, 7 MAY

George Taylor
Went along tonight to hear Dr Midgley Turner, the Clinical Tuberculosis Officer, speak of Health and Sanitation. Before the lecture, Dr Turner told me that he had little faith in lectures to lay audiences, and he thought that most health propaganda of no good effect, and that it might even be harmful in creating an over-consciousness of illness. He developed this topic in his lecture as well as dealing with the development of various health services. One thing in the new Health Bill gratified him, and that was the separation of the hospitals from the preventative side now under the control of Medical Officers of Health. Preventative and clinical methods were quite different, he thought. He was not optimistic about research under government control, however, and urged the maximum freedom for medical men.

Questions came without any difficulty and continued right to the last permitted minute. There were a few people with bees in their bonnet, such as an obvious anti-immuniser.

Herbert Brush

It seems to me that the Government are doing a very serious thing by withdrawing all our troops from Egypt; the next thing is that we shall not be allowed to use the Suez Canal route to India. However, if we are to lose India, that won't matter very much. The King will be King of England but not Emperor of India, so some of the coins will have to be reminted. No foreigners will look upon the English as people who cannot be sat upon with impunity.

I wonder whether we shall live long enough to see the end of the British Empire, brought about by the Labour Government. The next thing our Government will want to do is give up the Rock of Gibraltar to Spain, if she asks for it nicely.

B. Charles

Mr Durie seemed to think 56 Bruntsfield Place would be in a bad state of repair and when I went in with Mr Erskine the solicitor this afternoon I found it certainly was! I have never been in such a filthy, disreputable house in my life! IMPOSSIBLE. But it has been a lovely house in its day. There are two lovely rooms, and the garden is delightful, but the cost of getting it into any sort of decent repair would be prodigious. It seems they have already had an offer for it for over £3,000. Before prices reached these fantastic levels, it would not have sold at any price. It might be worth £2,000, but not to me. I hope to find a suitable place soon.

WEDNESDAY, 8 MAY

Maggie Joy Blunt

Cleaning is finished. Cottage now tidier and brighter than it has been for years. I have done it without any help. Mrs Mop has quite deserted me. Cleaning materials used – Octim, Gumption, Scourine, soap flakes, Voltas bleach, Ronuk furniture cream, red tile floor polish, remains of age-old green soap, sugar soap. With 'heatless solder' in tube have repaired bucket, saucepan, watering can, small Valor oil stove – in all of which small holes had appeared. NB for housekeepers: Octim is a wonderful cleaning agent.

Now it is all done I feel enormously triumphant. Want everyone to see it. But the sad fact remains that most of the walls need distempering badly, paint is wearing off here and there, covers and rugs are shabby . . .

THURSDAY, 9 MAY

George Taylor
With a WEA party to the CWS Glass Works at Worksop. We have been fully booked for a long time and have had to turn down several would-be members of the party. Eight people from Worksop joined us on arrival, and we spent an interesting evening watching milk bottles and jam jars being made.

B. Charles
What an extraordinary thing it is that people seem, in a truly amazing fashion, to HAUNT me! This morning Mason asked me if I had seen an advertisement in last night's *Dispatch* about a flat to be sold here. I said no and he phoned his wife for full particulars. The flat is in Chester Street, where I went to try to buy the satinwood cupboard a few weeks ago.

I went with Robertson this afternoon to see the place, and I have an idea I shall buy it. In a great many ways it will suit me excellently, but it is a pity that, as I want three sitting rooms, there will only be two bedrooms. But when it is reconverted, it will be very attractive. The rooms are large and lofty and the entrance good.

SATURDAY, 11 MAY

Edie Rutherford
Spam yesterday, Spam today and Spam tomorrow . . . oh well, I'm sorry.

SUNDAY, 12 MAY

Maggie Joy Blunt
My cousin J was here this weekend. She is still doing work as a dispenser but wants to change into something else as soon as she can. Complains also that it is a dead-end job with little scope for initiative and progress. She has to deal with all the sort of silly people who visit

a doctor's surgery, none of them serious or interesting cases, but all wanting to talk about their imagined ailments to someone. She makes up what are known as 'pacifying' medicines for them – usually coloured soda bicarbonate and water. Something to keep them quiet.

J is, of course, always full of complaints. She was 'born with a grievance'. I admit that her grievances always appear fully justified – she has had to work hard ever since her very inadequate schooling. She can, when well dressed and with the right make-up, command favourable attention, but she is physically unattractive, harsh-voiced and rather brittle in her manners – like a frustrated schoolmistress. As a little girl I remember her pasty, ugly, sullen, and all the family, the vast family of Blunt cousins, laughed at her, her and her mother's ideas, which were considered affected. We were all thoroughly nasty to her. She has told me since how sensitive she was, how often she cried. Yet now I have more in common with her than any of my other cousins who have long since married and been lost to me in the concerns of their families. J and I are the two Old Maids of our generation.

NB: I spent about seven years at a good girls' public school, five years at University College London and three years in my father's office . . . yet follow instinctively all my untrained, domestic, feminine inclinations. Excepting only the inclination which I should have, and haven't – to have children.

TUESDAY, 14 MAY

George Taylor
The new railway timetables have been in operation all week, but I have still to see a new guide, or even a list of the main alterations. The stations have none for sale, the local guide for May is not yet published, no *Bradshaw* or any official guide is available at the public library, and there has been neither public advertisement nor even a news paragraph in the local press. The railways have certainly preserved the mystery of their running pretty well, and I don't think a Government department could do much better in that direction.

THURSDAY, 16 MAY

Herbert Brush
The BBC gave notice of a frost in this area tonight so I have been busy covering my tomatoes with newspapers. Of course it gives people the chance to say, Never put tomatoes out in May, for you may be sure some will be lost, for certainly there will be frost, or weather cold enough to kill; however, risk it if you will. Note the rhyme in the above sentence.

FRIDAY, 17 MAY

B. Charles
When I was reading *Cavalcade* last night I saw a long notice, with a photograph of Antoine, of his recent drivelling autobiography. When one considers this has been published during the paper shortage, and when one reads the most eulogistic reviews of this book, one realises, I think, how very deep the utter rot has set in with regard to the vast majority of women. Unless there had been an enormous demand for this sort of drivel among all sorts and conditions of women, such a book would never have been published at such a time as this.

The following is a sample of what may be expected in this book: 'The Duchess of Windsor, who painted the rooms of the Governor's Palace, at Nassau, the colour of her face powder; Joan Crawford with red nails, toes and mouth . . . This cavalcade of lovely women adds a small glittering page to this history of our time, reflecting, as it does, the elegance, hedonism, vanity and futility of the international smart set whose pleasure, between the wars, appeared to be the result of industrial civilisation.'

Went to the meeting at 17 Chester Street at 4 p.m. and have agreed to buy the house. I don't think I shall do better. Of course £3,500 is quite enough to pay. It is supposed to be ready for occupation on 28 November. I like it very much in a great many ways, and think I shall be able to make it very attractive. It is a relief to have got a house after all this wandering around.

SATURDAY, 18 MAY

Herbert Brush

From the news this morning it seems that we are to go with less so that the Germans may have more. I wonder what excuse Morrison will have for letting the Germans have our wheat, wheat sent by Canada for hungry mouths in England, not for the greedy guts. Personally I don't believe in starving myself so that my past, present and future enemies may have plenty to eat. Our present Prime Minister seems to be a nonentity, unless he is really pulling many strings in the background, and I don't think he is clever enough to do that.

The revolving bird scarers which I made for the plot in 1940 are still working perfectly as far as revolving goes, but birds have grown used to them now and don't mind perching on them.

TUESDAY, 21 MAY

Edie Rutherford

I regret the purchase of the Jones sewing machine as have endless trouble with it. Wonder if I could get it overhauled, or if I should cut the loss and buy a new one.

I wonder why starch remains scarce. During the war we were told that shortage was because nurses in hospitals needed so much. Now I suppose if one pressed one would be told it is owing to export trade. Starcheen is off now also.

Poor David Niven. What a terrible way to lose his young wife. I remember we read a book a few years ago, titled *Hollywood Through the Back Door*, or something like that, in which the writer suffered a similar accident, walking through a door which led onto a staircase, and being taken to hospital where he lay for many weeks before he recovered. With all her swank, USA has her faults in many ways, architectural among others.

WEDNESDAY, 22 MAY

Herbert Brush

I had toe ache for hours in bed last night. Then I dreamed that there was a knock at the front door and when I opened it two men with nags said they had been sent by the Government to billet themselves here. While I argued with them that there was no room, two more came and managed to get into the house, then some more men and two women appeared and they all crowded into the various rooms and began to make themselves comfortable and to read my books. I counted them up and found there were twenty-three with others coming. One was drunk so I began to put him out, but suddenly thought that a really drunk man would be less trouble as he would go to sleep in a corner.

Can you interpret a dream like that?

B. Charles

Before I went out this afternoon, I wrote a letter to the *New Statesman & Nation* about the dramatic criticism of the revue *Sweetest and Lowest* by Stephen Potter in the recent issue. The way it is now the fashion to joke about homosexuality in many revues is an amazing change in public taste. Why, a few years ago, if you *mentioned* the subject, in the most guarded way possible, you were criticised: now it is the subject for jokes! It is very difficult to know what the average person thinks about it. I feel, of course, that there are a very great many people who do not realise that there is such a thing as congenital homosexuality at all. They seem to imagine that when a man indulges in such a thing, that he is merely giving way to a passing phase. And, of course, I am sure very many people do not imagine that anything really sexual takes place.

There was a letter from the British Peoples Party this p.m., telling me there is going to be a meeting, in Edinburgh, on 7 June to try to get a branch of the party going in Edinburgh. They want me to attend. I have replied that I shall try to do so.

MONDAY, 27 MAY

Herbert Brush

The Reading Room at the BM is closed until next week, so I went to the Victoria and Albert Museum. It will be a long time before the museum is complete again, and there are so many huge rooms still quite empty and bare. At Kensington Gardens barricades are being put up to control traffic on V day. I don't think I shall venture into the crush. The authorities evidently expect a little roughness, as they are protecting things in Trafalgar Square. I call this Victory March just damned foolishness, a waste of money, a thing which no one wants as far as I can hear.

Went with W to the Odeon Cinema in Goose Green. The picture was not very accurate, as Ronald Colman, after being wounded in the Zulu war, came back to London and the Tower Bridge appeared in the distance, though it was not built until a long time afterwards.

Maggie Joy Blunt

At hairdresser's this morning I was asked if I was going to see the Victory Parade. Have no intention of doing so. No interest. No one I have met has any. As hairdresser says, we feel, 'It is all such a waste, so meaningless, with people starving in Europe and things no better and even worse than they were a year ago.' But we suppose many people may go at the last moment. There are sure to be thousands there who would go to any sort of pageant and like being pushed around.

Journalistic work for myself rather difficult at the moment. All periodicals so short of space. Am making interim plans. Influence, or 'knowing the right people', has its value. Take CL, for instance – she is an extremely capable young woman with her needle and can design clothes; she is also very attractive and has charm, but she knows through her artist parents and her well-connected (socially) husband a great many people with the right sort of influence and is never without work of some sort or another. It was by introduction that she got some work as photographer's model, and also training as a mannequin, and, again by introduction, she is to start in August, I think, as a full-time mannequin to a designer opening an establishment in London. She will be his only model and will have clothes specially designed for her to display, and will receive £7 a week. She should be a huge success.

My friend June said last week: 'Do you remember, we used to have a 9 p.m. post delivery before the war?' (they are getting two to three deliveries a day now in Hampstead), 'And those gorgeous fat dates we could buy in long pink boxes? How one does forget! I wonder when all the nice things *will* be back in the shops.'

TUESDAY, 28 MAY

Edie Rutherford

I can understand that Eisenhower is too booked up to come for our Victory Parade, but I think it is an insult on Russia's part in not accepting our invitation to send a contingent of men, who just cannot be too booked up to come, out of all the Red Army. I expect it is the usual desire of that country to keep their ordinary folk behind a wall.

WEDNESDAY, 29 MAY

Maggie Joy Blunt

Flowers out are: Spanish iris, geum, violas, pansies, rhododendron, wild garlic.

Nearly over are: forget-me-nots, lilac, polyanthus, tulips.

In bud: rambler roses, oriental poppies, foxgloves, peonies, ever-lasting pea, Madonna lilies.

THURSDAY, 30 MAY

Edie Rutherford

I omitted yesterday to record a comment on *The Brains Trust* of the previous night. The question asked whether the phone had destroyed the art of letter writing. From the answers you'd have thought every home in the UK has a phone. No doubt all those round the table had phones and have had for years, but that obtains in so few homes that I could not help realising how *The Brains Trust* is NOT representative of the people. No one thought to point out that phones are the luxury of the few. We, for instance, have never been able to afford one.

To refer to another *Brains Trust* matter, I agree with the *Daily Mirror* which has a leader on it. Railways should be all one class, but I would have non-talking as well as non-smoking compartments, so that when a person needed quiet time for study he or she could be sure of it. Also, anyone so snobby they can't talk to fellow beings can stay in a no-talking carriage and good luck to same.

B. Charles

A long letter from Bobby this morning. He sent me a cutting from a Newcastle paper, a letter from some woman who said the men of today seemed to be very effeminate, and seemed to wish to be as glamorous as a Hollywood film hero. It seems he has seen some of them combing their hair in the street while looking into shop windows. He goes on to say that with men like this, and women dressed in trousers, and with bobbed hair, it is at times difficult to know which is the male and which is the female. This masculinisation of women and effeminisation of men is an interesting present-day phenomenon.

FRIDAY, 31 MAY

Edie Rutherford

I'd like to be in London for the Victory Parade but not unless I had a seat. No signs of any preparations in our city. Description by BBC reporter of London's preparations makes one envious.

SATURDAY, 1 JUNE 1946

Edie Rutherford

Cricket balls rationed. What a calamity. Ha ha.

I see that bread rationing is again being mentioned. Good. A whole good cauliflower was in our pig bin yesterday. Folk ought to grow their own vegetables, then they'd know what it means . . .

Herbert Brush

Why do people on the broadcasts always say 'Well' before they start a remark? And why do announcers always shout the last word as loud as they can, especially when introducing a performer whose name is supposed to be well known to listeners?

B. Charles

There is a great deal of cynicism about the Victory Celebrations. People seem to think it is positively absurd to pretend there is any cause for them. I agree. It seems amazing to read in today's paper about everything being in readiness for bread rationing, and then to recollect that next Saturday there are these absurd celebrations!

I believe everything is going to be closed: shops, restaurants, etc, so there will be nothing to do but stop at home, as everywhere will be packed and there will be no chance of getting in anywhere for a meal. The international situation seems to be extremely ominous at present, and possibly as I feel a bit dull and lonely tonight, I can't help remembering what H. G. Wells wrote in the book *Mind at the End of Its Tether* about a fearful 'queerness' having come into everything. Certainly just now things to me seem excessively 'queer'.

Chapter Nine

THE IMAGE OF HER MOTHER

KILL those PESTS
that *CRAWL* or *FLY*
the **EXTRA POWER**
makes sure they *DIE*

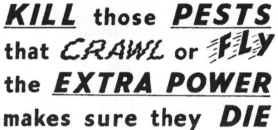

SECTO
EXTRA POWER.
D.D.T.

'Britain's Super Insect Killer'

Liquid & Powder from Chemists, etc.

INSIST ON SECTO

Gave the chest another going over with DDT: new uses discovered every day

'Why is reception in many parts of Britain so much worse than before the war? Is the BBC treatment of authors as unfair as the Society of Authors believes? How much justification is there for the complaints so widely made by members of the BBC staff? And finally, can an adequate Parliamentary control of BBC policy be discovered, which avoids the danger of Parliamentary dictation?'

New Statesman & Nation, *29 June 1946*

'Two British films take the floor this week; on average two British films take the floor every week, and whenever that happens it is D-Day for quite a lot of people.

The process that put them on the floor probably began before Christmas 1945. It began with a man sitting in a West End office worrying about a girl in the Midlands he will never meet. She is aged between 17 and 22, goes to the cinema 30 times a year – mostly in March and April, sits in the middle stalls, stays 3 hours 10 minutes 10.23 seconds, and has 1s. 9d. in her purse. She is the Average British Film Fan; he is a Film Producer. He has a hunch that he knows what she wants . . . and is prepared to back this hunch to the extent of £20,000 or £200,000.'

Picture Post *on a booming industry, May 1946*

MONDAY, 3 JUNE

Herbert Brush
Green Park is full of planes of all sorts and sizes for the Victory
Parade, and they are busy fixing up chestnut fences in Hyde Park. I
went to have a look at the demonstration allotments which are still
being kept up by the Ministry of Agriculture. The land girl, or rather
the land woman, was there, and I talked to her about the various
vegetables she was growing, some of which are better and some not
so good as mine.

I met Mr Ing in the street, and he had a lot to say about the mighty
pageant prepared to celebrate victory before the victors begin to
starve.

Edie Rutherford
Paper today lists the animals to be used in atom bomb tests –
Husband says the animals should be spared and Goering & Co. be
sent to take their places.

I omitted to record my disgust last Friday of the Radio Doctor
actually saying constipation is made too much of, that it doesn't
matter as much as some say, that indeed many people feel better
when constipated! Really, it is time that man was shouted down.

We aren't making any headway re our annual holidays. I shudder
when I think of bulging trains and my tired feet and Husband's tired
spine. Then if the bed isn't comfy and the food poor, we'll want to
come home. All the same, we would like some sea air. We feel we
deserve it too.

TUESDAY, 4 JUNE

B. Charles
Thought Ruth Draper last night absolutely MARVELLOUS. I don't
know when I have enjoyed anything at the theatre so much. It is
uncanny how she seems to manage to create the impression that the
stage is crowded with people. I think 'Opening A Bazaar' really a
perfectly lovely thing! But to me her greatest *tour de force* was 'Vive La
France'. She gave it in French, and I don't suppose half the audience
understood a word she was saying, but her genius is such that she held
the whole theatre spellbound by the nervous intensity of her acting.

This morning I went to West Linton to the view. It is needless to say that the bus was crowded. WHERE DO ALL THESE WOMEN COME FROM? It makes one wonder if, perhaps, the ancient custom of female infanticide may not have been necessary after all! But seriously, where do all these women come from?

WEDNESDAY, 5 JUNE

Maggie Joy Blunt
N has persuaded me to stay with her next Friday and Saturday night. 'I propose,' she writes, 'that we both go down to this club (near the Haymarket) somewhere in middle of Saturday morning. They are putting on a Victory meal with drinks for 5/-. We shall be in the midst of what I feel to be rather a ridiculous procession and celebration with "atomic warfare" written across the future skies, and "starvation" across the present earth.' But as somebody has said, 'it is a poor heart that never rejoices', and therefore I shall rejoice that these terrors didn't come to us under Nazi domination of Europe.

THURSDAY, 6 JUNE

Edie Rutherford
In town yesterday the only sign of decoration I saw was one Union Jack outside Woolworth's, though Husband says LMS station was being decorated till the gale threatened to blow the men away, so they had to postpone the job to a calmer day.

So Italy is done with its King. One by one they go. I wonder where this family will go. Husband says Bucks or Surrey. I say no, Egypt seems the haven for kings now, Zog and Umberto's pa recently gone there, so let the rest follow. How Moseley can deny that he had money from Italy in face of the evidence is difficult to understand. How we can let his kind have their freedom is even more difficult to understand.

As for that poor eleven-year-old king of Iraq who arrived yesterday for a holiday here, poor little wretch. Will he ever reign?

Herbert Brush
Coming back I met Ing in the road. As usual he had yarns to tell. He always has the latest bit of news. Apparently the tall postman who

has delivered letters and parcels here has been caught pinching things and when the police visited his house they found about a ton of things which he had stolen. I don't think that he took any things addressed to No. 25.

According to Ing, the landlord of the Woodman, PH, went as usual to see the Derby. When there he telephoned and told his family to tell all his friends to put their shirts on Airborne. Of course his family rushed out and put money on the horse, which won. Ing was of the opinion that there was a wangle somewhere.

FRIDAY, 7 JUNE

Edie Rutherford

Children are on holidays and building up a bonfire for Saturday night. Up to yesterday the wind blew away their pile as fast as they accumulated. I could not number the times they've been door to door for stuff to burn.

Authority has turned down my application to send a fiver to my god-daughter in British Columbia for a wedding present. I want to go out and kick someone.

SATURDAY, 8 JUNE, VICTORY DAY

Edie Rutherford

Midday. So, it has started to rain on London's procession. I turned on radio at 10 a.m. to listen in as I did housework. When it got to the piping, husband could bear no more and switched off. So I went to fifth floor to feed cat in our care over the weekend. Am now back and, as Husband is out, am listening in.

Went next door a few minutes ago. Both teachers sewing and listening in – won't miss a word. Thrilled. When Churchill's behaviour was mentioned, Husband said it sounded as if he woke with his whisky bottle this morning. Knowing his reputation, that is possible. On the other hand, I think if anyone on this earth is entitled to lose his head today, that man is WC. This is what he lived and strove for for years, defiantly, confidently and magnificently. This day is enough to go to his head without whisky.

It is just one continual cheer now. What a sight it must be. I do hope we see the coloured film. Husband wants to see it but not if it

230

means a queue. How the crowd responds to music! What defiance to the rain! Well, if we let our climate hinder us ever, we'd get no place, never.

Now the Dominions – Canada. Now the Aussies. Three VCs . . . New Zealand, VC & bar. Oh, I'm so glad South African natives have been included. I'd give a lot to hear one of them describe it all afterwards.

I think Goering & Co. should have been brought over to see all this. I hope that young King of Iraq or is it Iran (I never can sort them out, Iraq I think) will read, mark, learn and inwardly digest what he sees today.

I MUST get lunch or I'll be divorced.

Got the dinner all on . . . I do think the souvenir programme of today in London should be on sale outside London. Have just been to pig bin. The children are building up their bonfire.

George Taylor

We celebrated Victory Day by having an extra hour in bed, but later I had an hour in the garden. After lunch we had arranged to go with the WEA to Ashford. Most of the members joined the dance, and the district secretary of the association even acted as judge of the fancy dresses. He told me that he played safe by awarding the prize to the youngest competitor.

B. Charles

I have seen no 'celebrations' at all. There are a good many people milling around the town, much in the same way as they do on any Sunday night. There are big crowds outside the cinemas, but all the pubs seemed to be closed by 8 p.m. Probably because they are sold out. There is very little rowdyism. I think various public buildings are going to be floodlit later and I think there is going to be a fireworks display. But I shall be in bed before these festivities start.

Maggie Joy Blunt

With N at Swiss Cottage. We did not feel very enthusiastic about celebrating 'Victory' but wanted to see something of what was going on. We got up and listened to the BBC broadcast of proceedings. N could not decide what to wear, weather uncertain – looked as though it might turn fine later, so she put on new cotton frock coat and smart straw hat. But as we left the house it was beginning to rain so we went back for mackintosh and umbrella. Travelled by tube to Piccadilly without any discomfort. People coming and going at station entrance wearing emblems and silly hats. We went straight to the club, off the Haymarket, run mainly for Canadian women. Lunch for about seventy had been prepared by the staff, two of whom had been up till 5.30 previous morning. Large plates of mixed cold meats (ham, tongue, sausage meat) and generous helpings of salad, trifle with fresh strawberries, cheddar and camembert, cream cracker biscuits and draught beer at 5/- a head.

About 1 p.m. N's friend and her husband arrived – they had slipped out with periscopes to see what they could. They were very surprised that the periscopes worked. Very soon after this we heard the planes passing over and dashed out to watch, N's chief interest being to see the Vampires. Decided to have a look round immediately afterwards, but by then it was raining far too hard. We waited in comfortable lounge about half an hour, then decided we would go home, rest, and come back later to see the fireworks. But when we reached Piccadilly tube, bedraggled sightseers were queuing into the streets outside each of the station entrances. Too much for N, who felt quite unable to cope with crowds, so we returned to club where we stayed until 4 p.m. The rain just fell down as though tipped from a bucket. This was the BBC's 'thundery showers'! People looked sodden and sorry for themselves. Several groups had picnicked in adjacent doorways and stayed there.

At about 4 p.m. we left for home without difficulty. We listened to the radio, I knitted, and we supped off haddock, salad and an apple each. At 10 p.m. we went out to Primrose Hill. Rain had stopped. Many people with the same idea. We could see dome of St Paul's floodlit, and the Abbey Road Building Society tower. Fireworks had begun. A searchlight behind us was circling the sky, answering distant searchlights. For one moment it swung low and spotlighted St Paul's and the trees and roofs in its path were lit dramatically. The hill was muddy. People moved from point to point. Many children and dogs among them and babies asleep in prams. The crowd sighed delightedly 'ooh – ah!' every time fireworks shone through drifting clouds. N supported herself against a tree. We didn't stay to the end but came back and made ourselves cups of chocolate from a packet sent to N from America.

SUNDAY, 9 JUNE

Edie Rutherford
We had friends in to a meal last evening. I had a tin of Heinz tomato soup so we had that, lengthened with stock from pressure cooker last Sunday. Then cold beef from tin sent me from Durban, with salads. Then the tin of peaches we got on ration some weeks back, with jelly from my sister and mock cream. All very good and self highly praised. We played cards afterwards. Gave up a quarter after midnight, and settled up the 2d. I was down.

Herbert Brush
Last evening we went out in the car to try to see something of the firework display on the Thames, but the air was misty. Every high spot was crowded with cars and people, all looking towards London, and someone had a wireless set in a car and we could listen to a description of the firework show.

TUESDAY, 11 JUNE

B. Charles
This morning, while waiting for the tram, I got into conversation with a young Egyptian at the university here. He told me there is no food rationing at all in Egypt, that life there is just like it was before the war, and less expensive than here. Of course, I really ought to pack up entirely in Europe, and go and live quietly in Cairo. He told me the English are far from popular at the moment, but he thinks when the British troops are all gone that things will be better in every way. I gave him my address, and asked him to call and see me sometime, if he has nothing better to do.

I see by today's paper that the amount of litter and destruction left behind by all the stupid Victory celebration crowds is enormous. Scores of German prisoners of war are being drafted in to London to clear up the mess.

Gave the chest another going over with DDT.

Edie Rutherford
My worry at the moment is that the cat, Smudge, of which we have the care over the holiday, has gone and got lost. We had him here on

Sunday but he was so obviously unhappy that we took him home on Sunday evening. When we went yesterday evening to feed him, he had gone. A small window had been left open and his owner was quite sure he would not attempt to get out. But he MUST have done so. I have been on the roof calling four times now, and into the basement, all round the grounds and surrounding streets. I gave caretaker a notice for board the moment we discovered the loss and went to him just now asking him to please display it, as I may be wasting time searching while someone has the cat in a flat. I feel wild about this loss. Whatever shall I say to Dorothy if Smudge isn't found when she returns? I'm not clear if she comes today or tomorrow.

WEDNESDAY, 12 JUNE

Edie Rutherford

I liked Mr Attlee's speech at Bournemouth yesterday. The more I hear the man, the better I like him. Sober, calm, dignified, just what we need for this time of pulling up our socks. I think, given time, he will grow on the people and become gradually liked. It always takes longer for unspectacular goodness to be appreciated. I've noticed that.

Dorothy came back last night and met someone who told her Smudge is lost. So that relieved me of that though I felt awful about it. She searched from roof to basement, calling, as I've done more times than I can now number. No luck. I asked her to have coffee and sandwiches with us but she could only take coffee, too upset to eat. She doesn't blame us, of course. We've looked after her cats for years. He is no doubt cowering in a dark place somewhere, too terrified to move. I am constantly dashing out to look for a black and white cat which someone tells me they've seen here and there.

THURSDAY, 13 JUNE

Maggie Joy Blunt

Letter from brother in Alexandria dated 9 June and sent Air Mail, received yesterday morning. He says: 'There have been two demonstrations recently where the crowd was shouting "Long live the British", "Bring back the English soldiers", "We want work", and so on. As the British are closing down and moving out, thousands of Egyptians are becoming unemployed. They say there are already

120,000 in Cairo and some 80,000 in Alexandria who have lost jobs owing to the British installations shutting.'

FRIDAY, 14 JUNE

George Taylor
One of our farmer clients has been complaining of opencast coal mining. It seems that one of his 20-acre fields was threatened, and he consulted the superintendent of the work as to the probable date when it would be required. He was told that it would be safe to sow. He sowed, and the crop was nearly ready. Then he was warned that working would start the following Monday. He asked for a fortnight's grace in which to gather the wheat, but was refused. It was no concern of the opencast department that 20 acres of wheat would be lost. However, the men did not turn up on the Monday, neither did they on the Tuesday. On Wednesday a few came and worked until Friday. Next week was August Bank holiday, and no work was done all week. Finally the field was torn up, and the crop destroyed the week later. Thus, for the sake of three days' work, a good crop of wheat was wasted.

Edie Rutherford
Yesterday afternoon I went for our ration books, only about ten minutes wait. Suppose we dare not hope these will be our last. When I said so last evening, Husband said we'd be rationed for five years yet. I told him not to be so daft. Another year perhaps but not longer than that, surely?

In the little street over the way where the bomb fell which took our windows out that time, the eight houses that were demolished are now to be rebuilt. Foundations are started on. Not prefabs, real houses.

Found the cat Smudge yesterday, thank God. There is a 6-inch slit between ground floor verandah and rock garden, which opens out wider to a small hole. There he crouched, a friend airing her two dogs saw him and fetched me. I had a job coaxing him out and then he struggled so hard that the friend whipped off her coat and we threw it over him. I was determined that I would not let him go. Got to his fifth-floor flat safely and Smudge purred like mad when he realised where he was. I fed him and his owner brought him to see us when she got back in from work at 5.30. She is of course thrilled to bits to have him back. Little beast.

Herbert Brush

Last evening W, D and I went in the car to see the illuminations in London, but we did not see much except cars and crowds of people. We wanted to go through St James's Park but every route was blocked and we had to crawl along Whitehall at less than walking pace. We thought there might be a chance to go along the Mall from the other end, but it was no use. We spent about a quarter of an hour passing the back wall of Buckingham Palace. Then we thought it would be clever to go along the river and past the Tate Gallery, but we found the way blocked and had to cross Lambeth Bridge. After that we gave up and went home.

On our return there was a notice from the police that on 29 May W had committed some offence against the Highway Code. W had no recollection of doing anything, so off we went to the police station to inquire what it meant. Found out that W was supposed to have killed a dog by running over it with the car, and the owner, a woman, was trying to claim £2.

I looked up in my diary and found that I was not with W in the car that day, so could not say anything in the matter, but W is quite certain that she did not run over a dog.

MONDAY, 17 JUNE

Edie Rutherford

I thought our new Food Minister very good last night. I am quite sure his aim to be frank with us at all times is right. At first, it was odd to hear the Strachey voice speaking other than a war commentary. I liked his emphasis on the moral reason for feeding others even at great cost to ourselves, even our ex-enemies. I hope still that bread rationing comes. It won't be a calamity but a blessing, to us and to others. I'm all for forcing folk to do what is right if they won't bother to do it otherwise: why should a child die in India because a woman here is thriftless and thoughtless?

Dorothy just called to say she has lost Smudge again.

TUESDAY, 18 JUNE

Herbert Brush

I was on the plot for a couple of hours this morning. I think that every bird that comes into the field perches on the crossbar over my runner beans and uses it as a lavatory.

I was busy cutting grass along the edges of the footways when I saw three men with large sheets of paper going from plot to plot, evidently judging the merits and awarding points, so I packed up and cleared off just as they were coming as I did not want to influence them in any way, not even by pointing out the flooded nature of the ground.

Maggie Joy Blunt

Still no Mrs Mop. Am going to advertise in local papers. But classified ads restricted. In some papers, e.g. the *New Statesman*, one has to wait at least eight weeks before insertion.

Yesterday hairdresser suggested that people smoking more because they were hungry. A cigarette does often seem to fill a gap one would have filled at one time with a biscuit, apple or chocolate.

Am now reduced to rolling own cigarettes.

WEDNESDAY, 19 JUNE

Edie Rutherford

Now that Princess Elizabeth is being dressed ten years above her age, she looks the image of her mother. There are comments on all sides about the too-grown-up way she has appeared since the Victory parade. It makes her sister looks very juvenile by comparison too. Are we being got ready, as an Empire, for the betrothal of the heir to the throne, and is she being made to look of marriageable age, so that no one can think what a kid she looks, given as a lamb to the slaughter?

THURSDAY, 20 JUNE

Herbert Brush

I met Ing in the road, and he told me that he went to Brighton on Tuesday, a church outing arranged by his wife without his knowledge. It rained in torrents all the time and the wind nearly blew some of them into the sea.

'Never again,' said Ing. 'Fourpence for a half-full cup of tea and 18 pence for a sandwich is not playing the game.' Then he told me of a new dodge in the ladies' lavatories. A woman can get in all right, but she has to put a penny in the slot before she can get out. I wonder whether that yarn can be correct; Ing said his wife told him about it. I pass on the yarn in case you might get caught without a penny to get out.

FRIDAY, 21 JUNE

Edie Rutherford
All this Palestine business is ridiculous. We can't be being firm enough. Kidnapping our men, three days they've had them now. Ridiculous.

To town yesterday to lunch – my turn to take a friend. Cost me 8/- and I could have done far, far better at home. We had a salad composed of two lettuce leaves, one tiny piece of tomato, one slice radish, three new potatoes and a small piece of mayonnaise-smothered fish called salmon on menu, in fact our old friend cod. Then a sweet with a fancy name which turned out to be a piece of two-coloured sponge cake with a blob of ersatz cream on top. I came home hungry.

SATURDAY, 22 JUNE

B. Charles
Met an interesting young fellow at dinner. He is now demobbed and has done a lot of time in Germany in the army. He says the devastation is awful, a town like Cologne just flat. He told me when he saw all the havoc the RAF had wrought that he did not feel proud of the achievement. He told me that the old people and the young ones are suffering very badly through privation. I asked, as the devastation was so awful, where the people were living. And he could only infer that they were living in cellars, though he had never actually seen any people living there. In the daytime it seems the streets are crowded with people.

Herbert Brush
A police sergeant came to see W about her alleged running over the dog in Lordship Lane. W never felt anything or she would have

stopped. The owner of the dog says she has a witness to prove her case, but I am doubtful.

SUNDAY, 23 JUNE

George Taylor

A WEA weekend school in Sheffield. It was a gloriously hot morning, so we had the lecture outside on the lawn. And what a lecture. I was certainly enthralled with Mr Packington's talk on 'The Origin of Life'. He started off with an explanation of the laws of probability, then showed how through these it might be expected that the extremely rare but absolutely necessary condition of a strictly limited range of temperatures, humidity and atmospheric pressure would occur and so make the commencement of life inevitable. He went on to discuss the possible origins, and as his considered guess hazarded that viruses might be the first form, followed by bacteria and then the unicellular plants and animals. I have never heard this line of development so clearly and convincingly argued, and I think that all the students were spellbound. The chairman, a politician, was certainly out of his depth, and I could not but compare the unsatisfactory shallowness of a normal political discourse with the very profound discussion of Mr Packington.

B. Charles

There is a long article in today's *Sunday Times* about a new biography of Oscar Wilde. It is interesting to see today how freely the subject of homosexuality is discussed, even in the most 'stodgy' sort of papers. Yet I doubt if this free discussion of the subject is any indication that the general public view it in any more tolerant way than they did when the Wilde scandal was on the go. Sometimes I think they are less tolerant.

I have always thought, and I still think, that all the hullabaloo about sex is due to the fact that it produces a pleasant sensation. Had it produced an unpleasant one, I am sure we should all of us have been driven, if necessary with whips, to indulge in it.

Maggie Joy Blunt

Finished knitting a dishcloth to the Alf Hale programme. I like the Hales and have been an admirer of Binnie since I first fell for her in

239

Bow Bells (1932 or '33 I think). Those thirties – when I was in my twenties – didn't seem so long ago. The six years of war has been an interval when 'nothing' happened. That's how I feel about it, although a great deal actually did, to me personally as well as to the world in general. I think I mean that the thirties don't seem so out-of-date as the pre-war years of the last war did.

MONDAY, 24 JUNE

Herbert Brush

It has been spitting with rain all morning so I have done a few odd jobs under cover, such as soldering up a hole in a kettle and a couple of holes in a zinc bath. By the way, I noticed a word on the side of a bus today which looks like a mutilation of the English language: 'Schweppervesence'. It may be a good advertisement but it looks to me like German.

THURSDAY, 27 JUNE

George Taylor

My wife had an old friend to tea and I arrived home just in time to say 'good evening'. It is strange that although this friend has a fruiterer's shop, she cannot get rhubarb. We supplied her with some, which she is going to sell. I think that this is the first time that any of our produce has been marketed, although we are not getting any of the proceeds.

Herbert Brush

How very quickly this month seems to have gone. When I went to see my bank manager this morning for him to certify that I am still alive, we both agreed that it only seemed like last week when I called on him to do the same job.

I wonder what is really going to happen in the Pacific tomorrow night when they explode the first atomic bomb. I hope that we shall not feel anything if something goes wrong with the experiment. The explosion may have some effect on the atmosphere over a very large area, and this may spread round the world like it did when the mountain Krakatoa blew up many years ago.

FRIDAY, 28 JUNE

George Taylor

In the evening we walked over to Totley and spent the evening with my brother and his family. We stayed to hear the dropping of the atom bomb, but as reception was so bad, we left at 10.45 p.m. for our hour's journey home. When we arrived back, I rushed to switch on to find that the bomb had been dropped at 11.20 p.m. and the sound of the explosion had failed to come through. I think my sister-in-law was almost afraid to listen to the broadcast, and after reading the account of the Hiroshima bomb, the whole affair seemed pretty dreadful to me.

SATURDAY, 29 JUNE

B. Charles

As I was going to the Hallé concert last night George Hobson passed and said 'Goodnight', but he never stopped. I followed him down the road for a little way, and I saw him glance in a shop window to see if I was following! Really his behaviour is most eccentric. This morning, as I was turning into this street, I saw him some little way behind on his cycle. He did not come down Warrender Park Road, but went the long way round to Marchmont Street. An interesting case of Apprehension Psychology if ever there was one!

I went and tried to get some oatmeal this morning and found it had all disappeared under the counter. Not an oat to be found.

MONDAY, 1 JULY 1946

Edie Rutherford

Husband gets the idea the atom bomb has been a disappointment. I hope it has. I went to bed last night when he turned on for the relay. The awful atmosphere sounded to me too much like the wailings of the poor animals we beastly humans have put on the ships for test.

A woman was telling me yesterday that her baker says that what is worrying his customers is not the amount of bread allowed but the fact that they won't be able to eat bread hot as they are accustomed to doing. He says most of his customers come into his shop three or four times a day so that they can get bread hot from the ovens. Well, it is time that stopped. Apart from the extravagance of it, it is not good to eat hot bread and it is at the root of much illness.

The Government should put a dozen nutrition folk on the air for the next few months to enlighten the ignorance of the masses on 1. The amount of starch the body needs as distinct from its wants, 2. The need for chewing properly as the digestion of starch commences in the mouth, 3. What too much starch does to the system.

Herbert Brush

I had made a mental note to see 'Germany under Control' in an exhibition in Oxford Street. The place was nearly hot enough to satisfy my wish that Hitler should go to a warm place, but there was only one painting of him there, which made him look fit for a straitjacket. There were also a few old German weapons and various models of U-boats and such like. One weapon I noticed was a rifle with a bent barrel as though it was meant for firing round a corner. I can't imagine it would be very deadly.

TUESDAY, 2 JULY

B. Charles

I gave [recently purchased Persian] carpet a good do with DDT powder. There is a little moth at one corner, but it is a very beautiful carpet and it ought to look extremely well in Chester Street. It is the finest carpet I have ever handled.

I went out for a short stroll, but it seemed impossible to get a drink anywhere, as almost all the pubs were shut (this is usual, now, on Tuesdays). It is owing to the beer shortage. I didn't see anyone I knew, and came back about 8.15. I then read a review, in *Time and Tide*, of that book by Antoine, the hairdresser. The reviewer finishes the review by saying that this book is a 'terrible indictment'.

This book – I really ought to read it. It will be a valuable contribution to the future historian in getting at the contributory causes of the decline of the birth rate in Great Britain, and in fact the whole world. To say nothing of it shedding light on the decline of home life, the increase of divorces and the general 'rottenness' of present-day society.

WEDNESDAY, 3 JULY

Edie Rutherford

Last evening we went to City Hall – I actually had Himself with me – to see a show put on by the employees of Newton, Chambers & Co., an iron and coal firm near Sheffield, employing today between eight thousand and nine thousand people. Celebrating fifty years since the first Mr Newton and Mr Chambers started. Five hundred people took part in the show. Their own orchestra and brass band and male voice choir and dancers. Wonderful stage setting and beautiful dressing of everyone in every period of the past 150 years.

THURSDAY, 4 JULY

Edie Rutherford

Husband is much concerned re conditions in his timber trade. Says lots of firms have already had to close and unless Russia can be persuaded to trade, more will have to go. Moreover, we still don't get as much coal to Sweden as she wants so that we can get worthwhile shipments of timber from there. Is there nothing we can make that Russia wants so desperately that she'll discuss timber with us?

Spent 6/6d. on a tin of Cooper's insect spray today, contains DDT.

SUNDAY, 7 JULY

George Taylor

One of the few days in the year when we could sunbathe in the garden. I did this so effectively that my feet, legs and arms were a glorious red before I realised it. Accordingly, I had to use some calamine lotion, one bottle of which, significantly, has lasted already seven years, and is only one quarter empty now.

MONDAY, 8 JULY

George Taylor

Following a board meeting of an engineering company we had lunch together, and going back to the works my two colleagues remarked on the decorations in town to celebrate the jubilee of municipal transport here. Both were disgusted that considerably more display was being made than the few rags which were put out for Victory Day.

B. Charles
Visited the theatre with Bobby. It was fearfully hot. The play, *Clutterbuck*, rather like weak Noël Coward, but it was very well acted. We had a high tea at the British Restaurant and afterwards went to look at the outside of Chester Street, which Bobby thought very nice indeed. Had several drinks. Bobby went to speak to one of the Argyl and Sutherland Highlanders, who told him they will all be in kilts again quite soon.

Herbert Brush
W dropped me at Westminster Bridge this morning and I went by tram to the BM. When I was walking along Great Russell Street I noticed a crowd of people outside Zion House, and soon saw that they were all Jews, men and women. They were talking excitedly and going in and out of the house like bees in a hive, so I suppose they were cooking up something to say to the Government about Palestine. There was no mistaking the Jewish proboscis of the men, though it was not quite so apparent on the women. The Jews are always in trouble with some other nation, and always will be I suppose. Personally I should be inclined to let the Jews and Arabs fight it out among themselves, if that could be arranged without dragging us into the matter.

TUESDAY, 9 JULY

Edie Rutherford
Oh heavens, the horrors of being an aunt. My niece Ursula writes me asking can I get a job for her to last from 1 September till she starts nursing at Guy's next April. Something artistic, doesn't like animals, likes children, doesn't want to dirty her hands, and so on. Presumably live here with us? I can see Husband rearing up against that idea.

Our trams are celebrating their jubilee. For 1/- one may take a ride, very short, in a horse bus, brewery horses pulling it. Illuminated cars at night. And it's all very well to restart cheap railway trips, but would suit the public better if those who already travel could be sure of seats. Hasten slowly would be a better motto for the railways at this moment.

This land of no refrigeration cops it when we do get a bit of summer – the butter, marge and fat I've brought home today should be sold in bottles as it is almost liquid. And the women who serve still lick their fingers before they take up the greaseproof paper into which they weigh.

Husband says they had a man in their office one day last week who says he has never tasted tea. Asked how that came about, he said his mother never gave it to him (wise woman) and somehow as he got older he never wanted it. Wonder who has his tea ration?

Chapter Ten

LEN SQUELCH IS BACK

The damned silly measure may be shelved: the day before bread rationing in
Streatham High Street

Washington: Mr Snyder, Secretary of the Treasury, disclosed today that Great Britain has made a first withdrawal of £75,000,000 from the loan signed by President Truman on Monday.

Mr Snyder said that this first withdrawal from the £937,500,000 credit will be placed to the credit of the Bank of England tomorrow. 'I understand it is intended for the purchase of food and for a considerable amount of heavy machinery,' he said.

The Times, *Thursday, 18 July 1946*

'Groups of people carrying bedding converged on High Street, Kensington, from all over London at two o'clock yesterday to take over a large block of flats, the Duchess of Bedford House, Duchess of Bedford Walk, West Kensington.

Some families came from as far as Stepney. The operation had obviously been organised on a grand scale. All the parties were met and, as one body, moved through the streets towards their destination.

Within ten minutes, 1,000 people of 400 families were through the doors and were being directed to individual flats. They were mainly young married couples carrying the bare essentials for the night, suitcases with bedding. Some women had small babies in their arms and outside the flats were a number of furniture vans loaded with household effects. There was also a score or more of taxis carrying heavily laden people.

Daily Telegraph *on the Squatters Movement, Monday, 9 September 1946*

WEDNESDAY, 10 JULY

B. Charles
Bobby bought *Picture Post* for 13 July, in which I read a positively lamentable article on the Butlin Camp at Filey, Yorkshire. The article is fully illustrated, with snaps of the camp and the holiday-makers. It pretends to be organised 'Fun' the whole of the time. Of course, to me, to spend such a holiday would be torment. But I gather Mr Butlin turns down six hundred applications a week for accommodation, and next year he hopes to cater for a million holiday-makers, and I should think he will. It seems to me that this holiday camp is about the same sort of thing as a holiday on the French Riviera, only for £5 15s. 6d. a week, instead of for hundreds of pounds. In fact, it brings Monte Carlo within the reach of the working class. It used to be said that all the nonsensical 'goings-on' on the Riviera only influenced a tiny proportion of the world's inhabitants, but now the same thing is available to anyone.

Also in the week's edition of *Picture Post* is an article called 'Banned Broadcast'. The BBC asked some American to give his impressions of the Paris Peace Conference, but when they read the article they demanded so many deletions and alterations that the author refused to broadcast at all. I am so utterly sick of all forms of propaganda.

Bobby told me an extraordinary story about the 'French House', somewhere off Shaftesbury Avenue in London. He says two Scotland Yard detectives keep watch, just inside the door, and 'vet' everyone who goes in. If they think any person 'undesirable', they signal the barmaid who refuses to serve the person. Such technique, to me, seems to have more than a bowing acquaintance with *Alice in Wonderland*. I should have thought the police would have been better employed in trying to recover stolen property, and tracing murderers, rather than wasting their time vetting 'undesirables'.

THURSDAY, 11 JULY

Herbert Brush
Went with W and Maggie Hutt to pick cherries today. W fell off the stepladder and strained her shoulder muscles a bit. She felt herself falling and grabbed a branch which proved to be rotten and snapped

off. The lady next door told me that she had just heard of a child who had to go to hospital, and the doctor took three hundred cherry stones from her stomach. She was the small daughter of a cherry picker, who ought to have warned her to spit out the stones. W has made up several parcels of cherries to send away, and one of these parcels is for you.

FRIDAY, 12 JUNE

Edie Rutherford
Have been making a table lamp from a Shelley biscuit barrel which was given me, lidless, years ago to use as a vase. Friend made me a shade. It looks very posh. Now going to make another from a grey ginger jar.

At my grocer's this morning: Woman: 'I don't want that cheese. I'll come in tomorrow to see what you've got then.' Assistant: 'We won't have any other cheese in till next week so I advise you to have your ration now.' Woman: 'It's dry.' Assistant: 'No, it isn't. It is quite moist.' Woman: 'Is it strong?' Assistant: 'No, quite mild.' Woman: 'Give it me then, it'll do to light fire if nowt else.' Me: 'Oh no, you wouldn't waste food like that?' Woman: 'Oh yes. More often than not cheese ration in our 'ouse lights the fire in morning.'

Then I went to buy *News Review*. At the counter a woman was buying a 6d. kid's book for small boy about four years, and said, 'I'm sick of it. Every time we come downt' road, 'e 'as to 'ave one o' these books.'

Herbert Brush
I used to think that corduroy trousers were everlasting, but now I have changed my mind. Just now I was walking along the rhubarb patch when my left trouser leg caught on a marking stake and it tore a hole from the calf to the ankle. The material has been absolutely rotten since it went to the cleaners.

8.15 p.m. I went with W in the car to the State Cinema this afternoon. The main picture was good but not very probable. *Dragonwych*.

SATURDAY, 13 JULY

Edie Rutherford
Went to cinema last night. Saw Wendy Hiller and Robert Livesey in what I call a grand film, *I Know Where I'm Going*. Hadn't seen Livesey before – he's certainly a heart-throb for me all right. Also heard Mr Strachey in a short tell us why bread rationing is coming in.

B. Charles
A very dull day indeed. I should be very glad if I could get to know one or two people who would be willing to spend an evening quietly here, or we could go to a theatre from time to time.

Since the war it seems very difficult to make friends, I think. People are, I expect, 'upset' and not inclined to make fresh acquaintances. I shall go out presently, but I have no doubt that most of the pubs will be shut. I was amazed this afternoon when I asked if I could buy some bran, to be told that, no, it is necessary to have a doctor's certificate before you can purchase it. The number of fresh regulations now in force is simply staggering.

SUNDAY, 14 JULY

Edie Rutherford
So the pesky Loan is settled at last. No hurrahs. Am amused at *Sunday Despatch* leader warning Government that the money is not to be used to benefit the masses – how the capitalists give themselves away!

Herbert Brush
I wonder whether this American loan will make much difference to us. I dare say that our Government will find many ways to spend it, but what will our descendants think when they have to pay it back with interest? It will be something like a millstone tied round the necks of the people alive in fifty years' time; won't they curse us for doing business in this way.

MONDAY, 15 JULY

Herbert Brush

I went to the *Daily Express* Exhibition of '50 Years of the Films' in Regent Street this morning. A man dressed in an old-fashioned suit stood at the door of the 'moving picture hall', and a girl dressed in an ancient style with her hair done up on the top of her head banged away on a small piano.

One picture showed Charlie Chaplin in a boxing booth, where, before it was his turn to box the professional, he is shown inserting a horseshoe into one of his gloves. Of course the horseshoe made him the winner when he did hit the boxer. It made me smile once or twice, but it was more silly than funny, though I remember laughing out loudly when I saw the film many, many years ago.

Some of the slide shows are interesting. A model of a steamer with small boats and dummy figures showed how a wreck was filmed without danger to anyone. Very ingenious, but likely to take the excitement out of a picture if the onlookers know how it was done.

B. Charles

Went and got Adams to look at my top plate which broke a little the other day. He told me a particularly revolting story about some Government official calling to see a small joiner the other day, and trying to get him to do something that was illegal. Fortunately the man refused, whereupon this scoundrel told him he was a Government official and he now knew he was 'all right'! Adams said he hoped some of these *agents provocateurs* would get a jolly good hiding, and so do I. All this spying, and pimping, on the part of the Government is absolutely disgraceful. There is so much roguery now in the Government that it makes all sorts of really quite law-abiding citizens just break the law without thinking anything about it.

TUESDAY, 16 JULY

Maggie Joy Blunt

An uncle – the father of my cousin J, husband of my father's youngest sister – died last week. We buried him this morning. He was seventy-eight, had retired after fifty years or so devoted service in a small building society and was ageing rapidly. Auntie and he bickered constantly. Now she is like a stricken little girl. There must have been twenty to thirty mourners and no one was in full black, but wore what clothes they had.

I came home via Uxbridge and Beaconsfield collecting cigarettes en route. Yesterday left here with ten Player's and tobacco to roll if necessary, picked up ten Churchman and have come home with ten Woodbine, ten Player's and twenty Piccadilly. Sir Stafford Cripps has promised that the situation will improve very shortly.

Edie Rutherford

Spinster friend called last night, furious about bread rationing. Says she has written Strachey asking how he thinks a woman can keep fed on so little. I discovered she eats close on three times as much bread per week as I do. When I pointed out that she has chronic catarrh and said less starch would relieve that, she was unbelieving. She said her parents have always been big bread eaters and are healthy. I didn't like to say so but her father wears a strained look on his face which doesn't go with sound health, and her mother has a Derbyshire neck.

Two parcels from home today – eats. Lovely fudge from my sister. Her parcel had been slashed and someone got out 1lb. dried fruit and 1lb. peanuts. I hope they enjoyed them.

WEDNESDAY, 17 JULY

Edie Rutherford

Yesterday afternoon I went down to friend's flat on ground floor to have a cuppa tea with her, and on my way met three small boys who've all been born here in the last four years, so I gave them each three monkey nuts from the dish I was taking to shell while I had a cuppa. I hadn't realised these kids would not ever have seen monkey nuts and they all popped one into their mouths instantly. 'Here, spit it out!' I said, and then I showed them how to break the shells and eat the nuts.

A magistrate in Southend has deprived four boys of going to the pictures for a month for throwing stones at trains.

B. Charles

I should think it probable that there may be such a stink over this unnecessary bread rationing that the damned silly measure may be shelved. I wish everyone would band themselves together and refuse to carry it out. Strachey's stupid chatter about inflicting heavy penalties if the bakers refuse to co-operate is just empty threats. I was interested when Adams said this morning that the Co-Operative Society had started some banking business now! Whatever next?!

FRIDAY, 19 JULY

Herbert Brush

A man came to see W yesterday and demanded £2 10s. for a slight scratch on the wing of his car, which he said W had done while passing his car in a garage. W knew nothing about it and told him to 'go to blazes'. It seems to me that a female alone in a car is now the target of sharks.

SUNDAY, 21 JULY

Herbert Brush

Went to the Hutts at Dulwich and stayed there until after the nine o'clock news. Talked about the bread ration for about an hour, but did not find out for certain how it was going to work. It seems to me that mental homes will be required for bakers and their assistants before very long.

MONDAY, 22 JULY

George Taylor

As I am saving up current Readers Union books for my holidays I have been looking over old issues. It is only last November that I read the anthology *This Changing World* and I was astonished at how little detail I remembered. I think the political trends in the book dismayed me even more than in November. I, for one, do not wish to live in a world where everything is planned: I would much rather have liberty to make a fool of myself than become an ideal citizen by regulation.

THURSDAY, 25 JULY

Edie Rutherford

I'm glad Labour has so far held the by-elections. I note the jubilant headlines in Tory press because majority is less and theirs up but am not dismayed. The start of bread rationing was a hard time for a Labour candidate.

Bread rationing, but cakes on show for folk like me to buy, for the first time for quite six years. No cake queues. One corner hereabouts looks unfinished without its daily queue.

Herbert Brush

It must have been a wonderful sight to see the result of the atom bomb explosion in the Pacific last night. Even the record of the roar on the wireless this morning was impressive, but what is the use of it all? I expect that there are a few million dead fish floating about on the sea in that neighbourhood.

FRIDAY, 26 JULY

Edie Rutherford

For months I've tried to buy a skirt, but it was never possible to get my size and the colour I want, brown, which is the most economical for me and suits me best in every way. A friend has kindly said she'll make me one, and on Wednesday passing some remnants on a shop counter in town I saw exactly the material I'd like, only five coupons, 19/10d. My friend thinks she can make me a waistcoat with the material left over.

More and more people grab army huts and more and more do I sympathise with them. I am waiting to see when our anti-aircraft gun site is taken over. It is set on a hillside in clean air with a lovely view, about a score of various kinds of huts with water and light. Been standing empty two years or more now. I am of the conviction that every habitable dwelling in this land should be allowed to be habited these days and hope folk will continue to show it if authority is slow.

From disclosures being made it does look as if doing the pools needs control. Husband announces he is going to amuse himself with them this year. Says all the men at work always do and that he thinks it is fun. Well, as he is fifty next month I suppose it is something that he can find fun in so simple a way, and anyway, he always does just as he pleases. The most I ever do is express an opinion, which I do without reserve always, and he can do as he likes then. I try not to say 'I told you so'.

SATURDAY, 27 JULY

Edie Rutherford
Husband said this morning that he has only one sorrow about the Nuremberg thugs, and that is that they did not exterminate the Jews before they were stopped at it. Husband went on to say Jews are parasites. That they are never found with their coats off, that they are cunning, etc. I regret this wholesale condemnation of his but I know that he is sorely tried every day in his timber work by Jews.

I can't myself believe any of the monsters now on trial will get off. If they did, I fancy there'd be someone to take the law into their own hands.

The first paragraph of Opinion in *Daily Express* today makes me hopping mad. The Germans cost us £4 per person per head and the population of our Colonial Empire 4/- per person per year. How utterly disgusting.

George Taylor
My niece came for the afternoon and evening. She has just passed for entry into college as a trainee deaconess. As far as we are aware she had received no encouragement at home for this, and if anything she has been influenced otherwise. However, in spite of this she has saved up the necessary fees, and now given up a civil service job to undertake the training. Personally I am somewhat sorry as I do not like to see a young girl in her early twenties taking such a serious view of life, and I cannot but think that there will be a rude awakening when the glamour of the job has worn off, and the daily round of dealing with unpleasant people in often distasteful circumstances begins.

SUNDAY, 28 JULY

George Taylor
The joint ramble with the Rotherham WEA Branch was certainly small in numbers. On the way to Fulwood we passed a large

prisoner-of-war camp, and my wife remarked that she was sorry that the prisoners were still detained here without any promised date of release. Not much sympathy with this point of view was expressed, however, and one member, an intelligent works chemist, thought that they should be retained almost indefinitely on reconstruction work.

MONDAY, 29 JULY

B. Charles

Went out this afternoon, and got a seat for *The Rape of Lucretia* for 12 August. I don't expect I shall think much of it, but I want to hear it. As I was returning home I went to Boots and asked if they have any glucose. They have not, and the manager tells me it is in very short supply indeed: shorter than it has ever been. He says this winter will be absolutely lousy in every way. Everything, in the body-building line – cod liver oil etc – will be hard to get, and he thinks the situation with regard to soap may easily get worse.

WEDNESDAY, 31 JULY

B. Charles

Had an early dinner and got back here to wait for Sammy, who came at 1.10 p.m. He is very intelligent, very 'sharp', and has decided possibilities. So far he has none of the hateful 'modern' touches about him. He will be interesting to watch develop.

[Later] I have just come back from a couple of hours spent walking around the town. I was more than ever before impressed with the magnificence of Edinburgh as seen in the bright, clear light of a really sunny evening. There is, even today, an atmosphere of 'spaciousness' about Edinburgh, which is very delightful. I met an officer in the Seaforth Highlanders and we had a meal at the Brown Derby. He told me he was educated at Eton. He is just now going to Palestine for, he expects, about two years. He seems to think the situation there is very disturbing.

THURSDAY, 1 AUGUST 1946

Edie Rutherford

So our lads may marry foreign women now, except Japs. I should think so. As if love knows barriers of race. Isn't one way of ending wars to get together and understand other nations? All barriers to marriage are artificial and should never be attempted under any circumstances. And at last, after years of agitation, a British woman doesn't lose her nationality by marriage, and a foreigner marrying a Britisher must ask for the privilege if she desires to become British. Announced as calmly as if there has never been any rumpus.

FRIDAY, 2 AUGUST

Herbert Brush

We made a start on our journey to Truro at 6.55 a.m. and felt disappointed at the dull, damp weather.

10.30 a.m. A little rain then sunshine as we came into Salisbury market place, where we went into the Cadena Café for coffee and a jam tart apiece. Afterwards W bought a length of rope, just in case we required rope for some purpose. She always likes to be ready.

4.20 p.m. Mist came down as we left Moreton for the high land of the Downs, and it was far from agreeable. We began to look around for likely places where bed and breakfast were to be had. A little pub about a mile east of Postbridge was the first attempt, but they had no accommodation for visitors; W regretted this as she saw some large dishes filled with cream in the kitchen. We stayed at an inn at Merrivale.

Edie Rutherford

I'll take a bet we won't get the ringleaders of terrorism in the Tel Aviv clear out. They would not risk being there so long after the deed. Far too wily for that. However, if we get some underlings we may know ways to make them talk. I'm getting a Nazi mind about how to tackle folk who are such a damned nuisance to us in these days when all the world cries for peace and order.

How young women are falling for the family allowance! During the war years one noticed the many pregnant women and now it is more so. I'm sure this Government at next election time will be able to claim they send the birth rate up. How astute of them to get the family allowances going so early in their reign.

What a lovely cover picture on *Radio Times* this week. A Nissen hut is an ugly thing but with such a garden it becomes a thing of beauty.

SATURDAY, 3 AUGUST

Herbert Brush

I hope I shall not have the same trouble with my eyes as I did yesterday. My right eye went blind for a few minutes as I sat in the car. It may have been due to watching the roadway for so many miles at 30 or 40 mph.

We arrived in Truro in time for lunch, but no pubs have any beer for the holiday, so some people will not enjoy themselves as well as they hope to do.

SUNDAY, 4 AUGUST

Herbert Brush

We went across the Lizard Downs by a narrow road and came to Kynance Cove. It is a stiff climb to get down, but it was nice when we did at last reach the sand. Young people were playing cricket and I felt like joining in the game but had enough sense not to do so. Kynance Cove is well worth a visit when the tide is low. I imagine it is also worth a visit when the tide is high.

MONDAY, 5 AUGUST

Herbert Brush

Went along to Porthtowan. We went to the Shore Café for cups of tea, and there was a notice on the door that thirty-eight cups had been stolen this week, so it was not surprising that a large deposit was asked for from anyone who wanted to take a tray on the sands.

On coming out of the café I was surprised to see a large crowd waiting in front of the entrance, but soon I learned that it was waiting to witness the choosing of Miss Porthtowan, the most beautiful bathing girl.

Judges were chosen at random from the visitors. I found that I was standing at the end of the row of beauties. There were twelve in all, some very nice-looking girls among them with straight limbs and scanty bathing costumes. One by one they walked towards the judges and then away from them, and I had a good chance to pick the winner before the judges decided. But I made a mistake. The winner had a very fine body, but not a very pleasant face, though I noticed that her face improved when she smiled when she gave away the prizes to the winners of some sports competition that had taken place earlier in the day.

Tomorrow we propose to go to the Scilly Isles, so I hope the sea will be smooth as I don't feel like giving the fishes my food.

TUESDAY, 6 AUGUST

Maggie Joy Blunt

No cigarettes anywhere in village today. I had managed to collect a supply for the holiday but am now reduced to rolling own again. Outside one local pub is chalked:

> No cigarettes, no beer
> No bread, no soap
> You put 'em in
> You got some hope.

It took N to explain to me that this was a blunt stab at the Government.

B. Charles

When I went to cash a cheque, the manager of the bank wanted to see me. He is most charming, and says they will be very glad indeed when I transfer my account to them, and that they will do everything they can to help me. He has delightful manners, so unlike the majority of people nowadays! He made one interesting remark. During conversation, relative to me getting my Deed Boxes and the silver from Windsor to Edinburgh, he said how terribly 'honesty' had suffered as a result of the war. He continued that people who, before the war, would never have dreamed of doing anything dishonest, very often now seemed to think it was quite 'in order' to pilfer and cheat if they got the chance. I am sure he is right. Yesterday Alec said, quite as a matter of course, that he had got his suit without giving any coupons. And he seemed quite pleased about it. Of course, it is hardly to be wondered that people try to cheat such idiotic regulations. And, from cheating idiotic regulations, it is not a big step to cheating whenever one can.

WEDNESDAY, 7 AUGUST

Edie Rutherford

I am appalled to read in *Daily Express* what it costs per annum to get the quite appalling weather forecasts which are handed to us.

Husband's 'unbreakable' top plate of teeth which he had fitted just over a year ago has got a bad crack. Dentist wants it tomorrow till Friday, so that means liquid diet tomorrow. He has his old plate but says it is now as uncomfortable as a new one, but he may wear it for appearance's sake at work.

Have had a scrappy day: somehow when a man is at home one neglects things. Well, I reckon his leisure must be put first, and, thank goodness, he wants my company after close on twenty-one years of married life.

THURSDAY, 8 AUGUST

Maggie Joy Blunt

Shopping in Slough this afternoon. An electric kettle with flex and light plug fitting for 42/3d. A belt, after some searching, to match linen maroon suit, for 6/11d. Ryvita with difficulty. Was told in one grocer's that all Ryvita and Melba toast had stopped when bread rationing began. Some rollmops from a delicatessen. The assistant went through his stock carefully, shaking each jar. 'This hot weather,' he explained, 'makes them go off quickly. They begin to disintegrate. By shaking them you can tell.' Still no peanut butter. The manageress said it would come in time – she had been offered it loose but replied, 'My customers aren't the kind that carry jam jars.'

B. Charles

I have been reading the report of the Heath murder. It is a terrible indictment of the present-day young woman. Both the ex-Wren, who has been murdered, and the girl he spent the night with, from Worthing, belonged to what is called the 'Better Class people'. Yet both allowed themselves to be 'picked up' by Heath, the ex-Wren immediately consented to accompany him to one of the Bournemouth Chines after midnight, and the girl from Worthing slept with him on her second meeting. Of course the reason, or rather one of the main reasons, for the present-day promiscuity of so many of the women is the spread of contraceptive knowledge, and the complete decline of home life. It is an interesting phenomenon.

FRIDAY, 9 AUGUST

Maggie Joy Blunt
Might now explain my 'interim plans' mentioned in 27 May entry. Have realised for some time that I cannot depend for the extra income I need on my writing efforts alone. Considered having a permanent business girl lodger but turned it down. Cottage too small for two women to live here together for any length of time. I am not really very good at living with other people, though can adapt myself for a short while and be amiable enough. But after a time the strain of being cluttered up with someone else's life gets too much for me and I – very politely – grow restless and rude. Alternatively I thought of having 'holiday visitors'. Throughout the spring-cleaning the idea developed and has slowly been materialising.

Two rooms upstairs rearranged. Certain pieces of furniture had to be removed into store. Then in front room placed two small beds (a camp bed and ARP fire-watching bed – for this a mattress had to be remade, but was done in a week by a store in Slough), a small chest of drawers, a wash stand, two chairs and two bedside tables and rugs. Re-stained and polished the floor.

The back room, which is larger, I have made into a bed-sitting room for myself.

I intend to cater only for people who will go out all day – walkers and cyclists and such like. It is an ideal centre for exploring the Chilterns or Thames Valley. I have done quite a bit of it myself recently. Meals: breakfast, hot evening meal and sandwich lunch. With Emergency ration cards I have no qualms at all about providing adequate food for normal appetites.

I thought of advertising discreetly early in May in the *New Statesman*. But not having used their Classified Ads page since before the war thought confidently of having something inserted within a week of it being submitted. At the end of May I discovered with horror that there would be a delay of at least eight weeks before insertion. Actually the first ad appears this week, nearly three months after I sent it in. As an afterthought I sent one also to the *Spectator* which appeared in the middle of July and has drawn several inquiries and one definite booking. My first official guests to arrive for ten days on Monday.

One outstanding difficulty remains. I have failed to find another Mrs Mop.

MONDAY, 12 AUGUST

Edie Rutherford
I hope I'm not over-sceptical, but I'd like to hear that talking dog before I believe he talks.

Hurrah for those families who've taken over huts [near Slough] being prepared for the Italian wives of Poles. So like us to look after foreigners and forget our own, and so unlike us to object and, what is more, show we object. I am always glad to see signs that the British lion won't have his tail pulled all the time. Palestine is finding that out too now. They'll feel the lion's teeth shortly. They seem to think, from their actions, that he's old and lost them all, but no such thing. This morning the 8 a.m. news was ushered in with the music of 'Jerusalem the Golden'. Scarcely appropriate.

We were disgusted to read in papers yesterday that Princess Elizabeth is going shooting with her father. Whenever are we going to grow out of such barbarity?

TUESDAY, 13 AUGUST

Maggie Joy Blunt
The first two guests: schoolmaster Mr W and wife from Manchester. They wrote that they expected to arrive by car about 7.30 p.m. but turned up about six without it and nearly caught me in my bath. Met them without make-up and with hair uncombed after afternoon hairdo at hairdresser's.

(NB Hairdresser's friend went to the Butlin's camp at Filey and was very disappointed. Food was bad and they had to queue for it. Accommodation not what they expected – too few bathrooms and bad equipment. Had been an army camp and not yet properly reconditioned.)

Mr and Mrs W nice, homely, middle-aged North Country couple. Not what I expected at all but I don't know what I did expect. They were very tired and went to bed soon after evening meal. Seem so far quite satisfied with accommodation and food and are enchanted with cottage and surroundings. Have another definite booking for September and inquiries keep trickling in.

WEDNESDAY, 14 AUGUST

Edie Rutherford

So H. G. Wells is dead at last. Roman Catholics will be pleased. He was a highly gifted mind, and courageous, and he has left behind enough testimony to that for all time. Wells was what I call a God man, for all his atheism.

More honour for Churchill, this time Lord Warden and Admiral of Cinque Ports. I don't know why some folk are disgruntled about the treatment we give Churchill in his native land. Seems to me he gets another honour every week, and the only thing to stop it will be his projected Continental holiday.

Maggie Joy Blunt

They are a very easy, appreciative, friendly pair. I am getting on famously in my new role as landlady. The Ws – both are teachers and worn out as all teachers are at the end of term – like to go to bed early.

Mrs W teaches afternoon and evening classes in Domestic Science. She says that they tried to have a Make Do and Mend course, but it did not work. Has a very poor opinion of the average working-class young woman. Says she has no desire to learn or look after her house, and all she wants is as much pleasure and sensation as possible. State is doing too much for them, no sense of responsibility. 'It was the same with our cookery demonstrations. They'd come but would not carry it out in their own homes.'

Friends ask me if I have my meals with my guests and are surprised when I say no. But, really, it would be embarrassing for all concerned if I did – the effort of conversation and me popping up and down all the time to serve things from the kitchen – they might feel they *had* to help and I don't want them to do that.

Neighbour Mrs C's little boys have whooping cough. They had developed it while on holiday and had to come home early. On fine days they play in the garden, whooping and whining, poor mites.

Mrs C is going to America next month on the *Aquitania*. No flying accommodation for months. Our businessmen are the people who can travel now, and the ordinary globetrotter has to wait in a long queue.

FRIDAY, 16 AUGUST

Edie Rutherford

So the war, all of it, was over a year and two days ago. I think it passed unnoticed by most. The peace is so grim that it occupies all our time. I see Sir J. Boyd Orr reckons 1949 should see the world over the worst, but I imagine that is dependent on management. It must be done on a world scale as otherwise we shall have the old story – famine in one place and food burnt in another.

I'm not surprised that there is native trouble in my country. It has been hatching all my lifetime. I do not believe it has been settled already. I believe that, once again, the poor nigs have been intimidated. It merely postpones the showdown. Smuts gives the usual kind of comment. He has the peculiarly Boer outlook about the native and it is all wrong. This is a problem which grows with postponement and sometimes I think there will be dreadful trouble in my country one day, as it seems that nothing less will wake up the white people to what is just.

SATURDAY, 17 AUGUST

Edie Rutherford

Both Husband and self are surprised that in the list of men in steel industry to talk nationalisation with Government not one man is from Sheffield. How can that be? Are the bosses in this town proving awkward? Or isn't this THE steel town of the British Empire as we thought?

MONDAY, 19 AUGUST

George Taylor

Finished packing ready to go away on Wednesday. We made our list as usual a week beforehand and then steadily put in the things as we had a few moments to spare. Now, with the exception of shaving tackle etc we are ready with two days to spare.

Our lady dispenser friend brought her sister to tea, and what a surprise. The sister is almost a dwarf with a large-sized head. She was dressed in the most old-fashioned style, and everything was wrinkled up and creased. And yet she is a teacher, admittedly in a country school with a staff of two, but she is quite intelligent and a keen worker for the WEA. For a girl to be such is a sight just awful.

WEDNESDAY, 21 AUGUST

George Taylor
To York by the 8.20 a.m. train and scrambled into the 10.15 a.m. Scarbro' train there, securing what I believe to be the very last seats. Soon other connecting trains arrived, and people began to pour in. We finished up with two youngsters sat on the luggage racks; one girl sat on another's knee and two young fellows stood. However, we had only half an hour of this, when we changed into the Whitby train, where there was plenty of room, and caught the first bus forward from Whitby, arriving at the farm exactly on time.

THURSDAY, 22 AUGUST

Maggie Joy Blunt
The Ws went this morning. A very satisfactory beginning. They have been delighted with their holiday and want to come again. The Ws 'appreciation' in my first visitors' book is a triumph for me. They are just the sort of people I want – quiet, considerate, easy to please and happy to be here.

Reviewing my menus and cooking mistakes:

Corn beef hash – add corn beef only at very last minute to give it just time to heat through. The hash was too salty, maybe because beef was cooking too long or there was too much Bovril.

Macaroni cheese – too much macaroni and not enough sauce.

Scrambled dried egg – never goes far enough. Four/five 'eggs' at least for two people needed.

Beefsteak pudding – stew meat first to make sure it *is* tender and, possibly, add to pudding *hot*.

Fudge pudding – this from the *Listener* – an excellent recipe, but it is filling and sickly. Only small portions should be served and after a lightish first course. Would be good after salad.

The rollmops I bought a fortnight ago are still unopened. Cannot get the top off.

FRIDAY, 23 AUGUST

Edie Rutherford
A perfect morning, never seen a better. Oh, I do hope it is a good omen for our holiday [Whitby]. After much discussion we've decided to be up at 5 a.m. tomorrow, leave here 6.30 a.m. and get 7.20 a.m. train, which will have left Bristol at such an unearthly hour, and Birmingham very early, that maybe they'll be seats on it for us here. Of course we change at York, and have a scramble again round 9 a.m. but we'll have to take our chances over that.

So here closes this diary for the present.

George Taylor
Another of our familiar days. In the bay during the morning, paddling in the water and then back to lunch. Reading on the cliffs in the afternoon and back to the bay for the evening. We also went into Hinderwell to have a look at next week's cinema programme in case we were driven in by rain.

SATURDAY, 24 AUGUST

Maggie Joy Blunt
In London yesterday to have eyes tested. Last done in Malta, 1937. Specialist found that they had changed quite a bit. Entirely new glasses required. His fee £4 4s. New lenses will take at least two months to make up.

TUESDAY, 27 AUGUST

B. Charles
I went to London on Sunday 18th and returned today. I went to Windsor to meet Simms at the bank and got all the silver packed up ready to come here. Then I had lunch and saw Terry Skinner in the street. He recognised me and told me Ted Thackray had committed suicide a few weeks ago. Terry also told me Len Squelch is back, driving one of the Post Office vans.

I thought the price of antiques in London very much lower than when I was last there in February. The man at Harrods told me that now that the Yanks have departed trade is not nearly so brisk. And every other shop in the West End seems now to be an antiques shop. I went to Weymouth and couldn't help noticing that almost everyone travelling on the train, and staying in the hotel, were what used to be called 'Working Class'. It is astonishing how the working class now goes away for holidays and spends money very freely. They seem to have money for *everything*. When one sees how very irresponsible they are, it is not at all surprising that things, in general, are as they are.

I had an uncomfortable journey back: the carriage was very crowded with mothers and children and I had a beastly headache. On arrival in Edinburgh I went to the NB for dinner and Sammy was very much in evidence. He told me he had got me some salad cream.

SATURDAY, 31 AUGUST

Maggie Joy Blunt
A full week behind me and an absolutely blank week in front of me. An opportunity to tackle the writing problem seriously. But I don't want to do it. Have never felt less like writing in my life, never been so bored with my own company. As a rule being alone never bothers or depresses me. But now I'm restless, fidgety, can't settle to anything. Household tasks a real effort.

Have been seeing my friends. To Hampstead to stay night with June and Kassim and meet Paul whom I haven't seen since last summer. He's now out of the army and back in private practice. Very busy. Complaining of Jewish influence in BBC. And that certain famous German composers and musicians now banned because they were not openly hostile to the Nazis.

I saw the film *Spellbound* with Lys. We certainly were spellbound. An excellent production but incredible story. I think it will do more harm to the cause of psychoanalysis than good. As Lys said, all the doctors seemed much more crazy than their patients.

Spending the weekend now with stepmother Ella. As I began counting my damson stones (I nearly always do this), Ella said, 'Do as I did, dear, and marry late.' She was forty-five when she married my father and was very happy with him. So was my mother. He knew how to make his women happy – simply, I think, by being loveable. You just couldn't help loving him.

We had been discussing unhappy marriages earlier, in particular that of Ella's godson. He is demobbed now and working for a cosmetic concern, a young business but his prospects seem very good. But his wife is causing him much trouble. She nags continually, accuses him unjustly, behaves in a mean, small-minded way. A flat near his new office is vacant for himself and family but she will not go there. She wants to be near her mother. They could have had a prefab, but lost the chance because he thought he would have to travel for his firm for two months in Wales and she refused to live on her own with the children. She threatens to institute divorce proceedings, but there are no grounds. But for the children he would not care if she did. He loves his children. She sounds very unbalanced.

MONDAY, 2 SEPTEMBER 1946

B. Charles
Robert told me he has had an audition with the Sadler's Wells Ballet Company, and may be going to join the company in a few weeks' time. He has personality, in a way, and he is somewhat romantic looking, so I dare say he may do reasonably well in the ballet. He says that if he is accepted his call-up for military service will be delayed for two years. He is coming to see me on Tuesday evening and MAY (I think NOT!) be accompanied by a friend.

Maggie Joy Blunt
I wandered round Woolworth's, bought some sardine tin openers, some uncouponed washing powder for silk stockings and woollies, and waited in a long queue at GPO to withdraw £3 from Post Office savings. Several men behind the counter with a very 'just out of uniform' look.

Squatters have taken possession of army huts near here. Bus conductor was talking about them and council houses being built, but not enough to satisfy demand.

George Taylor
I had hoped to dodge my weekly directors' meeting, but I found I had to go along. The chief business was to discuss the possibility of installing central heating in the works and offices and the directors are afraid that coal or coke will be difficult to buy. The Ministry of Fuel and Power are urging the use of fuel oil, although England is

supposed to be predominantly a coal-producing country. What a commentary on the failure of the mining industry.

Yesterday I packed up 461 letters for the WEA and wrote a further twenty-two individual letters, making a total of 483 for the day.

SATURDAY, 7 SEPTEMBER

Maggie Joy Blunt

It is increasingly difficult to stand up for the present Government. In short conversation with two near neighbours this afternoon we agreed that probably most people were socialist at heart and wanted the working man to have a 'square deal' – if they will work. The complaint that they won't is general, particularly in the building industry. Men are always being seen standing about idle. A friend of June's had her house decorated a little while ago. She found the men one afternoon in the sitting room with their feet up, smoking and reading the paper, waiting to do 'overtime'.

Much scandal, too, is circulating at present about members of the Government. Bevin, it is said, is a 'soak' and makes a bad impression abroad, though I have heard several people express admiration at his strength. An Indian journalist who lives above June, although not agreeing with our Indian policy, agrees with Bevin policy elsewhere (it is a fact that it cost this Indian £3 in drinks to interview Bevin).

Coming home last night on last bus I was in a daze and went right past my stop and found myself in Beaconsfield (three miles on). Fortunately the bus turned round there and after a few minutes came back again. Bus conductor young and talkative. Only just out of forces, had done six weeks in present job. Didn't like it. None of them did. Men in another section getting £1 a week more and doing no harder work. Men did not like having to cope with the public, who, according to them, were often unreasonable and rude. This young man said he was going to give driving the bus a trial.

Expect my next official visitors on Saturday, for a week, a Mr and Mrs F, and possibly a single woman the week after. I pray with the farmers for fine weather. But although it has not rained since Sunday (when it fell down, tropical style) it is really 'sharp' now early in the morning. Cycling to work, says my hairdresser, she has to wear gloves. Our summer is over.

TUESDAY, 10 SEPTEMBER

George Taylor

One of our clients, a large sheep farmer in Scotland, wrote us today that he was sick of receiving forms from Government departments. He had just received one inquiring about the number of rats and mice killed on his farm during the past year. He replied, 'Ask my cats.' Continuing, he wrote, 'I thank them for permitting me to live a fair part of my life without the motor car, the telephone and the BBC; for allowing me to know an age when men had time and inclination to think; when the contents of the jam pot bore some resemblance to the label and kippers were not dyed; when men were capable of making their own amusements, when statesmen had dignity and common folk liberty, when there were poets worth reading and pictures worth looking at – in fact, when life was more or less civilised. What a back number I am! Never mind, I have had the privilege of living in what was, compared with these days, the Golden Age. That is something which even a Chancellor of the Exchequer cannot take from me.'

FRIDAY, 13 SEPTEMBER

Edie Rutherford

Went to grocer 9 a.m. to find two customers and woman behind the counter discussing the poor devils who are squatting. The other woman behind counter then said, 'It isn't RIGHT to take other people's property, empty or not.' I said, 'And I'll tell you something else that isn't right – it isn't right for folk to invest money in flat building, never do any work from cradle to grave, and own houses in England, Scotland, Ireland and probably elsewhere, and if this Government wants to be true to its name, it will begin with that sort of thing and do some confiscating. Furthermore the royal family should make a gesture and give up one of their several houses to the homeless.' I got agreement from one woman customer to this, and the others said nowt at all.

Maggie Joy Blunt

Two days of furious domestic activity preparing for tomorrow's visitors. But the word 'furious' is misleading. I work slowly, plodding, and have great difficulty commencing a task. 'The difficulty in finishing is getting started.' Yesterday morning I had to do lengthy shopping and fiddle about with an oil stove which was giving trouble. After tea some washing, a meal, felt despondent and listened to radio, then bottled some fruit with Camden solution and paraffin wax.

Today more shopping. Had to fetch sausage meat which butcher sells on Fridays and found I was due for some more liver. A South African friend of a friend of mine, who is recently come to this country to live, remarked on the way British women went shopping every day, which seemed to her unnecessary and labour-making. But unfortunately it is often necessary – one never knows for certain what will be in the shops.

About two years ago my friend C had a very bad confinement and lost the baby. She can have no more children and has now adopted one. She has had it for over a year and both she and her husband love it as much as they could one of their own. A little boy. But they had great difficulty in finding a baby wanting adoption – the formalities are incredible. This one is an American war baby, the mother married with one child of her own and husband abroad, the father an American. The mother's husband would not accept it into his family. When the child grows up and hears the story what will he feel? How will it affect his behaviour?

B. Charles
Got back early and Sammy came along, with a Pan Chromatic film! I am delighted to have it, and have asked him to try his best to get others. He may be going on the dining cars next month. He is a very good lad, and I think will do all right. There is an interesting report, in *Time and Tide*, about the recent publication 'Report on the State of the Public Health During Six Years of War'. I must get this report. It is interesting to read how tremendously venereal diseases increased during these six years. The Report goes on to say: 'Sexual promiscuity must have been practised on a scale never previously attained in this country.' This confirms what I said several years ago, that, broadly speaking, every woman in the United Kingdom during the six years of war had promiscuous sexual relations. People told me, at the time, that I didn't know what I was talking about.

The Government still 'talks big' about the way it is going to evict the squatters. I doubt, very much, if they dare to do anything of the sort. The whole Squatting Movement is, largely, backed by the Communists, egged on by Moscow.

SUNDAY, 15 SEPTEMBER

Maggie Joy Blunt
Lys came to tea and stayed as kitchen help for the evening. We had tea in my bedsit, to leave the sitting room free for the visitors who amble in and out at unexpected hours. They seem quite satisfied and happy. Fire on in kitchen. Lys and I both purple in the face with cooking etc. When visitors' supper was served we sat down to dumplings and small glass of gin and vermouth. This increased our good humour enormously and the colour of our cheeks and ears.

She brought a message from Cy. He and local go-ahead stationer and printer want to bring out a small brochure monthly (as an advertising medium), containing short articles of topical interest etc, and would I be interested in editing for them? I think I would, very much, but must hear more about it from Cy direct.

B. Charles
I am interested to hear how many Scots resent being ruled from Westminster. The average English person knows nothing at all about Scotland. They seem to think it is a wild country, with deer running down Prince's Street, and where everyone wears a kilt and has heather growing out of his ears. I myself, although I have been interested in old furniture and culture for years, hadn't the least idea before I came here that there were all the lovely old things there are in Scotland. It has come to me as a real revelation. And of course Edinburgh is one of the most intellectual cities I have ever been in. The Medical School is first class and the Scotch education is far superior to the English. So it does seem preposterous that the country should be governed from Westminster.

MONDAY, 16 SEPTEMBER

George Taylor
Once more we have the problem of a youth returning from the services. He left us as a junior of eighteen, and now returns as a man of twenty-two. During his four years' absence his little experience of accountancy

274

has rusted away, and yet he will now want a man's wages. We decided to give him over 100 per cent advance on the wages he received before going away, but I do not know whether he will be satisfied.

TUESDAY, 17 SEPTEMBER

Maggie Joy Blunt

I followed, unintentionally, a woman from shop to shop in the village today. She was buying cooking salt. One block from the greengrocer which she concealed in her basket and then another from the grocer. Expect she is salting beans. I wonder how many of us do this sort of scrounging for a quantity of something, with and without feelings of guilt? I do it for cigarettes and do have a twinge of conscience.

My visitors again very nice and easy to please. They sit in the sitting room reading, listening to the wireless. She sews or knits and he sometimes writes and they seem quite happy. Every scrap of food I set before my visitors disappears, dishes and plates come back scraped clean. This is, of course, very gratifying, or perhaps I don't give them enough, but they haven't yet complained.

Local tobacconist is ill and has been away from his shop for some weeks. His wife serves in his place and when she first started the work knew nothing about it at all, as she had never been allowed to have anything to do with the shop. She has no head for figures and didn't know prices of cigarettes. But she is managing very well and most of her regular customers do all they can to help her. But a stranger came in the other day and asked her for twenty Player's, had no change and neither had she, and he went off to get the change with the Player's, and never came back.

She calls me 'Mrs Er . . .'. A lot of tradespeople who don't know me as 'Miss' call me 'Mrs' and often it is Mrs Blunt. I always feel flattered when they do though – probably I look too old to be unmarried and haven't yet developed the old maid's acid countenance.

WEDNESDAY, 18 SEPTEMBER

Maggie Joy Blunt

I think the Communists were right, whatever their ulterior motives may have been, to draw attention to the shocking housing conditions that many of the flat-squatters have had to put up with. Rat bites! Just think of it. It seems to me scandalous that a Labour Government couldn't have done better for their own people in this last year. Bevan excused himself by saying that living in army huts would have been sub-standard and so on, but at least, one assumes, they are free of vermin and are damp proof, and would certainly have done as temporary housing for families living in two rooms or badly blitzed houses. It does seem to have been badly managed. And Government members are so smug about this year's achievements!

Edie Rutherford

How cautiously Bow Street has dealt with the Communist squatters today. I should jolly well think so. Public opinion does count for something and not all the populace are agin the squatters. It is mostly the haves who are. That disclosure at court by the woman who had to take her child to hospital fifty times for rat bite was more than enough for everyone I should think.

Had to listen to that beastly fight last night when I wanted to hear the concert. The whole thing is horrible and shouldn't be allowed. That anyone spends twenty guineas on a seat! Wish Lesnevich had been knocked out sooner [by Freddie Mills]. How they can talk about a 'beautiful blow under the heart' beats me.

Whiter bread soon! Dear God, when will folk realise that the whiter the bread the worse it is.

THURSDAY, 19 SEPTEMBER

George Taylor

A grocer client called today. He tells me that his son opted for the merchant navy, and is still serving. He is on the Hull–Antwerp run, and is making a good thing out of private imports. Watches are in great demand, and the crew combine to defeat the customs people. Even one of the legs of their mess room table has been hollowed out to receive watches. According to our client, the son pays 6/- plus a cycle tyre for a carpet, on which he pays £2 duty, and afterwards sells here for £20.

Maggie Joy Blunt

Mrs F's sister has just died and this morning she and Mrs F left here at 8.30 to attend the funeral at Pinner.

I went this afternoon with Lys and CL and CL's mother to see *Birthmark*, a new play by A. R. Rawlinson at Windsor, produced for the first time on any stage. A dramatic morsel based on the idea that Eva Braun did not die but escaped, bearing Hitler's child, married a few months later a young Englishman who met with a mysterious accident soon afterwards and was killed instantly.

Dinah's kittens arrived this morning. Dinah began squeaking at me in the way she does when she knows her hour has come, and I have to go and sit by her box, stroking her and telling her what a wonderful cat she is until the labour begins. Then she gets very busy and says 'Go away', which I did about nine o'clock and when I peeped at midday found her the purring proud mother of four tabby kittens. She always rolls over to let me see them and looks at me with such delight in her eyes.

Cy met Lys and I for tea and drove me home, discussing his journal idea. I think it has possibilities. I should have a practically free hand to produce what I like within the limit of what the men want to spend. The printer being one of the men concerned will be an enormous advantage and, as a stationer, we'll be able to get good quality paper too. I feel quite excited about it.

SATURDAY, 21 SEPTEMBER

Maggie Joy Blunt

Mrs S arrived at 4.30. Dark, older than Mrs F, attractive, quiet and a little shy. Her husband and friend brought her by car, took her to tea in Beaconsfield. Mrs S is one of the housewives who ran a home during the war and did a full-time job. She had husband and sister to look after, got up at 6 a.m. every morning and did everything before she left for work. She still gets up at 6.30 and cannot get used to staying in until 8.30. She worked, I think, in a bank as cashier. Is very neat, dresses quietly but in good taste. Is a very good knitter, the more intricate the pattern the better.

TUESDAY, 24 SEPTEMBER

Maggie Joy Blunt

Many people have not liked *Caesar and Cleopatra*. They feel the story is trivial and that the film doesn't justify the amount spent on it. Cy said to me this evening that he watched the faces of people as they came out from seeing it and he said they were blank, as though they were coming out of church. But my hairdresser enjoyed it as I did. I liked the Technicolor and all the glamour laid on with a trowel. It must have been luxurious, exotic, exciting and colourful living, and much more cruel. And what I enjoyed as much as anything was the length of the programme – one long, good film and a newsreel. Just right. No trash to sit through. Usually I find the full programme much too long. Makes me feel headachey and dazed.

WEDNESDAY, 25 SEPTEMBER

Maggie Joy Blunt

In the sweet shop this morning where the old man's daughter is taking a turn of duty, she has heard from those 'in the know' that the ration may be increased to 1lb. next month.

At the cobbler's was a woman with four delightful small children. When she had gone I said, 'What a mob – they're not all hers, surely?' The cobbler, who has an embarrassing stammer, answered, 'There are s-s-six altogether I think, yes, all hers. Her husband's a master at the local prep school. There's only about twelve months between each of them. We joke about it every summer breaking-up day. There's nearly always another due in a few months!'

Now I do call that courageous for middle-class parents. The mother looked strong and healthy and well dressed, was small but had a good figure, not at all 'gone to pieces' as many young married women fear, and reminds me of an article I read in a recent *Woman and Beauty* by a young married woman who did not want children, explaining just why she did not want them. She brayed all over the page about her sex appeal and charm and devoted husband and how happy they were in their respective jobs and sharing their leisure time doing all the things they liked doing together, and she was not going to give up all this and become a domestic nursery drudge by having children! It seemed to me one long shriek of fear that she lose her husband's adoration and all the pleasures they shared. She was grasping at everything she could get that would give her satisfaction and suffering nothing if it could be avoided – building defences so that her present pleasant life should be secure for all time – and heading for a most disastrous fall. I'm not criticising her for the things she finds enjoyable, or for enjoying them. It was her fearful, grasping attitude that appalled me, the attitude of the coward who will not admit her cowardice.

A cable this evening from brother in Alexandria. He and family sail on the 27th (Friday), due at Liverpool about 5 October. Wonderful news!

Chapter Eleven

BRITAIN CAN'T GET IT

Wonderful, fascinating, terrible: an exhibitor en route to Britain Can Make It

'The moral is, roughly, that what Britain always could make, she still can, and in the other things improvement is coming. There is room for more and more improvement, because it is not in the long run enough that people should say it's a wonderful display –"considering" it is so soon after the war. British products must be wonderful in their own right; and "considering" nothing at all. And that is why it is good that they should be exposed to the critical gaze of thousands of people who want homes and things to put in them. In the words of the penny guide to the show: "The future of British design rests, in the long run, with you." '

Picture Post *on 'Britain Can Make It', 19 October 1946*

Neville George Clevely Heath, twenty-nine, who was sentenced to death at the Central Criminal Court on 27 September for the murder of Mrs Margery Aimee Gardner in a hotel at Notting Hill Gate, London, was executed at Pentonville Prison at 9 a.m. yesterday. He has also been committed for trial on a charge of murdering Doreen Marshall of Pinner, Middlesex, at Branksome Dene Chine, Bournemouth, but that charge was not proceeded with . . .

Hermann Goering committed suicide in the shadow of the gallows by taking cyanide in his cell at 10.45 last night, three-quarters of an hour before the time fixed for his execution. The ten other condemned Nazi leaders, beginning with Ribbentrop, were hanged between one and three o'clock this morning.

A dozen deaths in The Times, *Thursday, 17 October 1946*

THURSDAY, 26 SEPTEMBER

George Taylor
I was somewhat amused when I picked up *Radio Times* this morning and saw that the BBC had christened the new programme the 'Third Programme'. Apparently the BBC is afraid of the word 'Cultural' and neither 'Serious' nor 'Heavy' appealed. It is curious how English people are afraid of being serious, and how culture is regarded as somewhat priggish. The 'Third Programme' is a title which is certainly safe, but very colourless.

Edie Rutherford
We are having far too many air accidents. I think that, instead of making speed records, we should concentrate on making the air safe. Female friend who visited us last night said she has no sympathy for air crash victims, as most of them are wealthy people and if they have money to throw away in their impatience to get about, they must take the danger too, and they are no loss anyway. However, there is the crew . . .

I suppose it is a good sign to have papers larger on some days from this week, but as I have always felt the space ill-used in dailies, I am not unduly thrilled. As for the Heath trial – what a vile life the man has led. All very well for the doctor to say he has one redeeming point, i.e. that he is fond of his parents – all I say is it is a pity his love for them wasn't strong enough to restrain him on the many occasions that his actions must have wounded them deeply, culminating in this horrible case . . . I agree with the papers in the belief that had they been allowed to publish photos of the suspected man after the first murder, the second might not have occurred. I'm so glad he isn't a South African.

Maggie Joy Blunt
So Heath has been sentenced to death. I have been following this case in the press, all agog and aghast. The news of his death sentence came a long way down on the BBC bulletin tonight and I found Mrs S waiting for it, as I was. I wonder how many other people were doing the same. I can't see that it makes much difference whether he was 'insane' or not. He was obviously dangerously abnormal and had committed shocking crimes. N was arguing about it when she was

here – that you couldn't condemn a man who was mentally imbalanced. This is a case that will be remembered and discussed in the far future when more is known of psychology. Where does one draw the line for a person being responsible for his own actions?

Was in a vile mood this morning. I had no engagements, no urgent work and very little to do in the house or for the meals. Not even any shopping. A lovely warm, moist day, too – I can understand what makes some housewives *over* houseproud. When they are overtaken by a mood like that, a feeling of unbearable emptiness, they pour themselves as quickly as they can into some domestic activity to escape it. Their pride goes into the house because it cannot go into husband or children – or whatever else it is they hanker after and find lacking.

B. Charles

I have been reading a lot about the Heath murder case, and I am amazed, really, at the way 'sexual perversion' and 'sadism' are freely discussed in the papers. In a way, there seems to be a more sane outlook on the subjects of what are called 'Sex Perversions' than there used to be, yet I doubt if this change is more than superficial. In some ways, I have an idea that people, in reality, are less broad-minded on these subjects than they used to be. But certainly they are discussed far more freely. I wonder, really, if this is a good thing? I remember when to mention such subjects, even in the most guarded way and in the most carefully chosen company, would have been enough for you to be socially ostracised!

There is an article in the evening paper on the subject of sadism. It really is extraordinary the way the papers are bandying about the word now. I have written a letter to the editor giving a brief summary of the career of the Marquis de Sade, so far as it relates to the origin of this word. We shall see if the letter is published.

FRIDAY, 27 SEPTEMBER

Maggie Joy Blunt

Mrs S another very easy guest. Makes her own bed every morning. Leaves sitting room tidy and cushions shaken. She said today that she thought she was having too much fruit and would I mind cutting it out for her, as it seemed to be upsetting her – it was too acid. She has a bottle of milk of magnesia and has been taking a lot of it. I fear that it may be my cooking. But she is a nervous type and it's more likely that this complete change of routine and environment after years of hard work is causing the disturbance rather than my food. She says she would like to have been a ballet dancer.

SATURDAY, 28 SEPTEMBER

Maggie Joy Blunt
Article in this week's *New Statesman* on the need for reform of the law against abortion. I would support a petition for its amendment. Have heard of three abortions in the past year. One, the woman was sufficiently well off to have it done safely in a private nursing home. The other two, quite separate, unknown to each other in London, had to have unskilled help in the most sordid circumstances and went through such agony as made me feel really ill to hear of it. Both as far as I know are all right now and the first suffered no ill effects. But I don't think I would have the courage to go through what the other two did. Moralists might try to sermonise on this subject – but I think it is very much a question for the individual to decide for herself and be able to have the operation done by a qualified practitioner in conditions of hygiene and comfort. All children should be wanted children. And it certainly isn't fair that safe abortion is available only to enlightened women with long purses.

All day yesterday and today my brother and his family very much in my thoughts. Have not seen them since 1938. They were at home on leave that autumn and left again just after Christmas. My niece now a long-legged schoolgirl of thirteen. My brother and I both seven years older.

Of my sister-in-law I feel a little scared – she always did make me feel uncomfortable and ill at ease. But I very much want us to be friends. I cannot picture at all what they will be like. I wonder if I shall recognise them! I hope to meet the boat train in London – I want them to feel really welcome and have as good a time as possible. I don't want the meeting to fall flat as these meetings so often do, or to do and say (or not do and say) all the things that will upset my brother's wife as I always seem to do. Surely I have learned how to be a little less fearful, a little more patient and objective in the past seven years. I hope they'll like the cottage and I hope they'll let Babs come and stay with me.

The burden of a thinking person is that they think too much. My mind scents the danger of desiring and expecting something fantastic, something that could not possibly happen actually, and of being badly disillusioned. But I must go to bed. Am exceedingly tired. Shall stay there as long as I want tomorrow.

SUNDAY, 29 SEPTEMBER

Maggie Joy Blunt
I fell into bed last night with the minimum of attention to evening toilet. In certain circumstances I can see myself becoming the most repellent old woman. Having long ceased to bother about public opinion I shall never clean my nails or trouble about scratches, rough skin, torn clothes or mud stains. My cough by then will be a horrible juicy one and I shall probably spit just when and where I please. My teeth will be dark brown with nicotine stain. My appetite will still be healthy and if I can afford it I shall have someone in to prepare, cook and serve my meals. I shall by then be so used to feeding from a tray with my feet up on a sofa that I shan't be able to eat in any other way. I shall gobble and dribble. Upon a capacious blouse front will reside in the creases not only cigarette ash (unless I have taken to a pipe) but droppings of many meals. I shall have developed a beard and moustache. Cats will be everywhere, hundreds of them, all rather thin and mangy as I shall forget to feed them.

Fine and warm again all day. Slept in deck chair most of afternoon. Am now listening to BBC's new Third Programme.

B. Charles
I was interested to see in last night's *Dispatch* that my letter is conspicuous by its absence!

Edie Rutherford
Yesterday was such a perfect day. When we went for a walk at 5 p.m. I took camera but Husband is grumpy about being photographed and won't without persuasion, threats and coaxing. I took one of his back.

MONDAY, 30 SEPTEMBER

Maggie Joy Blunt
My neighbour FG, who is a music critic by profession, thinks the Third Programme an excellent idea – there was never, he said, anything worth listening to on the others and when there was it was never long enough. But Mrs FG and I agreed that the light programmes have their uses while we do the chores and that listening often depends on one's mood. Perhaps I shall now make an effort to listen to and understand good music. I shall certainly listen to all the Third Programme plays that I can.

TUESDAY, 1 OCTOBER 1946

Edie Rutherford
Well, I don't know whether history will laugh or cry about all this Nuremberg business. The sentences on the horrible men are now being given. Von Papen has got off lightly, better than he deserves I reckon, though no doubt to live in ignominy won't ease what he has left of his life, and his son will have plenty to live down. Hess is lucky to get a life sentence though I reckon that is worse than death. Maybe his physical and mental state has had something to do with it. Reception is appalling, the ether is full of hideous howls, in a way fitting to the end of such fiends, sounds like fiends in hell welcoming them.

In a few years, I expect those with prison sentences will be freed. Tucked away in some papers will be an inch or two to the effect that so and so was released today, and no one will do more than say, 'Do you remember . . . ?' and some might add, 'Yes, the b*****', but most will not heed. It won't even be considered news.

WEDNESDAY, 2 OCTOBER

Herbert Brush
I am glad that they are going to hang Goering and Ribbentrop. It's a pity they can't have a more painful death.

> When Goering feels the rope around his neck
> His thoughts may turn to lives he helped to wreck
> And maybe on the other side he'll find

Their actions very far from being kind.
A moment, and the hangman's work is done
And Goering finds his pains have just begun
For through the scaffold trap his body fell
And instantly he found himself in Hell.

THURSDAY, 3 OCTOBER

Edie Rutherford

We could not have a better sign of the absurdity of the Nuremberg Trial than the way the acquitted men dare not move from jail now. The masses are in no doubt about the way all those men should have been dealt with. So much for all the blah blah about British justice and 'What an advertisement for it' etc kind of talk.

I agree that Emmy Goering and all wives of Nazis should be tried. Mind, Frau Bella Fromm in her book about life as a journalist in Germany as a Jewess has some good things to say for Emmy Goering, who used to take a risk by tipping her off at times when someone was in danger, so let Emmy take her trial and if anyone can speak for her, well, that's fair. We are not hesitant in saying wives influence their husbands if what the man does is praiseworthy, so I think it is only right to realise they also have some say when they are devils.

Went to local cinema last night to see *Brief Encounter* and loved it. Could not see any resemblance between Celia Johnson of the picture and Celia Johnson who we saw on the stage in Newcastle in *Bring Home the Heart*, but I suppose it is the same wench.

George Taylor

We were up early to catch the 7.15 a.m. train to London.

We had been told to have a look at Derry & Tom's Roof Garden, and it is certainly a little beauty spot, although it has the atmosphere of a charity garden party. You pay 1/- to the Red Cross on entering, and then take tea at charity high prices and garden party low quality food.

From there we went on to the 'Britain Can Make It' exhibition, and had no difficulty getting in. The exhibition begins like a peep show, or a fairy grotto in a fair, and the illusion is not dispelled for some time, in fact until one goes below into a miniature exhibition hall. There, set out in cases like shop windows, are tempting goods with no price labels but merely warning signs on most saying

'Available later' or 'Available soon'. Some indeed were marked 'Available now', but where was not shown, and catalogue seemed to be out of print. We wandered through the exhibition, peeping into the furnished rooms where someone with imagination had been wasting his (or her) time inventing occupations for the supposed occupants of the rooms, and through the Hall of Fashion, which appealed best to my wife, but which was somewhat severely criticised by male experts who were inspecting it at the same time. Finally we emerged, not much wiser about what Britain could sell, and took a bus to Oxford Circus.

Herbert Brush

W has gone to her firm to be inoculated against catching colds this coming winter: it seemed to be effective last year. Personally I have great faith in the Catarrh Cream made and sold by Boots in tubes. The nozzles of the tubes are long for insertion into one's nostrils. This stuff suits me better than Nostroline.

FRIDAY, 4 OCTOBER

Edie Rutherford

The Tories in Blackpool are funny. Can't see very far – as usual. Go on blundering along, apparently unable to see that they must change if they are ever to prosper again. Like putting life into a dead body now.

George Taylor

For a change, we caught a Green Line coach to Windsor, and saw a much brighter display of British Industry on the Great West Road. All the factories looked as if they were pavilions in some great exhibition, very different from the dirty and sordid barracks which form the old factories of the North.

We had booked in the evening for the Garrick, as Beatrice Lillie was appearing there, and we had heard her on the radio and thought she was worth hearing. The production was called *Better Late*, but I think that a better title would have been *Better Never*.

SATURDAY, 5 OCTOBER

Maggie Joy Blunt

The Nuremberg acquittals seem to have surprised and shocked most people. It certainly shocked me when I first read the headlines. Why should any of them have been acquitted? It makes one wonder if behind-the-scenes pressure was brought to bear, and one immediately rebukes oneself for entertaining such a reflection on British justice – which does seem to be an example worthy of world respect. These war criminals have been given a fair trial (though I dare say there'll be some people who will argue that it wasn't) – and as better brains than mine have pointed out, under the Nazis similar criminals would have been shot without further consideration. So they would and are in Russia.

There have been several new burglaries in the district recently. Am I nervous? Not unless I think about it. Coming home late at night sometimes I quail and call to the cats loudly as I walk down the garden path.

SUNDAY, 6 OCTOBER

Maggie Joy Blunt

Last night we put back the clocks one hour. This morning I put away all my summer frocks and white shoes.

To London for the 'Britain Can Make It' exhibition. Britain can make it – one wonders. I did not have to queue for more than five minutes, but there was too much of a crowd round the more popular exhibits to see anything in comfort. The display is wonderful – wonderful, fascinating, terrible. Here is the Brave New World. The Shape of Things to Come, the sweeping lines, the pastel-coloured walls, the curves and candy pillars, fabric swathed ceilings, the cunningly concealed and directed lighting, the air conditioning and central heating, glitter of plastics and light metals – all that one expects and fears of the underground world of tomorrow. I was dazzled and dazed in this modern temple. Perhaps that was the idea – to dazzle the public into thinking the goods were better than they were. The absence of trade labels and advertising gave a false impression of refinement – it was only a very refined version of the Ideal Homes exhibition – some good things, some bad, in a glamorous modern setting. And our feet – our poor feet – trod the undisguised, unnoticed mosaic floors (familiar to all students) of the V&A.

My local Fabians have been debating 'That the new Health Service is in the best interests of the nation'. This was a good meeting, drawing a large audience of local doctors and nurses. Motion proposed by David Stark Murray and opposed by Dr Leslie Hartley, an eye specialist. Discussion that followed was lively, full of good points from either side. But the Socialists won: 53–47 I think, or near it. Old established doctors seem to fear the administrative muddle the new system will bring in its train – the filling in of forms, *more* queuing not less, valuable time wasted and so on. They resent Bevan's attitude and his condemnation of the hospitals. So many of these have had to close down, largely because of labour shortage, that they fear there will not be the nurses to staff the new hospitals when they are built. The present housing situation makes them sceptical that the new Health Centres will be ready by 1948.

MONDAY, 7 OCTOBER

Maggie Joy Blunt

Last week I sprayed sodium chlorate on the crazy paving and brick paths. It seems to be killing the weeds most effectively. Have just sprinkled some, dry, on various persistent dandelions, but feel rather a murderess. I like dandelions. I love their shining, vulgar little faces.

SS *Ascania* bearing the family homewards arrives at Liverpool tomorrow. Shipping office told me this morning that boat train would leave about 5 p.m., arriving Euston 9–10 p.m. My brother has booked accommodation at Exiles Club, Twickenham, and I think they may decide to stay in Liverpool overnight. Both Ella and I want to meet the train. I have sent a cable to the *Ascania* asking Pooh to let me know what they intend to do and anxiously await reply.

I have been thinking of my family history today. Because of my mother and her family I am in this cottage. Victorian, City of London merchants, prosperous middle class. The youngest son was adventurous and invested his share of the family fortune, and my mother's which she lent him, in tobacco instead of becoming an accountant as his father wished. It was a good gamble and I inherited my share of the proceeds in due course. It helped to pay for my university education where I met Paul who introduced me to Miss M–y when she was looking for tenants for her property at a time when I was looking for a cottage. And so I am here.

But why am I here, instead of married with a family, or a successful career woman? That's too long a story but has something to do with the character I inherited from my mother along with her money, which has always been in conflict with that large part of my father's nature that I inherited too. It seems to have got me nowhere, but I am not so sure. The story is not finished.

TUESDAY, 8 OCTOBER

B. Charles

Went to Inverness this morning. Stupidly I travelled in the Through Carriage and had a most uncomfortable journey. I shall never travel in a Through Carriage again. Arrived on time at Inverness, and went to the Caledonian Hotel where I had booked a room. KS arrived at 5.15 and we spent the evening together.

KS has some rather funny ideas about things in general. For instance, he had a room at the Station Hotel but thought it better for me to stay at the Caledonian, just in case we should get on one another's nerves! Of course it is far better to see too little of a person than too much, but when I was only staying for two nights, it would hardly have been possible to get on each other's nerves to any great extent. He seems to think it would be nice to get a flat above me in Chester Street if it can be managed. I will do my best, as I should like to have him in Edinburgh. When I got back here I found a letter from Bucklands to say they had sold 57 for £3,250. I am thankful it is sold.

I am interested in this hotel strike and note the strikers seem to be certain to get what they want. All these strikes are, of course, extremely symptomatic of the times. And of course they are extremely serious, as they will retard any sort of recovery from wartime restrictions quite indefinitely. I note the bread rationing is now quite definitely not coming off 'at present'. I doubt if it ever does, within any measurable distance of time. The Government gets more and more rotten.

Maggie Joy Blunt

Have been waiting twenty-four hours – more – for message from brother Pooh. None has come. It is nearly 4.30 p.m. I phoned the shipping office this morning. Boat train is due at Euston at 9 p.m. I can't believe the family will want to arrive in London at that hour and then have to get to Twickenham on this chill October evening. Oh, what are they feeling, thinking now? They will be in Liverpool. It will feel very cold – the town will look as shabby as London does. Over seven years . . . and Babs now thirteen . . . They will be coping with baggage and customs. I wish I had been there on the dock to greet them.

And at that instant the message came. They are hoping to catch the boat train and proceed to Twickenham but are waiting for confirmation of accommodation from the Club. So really I'm not much better off. But think I shall risk it. Will have to leave here at 7 p.m. to be at Euston by 9 p.m. They *may* not be on the train, but I should hate to miss them and if the Club can't put them up I can bring them all back with me – if they'll be persuaded.

FRIDAY, 11 OCTOBER

Maggie Joy Blunt
Went to Euston. The train was half an hour late. A crowd of people awaited it. And when it came the mob was so thick it was just sheer luck if you met the person you wanted. The entire train-load seemed to be Egyptians, Greeks and Orientals. I felt I was in a foreign city.

I gave up and went home. At Paddington I phoned the Club. They were expected but hadn't arrived. Next morning I did at least speak with the whole family and arranged to meet them for lunch at the Empire Society. So there we were finally – 'Granny' Ella, Pooh, Ivy, Babs and Auntie Piglet – drinking sherry and talking hard – about the voyage and the crush on board, the arrival at Euston when they fell upon the first taxi, wisely, looked for us but gave up, about clothes, coupons, food, high prices in Egypt, how Babs had grown, how brown she was (solemn, quiet until spoken to then her little face was alight with friendly smiles), the ease with which they got through the customs because Pooh found he knew someone who could pull wires, the stuff they have brought with them and what they might have brought! Their wartime stories – raids, bombs, blackout – and later the riots. Then all on to tea at Granny's, then home. They are due for about ten months leave but will be lucky if they get three owing to shortage of staff. Pooh, as he came to meet me at the Empire Society, looked exactly the same. But later I could see how tired he was.

Wish there were some means of recording one's thoughts as one sits in a train or bus, walks in a street or peels potatoes. They've gone now, those teeming queries and memories as I journeyed to Euston on Tuesday. The habit my father had of grinding his back teeth silently when excited so that you could see the muscles between jaw and temple moving and knew that his stomach was in a-flutter just as yours was, although he didn't fidget. The countless times we have met my brother or seen him off on another voyage. Stations and trains, ships and docks. What will he be like now, what will he think of me, what shall I have done, be doing when we meet again . . . ?

Herbert Brush

Do you ever listen to the BBC's *Your Questions Answered* on Fridays after the ten o'clock news? I always found them very interesting, except the questions on music, which I can never understand. I have often wondered what it is I am really missing in life, when I see the open mouths and rapt expressions on the faces of some people while they listen to high-class music, and glare at people who make the least unnecessary noise. I must be losing some pleasure, though I don't know what it is.

7 p.m. Went with W to the State Cinema this afternoon. The main picture was *Concerto*, a coloured film all about high-class music which I do not understand.

SUNDAY, 13 OCTOBER

Herbert Brush

9 a.m. Some of the plaster ceiling in the kitchen, which was put up yesterday by men working overtime, fell down during the night and made an awful mess.

11 a.m. Some more of the kitchen ceiling has come down and D is busy sweeping up the mess. I believe she enjoys it, as cleaning and scrubbing is her hobby.

Maggie Joy Blunt

Had tea with the family at their club in Twickenham yesterday. They seem satisfied with it and comfortable for the time being. To me it looked shabby, tired and not too clean – obviously war-worn, like so many places. Pooh has been to head office and may be given four months leave, as was overhauled by the company's doctor and diagnosed as thoroughly run down and in need of a long rest. He may get sent next to Colombo or Brazil. They don't know what they will do with Babs. If they get appointed to a station where there is a good school (they were very satisfied with the one in Cairo) she will go with them.

Was interested to read Tom Harrisson's letter to Mass-Observers received last week and that he believes the diaries will 'be of great sociological and historical value in the future'. It makes me feel one is, perhaps, doing something worthwhile, though it seems trivial and unimportant at the time. Yet just reading through one's own one is fascinated and amazed – they cover only a very small field of action. Multiplied and representing as much as possible of the social structure one can imagine and understand their collective value.

MONDAY, 14 OCTOBER

Edie Rutherford
Burglars broke into Husband's office on Friday/Saturday night. Husband had two pipes and two boxes of matches in his locked drawer, which was forced and the cheap pipe and matches taken. In his brother's office (he's the boss) they made an awful mess of his desk, hacking all the front away in order to force two locks on the two drawers, and when they had done it all they found was two cigars, some presentation pencils with the firm's name on them (ha ha), and some notepaper belonging to Gold Club of which Harold is president. All three safes untouched.

TUESDAY, 15 OCTOBER

Herbert Brush
More of the kitchen ceiling fell down yesterday.

B. Charles
I have been reading in the *Telegraph* about this proposed film of the executions at Nuremberg. I have never heard anything as horrible and revolting. Really, today, there seems to be a positive wave of

sensationalism sweeping over the entire world. For the Allies to contemplate, let alone execute, such a project, revolts every decent feeling. I can't think it will be allowed. There seems to be an idea that such a film ought to be publicly shown in England! And then there is all the sensationalism about the last hours of Heath. There has been a fearful debasement of taste and feeling during the last few years.

Maggie Joy Blunt

Today entertained the family to lunch and tea. A tinned tongue, lettuce, tomato, shredded cabbage, celery, parsley, mint and a Russian salad of cold potato, chives, carrot, tinned peas and baked beans, with vegetable soup first and a cold semolina, apple and sultana sweet – made with fresh milk – and coffee. The first coal fire of the season in the sitting room as a celebration. Also a spot of hoarded gin to welcome them.

Now I feel lost. I always do when visitors leave and I have an evening alone in front of me. Doesn't seem worthwhile starting any big job. I wish someone would call.

WEDNESDAY, 16 OCTOBER

Herbert Brush

Current was cut off in this district for a short time at 7 a.m., just when W turned on the set to get the news. However, it was on soon enough for us to hear that Goering had committed suicide.

Edie Rutherford

So the Nazi devils are dead, and Heath dead, and the *Queen Elizabeth* on her peace-time maiden voyage, with appropriately a pilot named Mr Smith. I don't myself care for enormous planes but if such must be, let 'em be British.

Seems to me someone looked the other way or was grossly careless re Goering and poison. Not that it matters in one way, so long as he is dead, but that he cheated justice at the end may give some of his deluded followers something to commemorate.

Actually a woman crying for Heath outside the prison yesterday and hoping to the last for a reprieve. Oh well, everyone's loved by someone, as the old song has it. A joke which has been going round here – I think it feeble but the locals seemed to get a kick out of it:

Heath's lawyer was able to prove his insanity as among his papers was a season ticket for the Sheffield Wednesday ground. (It had to be explained to me.)

B. Charles
This morning Miss Scott rushed in and said how awful it was that Goering had managed to commit suicide! I felt so bucked that he had managed to do this, and make such fools of the Yanks, who were supposed to be guarding him, that I could have danced with joy! I am always so glad when either the British, or the Yanks, are made to look fools with regard to all this sanctimonious rubbish at Nuremberg! At all events Goering was a very brave man and I am very glad indeed to learn that all the Nazis died very bravely, though I was perfectly certain they would. In twenty-five years' time they will be 'heroes' and 'martyrs', and, in the Third World War, the Germans will be our 'Glorious' Allies, fighting against the Russians. Another cheering piece of news in the paper today is the fact that the hotel strikers have got all they want. Anything to make this Government look a fool.

George Taylor
My second turn of police duty this year. Tonight I was on duty at the Safety First exhibition, an exhibition organised mainly by the police with the valuable assistance of the Junior Chamber of Commerce. The highlight of the exhibition was the kiddy car section, where toy motors were run on model streets, with traffic signals, pedestrian crossings and road signs all complete. Round and round they went, under the watchful eye of a police inspector. When any rule of the road was disobeyed, or any particular act of courtesy shown, the inspector blew his whistle and announced through the loud speaker what was wrong, or congratulated the model driver, as the occasion demanded.

Herbert Brush
My seventy-fourth birthday.

> A man whose years are seventy-four
> Can't surely hope for many more
> However, now I'm pleased to tell
> You all that I am feeling well

2 p.m W and I went to the 'Britain Can Make It' exhibition at the Victoria and Albert Museum this morning. W joined the queue at 9.45 and it was already more than 100 yards long, formed up four abreast by the police, and by the time we arrived at the entrance it was 10.20. A woman next to me in queue picked up a sixpence as we slowly moved along, and after that I glanced frequently at the pavement to see whether there was any luck for me, but no.

There is far too much of the exhibition and so spread about that it took us close on two hours to walk round and catch a fleeting glimpse of what lay behind the crowd. There were thousands of items which did not interest me at all. In a large hall there was a revolving stand on which female figures were dressed in new designs, but the waxwork figures were so hideously slim and lanky.

On arrival in the Children's Toy Room it struck me that the modern child has stronger nerves or less imagination than when I was small, or they would be scared stiff by the gollywogs and other great glaring-eyed stuffed figures.

W was much interested in an arrangement for keeping hens in the smallest possible space. There were four old hens, each one confined in a wired-in cubicle, and it seemed very cruel to me. An ultra-modern bicycle was interesting and must have been made of some very light metal, or it would weigh much more than any cyclist would care to push about. There is a battery and dynamo inside the frame to help one along. This is in the sections where 'Designers Are Looking Ahead'.

I could not see much of the 'Space Ship', as one had to look through a round opening in the wall to view a large section of the moon and a space ship apparently just going to land on its surface. I am not one of those who firmly believe that in a few years time we shall be able to travel to the moon and come back alive.

We came back through the park, and W dropped me near Victoria, and then went on to her firm to be inoculated against catching a cold. I caught a tram.

SATURDAY, 19 OCTOBER

B. Charles
There is a very amusing article in today's *Scotsman* headed OOMPH! It relates to that stupid old judge who pretended he didn't know what

Oomph was. He was trying some case relating to some firm who want to register the word 'Oomphies' for some kind of women's slippers. I have always thought that if these judges are really as ignorant as they pretend with regard to common or garden everyday matters, they are the very last people to hold such appointments. But I believe they are merely lying when they claim this ignorance. You will usually find that if some revolting sex case comes along, but one where the sexual habits of the prisoner are very ordinary, the fool of a judge will say: 'I have never heard of such awful things', or words to this effect. Whereas the most elementary schoolboy, or girl, knows perfectly well about such happenings. After all, I suppose the average judge has had some sort of classical education, and it is impossible to read even the most ordinary Latin or Greek classics without coming across cases of 'awful' sexual perversions. I never trust these old 'he-virgins'. They are usually just liars and arrant humbugs.

George Taylor
We made an effort to see Walt Disney's *Make Mine Music*. Technically the film was well produced, but the music of only two of the ten episodes was decent. The other eight were jazz.

SUNDAY, 20 OCTOBER

B. Charles
Last night I made one or two interesting discoveries about French clocks. From information I get, and from several illustrations I saw in a book, I now feel certain the clock I got at Dowell's on Friday is probably the most sensational bargain I have ever got.

My impression of the film show I saw last night may be of interest, as I hadn't been inside a cinema since September 1929. First and foremost the distortion of the voice I had noticed in 1929 is just as bad now as it was then. All the voices sounded as if the speakers were talking into a foghorn. But here the comparison with the dreadful *Show Boat* in 1929 ends. I enjoyed the performance very much indeed. But I am sure, for me, the silent films are preferable to these talkies. The first film shown last night was *Cyprus is an Island*. The narrator was Valentine Dyall and his voice was dreadful, but the film was most interesting and I enjoyed it tremendously. It made me want to go to Cyprus for a holiday.

The next one was called *Swinging the Lambeth Walk* which I liked better than the other two. The reason I preferred it was because there was no attempt in it to 'make a play'. It was just variations on the music of 'The Lambeth Walk', and there was a colour accompaniment. I can't say the flickering colours on the screen interpreted or enlarged the music to me. I feel sure that IF the cinema is ever to be of real, artistic value, an entirely new technique will have to be discovered, and what is suitable for the screen will have to be discovered. I feel sure the cinema is NOT suitable for theatrical plays. Plays need living actors, I am sure. I think I might find *Fantasia* or *Mickey Mouse* interesting, as they have no relation to plays, or 'glamour' or 'oomph!'. But, although I do not like plays in the cinema, I must admit the acting of Françoise Rosay in *Une Femme Disparaît* utterly marvellous. I have never seen finer acting and I feel certain no actress of any age, of any nationality or of any period has ever acted better, or ever will act better. Because this woman acts as well as it is possible to act. Her performance left me completely thrilled. If only the film had been silent it would have been perfect.

MONDAY, 21 OCTOBER

Herbert Brush

W told me early that she heard on the seven o'clock news that a hundred thousand monkeys were being brought into this country. Of course I did not believe it, but she said that the announcer said 'monkeys' quite clearly. I began to picture the sailors on a ship which had all those monkeys on board as cargo, and I could feel sorry for the sailors. However, I listened for a repeat on the eight o'clock news and the 'monkeys' turned into 'bananas'. A hundred thousand bunches of bananas.

TUESDAY, 22 OCTOBER

Edie Rutherford

I've told Husband not to have an accident in his ragged underwear. He says he won't, but if he should he'll say he is Abraham Popoffski from Poland and has no friends or relations in this country. It is comical to see him puzzling to know which holes are for his head, arms and legs.

THURSDAY, 24 OCTOBER

Maggie Joy Blunt
A day in London. Lunch with S in Fleet Street. He has been all over Europe again and at Nuremberg for the latter days. Trial very well organised, he said. Hess, he thinks, was mad. During the reading of the judgement he made rabbits of his handkerchief and kept nudging Goering and giggling. Goering played his part to the end – handing his earphones to the Americans at his side after his sentence with a gesture of contempt.

Europe grows less and less in love with Communism. There is continued talk of fear of war on all sides. But the Russian army is not mechanised. Discipline is bad. Somewhere S was with an officer who, when he found a sentry slack and inattentive, beat the sentry on the face with the butt of a rifle till the man fell. 'I am sorry you had to see this,' said the officer to S. 'He won't have another chance. It is the only way we can maintain discipline.'

Their toast when being polite to foreign visitors is always to 'Stalin, Roosevelt and Churchill'. Attlee and Truman mean nothing to them.

Mainly I like S because he talks a lot of nonsense and makes me laugh. Some of his stories are not repeatable. A good generalised picture of him is Evelyn Waugh's Corker in *Scoop*.

FRIDAY, 25 OCTOBER

Herbert Brush
11.30 a.m. I heard this morning from the Allotments Competition and learned that I have not even won a certificate this year, in spite of the fact that I have gathered more and better stuff from my plot than ever before. However, the judges know best so I must suppose that my work is not as good as it used to be.

3.40 p.m. The more I look at my plots the less I can understand why the judges gave me so few marks. For neatness and finish I got four out of eight. I don't think that I shall trouble to enter the competition again.

> I'd like to meet the learned judge,
> The man who judged my plot
> And gave me fewer marks this year

Than I have ever got.
I worked away from day to day,
I dug and raked and hoed,
And thought that I was doing well,
That all my efforts showed.

SUNDAY, 27 OCTOBER

B. Charles
A very cold day. I have only been out for the papers and milk, and this afternoon Donald Blyth came along as arranged, and we had a very long, and interesting, chat. I have always said I would far sooner have to teach an ordinary clever lad who is keen to learn, than a brilliant one who is not keen! I like keenness in everything. I think I cleared up a good deal of mental confusion this afternoon. He is coming again next Sunday, he says.

I have written Professor Crew this evening about the question of bequeathing a sum of money to the university for the study I have in mind, if he thinks it would be accepted. I shall be interested to get his reply. Last night I went to the library and found out a good deal about curtain drapery.

Edie Rutherford
So Goering had the poison all this time. I query whether he could have had it in his navel though Husband says I could not imagine the kind of navel he'd have. As for it being in his back passage – seems to me his searchers want lessons from the Kimberley diamond mines where they give the natives a purgative to make sure of that kind of thing.

Unedifying picture of corpses in *Sunday Pictorial*. Also warning articles in *Sunday Pic* about Mosleyites. I believe our Government does make the mistake of not taking them seriously, forgetting that tall oaks from tiny acorns grow.

MONDAY, 28 OCTOBER

B. Charles
Surely this is a day to remember, as this morning at Herrald's I found a pair of perfectly delightful decorated satinwood elbow chairs! At

least, I *think* they are satinwood (they may be birch), but they are lovely, in every way. I got them for £27.

Went to see Dr Broadie about my new body belt and he took my blood pressure. Quite normal, and he said so was my heart. Is this unusual at the advanced age of fifty-four? I went to Gardiner's about getting the belt made, and they told me there is an elastic famine. The man said it will be about Christmas before they can supply the belt.

TUESDAY, 29 OCTOBER

Maggie Joy Blunt

A new book for my diary always pleases me and fills me with good resolutions. Since I began using Duplicate books (February 1945) I have filled four of them. The copies remaining lie on the floor now in front of me, newly decorated with white labels bearing description and dates of contents.

I went searching for fireworks in Windsor this afternoon. Called in at every sort of shop where I thought they might have them but was told nearly every time 'We don't stock them' or 'We are not having them this year'. In one shop only did I hear, 'Sorry, they've all gone'.

Have promised to give a fireworks party for my niece next Tuesday. Am asking Mrs C and her two little boys and Mrs FG and her young daughter. I can manage the tea I am sure, with some help over the milk – the fireworks are the problem. My brother has promised to look round London and Richmond. I have a whole box-full left over from Babs's last Guy Fawkes party eight years ago. I tried a coloured match and a sparkler this afternoon and the match flared beautifully. The sparkler was not so encouraging, but performed when thrust into the fire. I intend to keep the box under the kitchen stove where it is now, in the hope that it will dry them all. My brother exclaims, 'For God's sake, don't blow yourself up – the cats might not like it.'

Spent the weekend at Hampstead. June's birthday. Lys came to tea on Monday and then she and I went to a Spiritualist meeting. London School of Para-psychology I think it is called, the Mona Rolf group. I am just curious and a little fascinated by it all but don't want to take any active part. I think Lys feels she is mediumistic and would like to train. What hundreds of 'salvation' cliques there seem to be – political, intellectual and religious.

B. Charles

There was a very nice letter from Professor Crew about the proposed bequest to the Faculty of Medicine, and he has advised me to write to Professor Sydney Smith about the matter. I have just done so. If he thinks the bequest would be accepted, I shall alter my will to give it effect. It is a project I have always wanted to further.

THURSDAY, 31 OCTOBER

B. Charles

I noticed in Brown's fruiterer a lot of persimmons at 1/6d. each. I cannot think why the Government is importing things like persimmons when there is such a scarcity of the ordinary commodities. Surely any sane Government would import eggs, etc, from Denmark, rather than this exotic fruit at scandalous prices, and which no one wants! I see rubbishy unripe pineapples are 25/- each!

Maggie Joy Blunt

No fireworks anywhere. Tried Hamleys in Regent Street and Gamages today. At Gamages they told me that queuing for them begins at 8.30 in the morning. By 4 p.m. not a stick left. Met Pooh and Ivy for lunch. We went to the Bolivar; I had a braised lamb's heart.

Edie Rutherford

Speaking to my friend's husband yesterday, he said he reckons the £ is worth 9/- today, compared to 1939. I have never thought it out as far as that but would not be surprised if he is right. He says he agrees with the Mosleyites that the Jews run this country though he has no time for Fascism of course.

FRIDAY, 1 NOVEMBER 1946

George Taylor

My wife left just before 7.30 p.m. for her polling station. Fortunately she was posted only about a quarter of a mile from home, and when she arrived, found that our neighbour was the presiding officer. I exercised my business vote for the first time. The Labour candidate had won by twenty in 1945, and my solitary vote would therefore be of some use in supporting the Progressive candidate.

Herbert Brush

A woman sat opposite me on the bus this morning and I think that 'The Ugly Duchess' would have been considered good-looking beside her. Her chin stuck out about an inch beyond her nose, her face was fully as long as mine, she had a moustache, a black one, and the colour of her skin was like oily parchment. But I could not help looking at her and I think she knew it. She wore a wedding ring and I could not help wondering how her husband could possibly stand a face like that.

SATURDAY, 2 NOVEMBER

Edie Rutherford

Our man has kept his place on city council and Labour has gained three seats there. Hurrah. Mind, the percentage of voting is terribly low, about a third of the average. Friend has lent me her Boots library sub. I use it but what a poor lot compared to our public library. Fancy paying for it! Signs of our times, headlined in large print today: 'Toffee apples off points' and 'One ounce more butter for Christmas?'

Herbert Brush

I and W went to the State Cinema in the afternoon. There was a really wonderful picture of a horse, *Smoky*, which gave me several thrills when the animals acted in almost a human way. If you ever get the chance, go and see it.

MONDAY, 4 NOVEMBER

B. Charles

I enjoyed the Film Guild show last night very much indeed. The film *The Music Box*, a Laurel and Hardy one, although it did not amuse me, was, of its kind, extremely 'worthwhile' and the travel film *The Venice of the North* most interesting. I am glad I have joined this society.

TUESDAY, 5 NOVEMBER

Edie Rutherford

Children started with fireworks last night, much to the consternation of cat from 178 who was visiting us. I should have thought that

306

everyone on this island had had enough of bangs for ever, but I suppose there is a generation of youngsters coming along now who did not register the big bangs we all dreaded so.

At 2 p.m. I was getting ready to go out when there was a knock at the door, a man with a scrap of paper: 'The Caretaker's compliments and will you telephone as indicated on this paper.' It read Detective Inspector Turner, 23105. I said, 'Whatever for?' and was told that when out shopping this morning two plain clothes men had been knocking at our door. I didn't like it at all, though I haven't a guilty conscience. I went down to the public phone and rang, and was asked if I was coming to town, so I said it so happened I was on my way.

Well, it appears a man calling himself Westlake, alias Morrison, has been getting money by false pretences and among papers at his last lodgings was my name and address. Did I know him? I said I didn't. Asked could I ring my husband in case he did, which I did, but Sid couldn't throw any light on it, was intrigued to know what on earth I was ringing from CID HQ for. This man has been posing as a doctor, distributing birth control stuff and abortion instruments. The detective inspector advised me to forget all about it now. But I can't. I'm curious and peeved to hell. The detective said so long as the man hasn't cheated me out of cash, all is well.

B. Charles

This morning I went to see Professor Sydney Smith, who was very pleasant, and he thinks if I leave the money for the purpose I have in mind, that the Faculty of Medicine will accept eagerly. I shall try to do so, as it has been an idea of mine to found a Research Fellowship for the study of Homosexuality when I die. It was curious that when I was going to see Professor Smith about this matter, that Bobby should have sent me a cutting from a North Country paper, with an account of the case of some old man of sixty-five whom Justice Charles has sentenced to ten years' penal servitude, for a homosexual offence. Professor Smith said he thought Charles a terrible judge when dealing with sexual cases. It is true. He seems quite unfitted in every way.

THURSDAY, 7 NOVEMBER

Maggie Joy Blunt

Firework party a great success – four adults and four children, for tea split scones, sticky buns, jam tarts, apple jelly and blancmange. Only one in the whole collection of fireworks was dud. DFG's little girl (twenty months) crowed and squeaked with joy and ran excitedly about the garden falling into flowerbeds.

This year's Old Girls' magazine arrived yesterday. The school getting back to pre-war conditions: 'The lawns can now be mown more frequently and the Formal Gardens were planted with flowers this year instead of vegetables . . . Improved travel facilities have made it possible to play matches further afield and to restore half-term weekends . . . The Garden Party has started again, the array of cars in the drive making it feel really like peace again.'

FRIDAY, 8 NOVEMBER

Edie Rutherford

Incredible case in paper yesterday – husband got divorce on account of wife's cruelty. Judge sympathised with him. Beats me. Surely the man was a poor fish for him to ever have allowed his wife to become such a tyrant. The first time she told him to walk behind her, or the first time she put her paper over the chair before he sat down, he should have asked her who the hell she thought she was, whose home is it, or something of that kind. Imagine a MAN letting his wife start such behaviour. He deserves all that followed. The twerp.

God knows, I have the mildest of husbands, but I know I could not start any nonsense. In the first place, I respect him too much; and in the second he'd be the first to kick hard at the first sign of domination, for all his quiet, gentle, mild ways, bless him. I would not have him otherwise.

Tangerines in a local shop, 7d. each, poor little things they are too, ripened in captivity by the look of them. Nice to see them again, but not at that price.

SATURDAY, 9 NOVEMBER

B. Charles
There is an amusing little piece in the paper about that idiot Aneurin Bevan. It reads as follows: 'Our island is made mainly of coal and surrounded by fish. Only an organising genius could produce a shortage of coal and fish at the same time in Great Britain' – Mr Aneurin Bevan, at the Socialist Party Conference, Blackpool, 24 May 1945! So now we know! (We are short of both!) How on earth ANYONE can take any politician seriously, if anyone does, I really don't know.

MONDAY, 11 NOVEMBER

Maggie Joy Blunt
A weekend with visitors has come and gone. A Mr H who made the booking for himself back in the summer. I thought it prudent that I should have a chaperone, so Lys came. She was vastly amused at the idea of my wanting one, as I am not fussy over the conventions when I know people, but with a complete stranger it seemed sensible to have someone else about the place – not only for my sake but for his also. And I think he might have felt a little embarrassed. He was a nice, quiet, respectable young man with glasses and moustache and untidy corduroy trousers. Rather pale and thin – looked underfed and ate every scrap of everything I put in front of him. He brought me in dead wood for kindling when he came in from his walks.

The kittens are all gone but one. I put a notice in each of the local papers and I have never before had such a spate of inquiries. The one still with us would have gone too but I have promised to keep it for S.

B. Charles
The twenty-eighth anniversary of Armistice Day 1918! What a long, long time ago it seems! It is now 7.10 p.m., and twenty-eight years ago today I was in my dressing room at the Court Theatre, Sloane Square, dressing for the show *Twelfth Night*! It was rather a thrilling day, in a way. I recollect many restaurant staff 'walked out' to enjoy themselves, and people took possession of some of the London buses to joy-ride in! The performance at the Court wasn't cancelled, but there was a very poor audience that evening.

It seems Lady MacRobert was invited to give a two-minute talk on the radio yesterday, but the BBC banned the speech. It is printed in the *Telegraph* today, and I agree with every word she says about all the continued restrictions and frustrations. She deplores the totalitarian methods of the present Government. Freedom, has, of course, entirely disappeared now in Great Britain.

WEDNESDAY, 13 NOVEMBER

B. Charles
A very nice letter from Professor Crew who says he is much attracted by my ideas and arguments. He advised me to get a book by a Doctor Cadawias on human hermaphroditism. I got it this morning and think I shall find it interesting. Of course such extreme cases as these human hermaphrodites are not, in my estimation, much help in elucidating the problem of homosexuality in quite ordinary men and women. But, at all events, I shall find this book interesting: the one exception of which he was ashamed is the Hudson Family. He was, of course, 'peculiar' himself, and, being a human ostrich, buried his head in the sand. Well, at all events, I don't do that!

FRIDAY, 15 NOVEMBER

Maggie Joy Blunt
Have embarked now, seriously, on some research into early eighteenth century with a view to a biography. Moved to do this by state of my bank balance. This project will take some months and is a gamble, but am determined to do it. The proposed local MM business has more or less fallen through. Partly because the printer misled both Cy and myself as to his ideas of the thing and partly because he is too busy just now before Christmas to take on extra work. Damn all businessmen.

B. Charles
I read quite a bit of the book on hermaphroditism last night, and find parts of it very illuminating. But when the man expatiates on the characteristics of male homosexuals, he seems to me to be prejudiced and, in quite a number of instances, completely wrong.

It is queer how many so-called intelligent and informed people seem to think that homosexuality is, if I may use the word, 'infectious'. Such people think that if once a lad is 'corrupted' by a male homosexual, he, hey presto! becomes homosexual! Such an idea is completely ridiculous, as I have proved on innumerable occasions. I have ventured to assert, after careful investigation, that almost every boy, at some period of his life, has been 'got at' by some male homosexual. At least on one occasion, and often on more. Yet the average lad forgets all about it, marries and becomes a father.

MONDAY, 18 NOVEMBER

Edie Rutherford
Where was I now – I went to London a week ago today. I thoroughly enjoyed my few days off and am glad I got them in before the worst weather comes. Mostly seeing friends. Had lunch at DH Evans, then off to South Kensington for Britain Can't Get It. Long queue but as it was a moving one, we joined and in about ten minutes were inside. Oh my my, what a tedious business. Miles and miles, and we had already walked miles that morning. Made one mad to see so much only to be looked forward to.

TUESDAY, 19 NOVEMBER

B. Charles
I enjoyed the film show very much indeed last night. I am beginning to understand, I think, why so many film actors seem to 'get there' without any previous training. If a man, or woman, is a 'type', they, of course, merely have to play themselves all the time. Take the case of Ray Milland. Well, he is now exactly the same as he was when he was just a trooper called Reg Jones. He hasn't, so far as I can see, learned anything so far as acting is concerned. He merely plays Reg Jones all the time. I have written to ask Peter if he can tell me who bought him out of the regiment and started him on this film career.

Maggie Joy Blunt
Yesterday afternoon cycled to see Stoke Poges church. Although I have lived within two or three miles of it for seven years, my last visit was about the time I was leaving school, 1927–8. I read again Gray's *Elegy*. At the time it was published I suppose it was something new in

311

poetry – in idea, detail and mood. But I am afraid it bores me. We have had so many melancholy poets, accurate observers of nature and the rustic scene, better and worse, since. I suspect that it has outlived its time and will be of interest in the future to students of literature only.

Tangerines off the ration in the village today, at 5/6d. a lb. Other people exclaimed, as I did, at the price and left them where they were.

WEDNESDAY, 20 NOVEMBER

Herbert Brush
I wonder when we will find a cure for strike-microbe. It seems to rob people of their common sense, and turns grown men into boys who like to destroy something just for the pleasure of it. Look at those silly idiots in Manchester, the bus strikers; now what good can it do to let the air out of the tyres on a bus?

THURSDAY, 21 NOVEMBER

Herbert Brush
I wish that my father had made a few more entries in his little Churchman diaries. I for one would have found them interesting, even though he led as humdrum an existence as I do.

Most of my father's entries refer to the weather, but on 4 June 1887 he had five swarms of bees, and had to put two of them into one hive.

'On July 26th there was the School Treat, but it was a windy day and the tent was blown down, so we had tea on the lawn, until it began to rain. To make up for the disappointment we had a second tea next day and there was dancing on the lawn to the piano.' He does not mention who played the piano.

FRIDAY, 22 NOVEMBER

Herbert Brush
A dull, damp morning. I went to Peckham, changed my book and took out *The Dark Side of the Moon*. I don't know yet why the book has such a title, but as it is a story about Poland and the USSR,

probably the moon does not come into it at all. But the name makes me think of the Far Side of the Moon, which we on earth can never see, unless we do eventually send a rocket round it.

SATURDAY, 23 NOVEMBER

Edie Rutherford

I don't think Gordon Richard Long should be hanged for ending the life of his imbecile daughter. Poor wretch. Even if spared, his life is not worth much to himself, yet I'm sure he felt he was doing right. It must be awful to live with a child of the kind his daughter was, day after day, week after week, month after month, for seven years. How dare we judge the man and condemn him?

How very nice of H. G. Wells to mention in his will the love he had from his family. I have said that he was a good man ever since I read his autobiography, and this confirms it, no matter how much of an atheist or agnostic he called himself.

B. Charles

Yesterday I met a nicely spoken and seemingly intelligent telegraph messenger. He told me he is English, from Hampshire, and he wants to take the London Matriculation in September. It seems he will have to take French, and so far, his knowledge of this language is NIL! I told him I used to teach French, and that if he wants to get through in September, he will have to put in a great deal of work. I gave him my Chester Street address.

WEDNESDAY, 27 NOVEMBER

Herbert Brush

The Dark Side of the Moon is a description of the way the Russians treated the Poles during the war, and judging by it, there was not much to choose between them and the Germans. People were herded just like cattle, and most of the time they were wading in their own filth up to their ankles. Some of the descriptions of the treatment of prisoners almost made me feel sick.

FRIDAY, 29 NOVEMBER

Edie Rutherford

As I look round the world, and read the papers and listen to BBC, I'm damned if anywhere seems better off than we are, taking a broad view of things. We may as well realise it and be content. Who for instance can say USA is liveable just now? Or Palestine, or Greece, or Egypt, or France, or Russia, or India, or my country? On the whole I should think New Zealand is the next best, and I see she has returned her Labour Government again. Good for her. She has had them in power long enough now to know what it means and clearly she likes it.

Well, it looks as if transport is going to be nationalised in spite of all the anti talk. Speaking to a friend yesterday she said she was sure the Health Bill would have to be abandoned. I said I wasn't of that mind though maybe there'd be modifications. Discovered she was entertaining five doctors on Monday, all anti, so no wonder she got a very one-sided view.

B. Charles

I had a rather interesting chat to a lad at lunch in the British Restaurant, and we discussed the Scottish Nationalist movement. He says that, at bottom, almost every Scot is very interested in the Movement. I think it is a shame that Scotland has not got its own parliament and does not manage its own internal affairs. It is a cheek for England to suppose that when she makes such a hash of trying to govern herself, she has the impertinence to pretend to govern Scotland! This lad said it is only the extremists who want to be entirely free from all interference from England, but all the Scottish Nationalists want a parliament of their own and to be allowed to manage their own internal business.

Maggie Joy Blunt

Am spending the morning in bed and may even stay here all day. For the last three months private affairs have been worrying and depressing me.

It is time our 'class' took its medicine. The wealthy are living comfortably on their capital, the working classes are being cared for by the state, and it is the middle, professional, out-of-work people who are being most badly hit if they cannot get well-paid, steady jobs in (for instance) industry. Pooh at his head office the other day while waiting in a room for about half an hour, witnessed six or seven people, of both sexes and all ages, come in and ask for temporary employment. 'Any sort of work,' said one middle-aged man.

Chapter Twelve

THIS DESIRE TO SMASH SOMETHING

So polite and well mannered: German prisoners of war make new friends in
Gloucestershire

Cadburys are already making 22 varieties of chocolate products; Milk Tray Assortment and Roses Chocolates; 3 kinds of Dessert Chocolate; 3 kinds of Plain chocolate; 6 kinds of Filled Blocks; 2 kinds of blended chocolate, and a very little Cadburys Dairy Milk, also chocolate drops and chocolate biscuits. Although the quantity is far too small to meet the enormous demand, it is a contribution to the variety of food offered to the people of this country.

Newspaper advertisement from December 1946, in response to a comment from John Strachey, Minister of Food, that the main problem with the British diet was that it suffered from a lack of choice

Press and public are by now so resigned to a meagre ration of clothes that there was little excitement or speculation beforehand about what Sir Stafford Cripps was likely to say in his broadcast. But while the speech of the President of the Board of Trade may not have caused actual disappointment, it was not calculated to make his audience, shivering round reduced-pressure gas fires, feel any more cheerful. There is, in any case, a school-masterishness 'all for your own good flavour' about Government by Exhortation which is infuriating to the ordinary person whose intelligence is constantly underestimated in Government pronouncements.

The one piece of more cheerful news which the President had to offer was that blankets, which for some time have appeared abundant in the shops, are now available off the ration. So, huddled in blankets like the Red Indians of picture books, we will, after all, be able to enjoy the Happy Christmas which Sir Stafford Cripps considerately wished us at the conclusion of his homily.

Time and Tide *offers seasonal good will,*
28 December 1946

SATURDAY, 30 NOVEMBER

Edie Rutherford
This morning at 7 a.m. it was as dark as a bag. When I think back to a year ago when we were told there would be jellies in the shop next year, and realise now that it amounted to one pack per family, I feel annoyed, as it was just one of the many traps we walk into these days. It would have been better to have said a small amount of gelatine, sugar, etc had been allocated for a small number of packets of jelly, and then we would not have got the idea, which all did, that supplies would be had on points quite freely.

How agog the men are about the cricket in Australia. I am surprised that radio reception is still so poor from distant lands. Should have thought that by now radio would have been perfected, almost, allowing for acts of God.

Herbert Brush
Australia look like making a record score in their first innings. It is fairly certain that they cannot lose the match now, although it lasts for six days. It's a good thing for us that Morris did not get going, as a left-hander is very tiring for the fielders. Being a left-hander myself, I always tried to change ends as often as possible, to give the fielders a little more exercise, to their great annoyance. The fat old umpires often refused to cross over to square leg every time a run was scored.

SUNDAY, 1 DECEMBER 1946

Edie Rutherford
My only feeling about the rumoured engagement of Princess Elizabeth to Philip of Greece is that there is a blood relationship there, and I should have thought our royal family would try to avoid mixing their own blood further. However, I imagine they have little scope in finding her a husband who would be considered worthy of the job.

B. Charles
There is the report of a very distressing case in last Sunday's *News of the World*. It is the report of the case of some young Scout master, whom Mr Justice Oliver sentenced at the Kingston Assizes to ten

320

years' penal servitude for offences against boys. He is only twenty-five and it is stated he had an exemplary character before this case cropped up. It seems barbarous to sentence a man of twenty-five to ten years for a first offence.

In the same paper there is a long report of the case of the woman who 'married' another woman. It seems this is her fourth or fifth offence, yet she only got nine months' imprisonment. She admits homosexual practices while she was in Holloway prison.

Maggie Joy Blunt

Unpacked one stone of apples I have had nearly three weeks in packing case, sent from fruit farm in Norfolk (about 9/-). Laid them all out on shelf in one of the sheds. Two rotten, four slightly bruised, the rest in very good condition and look delectable. Spoke to Mrs C as she took her boys for a walk to look at remains of house that burned down near here last week. People were away. Local plumber doing repairs to bathroom with blow lamp. Something went wrong and lamp began to spurt paraffin. Man lost his head. Rushed out of house with lamp in hand, leaving trail of flame. House all on fire in no time. Nearest fire engine five miles away came as quickly as possible, but too late to save much.

C asked me again was I nervous living alone. Mrs C got very nervy when Mr C was away and imagined footsteps and so on. I said I did not think of such things – I don't ever feel 'lonely' in that sense. He thought there might be something in the idea that one attracts what one fears by fearing it.

TUESDAY, 3 DECEMBER

Edie Rutherford

So Monty leaves Palestine. I had hoped he'd stay a bit and do something definite, as it seems we just go on and on there without doing a thing to get matters straight.

As more and more lads are killed there, I begin to wish we had started the war a bit later, so that Hitler would have exterminated a few more Jews. All very well for good Jews to write to the papers saying ALL Jews aren't bad – oh yeah? Why don't the good Jews, then, use their influence with the bad Jews? Our benevolent attitude doesn't seem to stop their murderous deeds.

WEDNESDAY, 4 DECEMBER

B. Charles

Well, this is the last time I shall enter up my diary at Warrender Park Road! I leave tomorrow, to go to the Roxburghe Hotel, prior to going to Chester Street. What joy it will be to be in a house of my own again! Went to Chester Street with Mr Durie and we thought there seemed to be fearful muddle and delay. He thinks I shan't be in for about three weeks, and, if they dilly dally as they are doing, I certainly bet NOT.

SUNDAY, 8 DECEMBER

Edie Rutherford

Brownie girl I know tells me they have all been told, not asked, to bring a week's sweet coupons for sweets to be sent to German children.

Woman in grocer's yesterday with a long face doing a moan, turned to me and said, 'Makes you fed up, doesn't it?' I said, 'No, not me. I was brought up hard so hard times don't worry me much.' So she said, 'Well, there were ten of us so we didn't have it easy, but I think we were spoilt before the war.' Me, feeling nettled, 'I wasn't.' Nor was I. There is far too much grumbling these days and not enough blessing counting. When one compares the life of working folk with a hundred years go, the improvement is so striking that one MUST rejoice now.

Have managed to get rugger ball for friend who was seeking one for sons aged fourteen and thirteen. She and husband elated and can't believe it.

TUESDAY, 10 DECEMBER

Herbert Brush

How impossible it is to hear what a man looks like by hearing his voice. I always pictured Bertrand Russell with a long beard and slovenly dressed, and now I am looking at a photograph of him on the front page of the *Times Lit. Supp.* where he is shown as clean-shaven and stylishly dressed. I pictured him with a small nose and dark hair, and here he is with a large nose and white hair.

THURSDAY, 12 DECEMBER

Edie Rutherford

I wish to record, permanently, that I object to hearing Christmas carols in swing. The BBC should forbid it. Yesterday in *Workers' Playtime* a factory, Levers I think they said, was on the air with the works band swinging Christmas carols. The whole thing was upsetting.

I uphold the decision not to allow Oswald Mosley to travel outside England. Freedom is a farce if it means a man is free to corrupt. We have quite enough on our hands as it is de-Nazificating Europe. Men who act as Mosley does, and avows he intends to go on doing, forfeit their right to freedom.

Maggie Joy Blunt

Last week at Windsor Theatre Joy Malloy's *Sweet Aloes*. The part of coloured servant played by real Negro. When company took their call at end they stood in a line as usual, hand in hand, all except Negro who stood separately, a little behind them.

SUNDAY, 15 DECEMBER

Edie Rutherford

What is one to make of the Post Office announcement that last Christmas hundreds of people posted parcels without any address whatever on them? I could understand a few, but hundreds?

TUESDAY, 17 DECEMBER

Maggie Joy Blunt

When did this cold weather start? Last week we suffered bad fogs. I had to stay one night with the family in Richmond. It was worse all along the river than here. Trains were late. Hairdresser told me that one person she knew took twelve hours to get to Paddington from Slough and back again.

Saturday was gloomy and cold all day. It was Saturday evening that we heard the BBC's forecasts of frost and snow. It was bitterly cold on Sunday though the sun shone. Yesterday morning there were fine snowflakes in the air and I abandoned my plans for the day fearing frozen pipes and came home to light fires as soon as I could. A neighbour's teacloths hung out to dry were as stiff as paper. There is thick ice on the water tub.

Today is bright with a strong, bitter wind. All the little plants that keep their leaves through the winter – the violas, forget-me-nots, wallflowers, foxgloves, primroses, etc – are nipped and woebegone. The cats seek warm places away from draughts. I have the fire in the kitchen and live there, blocking the bottom of doors with mats and dusters. Mrs C thinks authorities are cutting the electricity as her electric clocks are slow and she never knows what the right time is. I break the morning chill in the bedroom with the old Valor stove.

FRIDAY, 20 DECEMBER

Edie Rutherford

A friend with a small son, aged five, recently had injections when he had whooping cough, and didn't like the performance. His mother is not a believer in such and so the child had not been immunised. Well, authority has subjected her to all the pressure they use on mothers on that subject, so at last, in a state of extreme fear, she gave in. Says a queue of mothers waited half an hour, standing in a draughty corridor, and were attended to by a woman doctor who did not take off her fur coat in a warmed room. As soon as my friend's small son saw what was to be done, he bawled, having had enough some weeks ago. When the doctor had done him she gave him such a push that only his mother's intervention prevented him falling on his face, and said, 'And I hope you have a bad arm to serve you right for bawling.' My friend was furious and turned round and said tensely, 'If he does, he won't have another injection', and swept aht. I should think so too. I would have spat in that doctor's eye. Mother I am not, but I have some idea how I'd feel if I were.

SATURDAY, 21 DECEMBER

Maggie Joy Blunt

Nothing makes me more frantic than inability to sleep. I will even give up smoking for a couple of days to regain tranquil oblivion at night. A slight cold which began last weekend has settled as colds usually do on my chest, and as soon as I lay my head on the pillow two grains of tobacco dust lodged at the top of my lungs begin to fight. Nothing painful. Just irritating and infuriating. I could tear my lungs out. Should like to go to bed now, but what is the use – I should not sleep. Besides, I have Christmas cake in the oven. I long to smash something. When I am tired I am often overwhelmed, almost, by this desire to smash something hard as Gertrude Lawrence smashes gramophone records in *Private Lives*.

SUNDAY, 22 DECEMBER

Maggie Joy Blunt
Slept well on a heaped pile of pillows, stayed in bed until after lunch and feel recovered enough to smoke again. I calculate that I smoke thirty a day – that comes to 31/6d. a week – that is £18 a year and makes me *blush* to think I spend that much on a habit bad for my health that I cannot break because I don't want to.

TUESDAY, 24 DECEMBER

Maggie Joy Blunt
Have nothing much to do but prepare for my Christmas visit to brother and family at their club tomorrow, where I stay the night. Have put up a few sprigs of green in the sitting room and a vase of it with the rather withered but still colourful red berries gathered early in November. With the Christmas cards the room looks festive enough and I'm sorry it will not be used this year, though it is a change for me not to be fussing with food and airing bed linen.

Christmas boxes. Never know what to do about these. Aunt Aggie says I shouldn't bother: 'They're most of them better off than we are now! The paper boy, perhaps . . .' But I never see the paper boy. I left 2/6 for the milkman this morning because of the extra milk he has let me have. I intend to give the postman 2/- tomorrow if he comes, and that is all. I gave my hairdresser 5/- yesterday. She was very pleased and seemed faintly surprised or perhaps I imagined it.

Must have a bath now and go to bed. Tomorrow I have to leave at 10.45 a.m. A very happy Christmas to all my readers.

CHRISTMAS DAY

George Taylor

We were awake early, and I got up to make a cup of tea, to find that it was earlier than we thought; indeed, it was only four in the morning. The tea was nevertheless welcome. We then exchanged presents, and we had been able to gather the customary assortment of small things which we try and disguise as much as possible. For my wife there were chocolates, sweets, four books, a plastic apron, a shopping bag and a couple of tangerines, and for me some sweets, a pair of socks, cuff links, a couple of books and some fruit.

We settled down for a further snooze, but were up to hear the short ration of radio Christmas carols. Then it was quickly time to set off for my brother's at Totley, where we had our dinner. We had a quiet afternoon and evening talking, listened to Wilfred Pickle's *Have a Go* after supper, and then came home by taxi, a new luxury for us.

Edie Rutherford

Bird is cooking, 4lb. of it. Have opened a tin of South African pork sausages to go with it and tied a rasher of bacon over its breast.

Just because we could have had a late sleep, we both woke at 6 a.m.-ish, as lively as if we were kids with stockings to explore. By 7.15 I had had enough of trying to go to sleep again, so said, 'I'm going to make tea', to which Himself responded, 'I'll join you', and that was that.

A friend brought me a hassock last evening. Every now and again Sid falls on it on his knees and offers up a prayer. He is a blasphemous man. Makes our tuffet look very shabby to have such a new friend, so I'll have to do something about it soon.

BOXING DAY

George Taylor

Listened to the broadcast pantomime in the evening, which strangely enough came from the Sheffield Lyceum. It was a very poor show, however, and Enoch and Ramsbottom failed to raise a laugh either with the audience present in the theatre or with us.

Edie Rutherford

I think the King's speech yesterday could be summed up as 'Quit your grumbling, count your blessings, look forward to the future', and I can't think of anything better he could have said at this time.

FRIDAY, 27 DECEMBER

George Taylor

Mainly Maigret by Georges Simenon, Readers Union choice for December, starts off with a long story in which Maigret does not appear at all. It is a crime story without mystery, where the criminal is known throughout, where the detectives pursue an unruffled course in unravelling the crime and the murderer is finally arrested in the most matter-of-fact way.

NEW YEAR'S EVE

Maggie Joy Blunt

Circus yesterday at Olympia. Don't know whether it was because we had not seen one for so long but we all agreed it was excellent. All the turns were good. Horses and dogs in superlative condition. Where have they been throughout the war? In America? The discipline was so good. Those elephants – going through their tricks as slickly as a well-trained chorus, their little eyes twinkling at us benevolently. As I heard one man saying afterwards, 'looking as though they really didn't mind making fools of themselves for us silly human beings'. But during the lion act I did find myself wishing they'd do something unexpected, such as giving the tamer a good box on the ear or curling up and going to sleep. The high roof acts made my neck and head ache. A man cycling upside down, holding a suspended woman with his teeth – it was almost too fantastic to believe possible, but there they were, hanging above the audience.

Edie Rutherford

My nephew Tony, fourteen, arrived last Friday, train half an hour late. He didn't know me, but I recognised him after six years. He is now 5 feet 6 inches and 9 stone 5lb., so is an inch taller than I am and almost as heavy. We have had four days happily together. Lots of humour and no nonsense. Like all only children, comes out with some whimsy. For instance he said quite solemnly once, 'The war ruined my life.' I didn't laugh because I do understand that kids who were evacuated etc had a tough time. I merely said, 'Oh no Tony, your life has scarcely begun so don't think it is ruined yet.'

We went to town so that we could visit hardware shops to get a ratchet screwdriver which Tony says he cannot get in Birmingham. He went all round the flat, tightening this, loosening that, soon found the tool box and was most upset that he could not straighten the steel window frames which our land mine twisted years ago.

NEW YEAR'S DAY 1947

Edie Rutherford
Sunny and dry. 1947 came in quietly, not a siren, not a bell, not a voice to be heard. I start this year with more hope than I have ever had, speaking nationally and internationally. Local shops all shut today and tomorrow but Husband goes to work as usual, and factory next door is hammering like mad. Drives us all crackers.

Imagine Ralph Richardson getting a knighthood. Absurd.

Maggie Joy Blunt
This morning I picked the first two Christmas roses.

S wrote me yesterday from Fleet Street about his Cretan wife: 'She is despairing with deep-seated weariness with England, its drabness, its weather, its . . . Englishness. As I am, but, as an Englishman, keeping stiff upper lip, playing a straight bat, up St Agathas . . . She knows I am restless and unhappy and toying with the idea of returning to the army . . . indifference, boredom is damnable. And . . . I am bored, screamingly bored. I HATE journalism.'

My major operation this year must be the biography.

FRIDAY, 3 JANUARY

Edie Rutherford
We have only enough coke to last till 4 p.m. today, and suppliers say they have no more for us. Same old story, we kick hard and we get fuel.

The Jew owner of these flats writes to local press upholding the violence in Palestine and offers to explain why to anyone who cares to ask him. He'd better watch out or some of his wealth will be attacked here. He is reputed to be the richest Jew in Sheffield and top Zionist. I see that Fascists are blamed for the 'reprisals' in synagogues here.

SATURDAY, 4 JANUARY

Edie Rutherford
At 5 p.m. yesterday we had a delivery of coke, so the situation is saved.

George Taylor
The New Year Social of the WEA took place under very great difficulties. The university was not in session, so we could not use the refectory and had to provide our own refreshments, borrowing the crockery from a chapel, collecting our own food from the shops, cutting up in the hall itself, and boiling water for the tea on the Porter's stoves. However, 150 turned up: more than we have had since before the war. And we had a really jolly time in spite of the fact that the university was quite unheated and the Firth Hall was like an icehouse.

Owing to the enthusiasm of our new socials secretary, we carried on until 11 p.m. instead of the usual 10 p.m. I shall vote for 11 p.m. in future.

Maggie Joy Blunt
Last night a local Fabian meeting on housing. Speaker was the late chairman of Borough Council Housing Committee who spoke about how people will do anything to get their names down for a house. Pregnancy is one priority and women have appeared at the local offices apparently in an interesting condition, but when an inspector has visited the home later there is no sign of a child or of mother being expectant. Another priority is TB in the family. People have scraped through their family records to prove TB, and have got relatives to visit them and so on. Any sort of fiddle.

SUNDAY, 5 JANUARY

Maggie Joy Blunt
Another cold spell, we are told, is sweeping down on us from Asia. The wind was colder yesterday and there is ice on the water tub today.

Am smoking less. Cough is better. Many people suffering similarly. Sister-in-law and Lys, for instance, both smoking less as I am and taking cough medicines and lozenges.

Slept this morning until eleven o'clock. It is often nearly 9 a.m. before I can make myself get out of bed unless I have something definite to get up for. I get my breakfast and return to bed calling myself a slut and all manner of names. I wish I could get the day started an hour sooner.

Edie Rutherford

Have decided to buy from Barkers, London, their vacuum cleaner advertised in *Sunday Express* today at just under £9. Cheapest new cleaner we can buy here is £17. Husband is quite sure that Barkers can be relied on to supply something worthwhile so I hope he is right.

MONDAY, 6 JANUARY

Edie Rutherford

Snow, started at 8.30 and still at it, 1.30 now. It is also bitterly cold. Children and dogs delighted with the snow. Teachers next door fed up as they start school tomorrow and say they'll get nothing done while snow lasts, kids too excited.

I was disgusted to hear yesterday that the Greek embassy in Moscow had had an extravagant New Year's party. When Greece is supposed to be hard up, it is wrong. In fact, no one should be having banquets anywhere in the world these days. Friends here went to a twenty-first party last week, daughter of a wealthy managing director (no names though I could name who) and they had at least 150 there, a bottle of champagne to every two guests, an open bar serving anything asked for, abundance of fruity decoration as well as flowers everywhere, superb food; must have cost hundreds. In her speech the girl said she owed all to her parents. What about the few thousand work people who contribute to father's wealth?

TUESDAY, 7 JANUARY

George Taylor

It snowed all day, so I was not surprised to find a crowd waiting for the tram in the evening. As customary, I set off walking to the next stop away from town to get on easier, but I waited and waited, and no tram appeared. After half an hour, I decided to try another route, walked to the Wicker, but still no trams. I waited for nearly an hour, with only buses streaming by, but no trams. Finally one did come, I jumped aboard, and then the conductor put on the chain behind me. Finally I arrived home at 7.20 p.m., it having taken me 110 minutes to do the four-mile journey.

It was a change to turn from the winter weather outside to drafting the Summer Programme for the WEA.

WEDNESDAY, 8 JANUARY

Edie Rutherford

Snowed all day yesterday from 9 a.m. to 6 p.m. without stopping a minute, so now we have lashings of the beastly stuff about, thawing, ugh. I'm ready to slosh hard the next adult who says to me in a surprised tone, 'Oh, don't you like snow?' It looks lovely from our windows, granted, especially at night when the lights from various flats reflect on the laden trees. But, seeing one has to sweep it away, and slop about in it . . .

Took Husband one and a half hours to get home instead of half an hour, and was he glad to be here.

THURSDAY, 9 JANUARY

B. Charles

I should think it likely that I shall be in the house in Chester Street at the end of next week. It is about time I got something of importance seen to, instead of doing nothing but detail work about the house. The glazier is actually getting on with his work, but the joiner is a thoroughly bad lot. How glad I shall be to see the back of them all! I discovered the joiner was trying to steal the lintel from the dining room, but I have got the decorators to remove it into the front room; so I hope it will be safe. I found several of the terminals of the curtain rods I got from Drummond Place lying in the garden! Two seem to have been lost. I think this is owing to the joiner. The concert last night was mildly interesting.

FRIDAY, 10 JANUARY

Edie Rutherford
Listening to *Have a Go* today I realised that Wilfred Pickles is really outstanding. His sympathy and tact are quite amazing. His handling of old people is superb.

This transport strike is the limit. Poor Londoners, once again they cop it. I can't help feeling sorry for the men, going on what the BBC industrial correspondent said in the nine o'clock news last night. They seem to have a case and it has been eight months simmering.

B. Charles
This afternoon I had a very interesting talk with two German POWs and I bought them a few cigarettes. Now that it is permitted for civilians to talk to them I always take every opportunity to chat. They are so polite and well mannered. One of these fellows told me he had been in the USA for quite a while during the war. When there he was told he would be repatriated to Germany, but instead went to Belgium and later came to Scotland. He says they are never told anything as to when they are likely to be sent home. I told him I thought it was hard luck being used for slave labour, whereupon he replied, 'Oh! We lost the war', which I thought had a sad sound. He and his friend are working in the Scottish Command, in the kitchens. He attends to the boilers and his friend washes up. It seems if they are invited they can visit civilians, and I gave them my address and said I should like them to come and see me when I am settled in my house. They said they will be delighted to do so. I think it will be years and years before they are all sent back to Germany, as we can't afford to lose their help.

SATURDAY, 11 JANUARY

B. Charles
The most remarkable thing today has been the recital I went to at the Usher Hall, given by Claudio Arrau. I consider him the greatest pianist I have ever heard. His programme began with the Chromatic Fantasia and Fugue of Bach and this was followed by the Appassionata Sonata. In the sonata he thrilled me more than I have been thrilled for years. It was not a classical rendering, but the

passion and elemental fury he put into it were simply amazing. The audience, which was a very poor one so far as numbers were concerned, were swept off their feet. They seemed breathless at the end but, on recovering their wits, let loose a veritable roar of applause. The man's technique is simply amazing; his glissando octaves, in one small piece of Debussy's, were astonishing in their speed, clarity and ease, yet his technique is never displayed to astonish; it is merely necessary for his rendering of the various compositions. He has fury, yet in passages displays the tenderest emotions possible.

It seems odd that Arrau was quite unknown in Great Britain until recently. He is forty-three years old, gave his first recital in Chile at the age of five, studied in Leipzig and toured Europe before the war. I gather he is very well known indeed in America.

George Taylor

A parcel arrived from Sweden this morning, and as the contents rattled fearfully, my wife assumed that her friend who had sent it had been careless with the packing. She did not seem at all enthusiastic about opening it.

After dinner, what a surprise. The rattle was caused by a packet of beans which had burst, but most of the contents were perfect. There were prunes, milk chocolate, a couple of tins of sardines, a box of home-made caramels, two packets of peppers, several packets of unidentified (flavouring) nuts, half a kilo of butter, half of a thick (smoked) sausage, some vanilla puddings, custard powder, a kilo of sugar, three different types of biscuits, four hand-embroidered handkerchiefs used as protection for the marmalade, two boxes of processed cheese, a mixed dried fruit salad, a packet of raisins, several wool golliwogs and a wall picture for decoration. It is the only time in our lives we have received such a present.

Chapter Thirteen

THOSE COSY-LOOKING BOOTEES WITH THE FUR TOPS

Walking in sloppy pudding all the time: the milk gets through in Surrey

'The big story is a curving, opulent day silhouette that is the most elegant fashion for decades. Its best blossoming is at the new house of Christian Dior, whose "Corolle" line is the first major post-war fashion; a tight, slender bodice narrowing into a tiny wasp waist, below which the skirt burst into fullness like a flower.'

The British edition of Harper's Bazaar *reports on 'The New Look' unveiled in Paris on 12 February 1947*

'Had Ellen Wilkinson lived longer, there is little doubt that the children of England and Wales would have had reason to bless her name. She would have made mistakes; she would have provoked bitter antagonism; but she would have seen to it in fact, as well as promise, that no child would be denied the opportunity that was his due.'

Times Educational Supplement *on the death of Ellen Wilkinson, the Minister of Education, who died from an overdose of barbiturates after depression brought on by illness and, it was believed, her failure to bring in more radical reforms, 8 February 1947*

MONDAY, 13 JANUARY

B. Charles

I took the advertisement 'Personality developed, etc' to the *Scotsman* this afternoon, and was very surprised when the sub-editor asked me to see him and told me that, unless he got more particulars about the method of teaching I proposed, he could not take the advertisement. I explained what I proposed but it did not satisfy him and he regretted they could not accept it. Neither would the *Evening News*. It seems very amazing to me. But, of course, nowadays, if one wants anything, no matter what, that is out of the ordinary run, all sorts of difficulties are put in the way of anyone attaining it. The whole world has become so utterly regimented that any sort of individuality is looked at askance.

TUESDAY, 14 JANUARY

Edie Rutherford

The transport strike goes on. I am sorry for the strikers, as they have a case, and I'm sorry for the soldiers, as they have to take abuse.

Speaking of that, the woman who cleans my windows has a son in India and tells me he expects to return here daily; says how horrid it is for our boys these days as the Indians call out to them 'Quit India' ceaselessly, and our boys have been told not to retaliate. How much they'd like to! They can't quit too soon to suit them.

WEDNESDAY, 15 JANUARY

B. Charles

Another day spent almost entirely running around to see that things keep moving at Chester Street. I can't think anyone has had more vexations than I in getting into this wretched house.

There was a letter from Dicky this morning. He told me his people had had a burglary, and all the food his mother had got in for Xmas had been stolen. The number of burglaries committed today is appalling. It is, of course, largely owing to the continued rationing and artificially created 'scarcities'.

It was interesting to find, when I went out this evening to buy some peroxide, that Boots had none and said it is in very short supply. I took them an empty bottle but they didn't seem to want it, though we are told there is a great shortage of bottles of all kinds. I managed to get some peroxide in the end at Baildons.

FRIDAY, 17 JANUARY

Maggie Joy Blunt
I toyed a short while ago with the idea of buying a pair of those cosy-looking bootees with the fur tops until I heard price was fifteen to twenty guineas.

Rereading *Tom Jones*. Really it is an enormously diverting and well-written story. What I like about the eighteenth century is the way it accepted the pleasures and sins of sex without sentimentality or hypocrisy.

Descriptions of Mr Jones's meals has increased my hunger for meat. Not quite of course for the same quantities, but for more succulent beef and mutton and tender and beautiful roast fowl than I ever see now.

Another sheet has gone. When I put it on the bed I saw it was very thin in the middle and it should be turned but I couldn't be bothered to change it. Then the strap of my watch, which I usually wear at night, caught in it as I slept.

SUNDAY, 19 JANUARY

B. Charles
This morning I went to Granton and inspected a number of prefab houses there. I must admit that inside they are very good. The built-in cupboard accommodation is first-rate. One of the tenants of the aluminium houses invited me inside. I asked if they noticed the damp on the walls inside. But they said they did not. All the gadgets these houses have must be extremely convenient and they are so well arranged. In fact, I think, if one had taste that they could be made extremely attractive. And they have got far more finished than I had imagined; I was told they are getting five up every day. Of course the cost seems to be very high: about £2,000 each.

The worst part of them now is the class of tenants who live in them: just the scum of Edinburgh, for the most part. I fancy, however, when the worst of the housing shortage is over that quite nice sites will be selected, so that the class of tenant will greatly improve.

I see, in today's *News of the World*, that the famous tennis star Tilden has been sentenced to some months' imprisonment in Los Angeles for an offence against a fourteen-year-old schoolboy who was one of his pupils for tennis. The judge made the usual fatuous remarks when sentencing him. Of course people who know anything about homosexuality realise that very many athletes have this taste; but it will come as a shock to the ordinary person to find a world-famous tennis star who is homosexual.

TUESDAY, 21 JANUARY

Herbert Brush

The BBC news at one o'clock said that there was a pea-soup fog in some parts of London, but in SE26 it was quite clear, so I went to the plot and sowed a row of broad beans. I had only just finished when I smelt fog, and, looking up, saw a wall of it coming my way. Very soon the sun was yellow and then vanished, so I came home as I don't like the taste of a London fog.

I thought I'd see what sort of verse came out if I put a pen to paper.

> Sometimes I sit and think
> Sometimes I only sit
> And do not even blink
> For quite a bit
> Is this a sign of age
> Does life just flow
> Like turning page on page
> I'd like to know.

It sounds morbid, but after my exercise on the plot I'm feeling very fit.

B. Charles

I didn't specially enjoy the film show *The Gold Rush* last night though Charlie Chaplin is, in many ways, a wonderful actor; but the sort of thing he appears in never appeals much to me. The film was not going to be shown until a later date but the billed film, *Blackmail*, had not arrived from London.

FRIDAY, 24 JANUARY

B. Charles
I left the Roxburghe this morning and came to Chester Street, where I am entering up this entry. As the gas meter is not yet fixed I shall have to get all my meals out, but it is good to be, once again, in a house of my own. It is so utterly unsatisfactory living with other people. This is the fourth flat, or house, I have been in since 1929, when I first went to Windsor. I hope and think this will be the last removal I shall ever have.

Edie Rutherford
Such a fuss altogether about this royal visit. Why on earth do we have to go in for so much costly pomp when we are so hard up? How ridiculous that the Princess Elizabeth is to be given all those costly diamonds by my country. As if the girl hasn't enough already. We do live in a mad world. Why on earth doesn't she issue a well-merited rebuke and chastener by refusing to accept them? That would be courageous and *right*.

I enjoyed *Animal Farm* on the Third Programme. Am amazed that BBC did it and am sure they will have had a lot of protests.

Herbert Brush
A slight fall of snow last night and a very sharp frost. Another struggle with the car to get the engine to start this morning. Can't imagine what the trouble is.

I wonder whether anyone at the Mass-Observation office ever reads through one of these letter-diaries of mine?

SATURDAY, 25 JANUARY

George Taylor
I really did not want to go to the district council at Rawmarsh as the snow made me wish to come home. However, I went. During the afternoon we had a discussion about the raising of the school leaving age to fifteen.

We had tea at the British Restaurant, and I thought it a disgraceful meal for 2/-. Some of the delegates were quite delighted, however.

Maggie Joy Blunt
Niece with me again. This afternoon we went with Lys to see *The Fairy Queen* at Covent Garden. Babs has never seen ballet before and I could have wished it was *Swan Lake* or *Les Sylphides* but it had to be a matinee and this was the only possible one in January. We had good seats in balcony stall, and Babs seemed to enjoy it all thoroughly. She is a pet and I do love having her around. In between bouts of chattering she is very quiet and solemn, self-possessed, aloof. But I don't think it is shyness, not of the kind I suffered. I have never had a youngster to take about before, to pay her fares, see her safely across roads, answer questions – it is all novel and pleasing. We had a meal with Lys on our way home, in Lys's room, and played darts, and now the young woman is in bed and I hope asleep. She likes staying with Auntie, she says, because she doesn't have to get up so early these cold mornings for breakfast, or go to church on Sundays.

SUNDAY, 26 JANUARY

George Taylor
We thought that the snow was going, but were deceived.

This snow clearing has already cost me a new fountain pen, for one dropped out of my pocket when shovelling last Friday night.

MONDAY, 27 JANUARY

B. Charles
I had a letter from Doris who told me rather an interesting item. It seems she went into Tunbridge Wells to try to get a dress, and the only thing in her size was priced at £27 11s. Wisely she refused to pay this absurd price and, the other day, managed to get what she describes as, 'A *very* nice dress.' Utility, of course, for just under £4. She says she has been satisfied with what little 'utility' clothing she has had in the past and feels sure that if only people would either go without needless clothing, or buy utility, the astronomical prices for the non-utility stuff would be ended shortly. It is the same with all this crazy fruit on the market. I see there has been a sensational 'drop' in the prices of those horrid tangerines.

The man came to fix the telephone. With life so complicated now, I think the telephone really a necessity.

George Taylor

An acquaintance, who lives near here in a hut on his own, came for help in filling up his application for an old-age pension. As recompense for the trouble, he has promised us a chicken.

TUESDAY, 28 JANUARY

Maggie Joy Blunt

Overheard a man this morning say something about Siberia.

WEDNESDAY, 29 JANUARY

Edie Rutherford

Walking in sloppy pudding all the time. It snowed hours into the night and now we are deep in it. This morning the sun came out and when I went to our library, in our park the scene was beautiful. Cup tie at Bramall Lane today. Husband bet me this morning there'd be forty to fifty thousand there. Well, any man who stands around and *pays* to do it in this weather deserves pneumonia or worse. I know one man who is so bad with rheumatics that he has a taxi home from work each night, but he goes to every football match.

Maggie Joy Blunt

Snow fell yesterday afternoon and evening but it is not yet very deep. The wind is colder than ever. Last night to local theatre with CL and boyfriend to see *Frieda*, and stayed night with her in Windsor. I arrived home by 10 a.m., have relit kitchen fire and am still wearing fur coat, thawing out. Sky is very grey, heavy with threatening snow, but sun is now trying to come out.

THURSDAY, 30 JANUARY

Edie Rutherford

I do think it is unlucky that we are having all this bitter cold just when fuel matters so much. Electric clock is almost an hour slow today, the most it has ever been behind. Talking to a railwayman this morning. He says, 'Of course we are exporting coal. From here all the best coal goes to Liverpool for export. The stuff we are using here is second grade and worse.'

I have sent to Gamages for six more RAF escape maps. I sent for three and when they came two days ago I asked Himself if he could bear the idea of our eiderdown being covered with them and he said he'd have a go. Our eiderdown is falling to bits and I pick up feathers daily. I have mended it and mended it but now the material just falls away when I put the needle into it. If the maps will hold the feathers until one can get eiderdowns re-covered they will have served, and as cheaply as anything today.

The luckiest people in England today are the royal family and anyone else who is leaving this cold island.

FRIDAY, 31 JANUARY

Maggie Joy Blunt
Heavy snow fell early this morning and everything is covered several inches. I live in the kitchen. If it were possible to put a bed in it I would. I get up – yesterday about 8.30, today just before nine – light the fire and dress by it at once and then have breakfast. Bedroom much too cold to dawdle in.

In buses, trains, cafés, conversations are frequently about electricity and gas shortage. Our electricity here was out on Monday morning until after 9 a.m. Had to boil kettle for breakfast on oil stove. June's children both home from school until further notice – not enough fuel.

SATURDAY, 1 FEBRUARY 1947

Maggie Joy Blunt
It is nearly five o'clock in the afternoon. The window frames a lacing of bare twigs and tree trunks against a deep ice-blue sky. No. It is a sadder blue than that, a love-in-the-mist blue and ice-cold, deepening every moment. I am wearing thick woollen vest, rubber roll-on, wool panties, stockings, thick long-sleeved wool sweater, slacks, jacket, scarf and two pairs of woollen socks – I am just about comfortable.

Lots of small boys tobogganing in village. In the other bedroom, where Babs was sleeping last weekend, the water in washstand has frozen solid, right to the bottom.

SUNDAY, 2 FEBRUARY

George Taylor
Still more snow, and I had to dig a way out in the morning. My wife had a real tottering day collecting rents from snow-covered streets.

B. Charles
This afternoon the two German POWs arrived as arranged. They are quite nice. One is called Heinz Sue and the other Helmut Wiegers.

Sue comes from Hamburg and Wiegers from quite near. They say the plight of the civilian population in Hamburg is extremely bad. They are living, literally, in cellars and sometimes in holes in the ground. I was interested to note how very 'correct' both these men were. So German!

I was rather surprised to learn that Hitler was never very popular in Hamburg. Goering, according to Weigers, was very popular all over Germany. Both seemed to have no doubt at all that Hitler is dead. Sue told me the American soldiers robbed prisoners of watches, rings and all other jewellery they could lay their hands on, and destroyed all papers and photographs found on all prisoners.

MONDAY, 3 FEBRUARY

Maggie Joy Blunt
I have been celebrating the birthday of the Prophet – yesterday with Kassim to an over-ornate building off Regent's Park where the Islamic Society gave us a free tea and two lectures from confirmed Muslims – one of them an Englishman. The lectures were pedantic and uninspiring and must have bored many in the audience. The number of different nationalities present was interesting. Olive-skinned predominating – probably Egyptians and Turks. Others included Indian and coal-black Negroes. Men were in a majority and most of the women present seemed English and quite half of them fat, puffy-eyed, in expensive fur coats. There was one English clergyman present. Like all religions and faiths it is, according to its supporters, the One and Only, and the solution of all problems personal and international is to be found in the Koran.

Spent this afternoon in Marylebone Public Library – Mavis is letting me use her tickets. The list of eighteenth-century memoirs I handed over to the librarian he said he had had very recently from someone else – was I by any chance working in collaboration? No. This is what I have dreaded to hear – that someone else is working on same subject. It doesn't follow though, just because they want the same books as I do. Most of them are in the London Library and if I can only find someone with a subscription . . .

Edie Rutherford

Although Mass-Observation has not asked for it (and probably never would), I am going to give comments I have heard about the royal family since Saturday.

Housewife: 'I wish all I had to do was dress up and smile.'

Typist, thirty-five: 'All that nonsense about not enough coupons and how they make over their clothes, as if anyone believes it!'

Housewife: 'Makes you fair sick it does. Going off to enjoy themselves while we have to put up with what we have to put up with. And all that nonsense about the King and five inches of bath water. What sort of people do the papers think we are if they think we swallow that sort of talk?'

Old woman of seventy-three, living in a tiny room behind some shops, old-age pension her only income: 'I feel sorry for the royalty going out in this weather to start their voyage to South Africa.'

It was pointed out to her that they have furs and cars to ride in, and will shortly be out of this weather, and that if anyone needs pity it is herself, but she said, 'Oh, but you don't realise what it is like to be royalty.'

Small businessman, a Tory for fear of losing the little he has got: 'Good luck to them. They have gone to represent you and me and the lot of us, and we wouldn't like them to show themselves badly dressed, would we now?'

Housewife: 'I thought we were supposed to be hard up. They are all the time telling us we are and yet we throw away thousands at a time like this for four people to swank at our expense.'

Girl, about twenty-three, post office clerk: 'It is OUR money they spend. No wonder we are taxed the way we are.'

Teacher, female, thirty-five: 'Well, we can't do anything about it so we'll have to lump it. It has always been so and will go on being so.'

TUESDAY, 4 FEBRUARY

Edie Rutherford
Will it ever stop snowing? Postman said it had snowed 5/- pieces all night. I declare it has been at it over twenty-four hours now and it lies deep everywhere. There is one main track to shops and we walk in Indian file, can only cross roads where there is a track. I have been out twice – it is exhilarating all right. The view from our windows is beautiful. I think this is the worst weather in all my nearly thirteen years here.

George Taylor
I had an appointment at Eckington and although snow lay everywhere I decided to risk the journey. First, I found that single-deck buses were running instead of double-deckers, then on the way out we got stuck in a drift at Halfway, and the passengers had to help to dig the bus out. On the homeward journey, we stuck on a hill just in front of a lorry which had skidded into a bank. We kept sliding back and across the road, but by valiant efforts the driver got going at last, and then kept on going, stops or no stops.

Herbert Brush
One can't rely on electric clocks driven from the main nowadays. The clock stopped this morning at 9.40 and remained stopped all day.

I see that the Australians are outplaying our men at Adelaide. That left-handed player A. Morris is on the job again. It must be very trying fielding against a left-hander when the thermometer is in the nineties.

WEDNESDAY, 5 FEBRUARY

George Taylor
The frost continues unabated, and today I saw a team of men with a species of flame-thrower, used for melting the Tarmacadam on roads, thawing out tramway points. We received delivery of newspapers for the first time for three days.

B. Charles

A very cold snowy morning. At the Lane I left for an interesting old cuckoo clock and got it for 34/-. It wants a lot done to it.

I asked Mr Mason for the name of that stuff he takes to immunise himself from colds and flu. It is Anti-bi-San. I have got some and have taken the first dose. It does the trick and isn't dear.

THURSDAY, 6 FEBRUARY

Maggie Joy Blunt

Snow again. Several inches, falling all night and most of today, very gently and quietly in small flakes. Electricity cut for three-quarters of an hour from 5 p.m. I surrounded myself with four candles. Medieval gloom.

Two women and a man talking of chilblains at bus stop the other day: 'Mine itch.' 'Mine are past that, they just ache.' 'Mine itch *and* ache.'

Edie Rutherford

Alas, poor Ellen Wilkinson, fifty-five is not old. Well, she went far and died in harness and did not have a lingering last illness. She has certainly left the world a better place for her having been in it.

It is two weeks today, if I remember rightly, since this lot of snow began, and it has snowed daily since. We are all sick of it now.

FRIDAY, 7 FEBRUARY

George Taylor

A party of sixty-four members of the WEA had booked for the Village Players at Great Hucklow tomorrow, but the secretary of the Players told me there were 10-foot drifts on all the roads and it was quite impossible to carry on.

Edie Rutherford

I have voted for Sunday cinemas. I gather not many are voting and I fear for the result, as teenagers are not entitled to a vote, and the weather is making it a poor day for going out to do a thing.

For the first time there are *NO POTATOES* signs here.

SATURDAY, 8 FEBRUARY

Edie Rutherford

By some oversight it is not snowing.

Later: Sheffield is to have Sunday cinemas, majority of twelve thousand odd. Eleven per cent voted. I bet the Wesleyans are wild.

Herbert Brush

More electricity cuts. Electric clocks are worse than useless now. I wonder whether the BBC will think it worthwhile to broadcast to people who can't listen unless they have battery sets.

I wonder how many more unpleasant surprises our Government will produce before the country rises as a whole and demands a change from imbeciles to sane men who can think ahead.

George Taylor

The roads have become so thick with ice that the Corporation is using pickaxes to break it up on the roads.

I went along to the meeting point for the theatre party in case anyone should turn up, but apparently all had received intimation of the change, for I was the only one there.

SUNDAY, 9 FEBRUARY

Herbert Brush

More than a foot in places. I have done some more violent snow shovelling. I agree with the experts who say there is likely to be trouble if current is switched off the underground mains for long period.

B. Charles

The papers today are full of the Electricity Crisis and the stupidities of that idiot Mr Shinwell. I just can't think how he can avoid resigning, yet I should think he is so case-hardened that he will stick in office until he, and his kind, are kicked out. I think if this miserable Government is in office for the full term that the country will be completely bankrupt and finished. The ineptitudes of this lot are past belief, and their lying effrontery past bearing. Of course, in a way, I was glad when they got in, as I thought they couldn't do worse than the coalition, but I am mistaken.

This afternoon Donald Blyth came and told me the clock I took him to repair is able to be made to go, but the cuckoo arrangement is all missing.

MONDAY, 10 FEBRUARY

Maggie Joy Blunt
The big electricity cut does not seem to have affected me here yet. But hairdresser when I looked in about an appointment said they had no power till midday.

9.15 p.m. Attlee's speech on fuel crisis. I remember guiltily having used vacuum and kettle this morning, but otherwise could hardly be using less electricity – after dark, one light, I think a 60W lamp which I suppose I could change for a 40W.

Edie Rutherford
Of course it would be a dark, foggy morning to start the fuel cut era. I see that Letchworth, like us, can ignore the cuts. In fact Sheffield is so well off that it is unloading power to others. It is a change for this town to be able to do summat worth mention. I am sorry but I have so little faith in my fellow beings that I believe thousands will ignore the plea to voluntarily economise. Not a few will look on it as a chance to make things harder for the Government – some are just feckless, some selfish and others downright dumb.

Funny to read what USA and Canadian papers are saying of us today. Fortunately to us here in the crisis, it doesn't look as bad as to them at their distance. Anyway, we should make it, we always do. We have to be right down before we get up, that seems inevitable with our mentality.

Herbert Brush
I went by tram to the British Museum. The lighting in the Reading Room is good so there is no difficulty. I had a go at Boys' *History of Sandwich* from 1792.

Then I went to the National Gallery and sat in front of *A Corn Field* by Constable. The colours are remarkable and it might have been painted yesterday. Wonderful clouds with patches of blue, which in these cold, dark days do one good to look upon.

TUESDAY, 11 FEBRUARY

George Taylor

The Corporation are having difficulty in disposing of the snow they are clearing from the streets. Apparently the rivers, or riverbeds now that the rivers themselves are frozen, will take no more, so today they have been busy tipping lorry loads of snow in the side streets.

Edie Rutherford

It is snowing. I thought Mr Attlee's statement last night was good: no panic, just a simple explanation. But, of course, it is a golden opportunity for the opposition and I fear I see tongues in cheeks when Churchill swears they are not pleased that this has occurred. It is obvious that the crisis is due to a number of things, wheels within wheels, and I share the hope that it may have roused folk to the importance of coal and miners to us all. Husband still says the weak spot is that we didn't stop exporting coal to conserve more for ourselves and says no one deals with that point. He says a fortnight not exporting would have kept us going. Husband also thinks we should have a Coalition Government. Says the best men should run the country, regardless of party.

Herbert Brush

I wonder what is going to happen to dear old England next. No dog racing; what will the poor working man do without his little flutter? Blame the Government I hope and write to his MP.

WEDNESDAY, 12 FEBRUARY

Herbert Brush

I shall not be surprised if some of the rowdy elements of the unemployed start riots in the big towns if this state of affairs lasts for more than a week.

The last hard winter equal to this that I remember was in 1893 or 1894, when we had six weeks of continuous skating on the River Trent.

I am trying to keep warm by chopping firewood. I'll try my hand at verse for a few minutes before I go out to chop more, but verse writing does not keep one warm.

I think that folk who have no coal will blame old Shinwell now,
And, as they shiver in the cold, each one will wonder how
That Minister is keeping warm, and whether he goes short
Of anything he wants to burn; their answer's always nought
So I have joined the numbers who are now inclined to swear
That Socialism means much more than we're inclined to bear.

George Taylor

The news grows worse, and the re-imposition of the blackout is the final blow. We seem infinitely worse off than at any time during the war.

Edie Rutherford

A fight between three dogs broke out under our feet in a shop and all three were kicked out by a man in the queue. Woman behind counter said, 'If I had had an animal I would have got rid of it long ago, when the war started.'

I must admit I have often felt it is crazy the way we feed thousands of animals in zoos and pets while we are struggling for survival. The woman to whom one of the dogs belonged said she thought it was a bit hard, and added, 'Life is drab enough as it is without having a wholesale slaughter of pets.'

FRIDAY, 14 FEBRUARY

Maggie Joy Blunt

To town again yesterday. Two well-dressed, attractive, married women behind me talking horses, hunting, riding, Ibsen and *Wild Duck*, Gielgud's *Richard of Bordeaux*, modern stage, Churchill in the House, could shoot Shinwell and 'Don't mind going short if there really is *not* enough, but bad organisation makes me angry.' Evidently recently acquainted and pleased to know each other. Their thin, cultured voices, so pleased with themselves, such nice people – yes, they were – but (what was the matter with me?) so BORING.

Candles and oil lamps in shops. Candles in café where I went for coffee and candles and oil lamps in local shops too – in local library only central room is heated, side rooms are icy. In town, tube trains crowded at 3 p.m. Wartime gloom on every face. Scarves, mufflers, wool and fur gloves, fur-lined boots and bootees, fur coats, all much in evidence.

Met N at Hampstead Everyman 5 p.m. She worried about job. Her firm (aircraft) have already sacked many weekly staff. A feeling of 1930s panic prevails.

Edie Rutherford

'So that's what Tom Harrisson looks like,' she said after looking at next week's *Radio Times*. A regular sort of guy. Yes, I think he'll do.

I am with Cassandra in *Mirror* today regarding football pools: of all the mug's games. Husband says the rich man telephones his bookie and lays his bet so why not a gamble for the working man? I agreed, but said one did not make the other right. I see in *Mirror* that Mr Cope of Cope's Pools is getting conscience twinges about his pools. Well, that is one way of getting round it. I favour a State Lottery, as in Queensland, as we know then where the money goes, whereas this private enrichment of a few makes me sick.

George Taylor

The WEA Socials Committee met to decide on final arrangements for the first post-war dance, which is to take place on the 22nd. We have not chosen a very good time to try to sell tickets.

SATURDAY, 15 FEBRUARY

B. Charles

This latest blackout is too depressing. Last night, when I was returning from the concert, to see all the people groping about with torches amid the gloom was just as if the war was still on. It only wanted the siren to go to make it just the same.

SUNDAY, 16 FEBRUARY

Herbert Brush

A man yesterday caught a glimpse of the sun and photographed it for the *Daily Express*.

MONDAY, 17 FEBRUARY

Edie Rutherford

What a lovely morning at the Cape for the royal family and all the population on holiday. I could see the whole thing as the commentator described it all. Dear old Table Mountain. It always brings lumps to my throat and tears to my eyes.

All this drabness and cold and eternal snow is so soul deadening, lacking in poetry and romance altogether. Where husband works, the lavatory has been frozen nearly a month. What upsets my old man most is that he can't wash his hands all day. He says if this goes on will I crochet him a wool nose cap as his nose gets so frozen in bed at night.

B. Charles

Well, the last of the workmen has gone! I feel as if I had got rid of an infectious disease. At the moment I feel as if I would rather have the roof fall on my head than get any workmen in to prop it up. I don't think I can ever face having any workmen inside the place again. They are so filthy dirty in their habits: flinging cigarette ends all over the place, and not tidying up. Their presence in the house is a continual source of disgust.

Maggie Joy Blunt

This weather paralyses me. Felt very tired and down over weekend. I miss the radio while doing chores, particularly mid-morning story.

Letter from brother this morning, written at sea on way to Lisbon. 'It's much warmer now and quite pleasant on deck without an overcoat . . . '

TUESDAY, 18 FEBRUARY

Maggie Joy Blunt

Day after day the frost continues. If it lasts till Thursday, said my hairdresser yesterday, it will be the coldest winter for a hundred years. Fierce argument going on in greengrocer's this morning. One woman said it was as bad in 1940, hotly denied by others. I can't remember. There was much snow. It's excellent weather for keeping one at one's desk (mine being a rickety round table by the kitchen fire). But I never seem able to settle for long. I tell my London friends that I'm hibernating and will emerge when the weather breaks. But I have to emerge for food and cigarettes and certain social obligations.

Cigarettes: this morning at midday had smoked my last. In village none at all anywhere. This afternoon out again at 2.30 on cycle, cursing myself for being such a slave to this vice. Tobacconist has been told on good authority that sweet ration is to be reduced next month.

Herbert Brush
I met Ing in the street this morning, the first time I have seen him for more than a month. He has been laid up with some kind of 'itis'. Something amiss with his nose, which gave him a great deal of pain, and prevented him sleeping with Mrs Ing, a great hardship according to him.

George Taylor
We visited the Playhouse to see *Love in a Mist*. It proved to be a laughable mix-up between a newly married couple and an eloping pair, all marooned in an isolated country cottage. Finally the mist cleared and all ended happily. We had some jolly laughs.

WEDNESDAY, 19 FEBRUARY

B. Charles
A very nice letter from Naylor (re horoscope he is doing for me). He seems to understand me quite well. I am sorry that I was obliged to tell him so much, but in the circumstances it was the best thing to do. I shall be very interested to hear his full report.

There is an interesting piece in today's *Daily Telegraph*. It seems the Chief Constable of Derby, Col. H. Rawlings, is attempting to encourage civilians to act as informers to help the police enforce the lighting restrictions! It seems as if Hitler has, indeed, won the war! THE GESTAPO HAS ARRIVED!

FRIDAY, 21 FEBRUARY

Edie Rutherford
So the Government wants women back in industry, whole time or part-time. I shudder at the thought. Willing though I am to do my bit,

the memory of crowded trams, standing around waiting for them in the dark and cold, scrambled meals, no time to do a thing properly. I just HATE and DREAD the thought of all that again. Especially as, if one works part-time, about 30/- a week is thought adequate return. It just isn't worthwhile for that. When a woman gets to middle life and is as capable as I am, her sense of values is outraged by such reward.

B. Charles
I shall not forget this day in a hurry. As I was bringing the chandelier home from Herrald's, I slipped and fell and broke the base and one of the arms! It was a great blow, I assure you. Then this morning I lost my ration book.

SATURDAY, 22 FEBRUARY

George Taylor
Our first post-war WEA Dance. In spite of the snowy night, and the unheated university in which the dance was held, some seventy came. It was very cold in the hall when not dancing, but when on the floor it was quite passable. Curiously, I also noticed that the hall was definitely warmer when a dance was in progress even if one was sitting out. Immediately the dance stopped, the hall seemed to go cold, just as if the heat had been switched off.

SUNDAY, 23 FEBRUARY

Edie Rutherford
I have started to make a padded quilt like one I noticed at the 'Britain Can't Get It' exhibition. It is a Victorian idea but in these days, when we can't buy what we want, it is a good idea. I have used all my own scraps so am now cadging from friends. It is already pram size.

B. Charles
Both the POWs are longing to get back to Germany and say they will never return to Great Britain. Heinz made an interesting remark. I asked him what he thought of the Nuremberg Trial. He thought it so extraordinary, and so wrong to hang the German generals instead of shooting them, as they were entitled to expect, as they were soldiers.

I fancy this hanging of generals will have 'shocked' the German nation very much. And they will never forgive us for having done this. It is this sort of stupid blundering on our part that is sowing the seeds for the next world war. It is a huge mistake to humiliate a nation in the way we are humiliating Germany.

THURSDAY, 27 FEBRUARY

Edie Rutherford
Oh the poor King and Princess, bathing with hundreds looking on. Well, I call it bad management. There are heaps and heaps of lovely bathing spots round the coast and it should've been possible to whisk the whole royal family off by car to some such secluded cove; a word to the public to keep off, and to the police to keep a look out for a mile round three sides and they could ALL (fat Queen too) have bathed in the warm Indian Ocean with enjoyment. Human nature is the same the world over, we MUST gawp at royalty. As bad today as they ever were.

Herbert Brush
I think that the change in weather is coming at last. The temperature in the summerhouse is now 35°F, the first time it has been above freezing for weeks. The feeling in the air is different now.

FRIDAY, 28 FEBRUARY

Herbert Brush
More snow last night. A man told me just now that in a week there will be no more green food in the shops.

I went into my bank for the manager to certify that I am still alive.

Chapter Fourteen

I WANTED TO HOWL
MY HEART OUT

Silence at the Robinsons

Sobell at the Smiths

SOBELL MODEL 717. 7-valve superhet
Receiver with a push-pull output stage giving
8 watts undistorted output. 4 wave bands.
PRICE £34.13.0 PLUS PURCHASE TAX.

The Robinson's Radio is away for repairs. But
the Smiths with their Sobell have Radio all the
time—because with every Sobell Model there's a 2
year guarantee which provides free maintenance,
including any necessary replacements, on the spot.

Husband quite depressed about it: a new radio promises unmitigated joy

'No one will deny the seriousness of the economic crisis that now confronts us. It is not merely the weather that has caused this. The weather has made things worse; but the origin of our troubles goes much deeper than that. The immediate cause of the breakdown has been shortage of coal and shortage of electric generators. The fuel and power crisis, coming just at the time when industry was regaining rhythm in post-war production, has been a cruel blow to our prospects. Its effects will be long felt . . .

I say to the Government: stop galloping down national-isation avenue, and pay attention to the things that matter most now – food and fuel, houses and clothes, the balance of trade, the balance of the budget, the fate of home agriculture.

Anthony Eden, Deputy Leader of the Opposition,
speaking on the Home Service, 20 March 1947

'Never since the beginning of recorded history has mankind been faced by so terrible a problem. Either we must within the space of a few years unlearn beliefs and prejudices and consent to an entirely novel form of political and military organisation, or, if we fail in this, we must expect a world-wide disaster surpassing in its horror all that past misfortunes enable us to imagine . . .

The removal of this danger, if it can be achieved, will release for beneficent undertakings the vast energies at present concentrated on wars and preparation for wars. There will be an end to the nightmare fears which have oppressed the human spirit in continually increasing measure since 1914, and which have led to systems of calculated cruelty unsurpassed in the previous history of the species. The pessimism of our gloomy era will vanish like snow in the sunshine of spring, and under the inspiration of returning joy a great renaissance will spread throughout the world.

Bertrand Russell contributes to the debate on atomic
energy, Listener, *13 March 1947.*

SATURDAY, 1 MARCH 1947

Edie Rutherford

Husband says it is once again a good thing we can't see ahead, adding that if we could have seen in 1940–41 what victory meant many would have committed suicide rather than go on with it.

Yesterday, in greengrocer's, there was a man who has twenty-one children, and the queue waited while his order was weighed up. It occurred to me afterwards to wonder if he had had one wife or more to achieve this, especially as he said they would not mind a few more. The man looked about forty-five and had the clear skin and ruddy complexion a farmer has.

George Taylor

The threat to remove electrical goods from the home market made my wife and I resolve to buy an extension loudspeaker while they were available. My wife had seen a suitable one from a tram, so I called at the shop today and bought it.

SUNDAY, 2 MARCH

B. Charles

I decided to inform the police about the door being forced open yesterday. Two constables called and said they will come again tomorrow and question the workmen. They asked if I had any suspicions and I told them about the disappearance of my cheque book and that the decorator had been in the house at the time. I also told them the same man had been here yesterday, and had seemed reluctant to go when I asked him, but I then said I really did not have grounds for believing he had broken open the door. This evening I found that the green lampshade the same man had admired had vanished.

Edie Rutherford

Last night we had the two teachers from next door for a meal. In all the years we have lived as neighbours that has never happened before. I had, from Texas a few weeks ago, a packet of Rice Dinner. The last of my 1939 hoard of tins was a tin of Libby's prawns so I prepared one with the other and served with roast potatoes and tinned peas. A mixed vegetable salad with mayonnaise and to follow plums (2/9d. a bottle) with chocolate sauce and tinned cream, and all went well.

Since dried eggs were put on points I have bought just two packets. Now that they are to go to 2/6d. in price I shall dispense with them entirely. I imagine the Government is now trying to ease us off the things and no doubt they will succeed this way.

MONDAY, 3 MARCH

B. Charles
What a day! One succession of household worries. I just could not survive another removal. To cut a long story short, it seems Robertson came, with some prospective purchaser, to look over one of the upstairs flats. As I was out and had shut the outside door he, being in a bad temper, burst it open! So it was he who had done it. He is, of course, stone potty. Then, later in the morning, I found one of the hessian curtains had disappeared and it has, I presume, been stolen by the man who has stolen the lampshade. I had to get in touch with the CID. They came to see me this afternoon and are going to see what action to take, if any. It is intensely annoying; fortunately I have enough hessian to make another curtain.

TUESDAY, 4 MARCH

B. Charles
It is, of course, the thirtieth anniversary of the death of dear Grannie. She had provided her last dinner for us: roast hare and that orange pudding we were so fond of. I remember I read the will after dinner and we arranged to bring away the sideboard. After Mother's death, she was my very best friend. I think now that I ought not to have taken part in the Park Street theatricals so soon after her demise.

WEDNESDAY, 5 MARCH

Herbert Brush
This is the limit. There were 4 or 5 inches of snow last night and I have been more than an hour digging ways out around the house. The storm has upset everything in London this morning. All the

buses and trams are stopped, and as I was working near the gate about ten o'clock a number of Dulwich College boys tramped past on their way to school. They had had to walk for miles, and they still had more than a mile to go.

B. Charles

A letter from Stephen Claude enclosing a photo of the royal family at some function in South Africa. Really I feel, after looking at the inane grin on the Queen's face and the completely vacant, meaningless expressions on the others' faces, that my name for them, 'the Smith Family', is more than ever suitable now. The Queen looks exactly like some fat, common cook dressed in her mistress's clothes, going out on her 'off' day after having imbibed too freely of gin. The King and two princesses are exactly like the average person one sees in any street, on any day, at any time, in any town in Great Britain. It is not surprising, I think, when such people are the heads of the British Empire that, say, Stalin treats us all with contempt.

THURSDAY, 6 MARCH

George Taylor

It is many years since I first read Hammond's *The Rise of Modern Industry*, but it is now instructive to note the reasons given by Hammond for the rise of Great Britain. One of the main reasons was that industrialists first gained freedom from restrictions in this country. It seems that the loss of this freedom now is to cause the Decline of Modern Industry in Great Britain and a future Hammond would have to write of the rise in America, where there is comparative freedom.

SATURDAY, 8 MARCH

B. Charles

I went to the Pouishnoff recital this afternoon, and enjoyed it very much. There was not a vacant seat in the Usher Hall. Unfortunately, he did not play the F Sharp Major Nocturne, the one dear Mother was so fond of, but substituted another. I used to play it when she was dying.

I think there is no doubt that modern young people, generally, are far keener on music than their parents were. I suppose this may be owing to the BBC, which broadcasts many fine concerts. I thought the fact that there was only one door open to admit the audience to the Usher Hall this afternoon, causing a great crowd and much pushing and jostling, such very bad management. I asked one of the ushers why this was so, and he replied that it was to try to keep the hall warm. Then there was no electric light at the beginning of the concert. I shall never forget what Avory, the old van man of Fortnum & Mason, once said to me at Windsor. He remarked that petty economies are so very bad for business, in every way. I don't believe the saving they effect is in any way commensurate with the bad impression they cause. It is to be hoped that at the forthcoming Festival there won't be any of these silly 'economies' otherwise the visitors will be certain, after all, that the Scots are a very mean nation.

Two police officers called this evening to say they have done all they can in the matter of the missing curtain.

SUNDAY, 9 MARCH

Edie Rutherford
Bertrand Russell's atomic talk was the best yet from the point of view of the ordinary man. I want to die before the next war. I'm sorry to say I don't feel man has yet enough sense to settle things in better ways. Husband says atom bombs won't be used next time for the same reason that neither gas nor bacteriological warfare was used last time – fear. I am not so sanguine because it seems to me that a cunning nation could steal a march and drop enough atom bombs in half an hour to get the upper hand.

I see in *Daily Express* a quote from Hearst Press about demise of British Empire, leaving USA and USSR the only worthwhile world powers. Good. Let those two fight while we form a gallery for a change, and come in just towards the end when we see who is winning.

George Taylor
The sun came out, and the temperature rose above freezing point for a change, so I set about clearing the yard from snow and de-iced the roof of the shed, removing most of the roofing felt in so doing. I hope that this will be the last of snow shovelling for this season.

MONDAY, 10 MARCH

George Taylor
Hopes again dashed! A heavy fall of snow during the night.

TUESDAY, 11 MARCH

Edie Rutherford
My German friend Elfie on ground floor has at least had news of home. Her father is dead, her one brother has survived the war but of the other no news. Her letter is from a woman friend who tells her the brother wrote our Home Office and Harrods, where Elfie worked before the war, endeavouring to get in touch with her shortly after war ended.

Elfie is terribly upset, though she says she has felt all along that her father would have got in touch with her by now had he been alive. Poor lass. All very well to talk about Germans but a human is a human and grief is the same to us all. Her brother has married since the war and is the father to twins who need nourishment, the friend says. So, I am trying to get Elfie to concentrate less on grief by being constructive about getting a parcel together for her brother, who survives for sure. She has plenty to send so she must rejoice in that.

THURSDAY, 13 MARCH

B. Charles
One of the worst days of the winter. It started to snow last night and it has continued all day. There are big drifts of snow all over town and all trains to England have been cancelled. At midday there was only one English paper on sale. I hoped we had finished with the snow for the winter. This morning I was terribly busy and some man arrived from some Ministry to give a certificate that the house was fit for habitation. I was too busy to let him over and said he would have to make an appointment. He was most off-hand – just walked in. These officials are just little Hitlers.

Edie Rutherford
I think Attlee coped with Churchill very well last night. It is no use the opposition shouting at the Government for nationalisation and so

on. Conservatives just don't see what it is all about. They refuse to see it, always have, because they don't want it to happen. Why doesn't Mrs Churchill, or someone, get at Winston Churchill and MAKE him see he's old, deaf and finished. The day of living on rhetoric is passed.

Maggie Joy Blunt
Much worried about Twinkle, and myself with chest and throat like the wrath of God. Cat doctor whom I've been consulting by phone thinks cat may have septic throat and I'm quite sure I have. I would have taken cat to clinic today but they were busy neutering and would rather see him tomorrow. He is very thin, weak, pinched looking, eats nothing and drinks very little. He smells awful.

B. Russell's broadcast very depressing.

FRIDAY, 14 MARCH

Maggie Joy Blunt
Twinkle died this morning as I took him to the cat clinic. I wanted to take him yesterday. I wish I had not been so obedient – though I know the vet there must have to deal with dozens of hysterical women over the phone who think their cat is dying when all it needs is castor oil. Twinkle was obviously (now it seems so, but I *never* give up hope with my animals) dying last night and in great pain and I didn't know what to do. Felt if only I could keep him alive till I got him to the clinic all would be well (that blind, primitive faith in witchdoctors and magicians). I had him in my room all night with all his paraphernalia and kept the fire going – every hour or so awake to listen if he still breathed, to move him nearer the fire when he had moved away. In the last twenty-four hours he fought pathetically both to live and to die. He tried to jump on to the draining board to watch me while I washed up, climbed on to windowsill to have a last look at the birds and garden, jumped on to edge of bath as it was running in and tried to play with my toes as he always loved to do.

These things tore me to pieces; he was so weak, so exhausted after each effort. But when I started to feed him he fought desperately and again and again moved into a quieter, darker, colder place when he could. His ash box he used not at all. This morning as I put him in the basket – he was a frame covered with matted fur – he made one last effort at resistance and then subsided. He was on a down cushion and I covered him warmly. It was snowing and the wind was bitter. Children in the bus – as they always do when they see the basket, grew excited for the poor, sick pussy which they couldn't see. He was still breathing. The bus journey seemed interminable. A few minutes before we reached the town he cried out, struggled frantically for a few seconds, and the children strained forward eagerly. 'He doesn't like being in the basket,' I said. I always say that. But I knew he was dead. I wanted to howl my heart out. At the clinic I was hard, bright, practical. The vet said that he had had a haemorrhage and died of that, that he had had some trouble with his lungs and an enlarged liver and the prevalent deadly cat sickness. He could have done nothing if I had brought him sooner but put him to sleep. My dear Twinkle. He must have been dying all this week and I did not or would not know.

Now I have to wait and see if Dinah is infected. She has been so well all this week and normal again and this vet thinks she may have escaped – but I must watch her for forty-eight hours. All last night and until midday today she has been out with her boyfriends making up for lost time, this afternoon in for a meal, hugely hungry, impudent, beautiful and full of life. She *must* be all right! I couldn't live through another episode like today's just yet. Death is so terribly remorseless. Little animals in its hands are so lost, frightened and far away, and we can only stand by watching.

The cat died. Such an insignificant event. A dead cat – target for mockery, small boys and dust. There are too many cats in the world. Why make all the fuss because now there is one less?

Every cat is a miracle of independent, loveable life, if you have the eyes and the feeling to understand it as such. I have loved many cats and shall I expect love many more. Each one becomes a friend with a distinct individuality, and the loss each time is a deeply personal one. No one else ever replaces that person exactly, but new personalities help you to forget your grief at the loss of others. Living would be quite unbearable if you could not transfer your affections in this way.

Meanwhile, Dinah, who insisted with persistent, feminine eager-ness on going out again, sits inside a coke bin tormenting a brute tabby and an ugly black and white – she sits just inside the place where the shovel goes, safely out of harm's reach, making outrageous eyes at both of them.

SUNDAY, 16 MARCH

Maggie Joy Blunt

'Morning, miss,' said the little gardener next door, putting his head over the fence. 'Shocking weather. More snow coming, so the wireless says . . .' And sure enough this afternoon about tea time it comes and has not stopped since. Several inches now everywhere. One begins to feel suicidal. Twenty-five-foot drifts in Scotland. My stepbrother's brother and his wife near Worcester completely isolated and snow up to telegraph poles. And as the thaw comes, so do the floods. All east London without drinking water.

Yesterday Lady A, who knew all about my poor Twinkle from her housekeeper from whom I had had to borrow 6d. for bus fare, saw me return and phoned as soon as I was back to hear the news. It was rather trying to have to tell her at that moment with tears streaming down my face but she was very sympathetic; then proceeded to tell me how infectious the disease was (someone else's cat nearby is ill with it) and how careful I must be for Dinah and so on, all of which I knew from vet. So have been trying to disinfect the kitchen and all the things the little cat used but difficult to know how. Turned out all mats and cushions in kitchen, cleaned floor and then mopped it with methylated, cleaned sink and draining board with it too, soaked his plates in it and boiling water. But it's impossible short of fumigation to be sure of everything. There's my dressing gown and bedroom slippers. Have also sprinkled Jeyes powder liberally over floor.

Dinah seems very well indeed but shall be in a nervous panic till tomorrow is over. I managed to get her in last night, but she is out again now with snow inches thick and whether I can find her before I get to bed or if she'll come I don't know.

MONDAY, 17 MARCH

B. Charles

In the afternoon there was a proper calamity here. I noticed a small patch of wet on the drawing-room ceiling and, on going upstairs, saw the water pouring into the flats owing to the gullies being blocked with ice. Fortunately, the two POWs started cleaning up the mess. The plumber's men came, and are here still, trying to clear away the ice and stop the dripping. Really, it has been one damned thing after another with this flat.

Edie Rutherford

Had a good laugh at Husband on Saturday when he told me a tram conductor had addressed him as 'Dad'. At first he was annoyed then, on looking at the young conductor, he quickly became philosophically resigned, especially when he thought how tickled I would be.

Last week there was an ad in *Daily Mirror* for pipes, surplus USA services, so I bought two as a surprise for husband. He had seen the ad and decided the pipes could not be any good, but condescended to try. They are fantastic to look at, marked pure briar. One is now broken in and husband says it is quite all right.

Maggie Joy Blunt

Dinah continues well. Is looking better than she has for a long while, eyes big and clear, coat clean, fluffy and in good condition. She's a tough little creature. There is a lot to be said for having more than one cat. She sits now by open kitchen window and the latest boyfriend under yew tree watching her. Do they talk to one another? She'll sit like that in the sun for hours – he was at one time right under kitchen window, until I disturbed him. Occasionally one hears low mutterings.

I like Solon's article in today's *News Chronicle*. Why *must* we go one being an arrogant, greedy power although we may be better colonists and conquerors than anyone else? Why not change the emphasis from wealth, power, importance (aggrandisement) to cultural and spiritual things – from quantity of possessions to *quality* of possessions? This seems to me much more important. I think that if we did, we could contribute something of much importance and value to the whole world. I have a feeling that our people, the ordinary, everyday, humdrum classes from the middle-middle downwards have more in them of potential creative ability, imagination, initiative, character and inherent wisdom than in any other race in the world – if given the chance to develop, released from this frightful, stupid strain of 'keeping up appearances'.

WEDNESDAY, 19 MARCH

George Taylor

Because there is a threat to the continued supply of electrical appliances we have decided to indulge in an immersion heater. If we let this chance go by like we did that of an electric cooker in 1939, goodness knows when we shall have the luxury of hot water on tap.

B. Charles
I have just returned from the concert and have much enjoyed it. I saw a little lad there with his father, I suppose aged about ten, who was enthralled with the music. His father seemed so devoted to him and was explaining various points in the music to the little lad. I think, probably, in a way, my father, when I was very small, tried to take an interest in me but, as I never liked the things he approved of, his interest soon slackened. Had I been a child now, the fact that I am so passionately interested in what are called 'artistic things' would not have been the great drawback to me that it was when I was a child. Then, for a boy to be interested in Art was scarcely respectable. Yes, things, in many ways, have improved greatly since I was a child.

FRIDAY, 21 MARCH

George Taylor
Eight weeks ago I lost my fountain pen when clearing away snow. This morning my wife came in crying, 'Eureka!' After I had cleaned it, and filled it with ink, it wrote perfectly.

Maggie Joy Blunt
A poem from S this morning. He turns out this sort of nonsense with great facility. 'Moog' is nickname for me.

> Weep not, dear Moogness, o'er the cats,
> But buy a brace of feathered hats
> And sing
> Hey Nonny no
> For Spring . . .

> Weep not, dear Moogness, for the State
> Or on the awesome Atom's fate,
> But sing
> Hey Nonny no
> For Spring . . .

Weep not, dear Moogness; gaily dance
Through Slough's despond and life enhance
With beauty e'er it's fatal kissed
By Planner or by Communist

Weep not, dear Moogness, let thy fears
Thaw away with winter's tears
Hey Nonny no
For Spring . . .

SATURDAY, 22 MARCH

George Taylor

I should have taken a party of sixty-four to the Village Players at
Hucklow today, but as the theatre was snowed in at the early part of
the week, the production was postponed for the second time. It is
now billed to take place in May, when it is hoped that the drifts will
be somewhat less deep.

We had the opening social of our Summer Programme at the university. As we had to be content with the Medical Library for the
function, parlour games predominated, and I spent most of the evening dodging them by helping with the refreshments. For this labour I
received a reward of a lump of cake.

WEDNESDAY, 26 MARCH

George Taylor

Another social! This time it was the WEA Philosophy Classes who
gathered together. As it was the same MC as last Saturday, parlour
games were the order once more. During the interval, however, the
tutor of the classes, a Unitarian Minister, gave demonstrations of
jujitsu. He is certainly a versatile fellow.

Maggie Joy Blunt

In London since Saturday. Saw S. Thinks that Russia will soon withdraw altogether from Europe and retire behind impenetrable 'iron
curtain' to prepare for war. Says they (Russians) are realists, out for
the good of their own country and their unborn millions, determined
to get it in their own way and just think us foolish. He said, 'I don't

like the Americans but I'd rather live in America than a Soviet-controlled Europe.'

A practical point raised at Fabian discussion the other night. The discussion was about the new forty-four-hour week. About ten present: one TU man on Trades Council, a shop steward and real workers' representative, the rest of us ordinary middle-class 'clerks' and professionals. We said it was the wrong time to insist on this now. All but the TU man agreed. Argument was heated. But he couldn't see it. Power is in TU hands now but their vision is so limited.

London cold, drab as ever. Worked in libraries. Best reference library I know is at Marylebone. Convenient, comfortable, a desk for each worker, light, shelves, ink. Have discovered a tea room in Marylebone main railway station.

FRIDAY, 28 MARCH

Maggie Joy Blunt
I subscribe now to the Cats Protection League and receive each month their journal *The Cat* ('The oldest magazine devoted entirely to cats'). It is full of interesting information, advice and anecdotes and makes me feel that I have in the past been needlessly cruel and careless. 'Pain and fear are common to both humans and animals', and an animal can suffer as much mentally and physically as a human.

We can be cruel from ignorance, laziness and carelessness or from being too sentimental and fussy, though the CPL only stress the first point. I have I am sure made my cats stay out at night and in bad weather when they should not have done. A cat, they say, should never be left out all night. I still feel guilty. The cats' illness and Twinkle's death and what he suffered – I can't forget it, and I am afraid it all started because I was making them sleep in the shed when the snow was on the ground.

Made lemon marmalade last night and overboiled it again.

SATURDAY, 29 MARCH

B. Charles
I have made some grapefruit marmalade but I am not certain if it will 'set' as firmly as I like. It took a very long time to cook. I have been baking this evening and no one has come along, except the Germans, all day.

George Taylor

To attract the members to our Half Yearly General Meeting of the WEA we booked Mr Holland, who has been the British Education Control Officer in the Rhineland. Mr Holland gave a very interesting account of his work in Germany. At first, the British were accepted with open arms, but thanks to the lavish promises made during the war by the BBC, there was now much disillusionment. Lack of physical remedies and shortages of non-Nazi staff had all made it difficult to set up a genuine educational system. Mr Holland thought that there was still time to do something, although the time was perilously short.

MONDAY, 31 MARCH

George Taylor

I heard from the ex-secretary of one of our clients that, like many of the wartime marriages, her marriage seems to be going awry, and since her husband left Chesterfield for a post in London he has acquainted her of his preference for someone else. She asked me to give her a reference in case she has to return to work to support her six-month-old son, and of course I did this. It is a real tragedy when marriage goes wrong.

TUESDAY, 1 APRIL 1947

Edie Rutherford

So children born of artificial insemination are illegitimate even with husband's consent? It needs more than the human opinion of an MP to decide that ticklish point . . .

WEDNESDAY, 2 APRIL

Maggie Joy Blunt

The battle against the cold this long winter, the continual Government crises and blunders, the cold, wet, delayed spring and everlasting austerity has exhausted us all to the bone. Our nerves are on edge, our anxieties and depressions enormous. Celia, whose film work and dress shows have been seriously checked so that she is thrown back entirely upon dressmaking, says that the least difficulty will upset her for at least two hours. June thinks she may have lost a pair of T's sandals at the nursery school, a new pair not a week old, a really good non-utility, well-cut pair of good material costing 8/2d., and can think of nothing else – the calamity is huge, out of all proportion. I find myself worrying unduly about the possibility of burglars or fire at the cottage; I have felt mentally worn out for nearly a month now, I sleep badly and all sorts of silly things fret me.

Middle-class dissatisfaction with the Government seems to be increasing. All the professional people I meet or hear of are gravely uneasy. We seem to be in a tangle that only gets worse and which will never unravel. Foolish restrictions are hampering honest private enterprise to such an extent that many people who were socialist are turning anti-socialist. Architects are particularly badly hit in this respect. Some young men who since the war have sunk all their available capital in independent ventures fear that they will lose it all and have to seek other jobs. The Government seems to be doing everything for the working class and completely ignoring the fact that other classes do exist and have as much right to existence – and have important value in the community.

Sarah, of tolerant, liberal outlook, living in a very conservative, well-to-do country district where everyone grumbles as they do here, obtained via her MP a ticket for the House one evening and sat in Members' Gallery. Heard Eden and Shinwell and said it was very interesting, but thought they wasted too much time talking for the sake of it and on schoolboy backchat.

THURSDAY, 3 APRIL

Edie Rutherford

Alas for the poor nig who jumped on the royal car in South Africa. At first I thought he might be a Communist with a petition for his friends in jail but seemingly he is just one of those so uncivilised that his feelings ran away with him. The Queen seems to have been scared. I am surprised that the nig got as near as that, seeing that nearly every bobby in the Union is moved to wherever the royal party goes.

We are to have a new radio. The manager of a local shop lives on first floor so husband called last evening and arranged for a Sobell to come on trial for lunchtime today. We are advised to sell our twelve-year-old Philips privately and this man says we should get £10 for it.

As it cost us £13 we are amazed and can't quite believe it. However, the Sobell costs about £30.

How much easier housework is with a vacuum cleaner and, heavens, the dirt there is in the bag at the weekly turnout. One of the teachers next door actually told me last week that a certain amount of filth in the air is good for us.

George Taylor

Had lunch and a business conference with a very special character. Prior to the war he had acted as technical representative to a Sheffield steel firm, but his secretary told me that he had always been more interested in technical questions than in orders. When the blitz on Sheffield occurred, he walked into the secretary's office the next morning and asked if he could speak to Lord Beaverbrook on the phone. The secretary was aghast at the idea, but eventually agreed, and got in touch with Lord Beaverbrook's office, where the scheme was briefly explained. They were much interested, and asked for details in writing. These were sent, and the secretary thought that would end the matter. However, in a day or two a phone message from the Balloon Barrage Commander here came through stating that he had received instructions to place the whole of his resources at the disposal of the scheme, and from this commenced the service of compressed gas for blitzed areas. Eventually our friend, at the request of the Government, built up a whole organisation, with special lorries and trailers, which rushed compressed gas to areas affected, and so enabled many works to keep in production which otherwise would have been shut down.

GOOD FRIDAY, 4 APRIL

Edie Rutherford

We have the Sobell radio on trial. Unfortunately our suppressor conked out when we disconnected our Philips radio, and using the Sobell direct from plug makes the lift, and other interference, worse than it was with our set. Husband quite depressed about it. He had so looked forward to hearing the Sobell.

What a nerve that Palestine rabbi has to say that our present misfortunes are because of our treatment of Palestinian Jews. By that argument I suppose the sufferings in Germany are because of their treatment of Jews. I wish the Germans saw it that way.

SUNDAY, 6 APRIL

B. Charles

Heinz and Heinrich arrived on time and we went to the exhibition of 'Germany under Control', which I found interesting. I can't, however, imagine WHY it is being held, unless it is to try to prove to the British people the enormous amount of work being done by the British in their Zone, and so try to justify the enormous expense this occupation is costing the country. The POWs seemed most interested in it. I couldn't help remarking how very little notice they seemed to create among the crowd of people there. People seemed to take them for granted and I think this is very praiseworthy of the British people. I have seen no signs at all that German POWs are resented or disliked; quite the reverse.

Heinz is the more patriotic of the two, I think. I was interested to hear him lament the fact that only the worst of the German uniforms were exhibited this afternoon, none of the best ones. The Germans love uniform. As we were going to the exhibition there was a procession of the Lad's Brigade going to the meeting at the Usher Hall. The two POWs were extremely interested to watch the procession go by and said how very like the Hitler *Jugend* it was.

TUESDAY, 8 APRIL

Maggie Joy Blunt

Village this afternoon bleak, deserted, dead. Very little in shops. Fishmonger closed. No food anywhere for the cat. Went round asking for Chappie or something similar and cigarettes. Everywhere 'No, so sorry' except at cake shop where I got twenty Piccadilly and twenty Top Score. Off points now are tins of anchovies (1/6d.). I bought one and can now use a tin I have had in stock since beginning of war and haven't liked to open.

Good watercress and cress in greengrocer's but little else. Rhubarb still very expensive. I don't like looking at my greengrocer's book nowadays, the amount always seems so enormous. For the last four orders, including the one for Easter weekend, it is 18/6d. I see that they have forgotten the rhubarb I had for Easter. This will be a burden on my conscience. I must point out the omission and pay for what I had. I don't usually go over the account and may have had many similar gifts or paid for something I haven't had. The woman in the shop puts it all down after one has left the shop, relying on memory. The eldest is very good at this, but the others, following her lead, evidently are not.

Yesterday by car to the river to view the floods, or what remained of them. Many fields are still underwater around Cookham, and traces of where water reached the bits of straw and rubbish are still hanging on the wire fences. Along one road the ditch edges were marked at intervals by stakes – evidently to show the line of the road. We went into a small pub, old, dark, low-lying where floorboards or flooring had been replaced with planks and dank chill struck up from the floor.

Shall now listen to *The Brains Trust* and put another patch on my pants.

Herbert Brush

12.10 p.m. Am now parked outside the Scotch Wool shop in Camberley High Street, the whole street is full both sides with parked cars and we were lucky to find a place. All the way W has been on the lookout for a fish shop where really good fish are sold, but up to now has had no luck. She gave 2/6d. for a small cauliflower just now which I regard as robbery, but unfortunately I can't grow them on my plot; club root takes them quicker than any other green.

2.30 p.m. Got some plaice.

WEDNESDAY, 9 APRIL

Herbert Brush

10.40 a.m. I am in the car parked outside the 'Kenolite' factory in Bournemouth. A loudspeaker on a car has just gone past and people are requested to 'Vote for Sunday Cinemas' tomorrow. Everyone over twenty-one has a vote, so I assume that there will be a little excitement in Bournemouth tomorrow.

11.40 a.m. My word it is getting hot in the car, and still no sign of W coming back from the factory. Another loudspeaker has just passed, and this time it bawls out, 'Think about your children's welfare and vote against Sunday cinemas'. I wonder which side will win.

THURSDAY, 10 APRIL

Maggie Joy Blunt
Our first day of spring. Wonderful. One daffodil is out. Sky clear, sun golden and tender, birds in happy voice. Everything seems too surprised to do anything but enjoy it. Have just finished salad lunch sitting in deck chair in garden. Neighbour's small boy G trotted in as I was preparing it (there is no division between the gardens and the children wander freely) and when I said I was going to have it outside he said, 'A sort of picnic lunch in the garding? What a good idea to do', and went back to his own house when called, telling his mother in a loud voice all about it.

Later. Another neighbour's small girl pranced in with enormous toy rabbit her father had just brought home for her. It was a splendid animal, sitting on haunches and all colours, pink front, white back, mauve face and ears, brown nose, blue front legs. She was very excited and all the children scampered off screaming with delight.

FRIDAY, 11 APRIL

Edie Rutherford
Have asked for Sobell radio to be called for, and hope it is taken before visitors come tomorrow, as a flat is small enough without a thing extra in it. When we reconnected our old Philips we realised it is every bit as good as the new Sobell.

Herbert Brush
> A gardener is an angry man
> When he has dug and raked and hoed
> And done all any gardener can
> To make grow every seed he sowed;
> And then the neighbour's cats come round
> And hold a 'beano' on his ground.

SATURDAY, 12 APRIL

Herbert Brush
W and I went to the State Cinema this afternoon. The main picture was *Margie* with Jeanne Crain in the main part, a pretty girl who

acted her part well and kept me interested all the time, but her bloomers came down several times, and a lot was made of the idea.

SUNDAY, 13 APRIL

B. Charles
I see General Montgomery is reported to have stated that '60 per cent of the recruits for the Navy don't know who Christ was'. If this is indeed the case, it is to me simply extraordinary how the Church STILL manages to exercise such great influence in public affairs. I think the general public is utterly indifferent to all things religious, so long as these things are not definitely attacked. If anyone openly says religion is all a humbug nearly everyone, even those who don't know who Christ was, will get on their hind legs and become extremely annoyed. I have been of the opinion for a very long time that, with measurable distance of time, organised religion will die of inaction, so long as people keep quiet about it, but, as I have said, IF they attack it, it will take on a new lease of life.

TUESDAY, 15 APRIL

George Taylor
The one blessing of the fuel crisis has been the reintroduction of double summer time. We thoroughly welcome this, and particularly its early introduction. Both my wife and I like to be able to go to bed while there is a trace of daylight, and we shall soon be able to do this with DST.

Doubts as to the future are still deterring businessmen. Today I was at a meeting where a small new factory was under consideration. It seems that the local authority will only grant a building licence subject to a ten years' limit, and there is a proviso that the company may then be required to demolish the factory at their own expense. No wonder that there is hesitation about starting.

The budget was quite a relief to me. I shall gain by the raising of the earned income relief and by the revision of the dependent relative's relief. The increase of the tobacco duty leaves me cold. But what a disgraceful broadcast was made by Dalton. He might have been speaking from a soapbox. Dalton is certainly not a statesman.

Maggie Joy Blunt

Heard ten minutes of Dalton's budget speech. He sounded just like scout master talking to his Cubs. I can think of nothing but huge increase in tobacco tax! My first reaction was dismay – I must earn more to pay for what I want. Then, how damnably unfair. The people with enough money will go on buying tobacco as they did before and it'll be the middle and small man who'll be making the real sacrifices, not from any virtuous patriotism but from stark economic necessity. One wouldn't mind cutting down and doing without if one felt all were compelled, as with food and clothes rationing (though black market stories are common enough). But will that 50 per cent increase do that? *Shall* I cut down, or shall I raise money to pay for the increase? Well, I'll try to keep twenty a day maximum and so save at least 8d. a week.

Mosquitoes – the large, vicious variety that thrive here – are already active. First of the season woke me early one morning about a week before Easter, buzzing so loudly that I thought at first it was a bee or a wasp. Today one has stung me in two or three places. I apply Dettol, which I find very effective.

WEDNESDAY, 16 APRIL

George Taylor

There seems noticeably less smoking on the trams today, and the decrease in tobacco fumes is welcome.

Maggie Joy Blunt

To British Museum after early lunch, arriving about 2 p.m. The first time I have used the Reading Room. A bit awe-inspiring. I felt rather as I mounted the portico that I was entering the abode of death and might be discovered some years later by despairing friends. Some of the attendants in uniform seem dead already and awfully peevish about it, 'I'd've *told* you, miss, before, if you'd *asked* me . . . Down there and second floor on the left.' Officials (all men) were very kind and helpful. Obtaining a ticket is really astonishingly easy. That *anyone* can get access to so much wisdom and work in such quietness and comfort for nothing makes me feel humble with admiration. It's now open until 5 p.m.

Less people seemed to be smoking – women particularly. I heard no grumbles. As I left this morning Lady A called out, 'Are you cutting down? It will be very good for you!' I heard one or two people say without much conviction and with a smile that when they had finished 'this lot' they would give it up.

THURSDAY, 17 APRIL

Edie Rutherford

Teacher next door says double summer time is disastrous in her class of fifty-one five-year-olds. On inquiry she found that only one is put to bed in a darkened room at a suitable hour. All the fifty run the streets till dark, sleep all morning in school, and it is 3 p.m. before they are fresh enough to hear what is said to them.

Husband says he is finished with his pipe.

Herbert Brush

I have again put my name down as an entrant to the allotment competition though I nearly made up my mind to give it a miss this year, as I was not at all satisfied with the judging last year, and suspect that the Labour Council in power were responsible.

FRIDAY, 18 APRIL

Herbert Brush

I listened to the BBC account of the blowing up of Heligoland; it must have been a fine show. Hitler's ashes would blow about if he could know the end of his scheme. I meant to go and watch the pond for ripples, but left it until too late.

SUNDAY, 20 APRIL

Edie Rutherford

Yesterday while getting luncheon served a cracked Phoenix dish fell apart in my hand and middle left finger on left hand has a nasty cut across top. I reckon Pyrex ware has Phoenix beat and will never buy Phoenix again.

Maggie Joy Blunt

Rereading volume one of Arnold Bennett's *Journals*. On 13 September 1907 he notes:

'I bought Taine's *Voyage en Italie* and was once again fired to make fuller notes of the impression of the moment, of *choses vues*. Several good books by him consist of nothing else. I must surely by this time be a trained philosophic observer – fairly exact and controlled by scientific principles. At the time one can scarcely judge what may be valuable later on. At the present moment I wish, for instance, that some schoolmistress had written down simply her impressions of her years in training; I want them for my novel. The whole of life ought to be covered thus by "impressionists" and a vast ware of new materials of facts and sensations collected for use by historians, sociologists and novelists. I must really try to do my share of it more completely than I do.'

This makes me pause once more to consider my value as an 'observer' – we all tend, as he notes of himself a day or so later, to go about blindly, wrapped up in ourselves. One's observations should be accurate, and recorded as sincerely and objectively as possible, and as consistently as possible. The difficulties here are immense. Another difficulty, as Bennett found, is to know or be able to select what may be of value later. How is one to know? One cannot possibly record all one's impressions – one must select and learn what to select. My diary seems to me much too spasmodic, impulsive and not full enough. Also I find it very difficult to be accurate – particularly when recording things such as overheard conversation some time later. It is so easy to put things down that one *thinks* one has heard. And one cannot be free, either, of a certain amount of subjective bias. Though that I suppose doesn't matter so much so long as the reader remembers it, i.e. that *this* is how this particular person saw the incident or scene (a different kind of person might have seen it quite differently).

Left my wristwatch in town on Thursday. Catch was faulty so I put it in handbag and it must have dropped out in Lyons Corner House where I had lunch. Inquired for it later and was told to come back again in case cleaners found it. Corner House 'Salad Bowl' was as good as ever – no wonder there is always a queue. My only complaint is that their mayonnaise is too vinegary.

Herbert Brush

As I crossed Bloomsbury Street on the way to the BM, the thought suddenly struck me that I would go and see what the office of 'Mass-Observation' is like, as that is where my diary-letters end up. I went

383

along to 21 Bloomsbury House, and was told by the doorkeeper that MO was on the fifth floor. I hesitated a moment, as I did not feel like climbing five flights of stairs; but when he said there is a lift, I went and waited for it.

Two men and a woman were waiting and when the lift came down, the attendant said that the lift could not take all, so I, the woman and the older man of the two got in, and the young man hurried up the stairs. I entered an office and a handsome young man greeted me and told me his name, but I forget it. As I had no real business there, I had to explain that I had come to see the kind of office it was where my letter-diaries found a home after you had finished with them. In a minute or so, Mr Willcock came in and we talked for about another minute about Caldwell, and I questioned the use of my diaries, as they very seldom contain any interesting matter for strangers to read. However, I was told that they were all read, and if anything of interest was there it would be found and noted. We shook hands and I left, feeling glad that I had not paid my visit at a time when the current was not available for the lift.

TUESDAY, 22 APRIL

Edie Rutherford
£4,500 worth of wild animals arrived in this country yesterday. I do think such could wait until humans are better fed and housed than at present. Can anyone put forward one good reason why these animals should be brought to our country just now? I read that last week we decided to take over the care of zoo animals being sent from Germany.

Both Husband and self amazed to hear seats will no longer be reserved on trains as we did not know that in this country one could ever book a train seat, and I bet most folk were unaware of it. Never have we even seen a reserved seat.

WEDNESDAY, 23 APRIL

George Taylor
It was the first of our WEA Spring Lectures, and as I was due to preside, I struggled up to the university, although I would rather have been at home recovering from my flu. I was amply repaid for my effort, as Mr

Boswell gave a most absorbing account of Biology in City Services. He dealt mainly with the problems of a pure water supply and methods of dealing with sewage. His enthusiasm for his subject was infectious.

Maggie Joy Blunt

All this week at British Museum, leaving early in the morning and not back till late at night. Quite like old times, having to do odd jobs in the evening and be ready for a morning dash. But now it is to please myself and I have no one to fear if I am a little late.

Noted on Monday: in front of me in bus, girl and her young sister. Powder-blue coat, crimson nails, mouth heavily made up and leather gloves and bag to match . . . a pretty colour combination. Girl's skin looked creamy, dark hair curled naturally. She wore light-framed glasses; eyes were grey-blue and lashes were dark and long. At first glance she intrigued me and I wanted to see more. Features a little heavy but she had young curves. Seemed as though she should be very attractive indeed. On station platform had chance of seeing all of her, full view and a good walk round. Very disappointing – coat too long, too full, too fussy. Mock nutria dabbed here and there and on large pockets. Brown leather court shoes, scarlet crimson handbag and gloves all wrong. Blue bow in hair, blue gauzy scarf and cluster-pearl earrings. Complexion was 'pancake,' not real, skin rather coarse, hair greasy at roots. And full face was plain. Her smile a painful shock – teeth badly spaced and an ugly colour, lipstick drew too much attention to it. Her movements nervous, affected. Conscious of many defects, immaturity and insignificance but determined to outdo nature and time with a result contrary to one intended. Instead of attractive she was repulsive. Make-up and nails would have suited debutante or sophisticated thirty-year-old. She was too young and inexperienced to carry it. I've seen dozens of young factory girls with paint as thick, but they've never looked out of character as this girl did. I felt sorry for her. She had possibilities but was making glaring mistakes.

Edie Rutherford

Mrs Braun at 174 tells me today she has heard from her sister that a pair of shoes I gave her reached Berlin safely. Being too small for the sister, they were handed on to a schoolteacher friend who kissed them all over in her joy at having them.

Today in post from Barrasford, Hexham, I got about five hundred daffodils from Rosemary, lovely of her. Eight of us have all had a good-sized bunch. They travelled very well indeed, and in water they have perked up as if freshly cut.

I am trying a corned beef curry today.

THURSDAY, 24 APRIL

Maggie Joy Blunt
Ella talking of several war marriages in vicinity that have crashed; one man with a child by a woman not his wife; a woman who has found a rich protector and refuses to go back to husband; another man who since his return from war finds his wife so extravagant and temperamental he refuses to live with her.

Characters in British Museum: man with large white pasty face, long moustache and hair like Rasputin. Woman with tousled bob, black leather coat, belted, three-quarter length, and I think shorts – her legs were bare and uncovered from above the knee. Many women now stocking-less again, some today in sandals. Got into conversation with French woman in British Museum Ladies this afternoon re the soap, a scrap that hardly lathers and is very slippery. How dirty our hands get from those dusty books.

FRIDAY, 25 APRIL

George Taylor
We went along to the open day at the university, and what a display had been prepared! We just found time to look round the dental department, and saw the new plastics, then to the bacteriology section to see the rather disappointing display of penicillin, on to the medical faculty where there was a very interesting if somewhat repulsive display of prenatal babies.

SATURDAY, 26 APRIL

George Taylor
I should have gone to the WEA District Council at Scunthorpe, but I did not feel very energetic, and did not want to get mixed up with the outbreak of smallpox in that town.

Edie Rutherford

Husband has spent two guineas on a smoking cure from Liverpool. I am watching events. I'm sure he will be better if he gets over the craving but realise the process may be unpleasant, to put it mildly. No matter what any doctor or other wise guy says about moderate smoking being harmless, I do not believe it.

SUNDAY, 27 APRIL

Edie Rutherford

Husband says, may he have some sweets – bull's-eyes – to take to work this week? He has finished his baccy and started his course.

Oh heavens, just as we were saying we might get fruit this year, as blossom would come after the frost, reports are that foul winter killed off bees so that pollination won't be coped with. Can nothing good happen for this benighted nation of ours?

THURSDAY, 1 MAY 1947

George Taylor

My wife joined the WEA party to visit the Batchelor's pea factory, where they saw peas and soup being canned. The party were surprised to see genuine vegetables being put into the Windsor soup.

FRIDAY, 2 MAY

Edie Rutherford

Husband's firm has had notification that 3 per cent of workmen must be disabled ex-servicemen.

Heard this morning of a doctor and wife, wealthy, who hate this Government so much that they are running up gas and electricity bills as high as £30, and smoking more than ever. Typical of the outlook of the greedy selfish rich, who think of themselves entirely, and nothing of England.

Also heard of another doctor who has three hairdressing businesses and three farms; doctoring being a sideline. Whenever he goes to a farm for a visit some beast is 'ill' and he operates. The knife slips and he and his pals have meat or pork for weeks.

Herbert Brush

I think that a good many people will be forced to turn on their electric fires today owing to the really bitter cold wind. We have a coal fire now, which D has just lighted, as the temperature was well down in the fifties. Imagine what England will be like in a few hundred years time when all the coal seams have been mined out. As the life of the country seems to depend on coal, the population will be reduced to about five million who will live off the land, like they used to do in the early days.

But we need not worry about that.

SATURDAY, 3 MAY

George Taylor

It is more than two years ago that I began thinking of a weekend for the WEA at Stratford, and at last has come the day when this was possible. But what a prospect. It poured with rain when was due to leave home this morning, and seemed absolutely hopeless. We sheltered in doorways until the coach arrived, then made a dash to get in. The drive through Derbyshire was almost wasted, for we could see scarcely anything through the steamed windows.

The Lord Leycester Hotel in Warwick was a bit frowsy, and the reception seemed sketchy, but the rooms were clean, and a first-class lunch was quickly served. We had a delightful summer's afternoon in Stratford doing the sights, and three of us had a very interesting conversation with the custodian of Shakespeare's birthplace. The chicken dinner at the Memorial Theatre was really excellent. One of our party was feeling so expansive that he ordered champagne, but when a full bottle was brought and he found, after argument, that he had to pay for it, his expansiveness was somewhat deflated.

Twelfth Night was the production of the evening, and a thoroughly enjoyable show it was.

SUNDAY, 4 MAY

George Taylor

It was drizzling when we set off for Whipsnade, and continued for the whole journey and the four hours we were there. Perhaps it was the dismal weather which helped to give me a feeling of disappointment about the zoo. I had previously imagined Whipsnade as an immense park, and I had been advised to take field glasses with me to see the animals. My impression, however, was that of a moderate-sized place, no larger than some Sheffield parks, and not a patch on Chatsworth, with a few animals scattered about in not too attractive pits. The solitary tiger looked lonely and ill at ease.

We had a good run back to Sheffield, just catching Lyons open at Bedford for tea!

MONDAY, 5 MAY

Edie Rutherford

Friend tells me this morn she has had her fur coat titivated: odd bits renewed and so on. Reckoned it would be about £20 and nearly had a fit when it was £65. Her husband shouted the roof off.

Turned out my miniature pantry today. Hasn't been thoroughly done for over three years so it was a filthy job. I did not, alas, find a tin of pineapple or asparagus tips.

Herbert Brush

I went along to the Royal Academy to have a look at the 1947 pictures. As there are about 1,300 exhibits I dare say that I missed a good many of them, but I did have a look at the two paintings by Winston Churchill. No. 57 (a prime number) is *Winter Sunshine* and it appears to my eye to have been done with a putty knife, but as there are several other pictures which look to me like this, maybe it is a style of painting which some people like. The other picture, *The Loup River*, I like better and the reflected light in the water of the river I thought very good. I wonder what the old man will turn his hand to next.

I noticed an oldish man, evidently an artist, making a sketch of the back parts of a black and white sketch of a nude female figure. He did this work very quickly, and as I watched, his little sketch grew and grew in a few seconds. He only did a small section of the buttocks and put it away quickly when he saw me watching.

Many paintings are of 'still life' and one of these I noticed included a pork pie along with empty beer bottles, and oranges. The pork pie was done so well that I could almost taste it and it made me feel hungry just to look at it. It was one of those pies with plenty of jelly between the meat and the crust.

Chapter Fifteen

THE PRESENT-DAY
YOUNG PERSON ALL OVER

No one at our table could say what the meat was: a holiday camp enjoys its dinner

Television Programmes
11 a.m.–12 noon Demonstration film
3 p.m. *Close Up*
3.25 p.m. Interlude
3.35–4 p.m. Wrestling demonstration
8.30 p.m. *Rococo*, a comedy by Harley Granville-Barker
9 p.m. Variety
9.20 p.m. *E & OE*, a macabre farce by Eliot Crawshay-Williams
10–10.15 p.m. News (sound only)

'The Post Office announces that the number of broadcast receiving licences in force in Great Britain and Northern Ireland at the end of May was 10,782,000, which included 18,850 television licences. This is the first official figure given for television receivers in use. The figure of nearly 19,000 sets represents an audience of possibly 100,000 for a popular television programme, although the BBC is convinced that a really important television broadcast would claim a great many more viewers.'

Television takes hold: the BBC schedule for Thursday, 5 June 1947, and news of the programmes' growing popularity in The Times, *27 June 1947*

TUESDAY, 6 MAY

Maggie Joy Blunt

Tonight I have completed something I thought I would never get done. For years I've collected recipes – cuttings from newspapers and magazines, and ones copied on to the back of envelopes and any odd scrap while having hair dried, or on a train journey or waiting somewhere with a magazine that isn't mine. Last year I got as far as dividing them roughly into folders and sub-dividing into envelopes. But now I have them all cut out and pasted into a special book.

This book pinched from my wartime firm – stiff-covered, foolscap size with alphabetical index. Have been having the time of my life. Once I started I could not stop. I think I started the collection seriously in 1936 when I moved into Hampstead flat but had been picking up oddments before then. Some are from Jamaican visit in 1933. Have several of my mother's, too, one from a newspaper dated June 1921.

Oh, those pre-war days! June says that when she hears good, unobtainable food discussed now her mouth waters so much she actually dribbles. *Foie gras* with whipped cream and hardboiled egg set in aspic with green peas. Pineapple cream made with real fruit. Strawberry meringue pudding made with whites of six eggs. A cake made with half a pound of butter, four eggs and cider. A jelly trifle with sponge fingers, fresh fruit, butter, egg, walnuts . . . peaches simmered in a rich syrup and served cold piled with fresh raspberries, cherries, redcurrants – nuts, icing sugar and five eggs with cake crumbs to make a special cake with cream filling. A poached egg on hot buttered muffin with ox tongue and covered with Hollandaise sauce. Lobster mixed with mushrooms and cream. Chicken soaked in milk and herbs for twenty-four hours before cooking. A special sauce of raisins, apple, banana, curry and cider to serve with white fish. Veal cutlets rolled in beaten eggs and grated cheese and grilled. Kidneys cooked with white wine. Pears baked in honey and butter and served with tinned cherries and lemon juice. Asparagus. I'm dribbling, too, now.

But it took a long time after the last war. I can remember vaguely my parents saying much the same sort of things that people are saying today: how expensive things are compared with pre-war prices and how much poorer quality. 'It's not the same as you could get pre-war.' I grew up on that slogan. I can remember my mother saying it about dress materials often.

What is the use of keeping such recipes? Because with a little cunning and effort they can be adapted. Instead of *foie gras* use meat or fish paste or nutmeat and some sort of gelatine. Homemade aspic jelly is not difficult with gelatine and I've not yet been without it. Cream can be 'mocked' in infinite varieties.

B. Charles

I was very interested to see in yesterday's *Daily Mirror* that the BBC is going to broadcast talks on venereal disease. It seems this decision has been taken at 'Cabinet Level'.

Herbert Brush

10.50 a.m. Through Wandsworth, Kingston, Staines and Egham to here, where I am parked in the car near a back entrance to the enormous building which I believe houses hundreds of mental cases, though I have not seen anyone this morning who looks like a patient. No sooner had I written that, when a bearded face came to the window of the building nearby and the man fixed me with a steady stare, and he was soon joined by several others who were evidently patients. They continued to take quiet interest in me until W returned, then they all watched as the car was turned to go out.

12 p.m. I am now parked outside The Beauty Parlour in Camberley High Street. From previous observations of the population of Camberley I judge that this place should do good business.

THURSDAY, 8 MAY

Maggie Joy Blunt

To British Museum on Monday and found Reading Room closed for week. This has upset all my plans, and delayed work. Am fidgety and moody. Smoking. Until today I have been keeping to fifteen limit. Cigarette supplies in all shops now, my favourite Du Maurier now obtainable almost anywhere at any time and, fatally for me, now at my greengrocer's where I have an account.

Phone call this morning from a mysterious stranger who wanted to know if I would be interested in Persian carpets. Said he had been showing them to a lady and gentleman nearby and thought I might be interested. Wish I had asked him who he was and how he knew my number but had no desire to encourage conversation. Persian carpets indeed!

The older I get the less London appeals to me. I never want to live in a city again. And most of my friends feel the same way. N has to move from her Hampstead flat in June and wants to get somewhere near her work at Edgware. June hungers to move her family into the country. Stella wrote this week that she and a friend have plans for a country plot, to grow and breed things for sale. She has been living some years now in a room near Paddington Station. It is, she writes, 'becoming more dirty and squalid each week. The police were summoned to cope with an attempted murder a few weeks ago . . . Another inmate plies a flourishing trade (by the half hour) and even has attempted to intercept another girl's friend on the doorstep and I have learned quite a lot of language which surprised me, and am getting to know when nocturnal shrieks are temper or terror . . . we now have five peroxide blondes, built on a heavy scale . . .'

Herbert Brush

[W's son] Jim is in charge of a Westinghouse stand at the World's Fair exhibition at Olympia, and he lent me a badge and took me there this morning to have a look round. He has fitted a wireless set in his car and we had music all the way to Olympia. Went in by a back way and no one questioned my right to be there.

The top floor was mostly children's toys and there was such a huge assortment that I could only glance at individual items as I walked slowly past the rows and rows of stalls. I was wearing an exhibitor's badge, so no one worried me to buy anything, but I think that most of the stuff is for export only. I saw more dartboards this morning than any other single item; nearly all the toy stalls had them and some made a speciality of them, with various kinds of darts in the foreground. I came down to the next floor and watched a couple of small boys riding on mechanical horses and roundabouts. A young woman who was speaking on a telephone mechanically handed me a paper as I went past her stall and I put it in my pocket. Now, on looking at it, it is a price list of carnival hats. I was interested in calculating and adding machines and am duly impressed by what machines can do if an intelligent person presses the right knobs or turns a handle the right way.

SUNDAY, 11 MAY

Edie Rutherford

If Churchill gets any more medals he will have to start putting them on his back.

I don't understand the mentality of people who are crowding at Portsmouth to greet the royal family in four hours time. Sunday dinner is not the institution in England it was.

Herbert Brush

Seeing that there were a couple of free exhibitions in Cork Street I walked along there to have a look, as free exhibitions of any sort are in my line. The first one I went into was the Redfern Gallery, where, according to a card, the paintings included the last works by Christopher Wood, 1901–30. I did not see anything which attracted me and as I thought that the two people in charge might regard me as a purchaser, as I was wearing better clothes than usual, I came out and went along to the other exhibition. This was by the PDSA (People's Dispensary for Sick Animals) and there were many fine portraits of Animal War Heroes by Mrs Shaw-Baker. There is a fierce looking German cat which was brought down over England. All the German crew were killed but the cat was found alive in the wreckage. I wonder if it went through quarantine?

The rooms in which the exhibition is shown used to be used by the USA army, and the walls of one room are covered with drawings of 'Ferdinand the Bull', made by Walt Disney's principal artist when he was there.

MONDAY, 12 MAY

B. Charles

How well I remember thirty years ago tonight! It was the last performance of the *Three Plays* at the Park Street Rooms: one of the most important nights of my life! And, I dare say, one of the most tragic, in a way.

This morning I phoned Black and he sent a plumber to see to the leaking pipe at the back.

WEDNESDAY, 14 MAY

B. Charles
Sammy called to see me. It seems he is to go to the Infirmary for an operation for circumcision next Tuesday. He seems to have been very frightened the other night at what happened, and was in very great pain at work. In the end his boss got him to tell him what had happened and gave him excellent advice. He went to the Infirmary and was treated and is to go for the operation next Tuesday. I have, of course, been very certain that the average working-class lad IS very ignorant of what are, euphemistically called 'The Facts of Life'. Sammy will be sixteen tomorrow, has worked for a long time in a big hotel where the staff is supposed to be very 'enlightened', yet his ignorance was really quite staggering. He seemed quite in a stew about having to tell his parents what had happened but I think I allayed a good deal of his fear.

THURSDAY, 15 MAY

George Taylor
We had a good party to the Glass Technology Department at the university; in fact we had to turn down many applications. In fact, the department did not want us, the professor was not there, and he left the visit in the hands of two assistants. I was in the first party, and in the testing laboratory our guide talked and talked, but all he showed us were a few test tubes etc, which were not at all interesting. We then visited the furnaces, which were not working.

FRIDAY, 16 MAY

Edie Rutherford
How nice to hear that the birth rate, infant mortality rate and maternal mortality rate are all the best for many, many years. Shows that folk are not in a despairing frame of mind, in spite of all.

Husband still has a desire for his pipe in the evenings. Now they are over the first shock, folk are smoking as hard as ever, by the look of things.

SATURDAY, 17 MAY

Edie Rutherford

Met a teacher friend last evening, she is head teacher at a school in a mining district, not far from here. She told me she had an instance this week of a father nearing seventy bringing his four children to school, just as children sat down to school dinner. 'Missus is badly and we o'laid,' he said.

Miss R said, 'But you can't bring them to school in time for dinner.'

'Oh but I can, they're ENTITLED to it.'

Miss R: 'Oh no they aren't, unless they come in time. I have to telephone for these meals and if your children are not here in time for my telephoning, no dinners come for them, and if I give them dinners today, which I will do, just this once, it means every child must have a little less.'

Man: 'Well, I'll go back now, doctor's coming. I don't rightly know if Missus is poorly or just reckoning.'

Miss R, indignant: 'Do you mean to say you think your wife is only reckoning to be poorly?'

Man: 'Aye, women do y'know.'

Miss R also told me this, said to have happened at a school in Ilkeston, Derbyshire. In the school are several children of a family, all going up in steps, a regular eighteen months between them. One morn they were late for school and announced with excitement that there was a new baby in their house. Teacher said, 'Another? Well, I should think you could give me this one, I have none and you have so many.'

'Oh no, Miss.'

'But you'd never miss it from so many, you can spare just one surely.'

'Oh no, Miss, we won't part with this one, you see we've not had a black one before.'

WEDNESDAY, 21 MAY

B. Charles

Heinz and Heinrich came this afternoon and they have waxed and oiled the beech chairs in the drawing room and they look highly pleasing. I never thought they would look so well as they do. I shall miss these two lads tremendously. They are coming for the last time on Saturday. Heinrich, in particular, is amazingly good.

Mr and Mrs Reid came this evening and Mrs R very kindly brought me a little bottle of chutney. Both seemed delighted with this flat and think my things absolutely first class. In fact, Mr Reid said I had got a perfect house. And he added that I was a real acquisition to Edinburgh! He is very knowledgeable and it is useful to know him. I fancy they were really impressed with the furnishings of this place. If I could make some sort of contact with some sort of publicity man, I feel sure I could make money by giving 'Talks' on how to furnish a period style at far less cost that in ordinary utility stuff. I will see if I can get to know a reporter, or something, on the *Scotsman*.

I never really cared much for this Mr How who has the flat above. He and his fiancée are common. Mr Reid told me some queer things about his uncle, which corroborated my own impression. It is unfortunate they are not more homely sort of people. I should think that they may be noisy and slovenly. The fool of a Revd Doctor, who has the top flat, is possibly a mere nonentity.

THURSDAY, 22 MAY

Maggie Joy Blunt

I have definite moods over a length of time when I cannot write this diary. Is it a good thing or not to obey such moods? If I had forced myself to it the results would have been more slovenly and inaccurate than usual.

Saw the French tapestries at the V&A on Wednesday. Very wonderful work, especially the medieval Lady and Unicorn set. What struck me was pomposity and vulgarity of the seventeenth- and eighteenth-century work. Have been brought up to such a reverence of the arts in these centuries that it was rather a shock. Modern designs: restless, uneasy, curiously typical of our age. Why should tapestry betray these characteristics more than other arts?

The need for some religious faith is very apparent in many of my friends. N and J have been seeking for years. Philosophy, psychology (Jung), spiritualism, the Quakers and the other night a theosophist meeting – we explore them all. To me so far the most satisfying is a combination of Graham Howe psychology and Quaker meetings. This need seems now very general among thinking people and is reflected in popular women's journals. On one, editorial centres on need for 'one reliable guide for the whole of life . . . an active faith in God'. An article discusses the difference between materialistic and spiritual attitudes to important questions such as use of atomic energy. And a great deal of reference recently in broadcast talks and articles to 'emotional immaturity'.

FRIDAY, 23 MAY

B. Charles
Yesterday afternoon Sammy came. He is still in a good deal of pain but the operation has been quite successful, I should say. He is a nice bright lad and, now that he has had the operation, I am sure will improve rapidly, in every way. He is most anxious to learn everything and seems to think he ought to have been told many things very much sooner. Of course, I think the suppression of truth in every case ultimately leads to the very troubles it is supposed to avoid. I never find the very least difficulty in telling people anything. And, I have usually found, people will tell me many things they refuse to relate to people who are far nearer to them by blood ties. I think I ought to have been a teacher in 'General Knowledge' or else an interior decorator.

SATURDAY, 24 MAY

Maggie Joy Blunt
Latest story (to reach mc) of Princesses. Margaret, when rebuked by Elizabeth: 'You mind your Empire and leave me to mind my own business.' I watched royal procession to Guildhall lunch over a week ago, from balcony of Kassim's office overlooking Ludgate Hill. Royal family looked tired; Queen magnificent, smiling and chattering to George amiably; Princesses upright and sullen. One of the RAF lining the route immediately opposite our windows fainted. I thought he was going to – had watched him growing greener and greener.

MONDAY, 26 MAY

B. Charles
Heinz and Heinrich came to say goodbye this afternoon. I had got them a packet of cigarettes for the journey tomorrow. Heinz was very

sorry, I could see, to say goodbye. He hopes they may return sometime here but I should think it doubtful. Both hope, if I got to Germany, that I shall pay them a visit, as I certainly shall. They are good fellows.

Herbert Brush

12.30 p.m. Arrived at Caister Holiday Camp.

4.30 p.m. Wandered round the camp awhile finding the useful places and looking at the visitors. Mr Dodds, the proprietor, came up and introduced himself and later found our table in the dining hall, which was No. 13. The food was plentiful and quite nice, but no one at our table could say for certain what the meat was, guesses from hare to turkey were probably far from the truth. The people here do not seem to be what is generally called 'high class', but as far as I can see they are good folk. From conversations overheard I conclude that many of us are factory workers, and that some of us come from the Midlands and Lancashire. This camp is really a large place, must be half a mile long, and as our hut is at the inland end, it is a good walk to the sea.

9.10 p.m. We had quite a good dinner, more than I wanted to eat. A man and his wife were at our table who came from Manchester and we talked on various subjects, mostly about food. Curiously enough they are in the next hut but one to ours.

TUESDAY, 27 MAY

Herbert Brush

8.10 a.m. The most uncomfortable bed I ever tried to sleep in.

10.45 a.m. Went to Norwich Cathedral and back to Caister in time for lunch. Two strangers had taken our seats, so we had to turn them out, and sat down as the usual party. One soon gets used to people when feeding is done together and the same man and his wife from Manchester sat next to us. The man – I don't know his name and will call him X – is mending W's petrol lights for her.

5.25 p.m. We went to the seashore by car, picking up Mr and Mrs X and Mrs Y on the way and paddled for a time in the sea, which at first seemed cold, but the warm sand soon put my feet right again. Mr Y came along later and he also paddled with us. Later we went and had tea and cakes in the beach café and stayed there for some time. Tried the strength of our grips on a machine in the café. Mr X was weak, I was fair but Mr Y sent the needle all round the scales.

10 p.m. After supper, or dinner, we went in the car for a ride round taking Mr and Mrs X (Harrison) with us to Yarmouth and along the front.

THURSDAY, 29 MAY

Herbert Brush
10.10 a.m. We left the camp about 9 a.m. and coming through Yarmouth stopped to buy some bloaters.

6 p.m. I imagine that Mr and Mrs X and Z are sitting down now for the dinner and probably speaking about the two absent ones, who contributed somewhat to their enjoyment of their holiday at Caister Camp.

SATURDAY, 31 MAY

B. Charles
A terrible morning. Just like mid-winter. Went to Marchmont, which always depresses me. It is such a lousy locality and it takes such a terrible time to get there and back. Both lots of washing were ready. When I got up this morning I found Madame de Sévignée [a clock] had stopped during the night! I must get Donald to see what is the matter. In the afternoon I went into Princes Street to see if I could contact two Germans to take the place of Heinz and Heinrich. I met a chap from Hamburg who said he and a friend will come tomorrow at 2.30. It seems they are at Gosforth Camp (where Heinz was for a time) and they both have bicycles.

SUNDAY, 1 JUNE 1947

Edie Rutherford
Yesterday we waited till 6 p.m. to do a walk, but turned back after about two miles and stopped on our way home at pub for refreshment. Once again, I have decided I don't like the folk who frequent pubs. I'm not snobby – they all, or 99 per cent of them anyway – look like Hogarth drawings and are sordid, physically misshapen in all manner of weird ways, and altogether have no

conversation and laugh at nothing at all. Well, we were glad to be home.

Herbert Brush
4.45 p.m. Jim has lent me his 'Biro' pen and I am trying it out, just to find whether it would do for my diary writing.

MONDAY, 2 JUNE

Maggie Joy Blunt
Heat is almost too much for us now. We find it exhausting and grumble madly. In the towns and close places it must be unbearable. It is too hot to sit even in the shade in the garden, and all heat seems caught and held in this particular dell.

Coolest place yesterday was Meg and Roger's bare little new house perched on open hillside. All windows open, a strong breeze blew through whole house delightfully. Roger was sure this summer was going to be good. He says they have occurred every seven years – 1940, 1933, 1926, 1919. Their house looked very clean, with new paint and fitments. Plaster already cracking in places, pieces of timber, not properly seasoned, have warped and so on. But it is a nice little house and has all the possibilities of a comfortable and happy home and they are, at least for the first time in their married lives, alone in a house of their own.

George Taylor
We were basking in the sunshine when a knock announced the arrival of some friends who had not visited us for years. They were an ex-tram conductor, his wife and son. The latter has bought a car out of his gratuity, and confesses that it takes every penny of his income to run it; in fact, he cannot pay his proper board at home. However, his mother prefers the convenience of a car to his money, and so a car it is.

Only last night my wife decided to bake some decent cakes and pastries for us, but two meals for the visitors tonight cleared it all off. We shall have to wait another month to collect the fats for a further baking.

Herbert Brush

Do you notice any improvement in the writing done with the 'Biro' pen? Jim tells me that he will never want to use any other kind. The pen was invented during the war for the use of the RAF pilots whose pens failed to work sometimes at the high altitudes.

TUESDAY, 3 JUNE

Edie Rutherford

Whew and Whew! Being a blonde I don't take kindly to fierce sun but wilt noticeably. Oh well, this is better than that hideous winter. The locals are bellyaching as usual. Men determinedly wearing waistcoats and bowler hats and sweating and grousing. Seem to think one is potty if one suggests waistcoat could be left at home.

The fish and chip shop in this road changed hands last week. The new owners are two coloured men, said to be Lascars, who are said to have paid £2,000 for it. They open at 7.30 and close at 10.30 p.m. Two able-bodied men with cash. Makes you think. White girls work for them while they serve.

SUNDAY, 8 JUNE

Edie Rutherford

After six weeks of no smoking, Husband started again last evening. Got milder tobacco than his usual and thoroughly enjoyed himself.

Well, I had two teeth out yesterday and was disgusted about it, as both were perfectly sound teeth as I saw afterwards. Most dentists here don't know about anything but extractions. I asked could the inflamed condition be treated since the teeth were good, but was told no, best thing to have them out. I said it seemed wrong and unwise, so he said. 'You'll have to have some dentures soon.' I could have hit him. There must be a huge profit in false teeth judging by the way dentists love to fix one up with them.

B. Charles

After dinner I looked through one of my tin boxes and came across a lot of old letters and photographs. It is a mistake to keep letters, I am sure. Photographs, as well, are usually better destroyed. There was one of Girolamo. Taken, it seems, in Gefara. It brought back such a lot of memories of Palermo. He was a rare lad for a lark! I think when he sent me this photo in October 1926, it was the last time I heard from him. I wonder if he was killed in the last war? If he is alive he must be about forty. I also came across a very unkind letter from Father. I wish I had destroyed it, as all the old recriminations make such unhappy memories. After tea I went out for a walk and spoke to two German POWs. I gave them both ten Woodbines.

MONDAY, 9 JUNE

B. Charles
A very nice, long letter from Heinz. He has now been sent to a small hostel in, or near, Motherwell.

This afternoon they fixed the bath panels. I am highly displeased with the whole thing. It is trumpery, vulgar and common and very badly executed. This bath is a common thing: a sort of domestic servant's 'dream of Hollywood'. And the way the bath has been fixed is disgraceful. How sick I am of Robertson and all the blasted workmen!

I see the French railway strike is spreading. I think it is only a matter of a very short time before France goes completely Communist. A rotten, lousy country. Churchill is a perfect fool to want a closer alliance with France. France is a real menace and scourge to the peace of the world. And always has been.

WEDNESDAY, 11 JUNE

Herbert Brush
I was on the plot this morning when nine four-engine bombers roared over not very high up, and I learn that these were the Americans on a visit to this country. I don't often see big planes so close nowadays. I had just dug up a bit of twisted metal, part of a rocket which fell close by, and it made one think of other times during the war when I should have dived for cover under such circumstances.

Ken and his wife came in during the evening and we played darts; the wife, a pretty dark-haired little woman, scored while we played several games. One was a curious game which I think worth recording as it shows the chances of luck in the game. We played 301 up, commencing and ending on a 'double'. I could not get my first double for a long time, and Ken had scored 299 before I started, and only wanted 'double one' to win. But before he could get his 'double one', I won the game.

B. Charles
There is an interesting report of some church congress in today's papers. The Bishop of Willesden has been saying there is a tremendous lot of immorality in factories. I doubt this. There may be a certain amount of dirty talk among the workers, but from my own observation, I fancy the amount of sexual indulgence among young people today is far smaller than it was some years ago. They seem afraid of sexual indulgence. They TALK a lot. But this is as far as it goes in most cases I think.

THURSDAY, 12 JUNE

George Taylor
We took a party of twenty-six to the Potteries, and I went with the group of twelve who visited the Wedgwood factory at Barlaston. It is a very attractive all-electric factory in the country about four miles from Stoke. The reception was off-hand, however, just one of the lady guides meeting us, and none of the management extending a welcome. We saw some delightful specimens of work – all destined for export, mainly to America. At the conclusion of the visit we were offered mementos in the form of china cigarette boxes and books, but at a price. We were not offered even a cup of tea, but fortunately we had made arrangements to take tea at the Wedgwood Memorial College nearby.

B. Charles
There was a most extraordinary announcement on the radio this morning: in fact I could hardly believe my ears. It took place during *Programme Parade*, about 8.15. It seems there is to be a 'talk' some time today, and during or after this 'talk' some woman is to give 'Hints on Make-up', firstly for a seaside holiday and then for an inland holiday. Surely this is about the worst inanity the BBC has ever perpetrated?

A nation that broadcasts on make-up for a seaside holiday, and then for an inland one is past all recovery.

FRIDAY, 13 JUNE

Edie Rutherford

I must say Princess Elizabeth looks well on her horse at the Trooping of the Colour yesterday. Even husband commented on how well she looked going into ballet the night before. Looks as if our future Queen is going to be a humdinger for the looking part. Well, that is the most essential part so all should be well. Woe betide her if she gets too intelligent. Good job it is her sister who is said to be the rebellious one.

B. Charles

Mr McWilliam came last night and we had a long talk. He told me about one of the men from the bank going to spend holidays in Scandinavia. It seems living there is VERY costly, but the food marvellous, just like 1938. I gather, too, that everything else is equally marvellous.

I see there is a small paragraph in yesterday's *Telegraph* about the ex-convict Stanley Thurston making a film as to his escape from Dartmoor. It is an astonishing thing how fashionable crime and criminals have become lately. The Glorification of Theft is now in full swing.

Herbert Brush

I had my hair cut in Peckham this morning. A small girl child sat near me in the bus, nursing a large doll, when suddenly on the floor of the bus she saw a sixpence. She grabbed it in a flash. I never saw such a transformation in the child's face, and a somewhat common face became a perfect picture of happiness. She was with a hard-faced woman to whom she offered the coin, but the woman would not take it, evidently thinking that someone might see her. The child carried the coin until they got off the bus. After that I lost sight of them, and I may be wrong in thinking that the child did not keep the coin for long when it was clear of the bus.

SATURDAY, 14 JUNE

Maggie Joy Blunt

Is this country going to the dogs? asks Meg. High prices, stupid Government restrictions, stories of bribery and corruption and black market activities are everywhere. If you have money you can get *anything*. Two seats wanted for particularly popular musical show in London were 'all booked till Xmas', but then obtained with £2 tip. Miners in the North now *coddled* and won't work. And so on. Our reputation for honesty and integrity is in danger. Middle classes are increasingly alarmed and bitter, resentful that so much is now being done for working people, for whom we are all paying, and that they aren't co-operating but are slack, insolent, indifferent. Where is it all leading us? Something somewhere will crack soon.

Dinah's latest brood now one month old tomorrow. She woke me in small hours to say they were coming, kneading the bedcover and purring loudly with excitement. I had to sit by her box for nearly an hour. She was purring all the time and giving little expectant squeaks, her eyes enormous. She was radiant, beatified with delight. It was her hour, the whole reason for her existence. I felt touched that she should insist I be a witness. As soon as the labour started I slid back to bed. In the morning – four kittens, but one dead. Her persistent tabby boyfriend (I think the father) comes every evening and spends large part of the night prowling round making hideous noises.

SUNDAY, 15 JUNE

George Taylor
[On annual visit to St Leonards on an audit.] It started to rain as soon as I went out from the hotel in the morning and I took refuge in the Sun Lounge, where a cup of coffee and two biscuits lasted me a couple of hours. Eugene and his orchestra were there again, and played popular tunes. After the performance I came to the conclusion that the xylophone will never be a musical instrument.

B. Charles
No one, so far, has phoned and no one has called. I posted a letter to a Mr Faithfull Davies, the former Secretary of some Boys' Club, as in yesterday's *Daily Mirror* there was a paragraph that some big house in England was being converted into a sort of camp for factory lads to holiday in. I gathered a number of people are going to instruct the lads, in their spare time, in what are called 'Cultural Matters': music, art, and so on. I wrote to this man to say that if there is any organisation in Edinburgh interested in giving working-

class lads instruction in interior decoration or antique furniture, I shall be pleased to receive visits from lads for chats on old furniture, etc.

WEDNESDAY, 18 JUNE

B. Charles
Had dinner at Woolworth's. The food there is not at all bad, far better than at the British Restaurant now. Have been in all the afternoon. Sammy came and I took some pictures. He has just about got over the operation now.

THURSDAY, 19 JUNE

B. Charles
This morning the postman told me there was a parcel for me at the post office. I suggested he should bring me the parcel tomorrow morning, as it was only a bottle of salad oil from Fortnum's, but he said it was too heavy for him to carry! I thought it isn't very surprising the country is in such a hellish state when the postman says a bottle of salad oil is too heavy for him.

FRIDAY, 20 JUNE

George Taylor
For the first time in my life I entered the sacred precincts of the Treasury. I had an appointment with a high official there, so I had a uniformed guide from the Inquiry Office. They seem to keep a pretty tight check on visitors, booking them in, being timed and signed for by the interviewer, and the pass collected upon going out. I wonder if it is all necessary?

I secured a promise of assistance which may help one of our clients, so the call was not wasted. My man was a very friendly type, although I have a faint suspicion that he was out to impress a poor provincial with his importance.

Maggie Joy Blunt
Man recently died in Ella's locality – worth £46,000. He had been years ago a clerk in her father's brewery, then bought a local wine

retail business and has been there ever since. A small, suburban wine and spirits merchant worth £46,000!

Local couple in village grocer's yesterday were discussing present situation. I know them – well-to-do and nothing-to-do, but nice people. Agreeing that it was all 'very serious indeed', and talk of war. 'I'm not afraid of dying,' one said. 'No, I'm not afraid of dying, I'm afraid of *living*.'

SATURDAY, 21 JUNE

George Taylor
I spent some time swotting the sheaf of documents which I have received in connection with our forthcoming Swiss holiday. There are meal order forms, return reservation forms, route preference forms and three different currency application forms.

Edie Rutherford
Next-door teacher tells me they have been informed that, owing to lack of premises, and school leaving age being raised, sixty must be considered the normal number in an infant class. She has had round that number for some years now but always hoped it was a war measure. At the moment thirty are away with chicken pox.

Mirror says the talking cat at Seaford has died. It recorded for the BBC last year, 'What! No sea wall, chum?' I didn't hear it and for once I say what my Husband so often says, 'I don't believe it.'

Herbert Brush
A man was fined £10 for bringing over a live Colorado beetle in a match box in his pocket. I wonder why he brought a live one and whether he intended to start a plague on his potato patch. The customs officer was pretty cute to find it, as he certainly was not looking for a beetle on the man.

MONDAY, 23 JUNE

B. Charles
The whole town is thronged with hordes of American sailors. They are a truly disgusting spectacle. There is simply no word to describe them but Loathly. Almost without exception they strike one as being

utterly decadent, mentally childlike and utterly worthless. Their appearance is truly awful. And the disgracefully bad behaviour they indulge in when in the street is most disgusting. All they seem to want to do is to eat ice cream, smoke cigars and get drunk. It is so awful to think Great Britain has thrown away everything, just too lazy to keep their heritage, to become the creditor of America.

In a way, of course, all these hordes of Yankee sailors resemble a Hollywood film come to life. The scenes last night when I left the concert to come home were disgraceful. Hundreds of these men were pretending to be drunk (some were drunk, but most were pretending to be so), rolling about the streets and behaving in a horrid way. Everyone is encouraged to 'develop their personalities' which is another way of saying: behave as badly as you can. I suppose the main cause of the trouble is that money has become the only thing the modern person thinks of the least use. They will do anything to get it. Just ANYTHING. So all commercial morality has just ceased to be. I believe these Yanks are here for about a week.

TUESDAY, 24 JUNE

Herbert Brush
I see by the papers that the miners are not bringing up as much coal as they did. I thought that would happen as soon as the novelty of a shorter week wore off. Workmen did exactly the same when their week was reduced from fifty-six and a half hours per week to forty-eight, and they started at 7 a.m. instead of 6 a.m. They worked hard the first two weeks and then gradually slacked off and watched the clock even more carefully, in case there was a chance to get a little overtime. I suppose that human nature will never change, and a workman will do as little as he can, unless he is working for himself.

Maggie Joy Blunt
I write with nails painted an exciting, alluring blood red. Rude little boys call out after me, 'Ooo! I cut a finger!' Nail varnish now very difficult to find in London shops. A few weeks ago it was to be had in variety, and good makes everywhere, now it is, 'Sorry, none at all.' I bought one bottle, 2/9d., in small chemist's, Oxford Street, and another at Ustrella in Shaftesbury Avenue, where they make all their own cosmetics and supply the theatrical world.

Also in Oxford Street, I was attracted quite by chance to a small shop window full of fountain pens and then read, 'Repair Service'. Inside I found they did repairs while you wait. The top of mine has been loose and falling off for months and I have been meaning to take it into Swan House but did not want to part with it. Today the top was tightened for me in five minutes for 2/-. Never so surprised and pleased since beginning of war.

WEDNESDAY, 25 JUNE

B. Charles

There is now this footling twaddle about a fresh fuel crisis, and when I got back from dinner there was a leaflet pushed into the letter box about this saving campaign. There is ALWAYS paper available for any drivelling forms. It is a case of forms and yet more forms. It makes me want to spew. What we want is more food, clothing and fewer forms. I had a beastly dinner at the Mayfair. I shall not go there any more. I have been in all the afternoon. No one has called and no one has phoned.

Herbert Brush

A man told me that a jay had been busy on the peas two plots away, as I put black thread around my peas which are nearly ready for picking, and are just right to the taste of a jay. I know from previous experience that a jay can soon destroy a row of peas. The man drove the jay away, but it is sure to come back again; with its mate probably. I've seen several jays about in the big trees where the owls hoot every night.

THURSDAY, 26 JUNE

Edie Rutherford

Last evening I gave a talk on SA to the 'Women of Intake Labour'. Spoke for about an hour, fifteen present. They seemed to enjoy it and asked me to come again. I was never at a loss for what to say. I admire those women. Every one of them had the worst kind of start in life except that they aren't handicapped by physical deformity. But all come from back-to-back houses and have lifted themselves to Council houses of the modern kind; they work and also try to do

413

their share towards making England a green and pleasant land for everyone. They deserve to be happy and well.

So Billy Merson is gone. Well, he gave us plenty of laughs in his time. With his lyre, and his Se–ora, Se–ora. And wasn't it he who used to pick his velor-or from the flo-or? I think it was. I can see him now tripping across the stage scantily clad as a fairy in pantomime.

In town yesterday Sybil Thorndike got on to a bus I was on. I greeted her as I feel I know her and, anyway, owe it to her for the pleasure she has given me. She looked much the same off stage as on. She is here this week with Lewis Casson doing a Priestley play which I would much like to see.

B. Charles
Sammy called this afternoon. He has not yet entirely recovered from the operation. He has been cycling a bit lately and has made himself a bit sore. He ought not to ride until the whole thing is thoroughly healed.

Herbert Brush
I was just digging my first potato root and stood up for a moment to cool down, when I suddenly found myself surrounded by a thousand or so bees, every one of them apparently eager to settle on me. I guessed in a moment that the queen bee had evidently mistaken my 'Huck Finn' hat for a suitable hive and I used it to beat off the swarm while I did a sprint to the other end of the plot.

A swarm in June is worth a silver spoon but a swarm in May is worth a load of hay. The saying does not give an idea which is the more valuable.

FRIDAY, 27 JUNE

George Taylor
We had great excitement last night: I discovered the first damson on our only tree, which we planted twelve years ago.

B. Charles
This morning when I went out I saw a pool of water and, on looking up, saw How's filthy corduroy trousers hung over the balcony in the front of the house, sopping wet and dripping. There is no doubt these two are going to be slatternly tenants.

SUNDAY, 29 JUNE

Edie Rutherford
Friend in one of these flats tells me she is taking in two small Austrian boys for two months from August, to feed them. I think she is splendid. Would do it myself if Husband would agree, which he won't. Can't do it without his co-operation. This friend's husband is in RAF so her life is lonely but for dog.

George Taylor
Discussing the purchase of new presses at an engineering concern. The best delivery promised is three years!

I got my loose change in Swiss money from the bank today. It is £13.

B. Charles
A very quiet day. I saw in a copy of a recent *Evening Dispatch* a long article by a Scottish poet in which he deplores the emptiness of modern peoples' faces. He writes that they have no individuality whatever, and that everyone looks exactly alike. I, of course, have stressed this characteristic for many years. It is, I fancy, a result of all the standardisation and regimentation that has come about. This poet says one has only to look through an old portrait album and see the different expressions of our grandparents to realise how vacant and silly the modern person looks.

TUESDAY, 1 JULY 1947

B. Charles
I am faintly amused to learn from the radio this evening that two Scotland Yard detectives have been found guilty of conspiring to steal and have been sentenced to terms of imprisonment. I expect the judge who sentenced them was 'terribly surprised' when he learned of this affair! I should think if he was, he is about the only person to be so! I have often thought how extraordinary it is that the police can 'get away' with their doings for so long.

WEDNESDAY, 2 JULY

Edie Rutherford

Chinese laundry near here has a new notice up, 'A few customers taken in.'

Today for the first time for years I opened the door to 'Will you buy something from a disabled ex-serviceman?' and he opened his case with alacrity. He seemed to have nothing I wanted, but, as I have done door-to-door selling, I always buy if I can. So I took two pairs shoelaces and bodkin, 10d. the lot. He then offered me elastic but, as I have enough just now, I declined with thanks. He was young and looked fit enough. One had hopes that this kind of thing would not follow the war this time. Husband has sent to Selfridges for sports coat advertised at 48/-. Prices here round £5 for a coat worth buying, and thirteen coupons.

B. Charles

This morning a HUGE refrigerator came from Adams, presumably for How. It is the largest one I have seen and it took four men over half an hour to get it upstairs. It is crazy of How to have got such a huge thing. With present-day rations, what can be the sense of him having this huge thing? But this is the present-day Young Person all over. They know nothing about household matters and, what is worse, they are not willing to be told. I saw him the other morning coming downstairs eating a stale bun (his breakfast), yet he buys this HUGE 'frig'.

I went to the post office to fetch the parcel from Fortnum's.

THURSDAY, 3 JULY

Edie Rutherford

Met a friend just now who tells me she and her husband are to go to St Ives for hols. Dreading train and, seeing ad in local paper offering a place in a car to Cornwall, they rang up. £25. Her husband said, 'I didn't realise you were selling the car as well', and rang off.

Husband much keyed up about the flying saucers over the American skies. One of his pet subjects. Papers can't report enough about them to satisfy him. Just like a small boy about it.

B. Charles

There was a really revolting picture in yesterday's *Daily Mirror*, the worst thing I have seen for a very long time. It represented four nearly nude men, apparently competing for the title of Mr America in some competition, and a foul-looking female 'sighing' as she gazes at these revolting specimens. I really think it is this utter vulgarity or decadence, so apparent everywhere now, that is a possible reason why Russia treats us with such utter contempt.

FRIDAY, 4 JULY

B. Charles

It is thirty years ago today since the garden fête at Brooklands, where I played in *Dick's Sister* with Eileen Downs! How well I remember the day! The garden at Brooklands was pretty and, I should think, when Grannie lived there, that it was most attractive. I fancy, after the fête I met Reggie for the evening. Well, well!

I was interested to see the parson fellow, who has the upstairs flat here, come down this morning at nine o'clock in a dirty dressing gown, pyjamas and obviously just out of bed, to get his letters. It seems, indeed, the fashion now to get up very late in the morning if one hasn't got to go to work. I can't think how people who rise at 9 a.m. ever get anything done in their house.

Herbert Brush

The judges came round this afternoon to look at the plots while I was working there; they did not say anything, except agreeing that it was hot. I have not the least idea what points they would give one, but as the plot is not in such good condition as last year I don't expect a certificate. If they saw the verse I wrote about them last year and nailed on the hut, I guess that they will get their own back on me. I saw them looking at my salsify plant, which I grew to see what kind of flowers came. This plant is now going to seed, and neither of them seemed to know what it was.

SATURDAY, 5 JULY

George Taylor

Our annual Weekend School at the home of Mr and Mrs Cole. Only ten had booked for the house, but visitors came for the lectures making the average attendance fourteen. Tonight's lecturer was Mr J. E. Tyler, of the university, and he gave a coldly dispassionate account of Anglo-American relations. He foresaw the possibility of Great Britain becoming less important to America, now that the British navy was no longer needed to defend the Atlantic sea coast, and with the growing importance of the Arctic Front between America and Russia.

SUNDAY, 6 JULY

George Taylor

Professor Potter was the lecturer today, dealing particularly with European affairs in a vigorous style, and at the conclusion he outlined the conditions which he thought necessary for world peace.

After tea, when we sat round discussing WEA affairs, a group of a dozen or so German prisoners arrived. The Coles act as hosts to them too, and give them a free house. Today Mr Cole was motoring them to Crewe Hall where they were to give a concert. I had an interesting chat with the senior officer, a lieutenant colonel, about the possibility of prisoners attending our WEA classes next session, and he was quite pleased with the idea.

B. Charles

I went out this afternoon and spoke to several German POWs, one of whom spoke very good English. I gave them a few cigarettes. When I got back the German who came here last Sunday called, and had a cup of coffee and some cake. I have asked him to call next Sunday and strip the clock for me. He seems to think he can do it in about two and a half hours. We shall see. Donald phoned this evening and was not at all obliging. I shall have a very straight talk with him when he calls on Wednesday.

MONDAY, 7 JULY

Edie Rutherford

There is a woman living in these flats to whom I have said 'Good Day' for a few years past, without knowing her name or which is her flat, or anything about her. This morn, going along the street I overtook her and started to walk along with her. She is about my age,

418

eldest of nine, she says. Husband has been dying for three years now of TB and sugar diabetes. A sister and both parents killed here in blitz, brother died at twenty-three under an operation. At the moment she has four close relatives in hospitals and, when not tending her husband, is going from one hospital to another visiting them.

TUESDAY, 8 JULY

B. Charles
A long letter from Davy Drye. From what he writes the housing position in Windsor must be just as desperate as it was during the worst days of the war. What a blessing it is I got rid of the house there when I did. Davy says my old house is now turned into two flats, and that two sinks and plate racks are distinctly visible in the front of the house. And, when I lived there, how nice it used to look!

WEDNESDAY, 9 JULY

B. Charles
I see German POWs are now to be allowed to marry British girls. Another of my prophecies come true! Isn't it just like the British Government to have condemned a German POW to twelve months' imprisonment yesterday, or the day before, and now to publish the fact that marriage is to be allowed! Still, the bigger fools we are made to look in the eyes of everyone the better pleased am I!

Herbert Brush
While reading *The Romance of Windsor Castle*, I gather that Charles II had a sweaty body like mine, and he so often caught a chill after a game of tennis by sitting about afterwards to cool down. Evidently Nell Gwynne or his other ladies did not make him change his vest when he got hot and perspiring, or even take a bath to get rid of the sweat. His symptoms described in the book were exactly like mine are when I catch a chill, so I feel fairly certain that he had a spongy body like mine.

Chapter Sixteen

THE SIGNS OF SNARLING

Long skirts give you a feeling of dignity: Christian Dior's New Look

'Hip hip hooray for the Holiday Uncle, that man of parts and patience, who keeps the children from self-slaughter and the grown-ups from grousing, who exchanges a smile for a scowl, who informs the fatuous questioner, dances with the dowds, rescues the reckless, and slaps the drooping spirit on the back.'

The life of Cecil Peck, host at Cook's Camp in Prestatyn, as described in Picture Post, *July 1947*

'Long years ago we made a tryst with destiny, and now the time comes when we shall redeem our pledge, not wholly or in full measure, but substantially. At the stroke of the midnight hour, when the world sleeps, India will awake to life and freedom.'

Jawaharlal Nehru addressing the Indian Constituent Assembly, 14 August 1947

THURSDAY, 10 JULY

Edie Rutherford

Now we have the betrothal of the heiress to the throne. Husband says it is only being done to boost public morale in the coming bad winter. Oh well, there'll be no need for priority dockets or a prefab or anything else austere for that girl, so I spare her no pity, except for the fact that she has to be at the beck and call of her job so much. All royalty get my pity for their uselessness, which they allow to entangle them.

I'm in the midst of packing, as we are off tomorrow. Windy, dull and cold. Not my idea of holiday weather.

FRIDAY, 11 JULY

George Taylor

We have now really started gathering the raspberries, for which I am duly thankful. I began to think that we should be going away for holiday before the crop ripened, and it would then have been all over when we returned. I think this is the best time of the year when we can go into the garden and gather strawberries, then gooseberries, and finally raspberries: only the cream is lacking.

TUESDAY, 15 JULY

Edie Rutherford

Bache Hill Farm, Kimbolton, near Leominster, Herefordshire. We got here at midday today. It is six years since we were here. All is much the same. Lovely country in all directions. Cousins not much altered.

Spent last Friday night at Derby, and went on Saturday afternoon to the school where my nephew Tony goes, then on to Cousin Iris who has a pub outside Birmingham, she is still the same darling.

Sunday we spent the day with Cousin Reg, her brother, and I spent the afternoon tidying up rosebushes and got much scratched.

Monday we went into Birmingham and did some shopping. Then home and Husband changed into silk tropical suit and we went to visit his elder brother. Had a lovely salmon for tea tinned in brine, which they brought back from Belgium a few weeks ago. Husband brought a saw with him as a present to our host and spends a lot of time using it. We'll leave behind enough sawn wood to last the winter. Haymaking going on everywhere like mad.

MONDAY, 21 JULY

Edie Rutherford
It has rained all day today. Lunch at Green Dragon, the best hotel in Hereford. Spacious lounge. Real serviettes!

Visited the beautiful spacious cathedral. In using the public convenience I saw the wall was covered in comments all either anti or for POWs, no half ways. It is the first time in all my travels that I have ever encountered writing on the walls of a Ladies.

Herbert Brush
I went to the British Museum and bought a 'Biro' pen on the way, after going into three shops where the pen was sold out as soon as they obtained a supply. I have heard so many good accounts of it that I made up my mind to buy one and use it in my diary. The pen runs well and seems to suit my style of writing, and goes very smoothly, no matter how hard I press.

THURSDAY, 24 JULY

Herbert Brush
12 noon. A lady with a perambulator caught me up in the road and asked whether I had heard that Mrs Chandler in Seymour Lodge had infantile paralysis.

1.20 p.m. W has gone to the hospital to have her chest X-rayed.

8.15 p.m. W was X-rayed this afternoon and did not have to pay the two guineas they usually charge because she subscribes 3d. per week to the Hospital Saturday Fund. Our doctor will report upon the X-ray plate in due course.

FRIDAY, 25 JULY

George Taylor
Arrived at Folkestone from Victoria, and we went down straight away for lunch on board ship and had nearly finished when a loud-speaker announcement informed us that a wire had been fouled by

the propellers, and that 'there would be considerable delay'. A few minutes before 4 p.m. the captain passed me, remarking to his companion that we were freed, and just five hours late, we set sail.

Boulogne looked frightfully war-scarred when we arrived. All the quays and neighbouring buildings have been destroyed, and much of the town is gone. I should think it is much worse than any English port. The Paris train was waiting for us, and finally we arrived – much too late, of course, to do anything but find our hotel.

We stayed at the Alcyon de Breteuil, near the Eiffel Tower. It was a typically small French hotel, but Madam was quite confused with the nineteen non-French speaking guests who had arrived. It took us a full hour to get the rooms allotted, and then a further hour to get a cup of coffee, at a cost of 35 francs each.

To reach the hotel we had to cross Paris and were quite surprised to see neon lights on the shops. This when in England, supposed to be much better off, shop window lighting is banned, apparently for eternity.

SATURDAY, 26 JULY

George Taylor
Travelling across France was pretty monotonous. The day continued to get hotter and hotter as we travelled, and at every station where we stopped, there was a rush out to the water tap to fill bottles. At many stations there was no tap, however, and at Delle we were only allowed out with an escort, as it was the frontier station. My wife suffered so much from the heat that her ankles swelled to twice their normal size.

Quickly after crossing the border the scenery became typically Swiss, and I was immediately impressed with the neatness everywhere. The stacks of winter wood looked to have been built according to an architect's plan, and all was set off by a display of gay flowers in window boxes on every available ledge, which made a very attractive picture. It was 8.30 p.m. before we arrived in Bern, and the reception office was crowded and as hot as Dante's Inferno. Luckily we picked up our documents fairly quickly, and were guided by a Swiss Esperantist to our hotel.

After our experience in Paris, it was delightful to find a spotlessly clean hotel, a large airy bedroom with a separate tiled dressing room, and four snowy towels. In a few minutes we were sat down to a substantial dinner, and then we made our way out on to the brightly lit streets. What a pleasure it was to see the shop windows fully lit, and crammed with good things which we have not seen for years, and are not likely to see in England for many a long time.

A programme had been arranged for the Congress members at the Kornhauskeller, at which Swiss yodellers were to sing.

SUNDAY, 27 JULY

George Taylor
We were late at the opening session of the Congress, and only obtained a seat on the side gallery. Hearing was so bad there that we did not stay long.

In the afternoon we paid a visit to the famous bears, and were lucky enough to see them climbing and descending the trees which have been set up in their pits. The bears seem to be the pets of the town, for there was a great crowd, by far the majority obviously Swiss, watching the antics. It was so hot, however, that we sought the shade by the river, and my wife bathed her feet in the swiftly running Aar. We even avoided the Congress photography, knowing that this would take a long time in the blazing sun, and we preferred to sip tea in a café balcony, and sample the marvellous Swiss cakes.

B. Charles
Kenny Reid told me that yesterday a diamond ring sold for £1,425 at their afternoon sale. He seemed astonished and said he thought it was only worth about £400. He said he thinks it revealing the huge prices that jewellery is now fetching. He says he is sure people buy these things to 'hide' their questionable gains.

MONDAY, 28 JULY

George Taylor
It was the first of our full day's excursions. Short of Interlaken we turned into the hills, and soon we had our first experience of the wide sweeps of an alpine pass. The views became more and more impressive as we climbed the Jaun until we reached the summit, and halted for lunch. And what a lunch. The hotels had provided lunch packets

consisting of sandwiches containing about six different kinds of meats, a hard-boiled egg and a Cellophane packet of salt, tomatoes, peaches and a banana or plum. We could not eat anywhere near the whole of what was provided.

After an hour's halt, we began our downward trek to Broe, where we had the opportunity of visiting the very modern Nestlé-Cailler-Kohler-Peter factory, and were presented with samples of six different kinds of chocolate, and a photograph of the factory. From there we made our way to Gruyère, had tea in a quaint terraced café, and only when it was too late discovered another where there were meringues with cream.

TUESDAY, 29 JULY

Edie Rutherford
When Husband got back yesterday he discovered that, from now on, their workmen start work at 8 a.m. instead of 7.30 and in future are to be paid for bank holidays as well as their usual holidays.

I hate to hear of the tense atmosphere in Palestine. I wish UNO would buck up and let us out of carrying that baby unaided. They move so slowly and all the time we take the rap. I wonder if public opinion here will at last be roused if the two captured sergeants are killed? What a tangle the whole thing is. No matter what we do, we offend one side or the other.

George Taylor
On the way out, at Interlaken, we had our first real view of Jungfrau, and very well it looks too. At the top we found a plentiful gathering of coaches and cars, and there was almost a Hampstead Heath bank holiday atmosphere, with even a trace of litter. We bought some peaches at a stall, and sat eating our lunch by the coolness of a mountain lake. The descent, although magnificent, was not quite so steep as the ascent, and it did not take us long to join the road through the St Gothard Pass, and then crossing and recrossing the railway and river, we came to Altdorf, the home of William Tell. We were more interested in finding some tea, however.

Our driver was a very obliging sort, and took us back to Bern by the ridge route. Just as the sun was setting he stopped on a hillside from which we saw the line of Alps all pink in the twilight. The effect was extremely beautiful, but very fleeting, and in less than five minutes it was gone. I am glad that I did not miss that view.

WEDNESDAY, 30 JULY

George Taylor
A holiday from excursions. For some years I have been searching for sandals to replace an old pair long since worn out, so first thing I went along to a shop whcre I had seen some reasonably priced. I got quite a nice pair for 36 francs, and my wife indulged in a pair for 26 francs. I started wearing mine straight away, and the shopkeeper volunteered to send my ordinary shoes back to the hotel. This first experience of Swiss service was a pleasant change from the take-or-leave-it attitude of English shops.

After lunch I went back to the Congress, and dutifully attended a meeting at which pious speeches were made to promote a fantastic world organisation using a new international currency etc. Not many of the delegates were impressed.

THURSDAY, 31 JULY

Edie Rutherford
I wonder if the Jews HAVE killed those two sergeants or not. Terribly anxious time for their relations. And if they have, what do we do then?

Looks as if Attlee has more austerity to break to us. Oh well, if the Government will make things plain, so that folk know there really is a need for it all, they will get all the backing necessary. However, so long as some folk can go to Switzerland, France, Morocco and what have you, spend thousands, and others slog at home, there will be discontent. The day when the rich could live in ease without comment from those not so well off is gone for ever.

There is also much adverse comment because midweek sport for the masses is forbidden but the boss goes to golf any day.

George Taylor
At Grindelwald we heard for the first time the long mountain horns of the Swiss shepherds. They are far from musical, and sound somewhat like a cow in distress.

429

B. Charles

I am not at all surprised to hear the bodies of the two sergeants in Palestine have been found hanging from a tree. I was sure they had been murdered. The Jews are a scourge to mankind. I should rejoice to know every Jew – man, woman and child – had been murdered! We ought to drop six atomic bombs on six different cities in Palestine and wipe out as many Jews as possible. There will be no peace until the Jews have been knocked into shape. And this now will be, I should think, almost impossible. This latest murder is appalling.

I am reading *The Anatomy of Peace*. It is a book of the very greatest importance, but, of course, its precepts have no earthly chance of being adopted.

SATURDAY, 2 AUGUST 1947

George Taylor

Even the Swiss hotels could not cope with us this morning, as we left at 5.30 a.m., half an hour before service of breakfast begins. We made the now familiar trip to Thun, where at 8.00 a.m. we had no difficulty in finding cakes. We were even able to buy a small one-cup Meta stove for which we have been looking for years.

Soon after leaving Meiringen, on the first hairpin bend our coach forced a private car into the rockside. My word, what a fuss there was. The driver, apparently a French-speaking Swiss, gesticulated and waved his arms about to reconstruct the scene, and his wife aided him with more windmill movements. After half an hour stuck on the bend impeding all traffic, a postal bus arrived and the driver tried to arbitrate. Still our friend refused to move until the police arrived. However, he was eventually induced to take his car away a few yards to free the traffic but our passengers got restive at the continued delay. One at last indignantly shouted to the driver that we had not paid 30 francs to stand still all day, and under this persuasion we set off again.

Soon we began to climb the Grimsel Pass. We safely arrived at the reservoir tucked away near the head of the pass, crossed the tightrope of a viaduct and climbed up the seemingly impossible road to the hospice and post office. I should think that this is one of the most romantically situated post offices in the world.

From the hospice we were soon at the top of the pass, where we crossed the Lake of the Dead, and then began the breathtaking zigzag descent to Gletsch, cheered on by the tale told by the guide of a disaster which occurred there to a school party of girls when eighteen of them were killed.

We arrived back at Bern at 8.30 p.m., just in time for dinner.

SUNDAY, 3 AUGUST

Edie Rutherford
The Sunday papers are full of guesses about the super-austerity to come. I do hope the bit about spivs being made to work comes true. What with them and army deserters, we are carrying too many passengers.

Husband says a man he knows has got pally with a German POW, and the other morn when paper showed the picture of the two British sergeants' bodies, this German said, 'Didn't I tell you Hitler was the only one who knew what to do with Jews?' The Yorkshireman had no answer.

MONDAY, 4 AUGUST

George Taylor
[Italy] We had a lazy morning looking at the shops and sitting on the lakeside reading. On the way down I found a summer coat for which I have been searching Sheffield for months without success, so bought it immediately after lunch.

In the afternoon we had a trip by boat to Ascona. It was only a twenty-minute run on the lake, and not a very attractive place when we arrived. I supposed the place is quaint, but I am not too fond of little alleys, which tend to be dirty. However, my wife sampled one of the fruit ices, which turned out to be delicious. On the way back to the boat she also purchased some coconut, a product unknown to the ordinary housewife in England for many years.

Maggie Joy Blunt
It has not been a bit like a bank holiday. I have two holiday visitors again and am chained to the house. Have not been even to garden gate. I have heard voices from the woods of holidaymakers and heard cars passing but noise has not been excessive. My two visitors, a Miss E and Miss C – quiet young women – seem very pleasant. Perhaps schoolmistresses. Appreciative of my culinary efforts and helpful.

Make their own beds but have not yet tried to invade kitchen. If this ever became a regular activity I would make a big effort to find a woman to help for two or three mornings, which would give me more time to fill.

But what does the future hold? The economic crisis is upon us, has been thundering away its warnings for months. It had to come sooner or later. Yesterday there was no *Observer* for me and only *Times* or *Express*; I dislike both, but chose *Express*. Perhaps the writer of one article in it is right when he says that the present Government is 'sentimental' and there are too many 'armchair' socialists in Parliament. I have heard so many of them on platforms and in discussion groups and read their pamphlets. They always seemed so confident, so convincing.

On Saturday the gardener cut down the willow tree, which was overgrowing the house. Light and air much improved and I now have whole stack of wood for winter fires and rose arches. He went off with two or three selected pieces, which he said he was going to season up the chimney and then make into a cricket bat.

Edie Rutherford

I am not surprised and quite glad people are taking their revenge on Jews in this country. The British have been long-suffering about Palestine for a long time, and two can play at the game the Jews are playing. I don't accept as sincere the comments of Jews these last few days. In their hearts I believe all Jews are glad to hit us British – they are notoriously lacking in moral courage on the whole. Anyway, to all who thought we were dying, the signs of snarling in the British bulldog will no doubt come as a surprise. Good.

TUESDAY, 5 AUGUST

B. Charles

Churchill has certainly flayed the Government. I wonder what measures they will advocate to try to mitigate this economic crisis? I greatly doubt if they dare advocate anything really efficacious, in case they cause a riot among their adherents.

I met Mason in the Lane and we had a chat. He seemed quite glad about these anti-Jewish riots in Liverpool and Manchester. I am too. I simply HATE the Jews and am certain they are largely responsible

432

for most of our ills at the present time: economic and otherwise. There will be no peace until they are, finally, put into their place. Napier came this afternoon to do the windows.

WEDNESDAY, 6 AUGUST

Edie Rutherford
Husband amused me at breakfast just now – said, and meant it, 'Life is full of nice things.' That, on a day when Mr Attlee is to talk gloom unto us.

THURSDAY, 7 AUGUST

George Taylor
In Lugano I noticed in the lift an official announcement that shorts were regarded as indecent wear when not justified by being on a walking or cycling tour. I shall risk getting locked up, as it is not often that I have the opportunity of wearing shorts and do not intend to deny myself this week.

This morning I tasted one of the famous 'Casata' ices, got up in the form of a large slice of melon, but in variegated colours and flavours and with a cherry in the centre. There was not too much flavour in it, and it was a bit disappointing.

Edie Rutherford
Well, Attlee hasn't scared himself and myself. One blessing about being on the floor is that one can't be knocked down. A pity to say that spivs and drones will be rounded up and not do it instantly as it gives them time to go to earth and to think up moves to outwit authority and so on. They are adept at getting round laws or they wouldn't be spivs.

SATURDAY, 9 AUGUST

Edie Rutherford
How stupid of Churchill to persist in his 'dictatorship' bogey. Who does he impress? Not the masses and certainly not his own party. His concept of freedom is not freedom for the masses, but only for his kind. No wonder they squeal these days! For the first time in history

his class has something to squeal about. It is their turn now and they don't like it, but, just as the masses have born it for centuries, they will find they can endure also. Every dog has his day.

SUNDAY, 10 AUGUST

Maggie Joy Blunt
I was caught nicely by the change in clocks this morning and had us all up one hour earlier than necessary. Visitors are very good tempered about it.

It has been a good week. The lovely weather continues. Visitors seem happy and satisfied and are getting browner and browner. Besides the usual chores, shopping and cooking each day, I have done quite a few hours of work in the biography.

I am in sympathy with *Observer*'s leading articles and comments on present crises. I like the leader on Attlee. He is a good man, but the Labour Party as a whole lacks imagination, the ability to make ordinary people understand what this crisis is all about and where it may lead us.

I get cross (quietly) when little people blame the Government for shortages and all difficulties. I keep hearing grocer's wife in village say she could 'shoot the lot' and people simpering in agreement with her. The cobbler gives them 'another four months'. This Government is making mistakes as all Governments do. They are human and fallible. I don't remember a time when the Government wasn't blamed and grumbled at. If there isn't enough wheat and timber in the world for everyone's needs at this immediate moment, no Government can produce them. People would understand arguments sensibly illustrated of this nature – why doesn't the Government try to put it over? Or *isn't* it as serious as they try to make out? Or is it so serious, so terrifying, that they daren't try?

S is taking wife and son to Australia this autumn, where job with his paper awaits him. There he says butter ration per person is 2lb. a week, meat 7lb.

George Taylor
We had been able to obtain a sleeper for the return home, and there was a reading light to each bed, and all the lights and ventilation could be controlled individually from each bunk. Of course there was

a washbowl with hot and cold water, and two towels. We thought there was a wardrobe, but found this led to the next compartment.

MONDAY, 11 AUGUST

George Taylor

War damage was much in evidence in our journey through France. It was particularly bad at Laon, and we saw still more destruction at Boulogne, and between there and Calais. The latter town had almost gone, and the quays look like a desert.

Although we have been away for longer than usual – our longest holiday during the war has been ten days – I did not feel so strange back at home as I have been after a spell on the farm. It was very cheerful for us to see a meal ready prepared when we arrived. I think that this is the first time we have had this pleasure after a holiday. My mother-in-law was responsible for this welcome.

Maggie Joy Blunt

I am in a mood where I can't stop. Overtiredness I expect. This morning after I had finished with visitors' breakfast, cut sandwiches and packed their lunch, washed up, cleaned out kitchen and store room, sweeping floors which hadn't been done for weeks. After lunch, I changed to have hair done at 2 p.m. Home by 3.30, had tea at once in garden, feeling exhausted. But recovered rapidly and felt inspired to try Peter Lea's (*Northern Chronicle*) recipe of today for spiced ginger cake for a slow oven. It has turned out very well.

I like my visitors very much though I do not see much of them. One suffers from either 1) strong sense of hygiene, or 2) acute delicacy, as she gets up in middle of night to use outside WC instead of conveniences provided in bedroom. They both look extremely well and eat up all the food I provide with apparent relish. I find cooking an exciting sort of game, taxing one's ingenuity to the limit. In other words, if you can keep leftover fish in good condition *don't* provide fishcakes for breakfast immediately after an evening meal of fish, but wait till the following day.

TUESDAY, 12 AUGUST

B. Charles

I read an article, in last week's *Time and Tide,* about the seriousness of reducing the numbers of the armed forces. But what can one do in the matter? The mass of people just don't care two hoots whether or not we remain a 'first class' power. In a way, I agree with them, as when we were such a power this did not prevent the Boer War and the two world wars from taking place. I think one must just face the fact that our day of 'greatness' as a world power is over for good and all. Will it make any difference to us all?

I had a few words with three German POWs who were returning to Germany. One said it is impossible to imagine the devastation there. He thinks it will take at least a hundred years to get things anything like right again.

George Taylor

The morning's post included the proofs for the WEA 1947–8 syllabus. I am soon back in harness.

At the office I spent quite a bit of time discussing the holiday with my partners. I was bursting to tell someone of the delightful time we have had in Switzerland – by far the best holiday we have ever had.

WEDNESDAY, 13 AUGUST

Maggie Joy Blunt

I am having a deliberately, deliciously idle afternoon on my bed. Weather is perfect; wonderful, brilliant, golden days. Why can't our summers *always* be like this?

The builder is here now, measuring up for the outside painting. I think there is something very exciting about maintaining and improving property. I sometimes think I could be content to concentrate the rest of my life to this cottage, if I could own it. In the present turmoil the safest investment certainly seems to be in a small property of this kind. I could make it pay adequate dividends I am sure and would guarantee for myself and friends a home, which seems to me quite as important, if not more so, as a well-paid job or winning big money in a football pool. What use is money if you have nowhere to live? No background, no anchorage?

Pages and pages of this diary form in my mind every day but never get written. Now there is never enough time and when there is it is because I'm too tired to be doing anything else. My energy is spasmodic and used up on immediate essentials.

THURSDAY, 14 AUGUST

Edie Rutherford
Another evidence of present madness: three brothers built a house and shop – knew nothing about it, just had the pluck and the will to do it, plus the cash. No licence. Result: fined £50. In these days when we are accused of loafing we would go and fine those who show they can work. I wish someone would strike a medal for those men.

In this town a man left the Co-Op and opened his own shop. Fined £5 yesterday for enticing customers away. Co-Op rep said they are not in business to make profits. Ha ha. The huge salaries paid out to high executives in the Co-Op are the reason mostly why I never set foot in their shops, that plus the fact that choice is limited.

Herbert Brush
12 noon. I have done a variety of jobs this morning. I fixed a pair of rubber soles on D's shoes, levelled off the end of a dinner knife, repaired two breaks in the garden hosepipe, cut some privet hedge, planted greens on the plot, picked spinach, carried many buckets of water, had a sharp twinge of lumbago which I cured by carrying more water, cut a 14lb. pumpkin and carried it home.

SATURDAY, 16 AUGUST

Herbert Brush
I have been to the dentist and had the stump of my broken tooth drawn. It was a very long root, and seemed to be very tight; however, it came out at last and the old man dropped it on the floor and could not find it at first. He asked me whether I wanted to take it home, but I replied that I had it for about seventy years and did not want to keep it any longer. He charged 8/- for the job, which I believe is cheap nowadays. I walked up the street about half a mile, spitting blood into the gutter every half minute or so, and I am still spitting it an hour after the tooth was drawn, and it is now becoming sore.

10 p.m. W and I went to the State Cinema this afternoon. *Tarzan and the Huntress* was good as an animal picture, but rotten in other ways. Tarzan has grown very fat and slow now, but he has a young man growing up to take his place.

Edie Rutherford
The BBC and press continue to stress India's affairs. I swear most folk couldn't care less, and I resent the inference that we have had them enslaved up to now. Most folk are simply glad to be shot of them, to put it vulgarly yet truthfully.

SUNDAY, 17 AUGUST

B. Charles
I left the Caledonian station this morning to go to Lanark to meet the Germans near their farm. I thought Lanark a very attractive, quiet, old-world town and as I sat in the park eating my lunch I found it hard to believe there had been a war. I met the three Germans at three o'clock and we had a very pleasant time together. I was interested to note they instantly, on seeing me, offered to carry my small leather case! They are so polite. So unlike the English counterpart.

Hein said it was being freely discussed on the farm where he works, what will happen if Attlee has to resign. Hein, in fact all of them, seem to imagine the £ will crash, in exactly the same way as the German mark did in the very early twenties.

Maggie Joy Blunt
'The crisis – where is the crisis?' asks the *Observer*. 'With Parliament dispersed, Ministers going on holiday – and the country bathed in a drowse of August sunshine . . . ' I have £15 in cash in my handbag for last fortnight's work, which will pay for all bills, rent, light and fuel and leave a profit. Why should I worry about a crisis?

On Friday evening I left a casserole in the oven for visitors and went to see *The Dominant Sex* at local repertory with Celia. I saw this when it first opened in London with Diana Churchill as Angela, but now found the play irritating and somehow out of date. Not one of the Angela class nowadays buys a luscious evening dinner dress on her way home from the office as just a 'little something'; nor do they move so easily into an all-electric garden city home; nor do their shopping by phone. Even the ideas on modern young couples seemed out of key. I wanted to spank Angela hard and frequently.

TUESDAY, 19 AUGUST

Maggie Joy Blunt
9.15 p.m. Positively I will go on strike, I will do no more work tonight of any kind. I earn every penny of the money I get on this job, and as one job alone it is not so exacting. What is exhausting is trying to write a book at the same time. When I should be and could be relaxing I'm using up energy mentally. But lately bad nights, full of frustration, nightmares from which I wake clammy with terror, are a warning. Another warning is my inner irritability. Every little thing that goes wrong is enormously exasperating. I have imaginary quarrels with all my friends, I beat myself, figuratively, to make myself get through the housework. I can understand why some women 'bang around'. It seems to release energy or manufacture an extra supply. But I am sure it is the sort of strain that leads to cancer if continual. Something gets knotted inside.

Not that I mind hard work. I'd be at my typewriter now if I thought I would sleep tonight without dreaming. I *long* to sleep without dreaming at all: just a deep, refreshing oblivion, I pray for it. But that just never happens to me. I resent it furiously. I want to *rest* at night, to renew my energy for the next day. I *love* my daytime life and hate not to have all the vitality possible to give to it.

Long skirts. Will the ordinary woman be able to afford them and cope with them? We agreed the other day that we liked the *look* of them: old family photos of aunts in expertly tailored costumes, ankle lengths, starched white blouses and sailor hats. Long skirts give you a feeling of dignity, make you feel immensely feminine and seductive.

WEDNESDAY, 20 AUGUST

George Taylor
At last I plucked up courage to stay a bit at the office. I do not mind working overtime in the winter, but I begrudge spending summer evenings there, particularly when the days begin to shorten as they are now doing, much to my regret. It is delightful on these continuing hot nights to arrive home from the office, and quickly don shorts and

an open-necked shirt. The freedom of summer is just what I like, and the poet can keep his 'welcome wild north easters'.

THURSDAY, 21 AUGUST

Edie Rutherford
Dalton was good on the air last night. Thank goodness we're getting tough at last. I hear the *Daily Mail* suggested Attlee is resigning. I know the *Mirror* last week said he should. Well, apparently Attlee is calmly going on and not going to be stampeded by anyone. Good for him.

This lad doing the decorating is twenty-one on Sunday, has been married fourteen months. Has no time for Churchill. He served in the war, was wounded, bullet near heart, gets a pension. Volunteered at seventeen. Started in business on his own at nineteen. Works quite well but he is in demand by his father for driving as his father was forbidden to drive for a year after an accident, and so his times are erratic. I try not to get impatient.

The filthy smoke from factories round here rolls along in clouds and my heart sinks when I realise how much money this decorating is costing us and then all the filth seeps in to spoil it all in a month or two. Smoke abatement is a farce here and it is time something worthwhile was done, to help empty the hospitals too.

Herbert Brush
Smut is looking ragged and thin but he always seems to be ready for food, and bites D's and W's legs if they don't give him prompt attention.

By Smut

> The weather's warm and I can lie
> Outdoors and in the shade,
> But, I am getting worried why
> I feel a bit afraid
> That car with which I did collide
> Has badly injured me inside.
>
> A nice old tabby cat I know
> Was killed the other day;
> Across the road he had to go
> But did not look each way.

440

Along the road a fast car sped
And then my tabby friend was dead.
His body in the gutter lay
Until the road-man came,
And in a barrow took away
My friend; which was a shame.

George Taylor

A client invited one of my partners and me, with our respective
wives, to spend a day motoring with him. It has been quite difficult to
arrange a date suitable for all, but finally today was chosen. We
selected Chester and the Mersey Tunnel for our objectives. The run
across the Derbyshire Hills to Knutsford was delightful. There we
had coffee in a dirty roadside café much frequented by coach parties.
It seemed the only café in the town, and in spite of diligent search our
host failed to find the ice cream for which he longed.

Although our host is an experienced driver, having owned and
driven a car for some thirty years, he confessed that the Mersey
Tunnel quite scared him. The rapid flow of traffic in the opposite
direction, the accompanying vehicles on the parallel track, the queer
lighting and above all the noise which drowned the sound of his own
engine, made him really afraid, and he was thoroughly glad to see
daylight at Liverpool.

FRIDAY, 22 AUGUST

Maggie Joy Blunt

I spent yesterday afternoon with Lys at our local lido. EM came
round in evening for cup of tea and gossip and exclaimed, 'You
haven't been to that *filthy* place with all the *filthy* infantile paralysis
about!' Our local policeman had once given her a gruesome account
of the swimming pool as he had seen it drained and waiting to be
cleaned. Well, I did go, and enjoyed myself thoroughly and could do
with days and days of such lying in the sun between bathes. Though
I must admit the lawns are very parched, dusty, and littered with
cigarette ends and plum stones.

SUNDAY, 24 AUGUST

Herbert Brush
I changed the wheels on the car this morning, putting the right-hand back to the left-hand front and the left-hand back to the right-hand front. Quite a job.

THURSDAY, 28 AUGUST

Edie Rutherford
More neglect of this diary, unavoidable. After living-room ceiling had had two coats and two walls were done, ceiling began to crack. The whole thing had to be scraped down. Of course we walked the stuff all over the flat. We are now emerging from chaos a bit. Phew. Never, no more.

Himself was fifty-one yesterday, and we were married twenty-two years on Tuesday. Husband says it begins to look like permanency.

George Taylor
One of my wife's friends wants a vacuum flask, so we asked at a chemist acquaintance. Much to our surprise, we found that a doctor's note was required, and then that this had to be produced to the Board of Trade for a licence to purchase. Our chemist friend produced a spare doctor's note, which on production to the Board of Trade has produced a licence and eventually, I suppose, a vacuum flask, although not for the person named on the note. If only we had known, we could have got one easily in Switzerland.

FRIDAY, 29 AUGUST

Herbert Brush
I went to get my tea ration tickets for those over seventy years of age, but I had the journey for nothing as they have not yet received instructions to issue the coupons. Expect to do so in a couple of days or so. Maybe the Government are trying to think of some way to diddle the old folk out of their tea.

Judging by the contours of the young women in the streets, most of them are trying for the 5/- per week in child payments and some I have noticed will probably qualify for 10/- a week. And all this when the country is overpopulated with a deteriorating race.

SATURDAY, 30 AUGUST

Edie Rutherford

Decorator left finally 5 p.m. yesterday, praise be. The woman on floor below who recommended the young man for the work tells me this morn she met Deryck as he was leaving yesterday, and he said, 'Isn't Mrs Rutherford wonderful? I've never met such a nice person in all my life. She didn't grumble once!' Bless the boy. He's very young and is sure to meet someone more wonderful than I am before he quits life. I hope so, anyway.

Herbert Brush

W and I went to the State Cinema this afternoon. The picture was *The Birth of a Baby*. All details were shown pretty clearly even to the actual appearance of the child and I learned how to deal with the umbilical cord.

TUESDAY, 2 SEPTEMBER 1947

George Taylor

The WEA syllabus is ready once more, and a pretty full one it is with thirty-two classes. Each year I make a determined effort to avoid any errors appearing in the final print, and I submitted the proofs to Dr Wood, an English tutor, as well as checking them myself. Then in the first of our 'subject' paragraphs I find a line misplaced.

Maggie Joy Blunt

Went blackberrying last week. Crop is lavish but fruit small, wizened, hardly worth picking. My own are better, the ones that grow at the back of the cottage and get scarcely any sun. But there are never enough for more than a dish or two with stewed apples. Have just cut the lawn for the first time for about three weeks, ground like cast iron, and the pebbles that met mower blades sent out huge sparks.

In the town this weekend, saw Priestley's *The Linden Tree*. After so much from the critics, a little flat, a little disappointing. I think perhaps it was a little too true to life. What was that line – 'We are doing a very wonderful thing in a not very wonderful way.' I think that is true. We none of us really understand what it's all about, what this Government is doing for the future. They are criticised for being in too much of a hurry, trying to impose their ideals too rapidly, yet future generations may bless their little hour of power.

Smallness of plaice. Fishmonger explained that young shoals were being netted instead of thrown back – 'Soon the North Sea will be dry of fish – that's what will happen.'

WEDNESDAY, 3 SEPTEMBER

Edie Rutherford
I do hope women aren't going to fall for the new long skirt fashion. Now we have our chance to take a stand for commonsense and I hope we don't miss it.

I don't like the news from South Africa, i.e. that police are to carry arms and bayonets and use if necessary, following the killing of three white constables by a crowd of natives a day or two ago. Sounds too drastic to me. However, the Union has her colour problem and has got to work it out some day, at times with violence. Nowadays there is more violence on the black side than has ever before been known, so great care will be needed.

Herbert Brush
The 'Biro' pen runs so easily it is a pleasure to write with it, no matter what I write. The mood is on me to write verse but I don't know what will come out until I write it down.

> In the summerhouse I'm sitting
> Looking at a garage wall,
> But in my imagination
> There's a huge Baronial Hall,
> Gardens, parklands all around it,
> Knights and ladies wander there,
> Surely this is dear Old England
> Nowhere else could be so fair
> But as I continue writing
> Suddenly the scene has changed
> Some things now have gone for ever
> Others have been rearranged
> Awful is the present picture

Conjured up within my brain
Life will soon be not worth living,
God grant I'm not born again.

THURSDAY, 4 SEPTEMBER

B. Charles
I was told the Festival here is likely to show a financial deficit. It seems many of the orchestras and performers are getting very big salaries indeed. I shall be very sorry if there is a big deficit, as it is really very first-rate. In the evening we went to the Usher Hall to hear Szigeti and Schnabel play some Brahms sonatas and I thought the whole concert extraordinarily fine. It is rare to find two such famous soloists play so well in chamber music.

A letter from Clive Gay in which he said we seemed to have a very great many interests in common, and he is looking forward very much to our meeting in October.

George Taylor
In the evening I went to talk to a group of German prisoners of war about the WEA. We are inviting them to join classes without payment of fee, and quite a number seemed anxious to take advantage of the offer. A lieutenant prisoner thinks that about thirty will join.

Our president does quite a lot of lecturing work for army recruits and prisoners of war. He is disgusted at the illiteracy of the army recruits, and thinks that the standard of the prisoners is far higher.

SUNDAY, 7 SEPTEMBER

Edie Rutherford
News of the World tells of a man who aims to bring a case against the Government for not keeping its election promises. Has any Government anywhere EVER kept election promises? Does anyone but a nitwit expect them to?

THURSDAY, 11 SEPTEMBER

Maggie Joy Blunt
The last three days in London. Banks still not open till 10 a.m.

Price increases from 1 September: café near British Museum that I often patronise. Their two-course lunch from 1/9d. to 2/-. This with 3d. tip, which a notice referring to staff wages makes one feel obliged to leave, and does not encourage me to continue. Place is quiet, clean and ever-so-refined, and there is no queuing, but they cater for the snippet appetites of old maids, wan widows and nice, home-fed little typists and I simply can't do a hard afternoon's work on what I get there. So I have been going to Lyons Salad Bowl (also up from 2/9d. to 2/10d.) where I can heap my plate and gorge and feel fed, not just filled. Lyons is a wonderful firm: I have said so often in agreement with other people and repeat it now. Before 12.15 one gets in without any queuing.

Going home Tuesday evening, tired and in a daze, myself quite elsewhere, I walked straight into the Gents instead of Ladies in Marylebone Road. Thought it looked rather odd and different and wondered what an agitated little man was doing shaking his head at me.

MONDAY, 15 SEPTEMBER

Edie Rutherford
I heard today from one of the Germans living in a flat here that Mrs Braun, who lives two doors away, is in London to fetch her mother who was flown over here on Saturday last. She was in the British Zone, in Berlin. The mother has gone very frail and needs looking after. It transfers a problem from our Zone to Sheffield where I'm sure it can be better tackled.

George Taylor
Twenty-one German prisoners of war have enrolled in our WEA classes, nine of them choosing 'Expression of English', four 'Appreciation of Music', two 'Current Affairs' and one each for Biology, Economics, Philosophy and Psychology.

Chapter Seventeen

NOT EVEN A SUPERMAN

A state of bankruptcy or worse: a man protests at the abolition of the basic petrol ration

'We are always hearing complaints now that people are becoming self-centred and selfish, unhelpful to others, disagreeable, rude and callous. If you don't like it, then lump it – that sort of thing. Women, especially the overburdened young mother or the weary middle-aged housewife, are particularly sensitive to this atmosphere, and perhaps it does more to depress them than all the planning and queuing and doing without. People are harder, more intent upon looking after Number One. They are more likely to snatch, grab, lose their temper. Now why is this? What has gone wrong?

I suggest there have been too many little changes and not enough big ones. Faced with a big change in our lives, and measuring ourselves up to its challenge, we soon become far more helpful, neighbourly, cooperative, unselfish than we are in normal times. Consider, for example, how people behaved during the blizzards and floods that followed last winter. It is no longer every man for himself. We are all, it seems, in the same boat, and must row together against the mountainous seas.

But a series of little changes produces the opposite effect. Instead of feeling that we are together defying a vast dragon, we feel that our lives are being nibbled away by mice . . . Nothing generous is expected of us, so nothing generous emerges from us.

We all accept the reasons for austerity. But what a chilly, unimaginative world! It is as if, every few hours, a cold finger were laid on our wrists . . .

J. B. Priestley on the Light Programme, October 1947

The Princess wore a dress and long coat of love-in-a-mist blue with a high bonnet beret to match and beige-coloured suede shoes, all of which became her immensely. The Duke was in naval uniform. After a minute or two of talk they boarded the Pullman *Rosemary*, and as they stood at the windows waving their hands to the throng on the platform the train quietly glided out.

Princess Elizabeth and the Duke of Edinburgh leave Waterloo for Winchester on their wedding day, as recorded in The Times, *21 November 1947*

TUESDAY, 16 SEPTEMBER

Herbert Brush
Last evening we sat and talked, mostly about the troubles ahead, and W is of opinion that by the end of the year the country will be in a state of bankruptcy or worse. I am hoping that some miracle will happen and that by the end of the year we shall be able to see daylight through the black cloud which everyone says will envelop us this winter. Apparently it is only the miners who can save us now and they don't seem to trouble about it.

Edie Rutherford
One good thing about the fuel cuts here is that we are not getting the hammering from the little factory next door. Thanks be. I am told there are women who say it doesn't worry them at all. Don't know if they are lucky to be so nerveless or whether to pity them for their lack of sensitivity.

I bet London milliners rubbed their hands together when the edict went forth that women guests at the royal wedding must wear hats. That's how royalty keep in favour – one of the ways.

George Taylor
I received the bulb catalogue this morning, and rushed off an order within an hour. We are very fond of hyacinths, and do not wish them to be out of stock when our order is received. I expect they will go off the market again in these years of austerity.

THURSDAY, 18 SEPTEMBER

Edie Rutherford
Yesterday I met the old German lady who has come to flat 174. She is a nice old thing. Doesn't know any English but we managed to get across quite a bit with her daughter's aid. She thinks we are in a land of plenty and just sits amazed at the table before each meal.

Friend who has a sweet shop in this street says a woman came in yesterday and said, 'Gi' us a bar o' chocolate – husband's gone to the pictures and kid's gone to mother's and I've got a 2d. love book, so I'm gonna put my feet up and enjoy mysen this afternoon.'

George Taylor
Our ornithology tutor is greatly disgruntled that he cannot have the use of the Botany Lecture Theatre this year, and has been allotted the Education Room at the university. He rang me refusing to continue with the new room. I soon told him that he was getting paid for the work, while I acted quite voluntarily. As he still was obdurate, I told him the class was cancelled.

FRIDAY, 19 SEPTEMBER

B. Charles
This morning an annoying thing happened: I had the milk stolen. I think there is little doubt who took it. This is the third time I had bother with it. I phoned the police about the matter and this afternoon a constable came to discuss the matter. He advises me to speak to the milkman about it. The tenants above me are most unsatisfactory in every way.

A letter from Peter who sent me a long rigmarole from a London paper about Mae West. I have always wanted to see the lady, and, if she and her show come to Edinburgh I shall make a point of going along. I have an idea she is very much the same sort of thing as Marie Lloyd only more blatant, as she is a Yank.

SUNDAY, 21 SEPTEMBER

B. Charles
Heinz and his friend, Margaret Hall, came to see me this afternoon.

He agrees with me that many of the Germans from the eastern part of Germany will probably want to stay in Great Britain indefinitely, for if they return to the Russian Zone of Germany anything may happen to them. Heinz thinks France will go Communist, I am sure Italy would follow suit. I was saying to Heinz that I think it is only a question of quite a short while before England and America quit Germany altogether. If this comes about Russia, of course, would take over the entire country.

Heinz has taken a lot of my shirts for Hein to repair, and he is going to see if it is possible for Hein to come to Edinburgh to measure the curtains.

TUESDAY, 23 SEPTEMBER

George Taylor

The ornithology tutor has thought better of his obstinacy, and has decided to try the new room. When I saw him there, he was careful to explain that it was better than last time he was in it, and that he would be able to use it after all.

Maggie Joy Blunt

In the kitchen, with the first coal fire I have had for nearly three months. A wonderful summer, now all over. One by one my summer frocks, suits and blouses are being washed and laid away. Next I shall gather together all the shoes and stow them in old family Gladstone bags as I did last autumn. Skirts, slacks and woolly jumpers reappear. I find myself viewing this coming winter with sadness.

Local builder, who keeps a rather more than fatherly eye on me, is full of gloom. He thinks he might be able to squeeze the outside painting and few repairs necessary in at end of October. But where I shall find the money for it all I don't know. Borrow again I suppose. (O God, let this book sell!)

B. Charles

I phoned the station last evening, about the train Davy was coming on, and was told it was running only two minutes late. Davy looks very well and we got a taxi home. It is extremely nice to have him here and he has told me all the news about Windsor.

During the afternoon How's brother asked if he could phone and he went to the bedroom to use the phone. He admired my four-post bed very much indeed. Mr How came to the door and looked extremely unlike a going-to-be bridegroom, but his brother said they were getting married during the afternoon. They are, in a way, civil enough to speak to, but they are slovenly and vulgar.

Davy wants to go dancing tomorrow.

WEDNESDAY, 24 SEPTEMBER

B. Charles

Davy has bought a kitchen table and some bronze figures. I have taken a number of photos of him and hope they will turn out all right. He is very civil and nice to have about the place, and I am sorry he can't stay longer. We both thought the dinner at the Cale Hotel very good indeed. Had there been a rather bigger portion of everything, it would have been quite pre-war. We found out from one of the porters all about the Hows' wedding yesterday. He showed me a photo in the *Evening News* of the pair of them with a very vulgar account of the bride's parentage. Davy is out at the Palais de Danse and I shall have to wait up until he returns.

THURSDAY, 25 SEPTEMBER

George Taylor
In the evening my wife's tailor called to fit her for a costume. He came about 10.30, brought his wife, and stayed for the best part of an hour. What a talker is his wife! She decides all the niceties of fashion, where the buttons are to go etc, and both my wife and the tailor himself had a job to get a word in edgeways. The tailor, by the way, is a Jew, and was the police tailor who fitted me with a uniform in the Specials. It is because of this that we have gone to him, but he is a pleasant little chap.

B. Charles
Davy seems to have enjoyed himself at the Palais very much, and is going again tomorrow afternoon. It is interesting to note how dancing has 'caught on' among all classes of the community. When I was young the idea of lads and girls of the working class going to these dances would have seemed utterly ludicrous! I fancy these pseudo-smart dances have had a very bad effect on young people.

SATURDAY, 27 SEPTEMBER

George Taylor
My wife, in full vigour of dyeing a handbag and flinging it up on the line to dry, sprinkled the ceiling with navy coloured spots. I tried first aid by chalking over the spots.

WEDNESDAY, 1 OCTOBER 1947

Edie Rutherford

At news cinema we saw the much-discussed film where a man has a sword put through his body. It made me feel ill and after the first moment or two, I could not look. I don't wonder some have fainted.

Charming pictures of Princess Elizabeth holding god-daughter in papers this morning. I expect it won't be long before she is nursing her own baby; she being in the fortunate position where everything is OK for her to have all the children she'd like to have. Five were my desire and here I am, scraping along just able to keep us two out of debt and properly fed, clad and housed.

George Taylor

We had a Birmingham pawnbrokers meeting at the office today. They are pretty good at getting carpets, and one of the directors brought me samples today of export quality, and I ordered some. He told me that last week he went along to the factory and could get only one roll instead of his usual six. The position is tightening considerably, he said. And this after two years of peace!

THURSDAY, 2 OCTOBER

George Taylor

For several weeks now I have been reading Hogben's *The Loom of Language* and in parts I have found it more interesting than many novels. Hogben's ideas about a universal auxiliary language are very theoretical. For over twenty years I have used an auxiliary language, Esperanto; Hogben admits that when the man in the street talks about an auxiliary language he means Esperanto, that language certainly works both in speech and writing; then why not admit it, and cut out all the discussion of theory?

B. Charles

I see there is a short article, in this evening's paper, about Mosley's new book. I think it was best to write direct for a copy as, if it is suppressed, the trade channels will be the first to stop its circulation. I don't expect there is really a great deal of interest in it, but I want to read it all the same.

SATURDAY, 4 OCTOBER

B. Charles
I had a great artistic and emotional experience at Artur Rubinstein's recital. He is one of the greatest pianists I have ever heard. The power and beauty of his tone is something utterly marvellous. The sweep of his interpretations is quite architectural.

Donald came this midday and says he has got a boil inside his nose which is very painful.

SUNDAY, 5 OCTOBER

Maggie Joy Blunt
I face (I hope) a month of intense domestic activity. Chutney, the next-door gardener and odd-job man, is going to redecorate internally throughout for me. He is a character, a village youth thought to be slightly 'simple'. They say he used to have epileptic fits. He can get all the paint and distemper necessary from a brother-in-law. Nothing inside the cottage has been done properly in the seven years I have been here. Walls have been peeling badly for a long time and are going to be properly stripped and patched with plaster first. Chutney seems to know what he is about (at 2/- an hour).

MONDAY, 6 OCTOBER

Maggie Joy Blunt
Last week, an article by Easterbrook in the *Northern Chronicle* on 'Britain is Being Poisoned' – our rivers polluted and creatures in it killed off by man's carelessness. Now an RU book on man-eating tigers (by Jim Corbett) in which the author says that this magnificent beast is being threatened by extermination. Man is a slovenly, careless, greedy creature allowed to live in a miraculously wonderful world, which he won't appreciate.

George Taylor
Four of us went by car to Drighlington in connection with a proposed new company. The instigator of this company is the typically cranky inventor. He lives in a large old house, accompanied by a bevy of dogs, fowls and three friendly geese. The gander is called Jim, and his wives Susie and Spot. While we were there he introduced us to

them by throwing open the window, calling loudly, 'Jim, bring Susie and Spot.' Immediately from the neighbouring field, but out of sight of the window, there was a great cackling, and a rush of wings as Jim came along, bringing, true enough, his two wives with him.

This inventor is so erratic that I fear it will be quite impossible to deal with him.

WEDNESDAY, 8 OCTOBER

Herbert Brush
Are you a long-skirt or a short-skirt fan? I am both because I think that so many women with bandy legs ought to be obliged to wear longer skirts. Probably they don't know what they look like to other people, as from their own viewpoint the legs may have an attractive appearance, as they can't see them in action, especially from the rear. Every woman should have a photograph taken, giving a back view of her feet when walking. Some women with short skirts look nice from both back and front, but they are not many. So I say 'Give shorter skirts to shapely shanks but longer to the lean and lanky lop-sided legs.'

George Taylor
Yesterday, after much struggle, I managed to find copies of the new railway timetables, so felt fully confident when I went for the 1.55 p.m. Leeds train this afternoon. I arrived at 1.50, only to find there was no such train. The ticket collector said there was one at 2.18. Another passenger was similarly marooned, so we went to the stationmaster, and later an inspector. Neither could explain the matter.

When I arrived home, my wife was very indignant about the 50 per cent cut in the bacon ration.

B. Charles
I spent a very interesting evening with Mr and Mrs Sheppard who have just gone. They are, in their way, quite a remarkable couple. They are, of course, what is called working class, yet they are artistic, interested in artistic things, speak intelligently on all subjects yet are not in the very least victims of class hatred. They treat you quite civilly, are anxious to do all they can to be agreeable and in every way

are just the sort of people I admire. Mrs Sheppard said that nearly all young people now are incapable of staying indoors, even for one night: they have got to be rushing around here, there and everywhere all the time. We all said it was amazing where they got the money from.

SATURDAY, 11 OCTOBER

Herbert Brush
Our next-door neighbour Mr Goebells has gone to hospital and has had a growth taken out of his throat. I don't often speak to him even though he is in the garden with only a fence between us, but I did not know that he had trouble of that kind until his wife told me over the fence yesterday. She is very much worried as she is expecting the War Damage people to come into the house to do repairs which ought to have been done years ago and her daughter is just going to have her first baby; so she has various things to worry about. She hopes that I shall cut down the big fig tree which overhangs her garden and back entrance.

SATURDAY, 18 OCTOBER

George Taylor
I was not too anxious to get a full dose of the WEA Conference, so had a look round the shops in Oxford Street, and then my favourite hunting ground, Charing Cross Road. I arrived at the Conference just in time to listen to the Minister of Education, George Tomlinson. He has a good fund of humour, is not too bombastic, has only a trace of bitterness of most of his colleagues. He did not tell us much, of course – I do not expect that of a Minister – but at least he entertained us for three-quarters of an hour and was as good as Tommy Handley.

In the afternoon I dodged the meetings again to attend the British Puppet exhibition in Victory House. I was surprised at the interest taken in puppets, and had no idea that such a good show could be given as the demonstration I saw there.

SUNDAY, 19 OCTOBER

B. Charles
A wonderful afternoon this, from a musical point of view. Menuhin played the Beethoven concerto absolutely sublimely. I have never heard such violin playing before. It transcended anything I had ever imagined. I thought the slow movement was just too perfect.

George Taylor
I was at St Pancras platform when the train came in, so I secured a good seat for the journey home. On the way I finished Readers Union October choice, *Man-eaters of Kumaon* by Jim Corbett. Apart from one short fishing interlude, the book is a series of short stories about how the author stalked and killed various man-eating tigers that were plaguing the north of India. The book ends very dramatically, when at the fifty-ninth second of the fifty-ninth minute of the eleventh hour on the last day of his tiger shooting career, after having given up his quarry, Corbett attracts a tigress by a mating call, and successfully shoots it.

Maggie Joy Blunt
Celia has recently spent eight days in Paris. Went to two fashion house shows and was entranced. She gave me this month's *Vogue* to look at. All that luxury and elegance portrayed – I like to feel that sort of standard is being maintained somewhere in this drab world. I can't pretend to despise it when I don't.

MONDAY, 20 OCTOBER

George Taylor
My partner went to see about a driving licence today. It is twenty-one years since he touched a motor vehicle of any kind, and then it was only to drive a motor cycle. However, that was sufficient to comply with the law, so he has been issued a full licence.

TUESDAY, 21 OCTOBER

Herbert Brush
12.30 p.m. I have just been listening to the salute to Nelson in Trafalgar Square. Of course the idea of putting Nelson so high up

was one to exalt his memory, but I think that if the column had been blown down in the war, he would not have been put back so high up that no one can see him properly. Some people I know generally show their friends the view of Nelson from close to the entrance to the underground near the Strand, as this makes the second hilt give Nelson a very indecent contour.

WEDNESDAY, 22 OCTOBER

George Taylor
Back-duty cases drag on for months, and even years. Today I brought to a head a small one which has been under discussion for two years. The tax lost is about £1,100, and I asked the client if he had any idea of the amount involved. After pressure, he ventured a guess – £200–300. I had then to give him his shock, and to point out further that the Revenue could press for a penalty of treble duty £3,300. I think that made him sit up. However, I still could not pin him down to any figure to offer the Revenue, and all he would say was 'I'll leave it to you – I know that you will do your best for me.'

Herbert Brush
I got nothing in the Allotment Competition this year, not even an acknowledgement of my entry; no one in our field has been any luckier. Some people must do very well on their plots if they have produced more food than I have this year.

SATURDAY, 25 OCTOBER

Edie Rutherford
Awful railway accident yesterday. I know it was foggy but surely one of the trains at least was on the wrong line? Seems futile taking care in life when folk meet violent ends through no fault of their own, all in a few minutes.

I sold our old radio for £9 day before yesterday to the woman who came the previous evening. This morning I have sold our two black floor rugs for £3/10d.

B. Charles
The Germans arrived about 5.45 this afternoon. The friend broke the

vase Jack and Freda Goujon gave me years ago. I valued it very much and I am grieved it is broken beyond repair. It is the first time that a German has ever broken anything.

MONDAY, 27 OCTOBER

Herbert Brush

The black population of London seems to be increasing. I don't often see really black women, but I sat opposite one in the bus today. She was well dressed and wore large earrings and a gold watch on her left wrist, which she kept on looking at, giving the usual flourish to her hands as she turned her arm to enable her to see the face. She seemed to do it in a way as if to attract attention to the watch, of which she was probably very proud. She had very thin legs and large feet but her body was uncommonly fat, also her face, which had a jolly kind of expression on it when she was not rolling her eyes around. As she was carrying an exercise book, I concluded that she was going to school or maybe the museum. I see Indian women around there sometimes, but this one was a coal-black nigger.

WEDNESDAY, 29 OCTOBER

Herbert Brush

W had left her car for a few minutes in London today when a would-be thief came along and wrenched off the handle from one of the doors, but luckily someone must have come along and disturbed him before he could open the door and steal W's coat. Nothing is safe in London nowadays.

FRIDAY, 31 OCTOBER

B. Charles

The complete change in feminine moral outlook was rather reinforced by a talk this afternoon by some woman doctor on 'The Change' in a woman's life. It is amazing how things that, even twenty years ago, were considered 'unmentionable' are now broadcast! Why, if anyone had suggested broadcasting on this delicate subject when I was a child, that person would surely have been certified as insane and promptly locked up. I was very tickled at the 'naice' 'refained' way this woman doctor spoke. She skated over the word 'flushes' and 'having a child after the periods had stopped' beautifully. I really doubt the wisdom of all this semi-sex talk 'on the air'. To me it has something very prurient about it. Smutty talk among young people is always frowned upon, but I have an idea it is far less harmful than this semi-medical stuff that is now handed out as a matter of course. Still, I for one enjoyed all this 'change' chatter! In these dreary, dull days, anything for a bit of amusement, and I am always one for a good laugh.

Maggie Joy Blunt

Chutney finished the kitchens and WC on Tuesday and I did more painting on Wednesday. Felt cold, tired and really miserable on Tuesday and slept all afternoon. Am sure nervous breakdown can be avoided by taking more care when really fatigued. I think many people are ashamed of sleeping 'out of schedule'. It isn't always easy I know when one has a regular job or a family to look after, but I am sure many women are too anxious for their reputation, afraid to let things slip now and again, convinced that if they take a few hours off occasionally their whole world will collapse. But sleep is also a means of escape from the difficulties of living.

SATURDAY, 1 NOVEMBER 1947

Edie Rutherford

Today we vote in municipal elections. I hope the usual apathy will be less this year, seeing that the opposition have got such wind up these days. Husband and I are both voting Labour. I am amused to note that our tenant who was a Blackshirt is now an ardent Tory. They're welcome to him.

George Taylor

My wife left home early on her duty as a poll clerk, and I voted on my way to work. During the day an ex-policeman came to vote, having walked with a struggle from some old folks' home over a mile away. He had come as he said 'to get those blasted robbers out', referring to the Labour council. Another person walked in and asked for a book of papers as he wished to cast them all in favour of the Progressives. When my wife refused, but added that she wished that she could let him have them, the presiding officer mildly rebuked her for showing bias.

SUNDAY, 2 NOVEMBER

George Taylor

What marvellous and quite unexpected news there was of the local government elections. Six hundred and forty-odd Conservative gains from Labour is a turnover which I had not dared to anticipate. The change is all the more surprising in view of the unbroken Government successes at by-elections.

MONDAY, 3 NOVEMBER

George Taylor

The result of the local government elections in Sheffield is disappointing. Four Labour gains, when the rest of the country is turning the other way.

In view of the impending budget, when purchase tax will no doubt be substantially increased, we decided to spend £29 in buying new watches for my wife and myself.

TUESDAY, 4 NOVEMBER

B. Charles

I got a sad letter from UM this midday. It seems he has been ill and went into a nursing home in Inverness, and the doctor seems to think there is something amiss with his stomach. He is waiting for the result of the X-ray slides. I hope very much it is nothing of a really serious nature, but as he seems to have suffered a good deal in that part of his anatomy for quite a while, it may be serious. I have written to say I will do all I can to be of assistance, if he will let me know in what way I can help.

WEDNESDAY, 5 NOVEMBER

B. Charles

I can't help feeling anxious to know the result of UM's X-ray. I fear it may indicate there is something gravely amiss. If he has to have an operation, the fact that he has been such a heavy whisky drinker for so long will NOT be a factor in his favour. He is a good friend, and I am very fond of him.

FRIDAY, 7 NOVEMBER

Edie Rutherford
In the tripe queue this morn I learned that all the events of this world have been foretold by a monk named Johann. There is to be another war, which will finish the world as we know it (I can believe that), and only a few faithful ones will be left to start anew. This last war will start between Russia and Turkey and then all will be drawn in. So next Wednesday is Budget Day . . . If Dalton raises the price of fags again he's had it, and so has the Govt.

SATURDAY, 8 NOVEMBER

Herbert Brush
War Damage workmen are busy on Goebells' house next door.

Went to the Capitol Cinema this afternoon. There was one very interesting picture, *Servant of the People*, which was a description of Parliament and the way a sitting is conducted, with apparently many MPs taking part, though I'm not quite sure of this. The other picture featured Bette Davies who may be a good actress, but her face does not impress me in the least, and her eyes, which are much too large for her face, always have a doped look in them, which repels me every time I see her in a picture.

SUNDAY, 9 NOVEMBER

George Taylor
Potato rationing is not an unexpected blow, but after two years of peace, this continuous taking in of the belt is becoming very discouraging. At 3lb. each, we shall have difficulty in managing, as we are very fond of potatoes. It was surprising, however, to hear that the sweet ration was to be reduced. And this at a time when the sugar supply is so ample that some think it might be taken off the ration altogether. When will austerity cease?

B. Charles

Two points of interest today. Potato rationing, and the fact that this morning I observed the Two Minutes' Silence in the kitchen here, with the two German POWs. If anyone had told me on 11 November 1918, that, twenty-nine years later, I should observe the Silence in my kitchen, with two German POWs from World War II, I should have thought they were crazy. I wonder with whom I shall observe it in, say, ten years' time, after World War III has happened? Hermann brought me two large turnips.

TUESDAY, 11 NOVEMBER

George Taylor

I nearly established a record for my radio listening tonight, when I listened to three programmes in one evening. They were all connected with the Jubilee celebrations, and I found the hour of recorded history very interesting. Is it a sign of my increasing age that I like to hear the retelling of the story of these last twenty-five years?

Maggie Joy Blunt

News that all women up to forty are to register, to loop in every able person to do 'essential' work. 'But they won't touch you, will they?' says my dear Ella who is staying with me. I am just the sort of person 'they' will touch. My socialist conscience approves and tries to argue how *right* that I should be doing something useful. My instinctively selfish Tory nature resents the idea furiously and puts up a number of defensive replies. But one plain, indisputable fact stares at each contending half: sooner or later a job of some sort for me is inevitable, economically. I can't exist on present income, or only by an overdraft. My main hope is in the biography, but when it is done (perhaps) by the New Year, it may well be quite some time before it is published. I won't consider the idea of it being refused by *every* publisher I approach.

WEDNESDAY, 12 NOVEMBER

Maggie Joy Blunt

The budget did not disturb me unduly. Nothing affected my convenience directly and it seemed fair that pools and dog racing should be taxed. It seemed a 'might have been worse', 'not so bad' budget. But after nine o'clock news a Conservative MP tore Dalton's speech to pieces. Dalton does seem to have made a mess of things: he talked down too much as though he thought no one but the half-witted would listen to him.

George Taylor
I am very relieved to learn that income tax is not to be increased. Nine shillings in the £5 is far too heavy, and this together with the higher prices reduces my present income almost to its pre-war worth and leaves me little return for my investment in a share in the partnership.

THURSDAY, 13 NOVEMBER

Herbert Brush
I have finished my tree-lopping this morning. The last one was a May tree, which managed to scratch me a few times before I got its head off. I put some creosote on most of the saw cuts to prevent rot setting in. I dropped my tin of creosote while I was up in a tree and it fell on the pavement; luckily no one was passing at the time or I should have been in trouble. I took the ladder back to Sparks, two doors away, and Mrs S showed me her television set, and invited me to see it some evening when there is a good show on.

FRIDAY, 14 NOVEMBER

George Taylor
So Dalton has gone. I am duly thankful. Dalton was the most unstatesman-like Chancellor I ever remember. I have never heard before a Chancellor so frankly out for the advantage of one class only, and so bitter in his debates. I do not suppose there will be less austerity from Cripps; rather the reverse. But I think that Cripps with his contacts in the business world will not be quite so biased as Dalton has been.

Herbert Brush
I wonder what will be done about the budget now Dalton has resigned. It seems to me that the whole country will be in an awful mess before long, and no one will be able to rescue it in time, not

even a superman. I guess that the shops will not wait for the purchase of new stocks before they increase the price of things. I bought some catarrh cream at Boots this morning, and it took the girl several minutes to find out what price to charge me, and that was higher than the last tube I bought. I feel sure that the catarrh cream was old stock, but it's no use saying anything.

SUNDAY, 16 NOVEMBER

George Taylor
I had confirmation of the death of an old acquaintance who lived, quite against the regulations, in a hut on his allotment near us. Sam Slinn was a real individualist. He was nearing seventy and recently I helped with his application for an old-age pension, which he never lived to receive.

Before the war he used to supply us with eggs and always said he would never let us down. In fact, we scarcely ever received any from him after the outbreak of war, but whenever we met him he was always going to call round. We could never be annoyed with him. Only a fortnight ago we went along with some food to his hut, but found it deserted and knew that something had happened. Now we find out that he died quite alone, and his body was found in the hut. We shall sorely miss him.

THURSDAY, 20 NOVEMBER

Maggie Joy Blunt
Forgot all about royal wedding till I opened paper this morning. Then, duly primed with various details of the day's function, I turned on wireless. A moving occasion. I do not need commentator to tell me this or doubt the cheers from the crowd broadcast. The feeling is genuine enough – a delightful sort of family feeling. I always get it watching any royal do when I'm there in the crowd. We do love our little ceremonies. And why not? *All* of us are hungry for colour, romance and adventure. Today's ceremony symbolised some dormant dream of perfection alive in the breast of every, well, woman, at least . . . I wept copiously into washing up bowl as I listened.

What a nice voice the groom has. And so surprisingly English – though I don't know what I was expecting. The Princess's voice too was becomingly virginal. One wishes them a long and happy life together, to set an example to the nation of what marriage *can* be like.

We do like some pageantry and fuss and to play at fairy tales now and again. And also we demand some sort of symbol of what is, perhaps, emotionally, the most important part of our way of life, the family. In youth I hated family life and its tyrannies. And I've known many people who've felt as I do. Yet I am strongly attached to remaining relatives and to certain memories, and I have made a compromise home of my own here which I adore.

There was a woman BBC commentator. I don't remember ever hearing one before.

FRIDAY, 21 NOVEMBER

B. Charles
When I went out this morning I found every paper was sold. I was astonished, but was told the reason was that people wanted to see the pictures of the royal wedding. I think, were they to disappear, the people would be very upset. Wherever you go there is damp and condensation.

Edie Rutherford
The royal wedding seems to go off without a hitch. I think the young man will hold his own in that marriage. I think people who slept on London pavements in the cold and wet are crazy, and likely some cases of pneumonia will develop this weekend.

Husband is now reading *Economics for the Exasperated* and each page gets him more exasperated.

George Taylor
At the second of our Students Evenings at the WEA one of our members attempted to summarise the history of England, Russia and the USA in just over an hour. He certainly did very well and made one or two telling points. His efforts were not highly appreciated, however.

SUNDAY, 23 NOVEMBER

Edie Rutherford

I have been thinking that our finest hour was not when Churchill said it was, but NOW. All who help England through at this time deserve the highest praise of all. The spectacular, unpremeditated courage which goes with war is not so good as that dogged, determined, calm courage which is needed for this recuperative time.

In this town last week there was a circus on at the Empire. A man had his arm clawed by a tiger and amputated afterwards. A friend of ours who was in a pub in town the next night was in a conversation about it. A black man who conveyed that he was in charge of the elephants, not speaking English well, understood the conversation and entered into it, demonstrating with his glass of ale, which he pushed away from him and pulled back, saying, 'Tease, tease, no tease, no arm go. I see, tease, tease' with more gestures. So we say serve the man right.

THURSDAY, 27 NOVEMBER

Maggie Joy Blunt

Spent weekend in Rye, a delightful old town. But why must we go always into the past to find dignity, beauty and good manners in our cities and villages?

FRIDAY, 28 NOVEMBER

Herbert Brush

I received a Certificate of Merit from the Ministry of Agriculture for my plot this morning. The judges' marks were 133 out of 200. I lost most of the marks for not arranging for much green food in the spring: apparently the judges did not think that all my artichokes and leeks were eligible for marks.

SUNDAY, 30 NOVEMBER

Edie Rutherford

How marked is the reaction to partition news from UNO for Palestine; the Jews rejoicing, the Arabs furious. Well, so long as our men are withdrawn . . .

The more I see of other lands, the gladder I am to be where I am. I heard this the other day: the Frenchman is glad to be French, the American to be an American, the Greek to be Greek. The Englishman is never proud to be an Englishman, he is only proud he is none of the other nationalities.

Mr Churchill has another birthday, his seventy-third. Time he retired.

TUESDAY, 2 NOVEMBER

Maggie Joy Blunt
A lovely dawn: frost like a lavender veil over grass, trees, hedges, door posts. Still freezing but BBC tells us It is Not so Cold so we all obediently believe it. The winter has now clamped down on us. There is no escape.

WEDNESDAY, 3 DECEMBER 1947

Herbert Brush
I went out to post my letter and found Mr Ing standing near the letter box waiting for someone to talk to. It was too cold to hang about for long but he had time to tell me that a lady had lost her handbag in a nearby street. She was walking along when suddenly a young man on a cycle turned into her, knocking her down, and before she could get up he had snatched her handbag and was off on his cycle, and got away. Ing, who used to be a policeman, always eyes a stranger suspiciously, and he started on another yarn about a Jewish-looking chap with a case, who asked him a question and then told him something which he knew was not true, about an old lady in a house.

George Taylor
I went with my wife to hear the Royal Philharmonic Orchestra under Sir Thomas Beecham and was surprised to find the City Hall half empty. Beecham seems to have lost his tremendous drawing powers in Sheffield. After several recalls, Beecham came back on to the platform to make a speech. Instead of the normal thanks which I expected, he began to comment in his dry and pungent way about the two Abyssinian lions which decorate the City Hall platform. Gradually he warmed to his theme, and finished up with a rounding denunciation of the arrangement, and of the city council which permitted such an atrocity. Next time, he said, he would need a telephone to com-

municate with his first violins and a telescope to see the other side. The audience rocked with laughter at his sallies, but I am told that the Lord Mayor, who was present, looked pretty uncomfortable.

Maggie Joy Blunt
This afternoon to sit in a spiritualist 'circle' with Lys and her sister and Julia. Very interesting. But how much does the medium pick up of one's own thoughts and wishes? Should like to hear a sensible psychologist's opinion on these matters. My father 'appeared' to the medium who gave a very convincing description of him and details known only to myself and father – reference to an old bicycle, for instance, which I had completely forgotten but that caused family at the time much amusement. My father also 'saw' me at a typewriter, hammering away. He sent many encouraging and warming messages that changes of the kind I desired were imminent and I should soon be getting what I wanted and was to 'keep smiling' (a term typical of my father). There was also present with him a young man who, by the description, I couldn't recognise at first, someone apparently whom I had known well but who had since passed over – he was very fond of me and interested. Well, that might have been a young South African I knew many years ago and have since quite forgotten. He might have been killed during the war, I should not know.

Everyone in the circle had similar messages of hope and encouragement – things were going to improve and change for the better with the New Year. If there is any truth in the idea of departed 'spirits' sending us messages and giving us guidance, then I can't help feeling my poor father must have been very surprised at being called upon to take his place in the company. He never had the least interest in spiritualism but I am sure he'd understand that I am moved by curiosity more than anything to experiment and 'see what it's like'. I think it would be immensely dangerous to rely on it too much, or at the sacrifice of our other abilities and faculties.

THURSDAY, 4 DECEMBER

Edie Rutherford
Going on the bus, I overheard two women behind me talking, obviously doing domestic work, one with a son aged seven, other sons fifteen and six. Both at a loss to know what to give them for

470

Christmas. From the lists each gave the other, the modern child of such parents has EVERYTHING: fountain pens, propelling pencils, bicycles, trunks full of books, railway systems which would sell for a fiver today, and so on. 'Grannie's giving a banjo for Xmas or I'd have got him that . . .'

FRIDAY, 5 DECEMBER

Maggie Joy Blunt
Short of cash. I decide to draw last £2 from post office savings and hope for the best. Income tax assessment arrived this week. My income is now so small I shall have *nothing* to pay in January!

Noticed woman this morning in station buffet avoiding drinking from usual side of cup. I know of several people who do this in public places where washing up may be sketchy, and also avoiding all cracks and chips in cups where germs may have settled, which I try to do myself when I think of it.

SATURDAY, 6 DECEMBER

Herbert Brush
W has had a new five-valve wireless set given to her by Philips: brought it home yesterday. Do you listen to the item *Twenty Questions*? Last night the producer was making out that quinces are not grown in England but this is not correct, as there is a quince tree within ten yards of me now.

TUESDAY, 9 DECEMBER

B. Charles
This afternoon I tried to get a new pair of corduroy trousers. None to be had in my size! I then tried to buy a new pair of braces. None to be had! I then made an effort to buy some more oatmeal in case Thomson doesn't get any. None to be had!

WEDNESDAY, 10 DECEMBER

Herbert Brush
W bought a new car today, another Standard 8. Sold her old one.

Today a dustman told me that he could remember me since he was a boy, but as he told me he was sixty-six, I had to contradict him. Then he said that he always thought that I was a retired police sergeant, and again I had to correct him. It's not the first time, by a good many, that I have been taken for a policeman; maybe the size of my feet. As far as I know, no one ever guessed me to be an electrical engineer.

FRIDAY, 12 DECEMBER

Herbert Brush

W brought home her new car, a light grey in colour, no. JLN 668. The number is very near that of 'The Beast'. I wonder who has car no. JLN 666.

SATURDAY, 13 DECEMBER

George Taylor

After a four-month wait we received the first instalment of the utility bedroom furniture we ordered. The tallboy and dressing table look very nice in front, but they are crudely built and raw in the unseen spots. One drawer in each article refuses to close by a good inch, the screw holes in one side of the mirror are too big for the screws with the result that the mirror is loose, and no attempt was made by the suppliers to see that everything was in order upon delivery. It was just take it or leave it, you are lucky to get it at all.

SUNDAY, 14 DECEMBER

Maggie Joy Blunt

On Wednesday I went to support Lys at her spiritualists' group sale of work. Like all church bazaars I have ever known. A 'reading' from the leading clairvoyant (an extraordinary, shabby little man, plump and rather soiled looking, works in a greengrocer's, but has very bright, clear eyes and an air of command with his workers and followers). My recent theories that these people pick up what is immediate in your thoughts now all overthrown. He spoke a lot of nonsense about people, relatives and so forth I could not recognise. He spoke of someone I knew well, just gone to Australia, works in newspapers, unsettled. I should be seeing him back. This must be S whom I certainly haven't thought of for weeks and do *not* expect back. Also the medium mentioned some 'big thing' I was thinking of selling and advising me not to do so until my plans are more settled. This man knows nothing about me.

WEDNESDAY, 17 DECEMBER

Herbert Brush

For the last hour I have been struggling to get the car to start, but I have now given up and W has asked the garage to send a man.

12 noon. The man from the garage has traced the trouble to the induction coil, the thing I suspected at first, but had no means of checking it. The garage man has gone to Camberwell Green to get another induction coil to loan until W can get another from The Standard Co.

3 p.m. We could not get the car to start even with the new coil, and finally we had to push it out of the garage, with the help of the men at the gate, and run it down the hill until the engine was made to start. After that, W went to Camberwell Green with it.

THURSDAY, 18 DECEMBER

George Taylor

At last I have got rid of my police uniform, nearly twelve months after my resignation. I wrote asking them to collect, and along came a Chief Inspector. He carefully checked off everything and then asked my wife for the few missing articles, such as my lamp, now almost rusted away, and instruction book. Regulations would not permit his leaving even the tiniest souvenir of my service.

SATURDAY, 20 DECEMBER

Edie Rutherford

So far, we have no hope of any poultry for Christmas. Husband trying, by ringing every few days, to pin butcher down to promising us a bird of some, any, kind. He says black market has them all and he WON'T trade with them, so his supplies are going to be very small indeed. We also don't want to deal in black market. I refuse to worry. We shall cope. Greengrocer says he may have a rabbit.

George Taylor

We had ordered a turkey from our greengrocer's and by chance my wife called when the first few were delivered. They were actually bigger than we ordered, but although the manageress said there would be some smaller ones in on Monday, my wife decided not to risk this, and brought one of the larger birds home. We had nowhere to keep the bird, so we decided to alter our plans, invite my brother and his family over tomorrow instead of Xmas, and have our festive meal then.

In the afternoon we made one of our rare visits to the cinema, actually to see the wedding film in Technicolor. This proved very disappointing, however, consisting merely of reconstructed scenes from the early lives of Princess Elizabeth and her husband, and of long shots of the arrival and departure of guests from the Palace and Abbey and very short scenes in the Abbey itself, but none of the actual ceremony. The supporting films were bad in the extreme, *I Married a Murderer* being a sordid tale with very ugly principals and a short featuring the usual precocious and repelling American infant.

SUNDAY, 21 DECEMBER

B. Charles

I am very interested to read about the suicide of Sir Bernard Spilsbury. He is another case of these old people being quite unable to carry on in modern conditions. They, of course, have had such a very pampered, easy sort of existence in the past: everyone has run after them, waited on them hand and foot, pandered to their every wish, that, now, with things so different, they just crumple up and haven't the guts to go on. If they don't commit suicide, many of them seem to live in squalor and are 'found dead' some days after they have died.

Herbert Brush

We put a hurricane lamp under the car last night to stop the sweating, and this morning it started without difficulty. Mr Goebells is pruning his quince tree about 15 yards away from where I am writing this.

MONDAY, 22 DECEMBER

B. Charles
Several letters and cards. A nice letter from Alice, who sent me a copy of the magazine *The Masque*, with many interesting pictures of interior decoration. There was a letter from Clive. He is 'resting' at the moment. Donald has just gone. He has given me four nice handkerchiefs. They will come in very useful.

CHRISTMAS EVE

Herbert Brush
W has gone out to get the turkey. Apparently she had her name drawn as one of the lucky ones at the Co-Op to be allowed to buy a bird at a high price.

CHRISTMAS DAY

B. Charles
Christmas Day! As on many occasions I spent the day quietly, alone. In the evening I went to dinner with the Sheppards. They had cooked an absolutely pre-war meal. I had not had such a meal for years. They are very kind and nice. His father and mother were there. The father is a remarkable old boy: he has done a lot of time in India and views with great concern the trend of events there.

George Taylor
For a change this year we decided to spend Xmas morning at home. After an early morning exchange of presents, my chief ones being a pair of sheepskin slippers and a copy of Lawrence's *The Seven Pillars of Wisdom*, and my wife's a handbag and an electric iron, we had a cup of tea and dozed off to sleep again. Then a taste of the Xmas radio programmes and a run over some of our special records followed.

Herbert Brush
I did not get up very early this morning, but lay in bed listening to the broadcast of a Christmas visit to a hospital and the sound of children who were in the excited state they always get into on Christmas Day.

Sometimes the verse which comes is too lewd for other's eyes and I have to tear it up or burn it.

TUESDAY, 30 DECEMBER

Maggie Joy Blunt
Food plentiful over the holiday. Snow today – a prelude to a repetition of last winter's severity? Presents that delighted me most this year: nylons from family in Lisbon, and bedroom slippers (much needed) bought with gift money. These cost only 11/3d. and are just what I want, from Dolcis.

Paper shortage getting serious. Cannot find any more of these Duplicate books though I still have one in stock. Julia, who depends entirely on cartridge paper, is having great difficulty in finding any.

I begin to wonder what I shall do for scrap. Have had a large stock, filched from my old wartime job, which is rapidly disappearing.

Herbert Brush
W made me a Christmas present of a pair of the garden boots you may see advertised occasionally up to No.12. They are just 5 inches across in the widest part. Have a look at 5 inches on your tape measure, and you will be able to imagine what my feet look like.

NEW YEAR'S EVE

B. Charles
Last Hogmanay I was with Brenda and had just got the last vanload of furniture off from Windsor. What a difference this day! Really, everything is in order. THANK GOODNESS. I could never face another removal. It would about kill me. I got the electric fire home and it goes all right, but emits a smell of rubber, so I have decided not to use it until Mr Sheppard has seen to it. I am very delighted with it. It is highly attractive and most original.

NEW YEAR'S DAY 1948

Edie Rutherford
I returned to the suppliers a Cozi-glow bed lamp and warmer, as it is a fraud. It takes only a 15-watt bulb, and if you use a higher power it

automatically switches off after about ten minutes. After four hours in bed, the container was as cold as it was when put in.

New Year's Honours seem in some cases to have gone to the right people, though I loathe all such. If you do good, the reward is in the doing, and really good folk would not accept knighthoods etc. All, all is vanity.

Herbert Brush

Another struggle to get the car to start. Last evening I and W went into the Sparks, next door, to wish them a Happy New Year and to look at their television picture of the Cinderella pantomime. My eyes are not good enough to see such a small picture well, but as, according to the announcer, it was the first time they have televised a theatre with its own light, perhaps I did not see the television under the best conditions.

I wonder how many people will begin to keep a diary today, and how many of them will keep it up for more than a week. I always think that it was a pity that father did not keep a fuller diary than he did. Mostly he just noted the weather but said not a word about what he was doing himself or what his various children were doing. I must have done a good many things of which he did not approve or he would not have said 'Go to the stable' so often. I remember going to the stable often enough but I can't remember why I was sent there on any single occasion. But I can appreciate that it was necessary for me to be under cover when father arrived with a stick, which he had cut from a tree in the garden. I made so much noise after the first stroke on my fingers that the whole parish would have heard if I had been in the open air; maybe, too, mother might have begged me off, if she heard the row I was making. Father had to cut a new stick every time, the old one could never be found. I took care of that.

I think it is a pity that boys are not brought up that way now; some of the little devils of 1948 would be better for a good tanning with a roughly cut stick.

FRIDAY, 2 JANUARY

Edie Rutherford

It's [nationalised] British Railways now. Well, they can't start brightening and reforming too soon, as I see it.

B. Charles

I met Mr Durie this morning and we had a stroll round. I asked his opinion about this new National Health Bill. He seems to think it won't work. With things as they are, I think it is probably a good thing. Nowadays, it is impossible to be nursed at home, so it is imperative to go to hospital in cases in which one would never have thought of doing so when one could have had attention at home. As this is so, some sort of state aid is essential. I am not against this measure and fancy it will be a good thing for the vast majority of people. I am more than ever of the opinion that future historians will consider the disappearance of resident domestic help one of the main causes of the collapse of the old order of things.

FRIDAY, 9 JANUARY

George Taylor

At the council meeting of the WEA we should have heard two German prisoners of war who had promised to give us their impressions of the Association and of its classes. However, a ban imposed on public speeches by prisoners, just made, prevented their coming, much to the disappointment of the members of the council. I was at first asked to protest to the Minister of War, but this was eventually watered down to an inquiry as to the extent of the ban.

Nearly a hundred attended the New Year's Social, and had a very bright time. Our new socials secretary varies things from the usual game and dance social, and tonight had a very capable illusionist-raconteur and an excellent elocutionist.

MONDAY, 12 JANUARY

George Taylor

We were back in the board room of our little engineering company for today's meeting. It was not very cosy, however, as the carpet has not yet arrived, and the managing director, thinking he had been particularly smart, had purchased the radiators in Doncaster where the electricity is supplied at 230 volts, compared with Sheffield's two hundred. So, although he had paid a few shillings less for the radiators, they gave out very little heat.

B. Charles

I have just got back from the pantomime and Mrs Sheppard told me a disgusting story about Margaret Lockwood being mobbed by a crowd of daft women in Glasgow. It seems that when this woman arrived by train there, she was besieged at the station by a crowd of hysterical females and a whole posse of policeman were needed to get this film star to her hotel. The crowd tore her bouquet to pieces to provide themselves with a 'souvenir' and generally behaved in a very disgraceful way. It is disgusting the way film stars have become the undisputed arbiters of taste and morals to seven-eighths of the female population of the entire 'civilised' world.

TUESDAY, 13 JANUARY

George Taylor

After seven and a half years, my wife finished her rent collecting for our firm today. The last man has come back from the forces, and we had to find him work. We did not need him on the accountancy side, so offered the rent job and he accepted. Accordingly both married ladies who helped during the war finished. My wife is sorry both to lose that little extra money, and the chance of working a couple of days each week.

WEDNESDAY, 14 JANUARY

George Taylor

I was on a small builder's accounts today and asked him the source of £100 cash paid into the business. After a great deal of pressure he admitted they were unusual transactions, such as the purchase of potatoes at 11/- per bag, and the sale of them, off the ration of course, at £1. I wonder how many other people are dabbling in stuff like this. It is a big temptation to the commercially minded, particularly when they think it is not assessable to tax. It is very difficult for we poor accountants to be fair to the Revenue and yet not to appear to be definitely against our clients, who pay our bill.

SUNDAY, 18 JANUARY

Herbert Brush
Yesterday afternoon W and I went to the Capitol Cinema. There was a queue about 100 yards long when we arrived, but we got in all right. The main picture was *Gone with the Wind* with Clark Gable and Vivian Leigh and Leslie Howard in the principal parts. Very good, but rather too long I thought.

12 noon. I have been on the plot for an hour or so. I planted a row of garlic, more for the pleasure of growing it than for its demand. So many folk seem to be afraid of growing it, in case they smell of garlic for days.

I have been trying again to appreciate modern verse, but I can't read much of it before I begin to wonder what kind of mind produced it. I bought a copy of *The Poetry Review* the other day, and in it I am told that it is really my fault if I can't understand and appreciate modern verse, but, so far, I have never come across anyone who will own up to enjoying it, like one enjoys rhythm and rhyme etc in old poetry.

Edie Rutherford
I got my money back from the Cozi-glow people the other day and put it back into the bank. First time for ages money has gone *in*.

My brother in Birmingham, Len, now has a pig. He has threatened this for years and now it has come off. His son, who aims to be a vet one day, will be thrilled.

Gandhi seems to know how to make Indians behave. They'd better keep him alive, as he'll be needed for more fasting before that country settles down peaceably.

FRIDAY, 23 JANUARY

Edie Rutherford
A friend of mine is furious because yesterday came a telegram to her husband condoling about her death. She promptly sent a telegram saying she was alive. I told my friend she missed the chance of a lifetime – it comes to few; she should have left things and then read all the letters the family wrote her husband and found out what they REALLY thought of her.

Letter from my cousin Reg this morn, taking me up because I won't have this Government slanged wholesale. Makes the comment that competition is the spice of life. I've taken him up on that. My dad was crippled in the Boer War, my husband a semi-wreck from the Great War, so I resent the idea that such men can only succeed if competing. Most of us want enough and a little bit over, and the ambitious ones can have their possessions and all the worry with them.

B. Charles
This morning several interesting letters. There was one from Heinz. I was very glad to hear from him. I am surprised Hein has never sent me a line. Yet another from Jack Clark. He asks if I have met a doctor of divinity of the name of Sherwin Bailey. I see his name is in the telephone directory and that he lives quite near here. I dare say he might be interesting to know, and I shall see if I can contact him. He comes from Alcester.

TUESDAY, 27 JANUARY

George Taylor
When on audit in Eckington, I take lunch at a cottage where the lady of the house is a farmer's daughter. This week, her father has killed some pigs, so today we had as a special treat pig's fry for lunch.

The decorators started work at home today. We have decided to have the hall and landing done throughout, as well as the lounge, cost what it may. We have become tired of doing without this and that, and have now entered an orgy of spending. What little money we have in the bank will soon be useless if this Government remains in power, so we think it wiser to use it on something which we appreciate.

WEDNESDAY, 28 JANUARY

Edie Rutherford
Last evening went to Foresters Hall to cabaret show by members of the Overseas Association. A poor do. There was one dark gent – in short, a nig – with a white wife, Dutch, and a very gifted and accomplished woman too, with eight languages at her tongue-tip. He was

born and brought up in this town, and his parents came from North Africa. They sat with clasped hands, obviously enthralled with each other. Although a lot more tolerant re colour than when I left SA fourteen years ago, I just could not hold a black man's hand, except maybe to dress it were he wounded. No thank you. I realise it is all wrong to be that way, but there it is.

Chapter Eighteen

ONE TRIES HARD NOT TO BE NASTY TO FOREIGNERS

Like dandies of a modern brand: a group of Jamaicans study an unfamiliar map

'The light has gone out of our lives, and there is darkness everywhere. Our beloved leader . . . is no more. The light has gone out I said, and yet I was wrong. For the light that shone on this country was no ordinary light. The light that has illumined this country for many years shall illumine this country for many more years.'

Prime Minister Pandit Nehru at the cremation of Mahatma Gandhi, 31 January 1948

'The united State organization which today takes charge of all social security payments "from the cradle to the grave" is a bold and costly enterprise. In its early years it will be making payments of about £550m. annually, including £60m. for family allowances, no less than £240m. for retirement pensions, and no more than £65m. for assistance conditional on proof of need. This machine will, in full swing, cost about £25m. a year to manage, and its total staff may grow up to 40,000.

The keeping of an insurance account for the lifetime of each registered citizen presents no great difficulty. In the cheerful, spacious, efficient, specially built central offices of the Insurance Ministry on the outskirts of Newcastle, each insured person has his own ledger sheet on which his whole insurance life history can be recorded. The 25m. sheets of the insurance ledger are located in 100 different rooms, each of which is occupied by a staff of 20. The last two figures of the citizen's insurance number indicate the room containing his ledger sheet.

If his number is not known or is misquoted, an alphabetical index of 26m. insured persons has to be consulted. In this register there are already 650,000 members of the Smith tribe, including some 8,000 plain John Smiths. The citizen who expects prompt service will do well to remember his number.'

A warning from The Times *at the birth of the Welfare State, Monday, 5 July 1948. On the same day, almost all hospitals passed into state ownership, and Clement Attlee restated that the National Health Service would soon be considered 'the envy of the world'. The healthcare and national insurance budgets were wildly optimistic; within three years the free supply of medicines was supplemented with prescription charges*

FRIDAY, 30 JANUARY

Edie Rutherford

Oh, who would have done such a dreadful deed as to kill Gandhi? What a terrible thing to do. I wonder the crowd did not tear the fiend to bits. Who can benefit from that good man's death? He was the conscience of mankind. We all know in our better selves that what Gandhi stood for and lived was the highest ideal.

B. Charles

Went to the concert at the Usher Hall and I thought the orchestra played the 'Eroica' very well. It always thrills me to hear this symphony. I was speaking to a lady about the assassination of Gandhi. She has been in India quite a lot and considers this assassination as one of the greatest tragedies of modern times. I have always thought Gandhi to be one of the most influential personalities in India that there has ever been.

There was a letter from the Victoria and Albert Museum about my proposed gifts. They will be very glad to accept and say the walnut candlesticks are a very rare type. It is gratifying to think I picked them up in the Lane and got them for 9/-! It is still possible to find attractive things cheaply. I half wondered if Dr Bailey would phone. He has not done so. In a way I am not surprised, and am a little sorry. It is always nice to get to know interesting people.

Herbert Brush

Went to see how Bill was getting on. Last Friday he was going up a ladder to the house loft when the ladder slipped and he fell and sprained his ankle badly. I sat with him awhile but he was very busy with his 'Freemason' work, so I did not stay for long. He lent me a book on 'Atomic Energy'.

1.20 p.m. Poor old 'Gandhi'. I wonder whether it would have been better for India finally if the old man had never been born.

SATURDAY, 31 JANUARY

B. Charles

Herman arrived first thing this morning. I made him a present of a large tin of treacle for his children. He leaves for a fresh camp on

Monday, preparatory to be repatriated. I shall miss him very much indeed. I think, really, he has been more useful than even Heinz and Hein were. He could be made into a real, old-fashioned servant. The man in Adams' this morning said we ought to give the German POWs British citizenship if they wish, in order to induce them to stay here.

SUNDAY, 1 FEBRUARY 1948

Herbert Brush

Maggie Hutt has invited me to go and entertain some young women this evening with my tricks with string, cotton reels and such like material and I have accepted with some hesitation.

8.30 p.m. It was a surprise to me when I went with W to the home where Maggie was waiting for us. I managed to amuse them for more than an hour and even then I had a trick in hand.

MONDAY, 2 FEBRUARY

B. Charles

The German friend of Herman's arrived this morning. He is a very quiet fellow, a bit slow, and I think he seems awfully sad. He is the only POW I have met who seems so sad. Tears came into his eyes as he told me he had lost everything and only had the clothes he stood up in.

WEDNESDAY, 4 FEBRUARY

Edie Rutherford

Fixed our holiday dates in the evening. As usual, Husband is last. All the rest say their dates and we get what's left. I said a piece about it as I don't *want* the last two weeks in July. However, we are obliged to have them again. So I then asked if we could book the last two weeks of August 1949 *now*. Himself received this somewhat coldly.

B. Charles

I went to Mr Adams and he has X-rayed my teeth. We discussed German POWs. It is interesting to see how 'popular' these lads have become. When I remember, about two years ago, how horrified people used to look when they saw me speaking to them in the streets, it makes me laugh. As usual I have 'set a fashion'!

THURSDAY, 5 FEBRUARY

Edie Rutherford

The top of the bus today was full of school kids. Boy about twelve said, when ticket inspector came, 'We get these things on the bus every time we use it.' Inspector turned round to the boy and said, 'Were you speaking of me?' No answer, so he added, 'I'll teach you some manners, my boy', and went on, 'You'd better stop that NOW or it'll be the worse for you, my lad', and went downstairs. Whereat the kid, private school product by the way, started repeating all that had been said by the inspector all over again, not one whit abashed.

An Austrian in these flats, who recently had six weeks in Austria with his wife, has returned quite sure the Germans are no whit chastened or wiser, only bewildered that they lost the war and determined to win the next one. This man says the Austrians are as bad. He is full of foreboding for us because he says we *won't* realise the danger and do something about it before it is too late.

Herbert Brush

Mr Ing came and talked over the fence just now. He was feeling annoyed with the butcher who had given him meat which he could not eat without great fear of breaking his new false teeth. I gave him half a dozen garlic bulbs, which he said he and his missus would eat and enjoy. I doubted it.

FRIDAY, 6 FEBRUARY

Edie Rutherford

Husband amusingly indignant that Orville Wright has left his *Kitty Hawk* to England. Asks how we'd feel if an Englishman left the USA such a thing? I said, well the old thing belonged to him to do as he liked, and no doubt he thinks more folk come to London so it is a better centre for anything so spectacular.

Friend on fifth floor has two little girls, six and three, both had injections against whooping cough, and both now have it. Doctor is shoving vaccine into the month-old baby, terrified she may catch it.

SATURDAY, 7 FEBRUARY

Edie Rutherford
My hair has had a lemon rinse today for the first time for many years and it looks the better for it too. It is a sign of better days in one direction anyway when one can use a whole lemon for such a job.

How long before one can use a raw egg shampoo without a qualm?

SUNDAY, 8 FEBRUARY

Herbert Brush
I went to the BM this morning and read in various books. When foot-and-mouth disease breaks out nowadays it is dealt with quickly, but I read today about the first time it appeared in England. It was 1275. 'A Spanish ewe brought into Northumberland by a farmer soon became rotten and infested the whole country. This plague of murrain continued for 28 years ere it ended and was the first rot that ever was in England.'

Even now we don't seem to be able to cure it, only to prevent it spreading.

TUESDAY, 10 FEBRUARY

B. Charles
I have just listened to the Eighth Mahler symphony and enjoyed it. I consider the Third Programme one of the greatest cultural events of the century. It is, probably, right to describe it as being THE cultural event of the century. It will be a national calamity if it falls through.

MONDAY, 16 FEBRUARY

Edie Rutherford
In the evening I went with other South African girls to the Gaumont to collect pennies for *Sheffield Telegraph* Poor Kids Holiday Fund. The film was *The Birth of a Baby*. Very good, everyone should see it. Four men fainted in the one and a half hours I was on duty down-stairs.

B. Charles

I heard a very sad thing this morning. ANOTHER suicide. This time it is the cashier at Lyon & Turnbull's. It seems he took poison in the office and wasn't discovered until one and a half hours later. He was such a quiet sort of chap (the last fellow one would have thought would have done such a thing) but now there are so many suicides that one gets quite used to them. I wonder if his cash is in order?

THURSDAY, 19 FEBRUARY

Herbert Brush

I hope that the doctors won't give in to Bevan, as I don't believe that a state-controlled medical service would ever be of benefit to the public as a whole; no patient would get individual service from a doctor who was not paid by the patient to the same extent as they do now.

FRIDAY, 20 FEBRUARY

George Taylor

A white world in the morning, and snowing most of the day. This was not at all welcome: memories of last year's severe weather are too vivid. No doubt the weather contributed to the absolute failure of our third student evening, this time devoted to ballet music. At starting time there was present the lecturer, the president of the WEA Branch, myself as secretary and my wife. After the lecture had been going for nearly half an hour, another student crawled in. In spite of this poor reception, the lecturer gave her talk and played her full programme of records.

Maggie Joy Blunt

I get to a state of exhaustion with this diary when I simply cannot bring myself to pen another word. There is always so much I want and mean to put down in it, but I need time.

I have been exceedingly busy trying to get book finished and have decided to type the manuscript out myself. This is for me a labour of ingratitude as I loathe typing, but I find the advantages (quite apart from saving money) outweigh the tedium. There still seems a lot to be done but manuscript is now nearly three-quarters typed and being read by various friends.

From Wednesday afternoon I have had constant hot water and permanent warmth. The new stove seems to burn less than half the quantity of fuel and will stay on all night and all day unattended if I want it to and give me constant hot water. It is amazing the difference that a really warm house can make to one's outlook on a cold day. Have yet to test out oven for cooking. Otherwise I am in heaven.

Herbert Brush
W dropped me in Peckham this morning and I changed my book for *Samuel Pepys* by A. Bryant. He was a gay old bird, when he was not hard at work on the business of the navy.

SATURDAY, 21 FEBRUARY

Maggie Joy Blunt
Weather very cold. Bought ice creams in village this morning and one for lunch and one for supper and can preserve them outside back door.

Am dallying with idea of joining Liberals.

SUNDAY, 22 FEBRUARY

B. Charles
When the German was here yesterday he said how depressing it is to see in all papers all this war talk. There is nothing else. He gave it as his opinion that the Third World War will happen in three to five years' time. I think it may easily happen earlier. He also said how much better it would be if Germany, England and America could join forces against Russia. Of course, this has been my own idea for years. He did a long time in Russia during the war and said the Russians are completely uncivilised and they are quite brutish. Many live all together in a hut of one room with their animals, and he says they never even take off their boots when they go to bed.

MONDAY, 23 FEBRUARY

Herbert Brush
I stopped to look in Foyles, and seeing that there was an exhibition of pictures on the fourth floor, free, I went up in the lift. The pictures

were done by patients in mental hospitals, and the exhibition was to encourage art, according to a pamphlet I purchased. I looked at them all and I am afraid that I shall remember some of them much longer than I want to do so. When I left there I went into the National Gallery to have a look at some of the masterpieces, just to rub out the memory of the others.

TUESDAY, 24 FEBRUARY

B. Charles
I remarked to Mr Adams this morning that he had a few icing sets in his shop. He said the traveller, who had got him to take these sets, told him he had an order for fifty thousand of them to be sent as soon as possible to Brussels! I said it seemed an enormous order, but Mr Adams assured me that the food position there is so luxurious that it isn't surprising at all! He says they have tons of sugar, cakes, fruits and meat and as for chocolates! He said a friend had brought him a box and they were the most marvellous he had ever had in his life. It seems it is the same thing in Holland and Denmark. Everything one can wish for and all at pre-war prices. Of course, all these countries had the advantage of being occupied by the Germans during the war and things were kept going in good order. Mr Adams agrees with me that this planned austerity is here for ever.

SATURDAY, 28 FEBRUARY

B. Charles
UM sent me an idiotic picture from some newspaper about this stupid woman who was televised the other night to illustrate 'Sex Appeal' in clothes. It is farcical, at such a time as this, when the word 'crisis' is dinned into our heads at all times of the day and night, to publish such a footling picture. What the BBC is thinking of to televise such a thing I can't think. As if this picture wasn't enough to show to what depths of inanity we have sunk, there was another, even sillier, in yesterday's *Daily Mirror*. This one depicted some lunatic mannequin displaying some petticoats. She looks utterly insane. If this sort of thing isn't a modern version of fiddling while Rome is burning, I don't know what it is.

About eight o'clock Davy phoned from Datchet. I heard him marvellously well.

MONDAY, 1 MARCH 1948

Edie Rutherford
At midday was very upset to have Husband slide into front door looking ghostlike. He had been involved in a street accident at 8.30 as he alighted from a tram to go to office. Had spent rest of morning at Royal Hospital, where he was X-rayed, given anti-tetanus injection and sent home with concussion, shock and bruises.

A milk lorry knocked him flying through the air, landing him heavily on his coccyx. He didn't lose consciousness or hold of the library book in his hand. I got his panel doctor who said there was nothing to be done except dope and wait for pains to subside. Meantime I crept about, doing nothing noisier than dusting.

FRIDAY, 5 MARCH

Edie Rutherford
We saw the sun for the first time for eight days. Sid not at all well, poor dear. Bought him a bottle of sherry.

SUNDAY, 7 MARCH

Maggie Joy Blunt
Cold spell: frost and snow, lasted about a fortnight. Stove behaving beautifully and a great comfort, but still no oven handle.

N has been here nearly a fortnight, following an operation. She thinks we shall have to choose soon between USSR and USA. She deplores both methods: Communist's police state realism and America's big business and commerce dictatorship. Of the two evils she would choose Communism as possibly benefiting in the long run the greater number of people. The democracies she thinks will talk and wrangle much and do nothing. She thinks there will be no war just yet. Russia does not want war and will get all she can without it. Britain will be left, an isolated and puny buffer between the two big opposing powers. America may become too occupied with Japan and South America to concern herself with Europe. A grim outlook.

Cigarettes. I seem to be smoking again as much as ever and the money I spend appals me.

Last page of this book. I have one more in stock. These Duplicate books are now practically unobtainable and I don't know what I shall do if I can get no more.

[This is Maggie Joy Blunt's last entry for 1948.]

WEDNESDAY, 10 MARCH

Edie Rutherford
Doctor came and advised Sid to get dressed and out, so in the late afternoon we got as far as library in park opposite.

George Taylor
We went for a short walk through Graves Park, which we seldom visit although it is just over the road from us. We were surprised to find so many people there. Among these we found two young urchins merrily digging up the bluebell bulbs and scattering them on the path. I accosted them in my best policeman's voice, and very grudgingly they stopped.

I made my annual visit to Chesterfield to visit a WEA class. The tutor, a new one to the WEA, Mr Mattam, was dealing with epic poetry, and there was a long discussion as to whether Longfellow ever wrote anything that could be described as epic. I was a long way out of my depth.

THURSDAY, 11 MARCH

Edie Rutherford
Went to police, found the one who came on the scene after Sid's accident, and he said the young driver admitted carelessness. Went on to lawyer who said he'd do what he could, but lack of witnesses was bad. Sid had tried to get some to admit they saw it who did see it, but not one would oblige. People are horrid.

FRIDAY, 12 MARCH

Edie Rutherford

Sid went to office and got two weeks' wages. Was told the young man who knocked him flying had called in one day to inquire how Sid was.

George Taylor

We determined to move round the furniture and our old radiogram, to make way for a Murphy console. I called in the shop at 9.30 a.m. and delivery was promised certainly today, probably this morning. This is something like service.

At 4 p.m. the new radio came, and in a few minutes the engineer had connected it. The new set brings in the Third Programme very well. The stimulus of a new set has caused me to alter the earth to a more convenient position. For fourteen years it has trailed directly from the dining room windows over a concrete path into the garden, and many times we have tripped over it.

Immediately the radio had arrived, we set off to the cinema for one of my few visits. It was a story of four generations, each of which were sacrificed to some extent for war. The plot was quite wholesome, and the acting clean.

SATURDAY, 13 MARCH

Edie Rutherford

Derby County vs Manchester United at the Wednesday ground, so the coaches in hundreds and humans in thousands went by. Sid went to see doctor and she assured him there would be no repercussions.

We had roast pork for lunch for the first time for years, as my brother in Birmingham killed poor Jimmie earlier in the week. Very nice it was too.

THURSDAY, 18 MARCH

Edie Rutherford

At the Overseas Association meeting last night I was nominated for secretary, but emphatically declined to take it on. Husband delighted.

A lady from local UN spoke on behalf of the children of Europe – I should say she SHOUTED at us. It was really terrible the way she shouted. In a hall that size her ordinary voice would have been adequate. We shuddered and exchanged looks of agony and were all glad when she left off. A collection was taken and £3 1s. contributed from about one hundred of us, which I thought not bad.

Herbert Brush

What do you think of Truman's speech last evening? He must know all the facts and judging from his words Russia fully intends to make all Europe Communistic, so it's about time something is done. We shan't survive for long if another war does start, as probably the Russians have as many atom bombs as anybody, but they don't tell anyone about it. I liked the way that Truman read his speech, just about twice as fast as the ordinary speaker and no hesitation at all.

I finished fixing a door on the dugout yesterday and gave it a coat of green paint. In the event of a third war the dugout would not be much use against atom bombs in the vicinity.

I hear that an allotmenteer whom I saw on Sunday dropped dead at a football match on Monday. He was a grumpy sort of fellow and I did not often speak to him beyond passing the time of day. He was sixty-four.

Four allotments adjoin my plots. One man is so deaf he can't hear a word I say. One man stammers and never gets beyond G-g-g-good d-d-day. One man is ruptured but can still do a lot of work in a short time. One man only comes now and then.

FRIDAY, 19 MARCH

Edie Rutherford

So the Queen calls her visit to the North a breath of fresh air. Don't make me laugh. The filth in our air takes away all the benefit we might otherwise get.

THURSDAY, 25 MARCH

Herbert Brush

If you are feeling feeble and disinclined to do digging or any kind of hard labour, take a good dose of 'Phosferene', especially if you are feeling a little thirsty, and I'm fairly sure it will pick you back up in a few minutes. I have tried it so often with good results. The other day I did not feel fit to fiddle about at all, so I took a strong dose and half an hour afterwards I shovelled a ton of sand.

GOOD FRIDAY, 26 MARCH

George Taylor
To Newcastle for the Easter holidays. My brother had recommended Herrons Hotel to us, and we found it a comfortable little place, although the plumbing needed attention. After a stroll round the town, we saw that there was a film of the Jungfrau at the News Cinema, so in we went. The film turned out to be very well produced indeed, and the neatness of Switzerland was very well caught, apart from an overfondness for the mountain horn.

Edie Rutherford
One tries hard not to be nasty to foreigners – I do anyway – but they make themselves disliked so often. We have several lots of Germans in these flats. All local shops hate the sight of them. They demand the best, unwrap each orange to see if it is as they like it, ask for more than they should, and so on. This morning one of my Communist friends who also tries hard to be internationally minded said she had occasion to go into the flat of one of these German families, and found they had been able to get furniture units, whereas she, recently having acquired her fourth baby, had almost to lie to get a few units for extra furniture. Also, these people said they'd had the chance of a prefab and laughed scornfully at the very idea of living in such a thing. This woman I spoke to would give her ears for a prefab. As a nation we are too tolerant, no doubt of that.

SUNDAY, 28 MARCH

George Taylor
Our object in visiting Newcastle was to see Hadrian's Wall, and this we did today. We had lunch actually sat on the ramparts, and it needs no imagination to people the Wall again with soldiers. We arrived back in Newcastle well in time for dinner.

Herbert Brush

[Folkestone] I read *Science News* during the evening and was much interested in an article on 'Glaciers'. A statement that if all the ice at the poles melted the level of the sea all over the world would rise 150 feet made me think a lot. There would not be much land left above water which would produce the food needed. Anyway, most of Essex and Suffolk would be under water. The least shifting of the polar axis would cause a flood which would make the biblical Flood a back number in floods.

From lunch until tea time we dozed in the lounge and then walked to the sea front and along to Butlin's Amusement Park, a huge place with every kind of amusement and every kind of gamble designed to make young and old spend money like water. I used to enjoy the Switchback, and skating and 'dodge ems' and all that kind of amusement, but now I am not likely to take any part again. W tried a gamble, taking three tickets for a mechanical device with many actors' names coming up in turn. My ticket had 'Ginger Rogers' on it, but she did not bring me any luck, neither had W or D any luck with theirs. A woman with a large family won a huge 'Teddy Bear'.

Apparently Felixstowe cannot stop Butlin from working his huge Amusement Park on Sundays.

MONDAY, 5 APRIL 1948

B. Charles

This midday brought a letter and a birthday card from Heinz. He asks me if I can send some insulin for his mother. I have phoned Boots and have written him to ask if it is forty or eighty units cc he needs. It is sad to think he can't get the thing in Hamburg.

When I saw the huge queue, and all the muddle as well, for the tickets for the [second Edinburgh] Festival, I just gave up all idea of getting tickets today. During the afternoon Dr Bailey phoned. He is coming to see me on Thursday morning at 11 a.m. I shall be glad to meet him. He sounded quite nice on the phone. I asked him about the Festival tickets and if he knew of any way of getting them without all the fuss and bother of queuing. He didn't. He added he thought it would, in all probability, be far easier to get them in London.

TUESDAY, 6 APRIL

George Taylor

The budget has not turned out too bad for me personally. The increased rate and maximum of earned income relief will help me, while the higher tobacco and beer tax will leave me quite unaffected. The relief in income tax will just about pay for the holiday abroad for my wife and myself, and I am duly grateful.

WEDNESDAY, 7 APRIL

Herbert Brush

What do you think of the budget? There are many worried, well-off people in England today. I can't foresee the final result when everyone is reduced to hand-to-mouth existence, but I don't think it will be pleasant for anyone except the crooks who are clever enough to beat the law. And yet we (they) encourage the filling of perambulators. Presently we shall need a special footpath for nurse girls or mothers who take up the whole pavement nowadays when they walk about.

Edie Rutherford

Nice budget. Cares for the poor and mulcts the rich. Suits me, but I bet plenty of folk are howling, and Churchill will find plenty to say in the House.

Post has brought me a beautiful box of Easter candies from Texas. I have never seen anything more beautiful; four layers of mints, all in flower designs, spring blooms, except some plain ones with letters spelling out HAPPY EASTER. Oh so posh.

Husband still enduring effects of his accident: fatigue, aches and insomnia. Patience seems the only remedy. He went back to work too soon, and unfortunately it is adversely affecting his damages claim.

George Taylor

Once more my birthday has rolled round, but I do not greet it with the exuberance which I did formerly. I do not like to think that I am near the fifty mark, but both physically and mentally I have to admit that I have passed the first flush of youth. I was quite surprised to receive no present at all from my brother and his family. They usually remember me.

THURSDAY, 8 APRIL

George Taylor

Once more I have decided to plunge. As the purchase tax on radios and musical instruments has increased, I decided to buy a record player for my new radio before the increased tax is charged by the shops. No sooner determined than done, and I called in this afternoon and bought an HMV player for £14 4s. 11d.

FRIDAY, 9 APRIL

Edie Rutherford

There was a to-do in tripe queue this morn. It appears some half-dozen women and one man stood in two doorways across the street, and when a queue started to form outside the tripe shop, they came and headed it. Instant and voluble protest, but they stood their ground. That tripe queue is the most unreliable ever. Women keep dodging out to 'just go to pikelet shop', run over t'fish shop, just fetch us eggs and so on, so that when one joins it, it may seem twenty strong, but when all the missing women return there are thirty ahead of me.

Complaints in tripe queue that we are worse off for food than in wartime. That was behind me. In front the conversation was on husbands and their loafing ways. Radio Doctor started it by saying on air this morn that according to recent investigations old men die first, and that they idle more than women who live longer. Every woman agreed. Me too.

George Taylor

In the afternoon I sat out in the garden in a deck chair for the first time this year. It is always a welcome occasion when I can do this, for nothing suits me better than to bask in the sun.

The record player arrived, so I spent the evening fixing it up and trying out my records. The pick-up is very light and should not scratch the records, and the tone through the radio set is very good. I think the player will be an acquisition, although like the old radiogram, I suppose that we shall use it only infrequently, mainly when we have visitors.

SATURDAY, 10 APRIL

George Taylor

My wife's birthday today, quickly following my own. She received a parcel from my brother's family, and found a present in it for me also, a record album. So I was not forgotten after all.

B. Charles

I forgot to record my impressions of Sherwin Bailey, who called the other morning. Like all parsons, so far as my knowledge of them goes, he is quite out of touch with what I call reality. He is very 'serious'. Of course, he tries to be very 'broadminded' (as so many people do) but I fancy it would be extremely easy to shock him, even by making the most innocuous statements. On the whole I prefer the old-fashioned type of cleric not in favour of all this modern 'broadmindedness'. It gets you nowhere.

Herbert Brush

I met Mr Ing in the road and as usual we talked, or rather I should say he talked and I listened with a word now and then to keep him going. Small children are his pet aversion just now, but he does not call them children, but b**g*rs. There is a woman in his street who has eight small children and is just having another, 40/- a week out of tax payers' money, and with all those cards they can get everything they want and the little bgrs get free milk. In their spare time they pull bits out of his garden fence for firewood. I sympathised with him on that because they seem to be making a start on our fence, after I so carefully did it last year.

TUESDAY, 13 APRIL

George Taylor

We went to see one of Priestley's plays, *An Inspector Calls*, at the Rep but did not like it at all. As usual with Priestley, sentiment is laid on thick and a whole group of people are each held individually responsible for the suicide, told times over in great and sordid detail, of a girl who was at once a strike leader, an impolite shop assistant, a pub crawler, and a prostitute. Priestley also brought in his pet theory of time reversal as well. No, I cross Priestley off my list.

B. Charles

This morning I came across the worst piece of racketeering I have yet discovered. In my grocer's they are selling tea seed oil for 16/- for 20 fluid ounces. This is exactly double the price Boots are charging. I went to Boots and reported what I had discovered. It is the same everywhere: the whole of life, now, is one long racket. It has debauched all classes of the community and is, I think, the most alarming feature of post-war life. I have written to the paper about this tea seed oil racket, but doubt if they publish it.

WEDNESDAY, 14 APRIL

B. Charles

I heard an unfortunate piece of news today. Miss Finlay has sold her house and bought a flat in Rothsay Terrace. I expect her house will be turned into these horrid flats. It is odd indeed how flats seem to attract the very worst type of people. Ex-prostitutes and racketeers. It is most unfortunate how Chester Street has gone down, even since I have been there! I expect, if I were to sell this place, that I should get my money back, but in a few years' time, I begin to think, I should lose on it.

THURSDAY, 15 APRIL

Edie Rutherford

Provided the Lords let it through, there won't be hanging in England for the next five years. Well, I dunno. One part of me hates it; another part of me says it is just. It is one of those things about which I cannot be clear-cut and I envy those who can.

I was disappointed in Mrs Roosevelt in *Woman's Hour* yesterday. She had a laugh in her voice at times when no laugh was suitable. I once again got that idea I get when women high-ups speak; they just have no idea at all of the viewpoint of the average woman. They try hard, but it is so far from them that it beats them.

Herbert Brush

So we have abolished capital punishment by a small majority, and the hangman is out of a job, without notice, so I suppose he will get a pension. We tax payers will have to pay for the keep of many murderers for many years at the cost of many pounds per annum per murderer, as they are sure to be expensive boarders as they will require extra care. Now, if a man wants free board and lodging for life he will only have to take the life of somebody else. I wonder how many more idiotic things this Government will be able to do before they are thrown out, with the curses of the country ringing in their ears. A good many, I'm afraid.

SATURDAY, 17 APRIL

Edie Rutherford
Combs I bought week before last proved as dud as any. One broke after four days, and the other five days later. Now I have one bought at a local shop which from feel and sound has metal in it. So far, after eight days, it is whole, so I'm hoping. Clever guys all too busy making atom bombs and such to make a simple thing like a good strong comb.

George Taylor
All our party of twenty-four arrived by the stipulated time for the trip to London, so we got them nicely settled in our reserved seats in the *Master Cutler* before the starting time of 7.40 a.m. The train is just an ordinary corridor train, not too clean, and certainly not new, which has been christened, and so made popular.

Mr Coleman had arranged to show the party Unknown London, and he was on the spot dead on time. Our first port of call was the Soane Museum, and the Pictures Room, with the walls hinged like the leaves of an album, was certainly a curiosity which none of us had seen before. From Soane we had a glance at Covent Garden, and the church there with the ashes of a famous actress, and so to the Temple for a look over the ruins. And so to Collins Music Hall, whose fame rests more in history than in its present-day performance. Now it is somewhat of a dismal theatre, and the entrance does little to dispel the gloom. The show, *Bearskins and Blushes*, included many bearskins, no blushes, but plenty of life and a very rude kind of wit. The audience were certainly appreciative, but the casual way in which people came and went during the performance was irritating.

SUNDAY, 18 APRIL

George Taylor
We set off at 9.30 a.m. for a look at the City, the remains of the Wall, and from there we went over to Southwark Cathedral and had a look at the site of Shakespeare's Globe Theatre on Bankside, commemorated by the LCC with a plaque erected on the wrong side of the road according to our guide. Then we had a rapid glance at the old George Inn with its balconies from which plays were viewed in the days of long ago, and due to the insistence of members of the party we called at Petticoat Lane, although we were warned repeatedly that our timetable did not allow for it. Then we took the tube to Wapping, wound our way through high and depressing warehouses along the High Street to the old inn, the Prospect of Whitby. Our lunch was to be served in the Cabin, an upstairs room, with a bow window and balcony overlooking the Thames, a room in which Pepys is supposed to have written much of his diary. I don't think Pepys would have thought much of the service today.

TUESDAY, 20 APRIL

Edie Rutherford
Post this morn has brought us a large piece of home-cured ham from my brother's late lamented pig, James. Weighs nearly 6lb. and I think my brother said the cost would be 4/6d. per lb. Whew. However, it is something we shall eat and probably share with others. Better to pay for something we eat and enjoy than something we can't eat and throw out, as, for instance, last Sunday's veal. It was so stringy, dry and tasteless that we left it all and dog on first floor had it.

WEDNESDAY, 21 APRIL

Herbert Brush
Yesterday I began to creosote the garden fence, but the brush is worn out and the hairs come out at every stroke so I did not do much.

The people next door (Goebells) have turned their home into two flats and the people are moving in. This was just after I had fixed a piece of old trellis on top of the fence between us, so they will probably think I did it to obstruct their view, but that was not the case as the trellis had been lying ready to be fixed for the last month or more.

George Taylor
To Birmingham for an annual pawnbroker's stock audit. We finished the audit satisfactorily in the afternoon, then all made our way to the Theatre Royal for one of the worst shows I have ever seen. The performance opened with a male chorus in a squirming dance, more dances followed, male and female. There was tap-dancing until one's ears ached with the noise, some wretched singing, an attempt at humour which did not come off, all hung together with a ridiculous thread about a service canteen in America. Fortunately the second part was short, and at any rate we had good seats.

FRIDAY, 23 APRIL

George Taylor
Seven hundred and fifty copies of our WEA Syllabus had been circulated advertising, among other events, the visit of the Danish Assistant General Secretary. Only eight members thought it worth-while to attend, however, but those eight were rewarded with a very interesting talk on the Danish High Schools. Still more interesting was to have a chat with Mr Hauerslev afterwards. His opinion of English hotels was pretty poor, and cafés, too, surprised him. In Denmark only a few begin to close at midnight, and the better ones carry on till one or two in the morning. Here in Sheffield, we had difficulty in finding him one open at 9.30 p.m., and he did not want to return to his hotel for supper, as it 'stank'.

WEDNESDAY, 28 APRIL

George Taylor
At a dye manufacturer's annual meeting. They tell me that the demand for dyes has fallen off considerably. Perhaps people are expecting to be able to buy new goods, and are getting tired of make do and mend.

I treated myself to a Rachmaninov concerto on four records, and enjoyed quite a concert with my wife this evening.

Herbert Brush

> Sometimes I feel that I am growing old,
> No doctor's medicine is of use to me,
> However warm the weather, I feel cold,
> So different from the man I used to be.
> Time passes quicker now with every year
> It seems to make me need for longer rest,
> A violent exertion makes me queer
> And rouses thoughts that I am going West.

THURSDAY, 29 APRIL

Herbert Brush

> When I have a morbid feeling on me
> Nothing seems to matter very much,
> Everything is black or drab before me
> Things are never pleasant to the touch.
> Weather is a factor that's important,
> Nearly always when it pours with rain
> Comfortless it makes my ancient body
> Which in turn will soon disturb my brain
> Making many thoughts which are just idle
> Wonder through the convolutions there.
> Making me attempt to find an answer.
> Problem, why I'm living anywhere.

How do you like the rhythm?

SATURDAY, 1 MAY 1948

George Taylor

After an absence of several months, we visited my brother at Totley again. My wife thinks that our reception was very cool, especially from my sister-in-law. The reason is probably that we have been spending money pretty freely on the house lately, and there is a note of envy. It is a pity, particularly as I do not think that we brag about what we are doing, and in any case, what is the use of a bigger income if it is not spent on improving conditions?

TUESDAY, 4 MAY

Edie Rutherford
What horrible people there are in the world. And what stupid ones, indeed insane – to order a house to be demolished because the man who built it didn't get all the permits we require in these silly times. I hope workmen continue to refuse to demolish. Any man these days who builds a house, especially if he keeps the bedridden mother-in-law as well as his own family, as in this case, should get a medal plus a cash bonus.

Shall curry remainder of rabbit for this evening. Strange that in a cold climate like this curry isn't popular.

WEDNESDAY, 5 MAY

B. Charles
A letter from Bobby enclosing a very interesting account of a book by an American: Dr Kinsey on *Sexual Behaviour in the Human Male*. This is a book of case histories of American men. He says that at least 37 per cent have some homosexual experience between adolescence and old age. I should think the percentage is a good deal higher. It seems odd indeed to read this account of his, and then read the report of Lord Goddard's speech the other day in which he brackets together fraudulent solicitors, 'fences', and homosexuals! The Yankee seems to think homosexuality a perfectly ordinary sort of thing, yet this old fool of a lawyer thinks that it is a heinous crime! I just can't figure out WHY homosexuality is, in many people's idea, a heinous crime.

THURSDAY, 6 MAY

George Taylor
[On the annual fishmonger's audit in Hastings.] By way of a change I visited the Ideal Homes exhibition on the pier in the evening. There were the usual gadgets for the kitchen, demonstrated by a voluble manipulator of a slab of pastry. I wonder how many times that was rolled and rerolled: I should not like to eat anything made out of it. Exhibits of plastic-leather-cloth-covered suites and furniture veneers also were very attractive to me.

FRIDAY, 7 MAY

Herbert Brush

Mass-Observation asks their members to say what their feelings are about the manners and morals and customs of the younger generation today (those born after 1918) and how they compare with those of the older generation. My own opinion is that they are very much worse in every way. Judging by the ones I come across, they have no manners at all, which may be due to a lack of control by their parents, but from whatever cause, London children are absolutely crafty little liars and clever thieves, and think only of what they can do for themselves: when they get beyond childhood, their parents and other elderly people should be done away with to make way for the rising generation.

TUESDAY, 11 MAY

Edie Rutherford

I've just curried two chops and only hope Himself won't come home saying he can't eat anything because he is so hot.

Husband has decided to buy a two-piece suit. Asked me to have a look-see in town today. Can get any price from £5 up and the look of them improves with the price of them. He has decided to buy a ready-made for the first time ever, as he knows several men who've done this lately and successfully.

Jolly good idea to put dots on knee of nylon stockings so that a woman can see when seam is straight. Good old British brain active. Bet the Americans copy the idea.

SATURDAY, 15 MAY

B. Charles

I feel sorry for all the nursing staff at the Blackburn Hospital where this little girl was kidnapped and later found murdered. I fear they will all get terribly 'told off' and I am sure it was just bad luck that the dreadful thing happened. It seems almost impossible for a person to walk into the children's ward in the middle of the night and kidnap a patient. I expect the night sister must have been either dozing or away for a few minutes. I feel certain a ward of children is never left in the middle of the night unless there is some extremely good reason.

SUNDAY, 16 MAY

George Taylor

Attended a lecture in the evening by a biologist, Mr Packington, who spoke of the Future of Mankind. He thought that all major evolutionary trends had come to an end, and that the organic evolution of man in society was now the important thing, and he was optimistic that man would be successful.

WEDNESDAY, 19 MAY

B. Charles

I had a very interesting conversation with a man from the Control Commission in Germany this morning. In his opinion, Hitler is still immensely popular, and he says this is not surprising when you think of all the good he did to the German people during the short time he was in power. This man thinks British prestige has gone down awfully since the end of the war. It seems all the stories we heard about the concentration camps in Germany were almost all true. But the only people in these camps were Jews and political prisoners. We both agreed that the Jews should be exterminated and that the political prisoners were just fools. It seems about 5,000,000 Jews were killed in Germany alone.

THURSDAY, 20 MAY

Edie Rutherford

Husband returned to work yesterday. Lawyer rang up and he went to collect a cheque for £50 as damages for his accident. We didn't have to pay lawyer or doctor, but income tax will take its haul. Sid says he'd rather not have had the accident or the £50.

Another railway accident. How can heat have buckled rails? According to that explanation hot countries would be having railway accidents daily. No, my private investigations show that our engines are old and in bad repair, and when drivers put them in for repair stating what is wrong, a busybody decides if they are right and says what is to be repaired. Then when the drivers get them again they find the old faults still there. I'm told they are all furious about it.

FRIDAY, 21 MAY

Edie Rutherford
Chief topic of conversation in tripe queue this morn was indignation that where coupons are abolished or reduced, prices have jumped, and shopkeepers quite unashamed in admitting it. Went on to other topics and the fact that there is so much more cancer than there used to be was agreed. As usual, food was blamed.

SATURDAY, 29 MAY

Edie Rutherford
When the 9 p.m. news came with news that Standerton had not returned Smuts in the SA election, I was stunned.

Friday morn we had the 7 a.m. headlines on just after we got up and I could have burst into tears when I heard that Malan & Co. were on top. What on earth is the matter with my beloved country? What did we fight the war for if a Dominion on a free vote can put Nazi lovers into power like that? Have they gone mad? Were the British apathetic about registering their votes? The poor nigs, they will be very downcast, far worse for them than the British whites. Husband predicts civil war. I hope not, though the stage is set for it, I admit.

SUNDAY, 6 JUNE 1948

Herbert Brush
I went to the plot this morning and saw that jays had paid another visit to my peas despite the cotton and the scraps of paper I used hoping to scare them off. An old man told me that he had seen 'three b***dy great jays in my peas having a fine time'. As they have taken all the full pea pods, I pulled up the peas and cleared the ground and hope that the jays will be very disappointed when they arrive for breakfast tomorrow morning. I would like to see those jays when they arrive and find only a bare patch of ground.

WEDNESDAY, 9 JUNE

George Taylor

We had a meeting of the WEA District Executive. After the meeting I went along to one of our tutors, a blind man, for the evening. His secretary was busy painting posters for his classes, whether by design or accident I did not learn, and during the evening I was introduced to his wife, his twelve-year-old daughter, an Indian medical student, another Indian at the university, a blind organist, and a dog.

Mr Kaulfuss, the tutor, showed me a new gramophone he has which plays records of complete novels. Each side of the record takes half an hour to play, and he can get quite a collection of records.

SATURDAY, 12 JUNE

B. Charles

About three o'clock Davy Brown arrived with a young friend. After tea we went for a stroll and saw a lot of the Camerons walking about in kilts. These conscripts look awfully shoddy and 'slack'. Two of them were walking along Princes Street each wearing different sorts of stockings with ordinary civilian shoes. They looked dreadful. The kilts hung badly and their battledress tunics were all rucked up.

We went into the Black Bull and it was interesting to see once more a real 'rough house'. I had no idea such pubs existed now. The place was packed with all sorts of servicemen and civvies with a good sprinkling of prostitutes.

When we came out we looked into Rutherfords, which was very well conducted, though there were a certain number of sailors there. With beer the price it is, I can't think soldiers and sailors can afford to go boozing more than twice a week. I didn't see one man drunk. Of course, now with the beer just coloured water it is almost impossible to get drunk.

TUESDAY, 15 JUNE

Herbert Brush

I went to the plot this morning. I am keeping a watch for the Colorado beetle, but hope that I shall never see one. They seem to be travelling around like locusts, judging by the newspapers. One more example of our own blessing is the English Channel, as they don't seem to be able to fly the whole distance, though apparently they don't drown if they fall into the sea; maybe the dead ones float and the others climb on to the dead bodies until they are washed ashore.

B. Charles

I see the Procurator Fiscal of Edinburgh has been fined £25 for a 'peeping Tom' offence in Spottiswood Road. He is fifty-two (the 'dangerous' age), married with two grown-up children. So many of these ultra-responsible men when they get to this age 'break out'. Either with little girls or in such a way as this. He must have been a fool. It is sad for him, really, and *very* sad for his family.

WEDNESDAY, 16 JUNE

Edie Rutherford

Husband reports that one of their customers works for the local corporation and when in yesterday to buy timber said that on one of the estates twelve lavatory seats were needed all at once. The inspector was told to look into it and discovered the tenants have turned the seats into picture frames in some cases, and mirrors in others.

As expected, immigration into South Africa is to be curtailed.

THURSDAY, 12 JUNE

B. Charles

During the afternoon I had occasion to go and see Davidson and he asked me if I thought men convicted of homosexual offences were 'mental'. He couldn't understand why so many apparently brilliant men were given to these practices. I said I did not consider homosexual practices necessarily meant the person was mentally deficient. Quite the reverse. He then went on to say a police inspector had told him there was a tremendous lot of homosexuality in Edinburgh and that the police could lay their hands on any number of male homosexuals whenever they liked, and that they did not consider the punishment for male homosexuality anything like severe enough. This inspector said, 'It had a most appalling effect' on young fellows. One sometimes imagines that nearly every male has had at least ONE homosexual adventure during his life. If this is so, it is difficult to think it has 'an appalling effect' on everyone.

I thought the concert last night was very good indeed. It is interesting to note the immense popularity of Tchaikovsky today.

SUNDAY, 20 JUNE

Edie Rutherford
The dock strike has gone on too long. We just can't afford such luxuries at this juncture. Somehow I can't find much sympathy for them, though, as usual, one doesn't seem to be able to hear both sides of the case. Why can't the matter be settled quickly? How can all those food ships be left indefinitely?

Husband keeps reiterating that this Government is silly to force on nationalisation, and seems quite unable to see that it is the foundation stone of Socialism; you can't have it without nationalisation. I am against nationalisation because no one can make a decision. Imagine returning a gift of sweets to the USA which was sent for some children because it weighed 2lb. more than the regulation allows. Why could not someone with some sense step in and say, 'Rubbish, let the kids have the sweets and mind you remember to thank the givers nicely.'

FRIDAY, 25 JUNE

Edie Rutherford
Thank goodness Palestine no longer hits the headlines. Even the dock strike now takes second place to Berlin [the Airlift began the day before]. What game are the Russians really playing? Obviously not the one we, the French and the USA are playing.

B. Charles
I had a letter from Heinz. Things seem to be moving to some sort of climax in Germany. He writes that as he is young he can make a fresh start, but 'it will be terrible for the old people'. It is hard, indeed, to predict what will happen in Germany. It looks as if the Allies will be obliged to clear out of Berlin and leave it to the Russians.

SUNDAY, 27 JUNE

Edie Rutherford
Let's note down these two prophecies: yesterday Churchill said he is positive Tories will win the 1950 election; Morrison said he was sure the Socialists will win it. They can't both be right. Both speeches were in public and both men ought to word things more carefully than that if they want to spare themselves the knocks that inevitably follow when one is proved wrong by events.

MONDAY, 28 JUNE

Herbert Brush
I went to the BM. I had a seat in front on the bus and during the journey two people had moved to other seats rather than sit on the same seat with me. The third one was a little vinegary-faced woman who looked at me sourly and showed clearly that she wanted half the seat. I looked out the window and took no notice, but she kept on pushing.

TUESDAY, 29 JUNE

B. Charles
Morton has arrived. He is, in very truth, a crashing bore. It seems he is threatened with diabetes. He eats enormously, drinks likewise, and seems to me to be thoroughly unhealthy. He went to sleep for most of the afternoon, which enabled me to get a lot of correspondence attended to.

I took him to the Bon Accord for our evening meal. Quite the best mixed grill I have had since the war. During the morning we went round to various antique shops and to several views. Morton's knowledge is infinitesimal. In fact, really he doesn't know one side of a chair from the other.

WEDNESDAY, 30 JUNE

B. Charles
This morning I had difficulty in getting a taxi to take him to the station. After he had gone I noticed he had broken off the large hand on the Thuret clock in the study. He never said a word about having done this.

Edie Rutherford

Thank goodness Mr Attlee's broadcast brought the dockers to their senses. I wonder how long it will take to clear the accumulation of work.

I have a telegram from my old friend Eileen to say she'll be here tomorrow [from South Africa], either road or rail, she doesn't know yet, 'Expect me when you see me.' Well, there is only one coach a day and if she is on it I will meet her in Blonk Street, where she is set down. Her room is all ready and so am I.

FRIDAY, 2 JULY 1948

B. Charles

I have been interested in buying a new pair of braces. I went to Binn's yesterday and they wanted 10/6d. for a rubbishy pair. I just walked out. This morning I got a pair of utility ones for 2/- and they are far better. It is far better to get utility clothes instead of buying the things that are not controlled. It is idle to pretend things would be better if all controls were removed. It would be impossible for ordinary people to live at all. I doubt if many controls ever come off. The war seems to have inaugurated such a collapse of commercial morality that controls will just have to stay.

SATURDAY, 3 JULY

Herbert Brush

Horace Bacon came last night and is staying a few days. He suggested that we should go to see *Oliver Twist* at the Marble Arch Odeon. The picture was very good, but we were rather nearer to the screen than I like to be. We went in near the end of the film, when Bill Sykes was murdering Nancy, so we saw part of the film twice. Fagin had such a long nose that I was all the time trying to see the join on his face, but if it was a false nose it was so well done that I could not see the join, even though I was so close to the screen.

MONDAY, 5 JULY

George Taylor

My neighbour, a garage proprietor, has decided to erect a workshop right up against my boundary fence, and include four windows in the building. So I have had to take up my rights, and consulted today a solicitor about them. I am sorry if it will cause any unpleasantness between neighbours, but I must preserve my right of light, and abate the nuisance as much as possible.

Our board meeting today was again cut short because the chairman wished to attend a cricket match in the afternoon. I wish there were a match each week.

WEDNESDAY, 7 JULY

Edie Rutherford

The whirlwind has gone. My friend arrived at lunchtime last Thursday. Since I last saw her fifteen years ago, Eileen has changed and not for the better. All the hard knocks life has dealt her have not put sense into her head. She still lives in a world far removed from reality. Won't see things as they are. I feel so sorry for her. She actually says she envies me and how lucky I am, so I pointed out that my life hasn't been flowers, flowers all the way. It was nice to see her, but I'm glad my life and hers are not closely associated any longer. She calls me a child, but in many ways I am an adult to her.

Now I am preparing for our holiday as we go a week tomorrow to Whitley Bay and, as always, there is heaps to do. Husband is taking his Panama hat, I my winter coat. One of us ought to be right.

Epilogue

Edie and her husband enjoyed their holiday, which they spent mostly with a couple called the Kitchens, and a nameless fat aunt whom Himself spent much time avoiding. At the end of the pier they saw a show with the comedian Maurice Colleano and a man who kept hitting a seal on his nose for laughs.

When she returned on 28 July, the Welfare State was three weeks old. She talked about the NHS with a man who came to repair her gas lighter; he reckoned the doctors would try harder to keep people well, as they were now being paid if people were well or not.

The Olympic Games in London was opened by King George VI on 29 July, but for some the impact was minimal. Edie Rutherford made no mention of it, but spent the day catching up on washing. ('I LOATHE housework,' she announced a few days later.) On the food front, the most significant new arrival was beaver meat, which she said reminded her of grey owl; at 2/6d. per lb she decided against it.

Edie continued to pledge her support to Attlee's sweeping reforms, and her conviction grew stronger the more her neighbours complained. The Prime Minister held on to power with a majority of five seats at the election of February 1950. His manifesto was entitled 'Let Us Win Through Together', and campaigned for further unity and nationalisation (sugar, cement). He was still clinging on as she wrote her final (surviving) diary entries in December 1950 at the age of forty-eight. In her last three pages she was not in optimistic mood: 'Just as we begin to get a Christmas which looks a little less like austerity, the menace of war clouds over our world again.'

The Cold War darkened everything, but there were other conflicts and inequalities on her mind. 'The Korean War goes on, and the Queen says she had a very sad day because her horse was killed racing yesterday . . .' The previous month she noted: 'I have concluded that I shall never live long enough now to read all the books I want to read and do all the things I'd like to do whilst in this phase of existence.'

She went out to lunch more often, despite the freezing weather. Petrol and clothing rationing had been lifted, but remained on many food items. 'We had the usual Christmas Day,' she writes at the end of 1950. 'No one called and we went nowhere, Husband to nearest pub, me at home all day. Didn't have a bird. Were satisfied with small tin ham.' Other parts of the country had suffered power cuts, but not Sheffield. 'Well, I wonder what 1951 has in store?' she asks on her final page. 'More war? Bigger war?' She received more than eighty Christmas cards that year, 'and lovelier gifts than ever we have had'.

* * *

George Taylor remarked upon the special Olympic Games flags when he arrived with his wife and some friends at Liverpool Street on their way to an Esperanto conference in Malmo at the end of July 1948. He was happy to get away, although unsettled by his inability to buy tea and cakes from a station platform on his way through Holland. Things improved a little in Germany: 'At Hamburg a party of German Esperantists were waiting to greet us, and for a quarter of an hour there was a buzz of conversation, although for much of the time I was chasing up and down the platform in my slippers trying to fill a bottle with water.' He had a high time at the conference, where he was able to mix with many like-minded souls. Even the social events went well – not too much alcohol. At the party following the opening ceremony he met four Swedes looking for foreign contacts. They passed the time drinking lemonade and eating hot sausages. His wife was wearing a home-made dress she had constructed from material brought back from Switzerland the year before.

In June 1951, George Taylor took part in what is traditionally regarded as the watershed between austere post-war Britain and a bright modern age: the Festival of Britain. He visited with some Esperantists from Sweden and his wife, whom he had begun to refer to in his diaries as Ida. They found large queues. 'I had intended on making our first destination the Dome of Discovery, but on the announcement that there were seats in the Telekinema, changed our plans and went there. This was really a success, for we secured good seats, and even though the television programme was of very little interest, and bad technically, the stereoscopic films were really well worth seeing. After a little wait we secured seats at the Polar Theatre, but this was a disappointment, the dogs being only used to bring in a sledge and nothing else.' They then raced through the pavilions, but found them of only medium interest. 'The Seaside a complete failure, and the Transport fair.' In the following days, the Taylors accompanied their guests on a swift tour of other sights, including Hampton Court and the Tower of London. After a trip to Kew they returned by underground, primarily to see the double escalator at Holborn Station.

A few months later, in the general election of October 1951, the Taylors helped to return Winston Churchill and the Conservatives. For his fifty-second birthday he was given Churchill's *The Gathering Storm*, and he found many modern-day parallels.

George maintained his diary until June 1965, by which time he was sixty-three. The world had been transformed, but the revolution did not appear to have had a great impact on his own life. He still lived in Sheffield, still worked tirelessly and usually thanklessly for the WEA, and he was nearing retirement from his accountancy practice. He had a new Pentax camera, and a television on which he watched cookery programmes.

In January 1965 the decorators had been in again. On 24 January 1965 he wrote: 'We spent the morning moving furniture and carpets. At lunchtime we heard of the death of Churchill. The 7.30 a.m. news we heard was not very cheerful, but we did not realise the end was so near.' The following week he watched his funeral on the BBC. 'With Sir Winston the last of the great statesmen disappears, and there seems no one else to replace him. [Alec Douglas-] Home seems a very colourless substitute, and Wilson a crafty schemer.'

On 20 March 1965 he visited the Ideal Homes exhibition at Olympia, and found it packed and very difficult to see the exhibits. 'It was just impossible! Thinking that the Food Gallery might be a bit quieter, I made my way up the depressingly ugly stone stairs, but on the gallery it was no better. I decided that I had had enough, so I made my way out. This was not as easy as it seems . . .'

He travelled back home on a coach from Victoria station. The M1, opened six years before, was busy. At the service station, he 'was horrified to learn that tea was only being served in cardboard cartons'.

His wife registered his death in Sheffield in April 1974, at the age of seventy-three.

* * *

Mr Charles did not go on holiday in the summer of 1948, but he had many people holidaying with him. A couple called Peter and Jess visited after staying at an unnamed Butlin's, where the food consisted of much poultry and game. Mr Charles was pleased to think that the new holiday camps were having an adverse effect on seaside land-ladies, whom he had always distrusted. He was still having trouble with the Hows upstairs, but the recent purchase of a pair of stools from Dowell's had cheered him up. And he was thrilled when Peter and Jess offered to pay for them. 'MOST thoughtful.'

In March 1949, Mr Charles mentioned 'ever increasing business' for his failure to maintain regular diary entries. His life continued as before – some fine concerts, much disillusion with young people. He mentioned a priest who had been extradited from Ireland for homo-sexual practices, and was more sure than ever that Communism would soon engulf Great Britain. He got some almost-bargains in the sales.

At the beginning of the month he learned that his friend UM was in a nursing home, and he doubted whether he would ever come out. He received many visitors in the following weeks, including familiar friends Jimmy Paterson and Mr Durie, and a call from a new lad called Gavin. He was delighted that Hein remembered his birthday.

On 30 April, his final entry, he wrote: 'These [last] five days have been so utterly crowded with all sorts of domestic things that I just do not have time to get anything entered. There has been nothing of consequence to relate, just domestic matters.'

Meanwhile, DDT played a large part in the eradication of malaria in developed nations, but was then banned for its high toxicity; its influence on furniture remains uncertain. Hollywood movies con-tinued to corrupt the nation, and Antoine the hairdresser enlarged his reputation throughout California. To this day, the University of Edinburgh has no chair in Mr Charles's name for the study of homosexuality.

* * *

Herbert Brush spent most of March 1951, his last recorded month, on his watery plot, growing a little garlic for the pleasure of it; he still didn't know anyone who liked it. There was an incident with a garden gate: 'There was a gale blowing and while creosoting the post I got a speck into my left eye and had to retire quickly and wash it out in warm water.' As he was creosoting, Mr Ing dropped by to admire his work, 'and told me about a friend who had just bought a new bath'.

He still exchanged his books frequently at Boots, and his last subjects of study at the British Museum were Cromwell and Venice. He weighed himself in Woolworth's, and was concerned to find that he was now over 16 stone. He read that a brown duck had recently fallen among the pigeons in Trafalgar Square and had broken its leg. Someone dialled 999 and the duck was taken away in a police van to the RSPCA. 'I wonder, would that have happened in any other country?'

He observed a modern phenomenon. 'I was waiting to get on a bus in Charing Cross Road when I noticed next to me a person I thought was a man, but seeing her ankles and her shoes I thought she was a woman. He, or she, got on the bus and I caught a glimpse of her face, which looked like a gaunt old woman, but she asked for a ticket in a man's voice. Her hat was pulled down over her face and looked like the bonnet of a woman, and she glared angrily at me when she saw I was looking. I wonder what she is, a man or a woman?'

And he remarked upon new social changes. 'What a lot of black fellows are about nowadays, and all of them dressed in well-cut clothes and almost looking like dandies of a modern brand. I saw one run today and I never saw better action of arms and legs. I was on a tram going at about fifteen miles an hour and he was on the pavement keeping pace with the tram for maybe 60 or 70 yards. The pavement was clear for a distance and he did not have to dodge any traffic and I watched him with admiration all the time and wished I could run like that. Then the tram accelerated and I lost sight of him.'

At the age of seventy-eight he still paid monthly visits to his bank manager, who certified he was very much still alive. His last entries bring forth new poetry; the muse is with him once more, but she is unusually vague.

I wonder, can I write some verse
To pass the time away.
It's possible, I can't do worse,
I think, some folk would say,
But while I have no work to do
I'll try to think of something new
It's curious that thoughts won't come
When I sit down to write
I feel quite sure there must be some
If I could start one right.

'A finch was chirping quite nicely in the garden this morning,' Herbert writes for his last entry. 'I have not heard that song for a long time and it somehow reminded me of my youth.' W registered his passing at King's College Hospital in Denmark Hill in February 1959 at the age of eighty-six.

* * *

At the beginning of 1950, Maggie Joy Blunt was still living alone. She had become secretary of her local Liberal Party, and was heavily involved with canvassing and fundraising. But she was not optimistic about their chances in the next election, and rightly so: the Liberals suffered a disaster, winning only nine seats and losing more than three hundred deposits.

In April 1950, Maggie Joy was still concerned about her finances, but she managed regular excursions to the theatre and lunches at a Lyons Tea Shop. She observed that her guests from abroad noticed many more goods in the shops than when they last visited a few months before.

On 10 May 1950 she wrote of the immense work she was doing organising the stalls and advertising for a local jumble sale. 'I feel my only way out of it all would be to stage a nice nervous breakdown.' Her last entry was headed simply Summer 1950. 'We went ahead with the jumble sale and made a clear £20 profit. At the same time I had visitors, and life was very hectic. By mid-July I was really ill and found to have anaemia badly – ordered two months' complete rest and to cut down work to a minimum. Much regret that I cannot find time at present to continue this diary. MJB.'

She lived for a further thirty-six years, until the age of seventy-five. On her death certificate her occupation was listed as Book Shop Proprietress. She was unmarried. There is no record of her eighteenth-century biography at the British Library.

* * *

The first phase of Mass-Observation was effectively over when Maggie Joy Blunt despatched her last entry. It had by far exceeded the ambitions and life expectancy of its founders. The vast amount of material was transferred to the University of Sussex in 1967, and the job of cataloguing the hundreds of thousands of pages began. That it is now an easily navigable and ever-rewarding resource is testament to the graft and intellectual rigour of those who have protected and promoted its treasures over the years, and in particular to the current Archive Director, Dorothy Sheridan. With the help of many colleagues she has ensured that the archive is a vibrant and stimulating place, concerned with improving access in the digital age, continually delighting those who discover its riches for the first time.

By the time Maggie Joy Blunt passed away, Mass-Observation was a force once more. A new Mass-Observation Project was established in 1981, and more than 3,000 correspondents have answered directives and maintained diaries. Recent themes have included mobile phones, owning pets, Saturday afternoons and the war in Iraq. The Project is keen to recruit new members to its panel, secure in the knowledge that what we now regard as commonplace might, in sixty years or so, prove to be another illuminating record of a distant world.

www.sussex.ac.uk/library/massobs

To enquire about taking part in the current M-O Project email: moa@sussex.ac.uk

The Mass-Observation Archive
Special Collections
The Library
University of Sussex
Brighton
BN1 9QL
UK

Acknowledgements

My thanks to all those who have helped me with this book. I am particularly grateful to the Trustees of the Mass-Observation Archive for their permission to use the material, and to Dorothy Sheridan for her support and guidance. The staff at the University of Sussex Library have also been a pleasure to work with, in particular Sandra Koa Wing, Joy Eldridge and Fiona Courage.

At Ebury Press I would like to thank my editor Jake Lingwood for his belief in the project and his unflagging enthusiasm. Hannah MacDonald provided the initial impetus for the idea, Claire Kingston conducted meticulous picture research, and I am grateful to them and all those who have shown so much commitment at Ebury and in the wider Random House empire.

Pat Kavanagh and colleagues at PFD provided the usual wise counsel. Finally, this book would have been far less enjoyable to work on without the help of David Robson, Sam Carroll, Jules Churchill, Karen Murphy, Piers Tomlinson, Charles Oakshett and, as always, my dearest wife Diane Samuels.

Chronology

1945

May
7   Hitler commits suicide in Berlin; unconditional surrender of Germany.
8   Winston Churchill and Harry Truman proclaim VE day.

June
4   Voters in Northern Ireland vote in favour of continued rule from Britain and Irish partition.

July
3   Allied governments agree to a three-way division of occupation of Berlin by American, British and Soviet forces.
5   Election Day, but results take three weeks to accommodate forces' votes.
15   Blackout ends.
26   Election results: Labour 393 seats, Conservatives 213, Liberals 12, Others 22. Clement Attlee is Prime Minister, Ernest Bevin is Foreign Secretary and Hugh Dalton is Chancellor, Aneurin Bevan becomes Minister for Health and Ellen Wilkinson becomes Minister of Education.

August
5   US air force drops atomic bomb on Hiroshima, followed three days later by Nagasaki.
14   Japan surrenders on condition that Emperor Hirohito retains his throne.
15   VJ day – the Second World War ends. King's speech announces a programme of nationalisation.

September
12   Ho Chi Minh declares the independence of Vietnam from French rule.
19   Labour proposals to begin negotiations on Indian autonomy.

October
4   Unofficial dock strike begins. Within a fortnight 40,000 men are out, and 6,000 troops are drafted to unload food.
20   Egyptian, Iraqi, Lebanese and Syrian governments warn the Truman administration that the creation of a Jewish state in Palestine would lead to war in the region.

November
20   Nuremberg Trials commence, with twenty-four leading Nazis indicted.

29   Establishment of the Federal People's Republic of Yugoslavia.

December
5       $3.75 billion US Loan Agreement signed in Washington, followed by the establishment of the International Monetary Fund and World Bank.

1946

January
1   Heathrow Airport opened.
10   First session of the UN General Assembly in London, with fifty-one nations attending.

February
10   Soviet general elections, the first since 1937, in which the full official list of approved candidates for the Supreme Soviet is returned.
12   Riots in India.

March
1   Bank of England nationalised.
5   Churchill delivers his 'Iron Curtain' speech in Missouri and advocates Anglo-American 'fraternal association' as a counterpoint to the Eastern Bloc.
21   Bevan announces plans for the National Health Service.

April
17   Government announces its intention to nationalise iron and steel industries.

May
16   Plans for Indian independence unveiled.
30   Bread rationing announced.
June
5   Victory Parade in London.

July
18   Initial British withdrawal from the £937m. Truman loan.
22   British HQ at the King David Hotel bombed by Jewish terrorists, killing ninety-one.

August
More than five thousand die in Muslim–Hindu violence in Calcutta.

September
1   The Football League restarts.
29   The BBC Third Programme begins.

October
1   The Nuremberg Trials reach a conclusion: 12 prisoners are sentenced to be hanged, 3 to life imprisonment, 4 are given prison sentences from 10 to 20 years, and 3 are acquitted.

November
6   National Health Service Bill passed.
12   King's speech announces nationalisation of railways and ports.

December
26   Fuel shortages close factories and mills, and a four-day week planned.

1947

January

7   Transport strike in London; food supplies delivered by troops.

24   The 'worst British winter ever' begins.

February

14   The conflict in Palestine worsens, and is referred to the UN by the British Government.

20   Mountbatten appointed Viceroy of India, with the transfer of power set to begin by June 1948.

March

The winter continues with the wettest month on record.

April

1   The school-leaving age raised to fifteen, while National Service is reduced to one year.

24   The Government bans the use of coal and gas fires until the autumn.

May

23   The Cabinet approves Mountbatten's plan to partition India.

June

30   Meat rations reduced. Reductions in dollar imports of petrol, tobacco and newsprint, and 75 per cent tax on foreign films.

July

12   Sixteen nations attend Paris Conference to discuss Marshall Plan for Europe.

31   The two British sergeants kidnapped by Jewish terrorists in Palestine are found hanged near Haifa, leading to anti-Semitic protests in Liverpool and Manchester.

August

6   New extreme British austerity plan announced by Attlee. Further food ration cuts and petrol ration abolished for pleasure motoring.

15   British rule ends in India.

24   First Edinburgh Festival.

September

7   Sheffield steelworks shut down after South Yorkshire coal strike.

26   UK mandate over Palestine relinquished.

29   Harold Wilson becomes President of the Board of Trade.

October

19   Bacon ration halved, followed by ban on import of US tobacco.

26   British troops withdraw from Iraq.

30   GATT free-trade agreement signed in Geneva.

November

5   Potato rationing introduced.

12   An emergency budget further increases duties and restrictions, and Dalton resigns the following day after leaking details to the press. Replaced by Sir Stafford Cripps.

29   UN agrees to partition Palestine, dividing the area into three entities: a Jewish state, an Arab state and an international zone around Jerusalem.

1948

January

1   Nationalised British Railways formed.

30   Mahatma Gandhi assassinated in New Delhi, followed by rioting throughout India.

February

10   Ceylon receives independence.

26   Communist coup in Czechoslovakia.

March

3   The American Loan exhausted.

15   Attlee announces removal of Communist sympathisers from Civil Service.

22   Talks begin in Washington regarding an Atlantic Pact between Britain, the USA and Canada; Russians start controlling western rail movements to Berlin.

April

1   Electricity nationalised.

16   Sixteen countries sign up to the Marshall Aid European Recovery programme.

26   GCE replaces School and Higher School Certificates.

May

12   Sheffield MP A. V. Alexander announces that the UK plans to make its own atomic bomb.

15   British mandate ends in Palestine and Chaim Weizmann named as first President of the State of Israel.

June

1   Private motorists limited to ninety miles per month.

21   The *Empire Windrush* docks at Tilbury.

26   Berlin Airlift begins.

29   Dockers return to work.

July

5   National Health Service inaugurated.

25   Bread rationing ends.

26   The Olympic Games opens in London.

30   British Nationality Act grants all Commonwealth subjects British citizen status.

Index

533

535

Important hours, importan[t]
) August in 1939 preceding th[e]
tension of a different kind, e[x]
made for a change in our [...]
tempo is slower. We wai[t]
official announcement by [...]
2 full days holiday an[d]
period of peace in Europe —
Hitler is raving as they sa[y]
commit suicide or be capt[ured]
that his henchmen are d[...]
t least seems balanced e[...]
Prince Bernadotte.
All the women of my a[...]
disapproved today of the t[...]
Mussolini & his mistres[s]